A
D
H
an

Atomic Diplomacy: Hiroshima and Potsdam

THE USE OF THE ATOMIC BOMB AND THE AMERICAN CONFRONTATION WITH SOVIET POWER

GAR ALPEROVITZ

Pluto  Press
LONDON • EAST HAVEN, CONNECTICUT

First published in the USA by Simon and Schuster Inc., 1975. An expanded
and updated edition published by Penguin Books 1985.

This revised edition first published by Pluto Press, 345 Archway Road,
London N6 5AA and 140 Commerce Street, East Haven, CT 06512, USA

British Library Cataloguing in Publication Data
A catalogue record for this book is available from the British Library

Library of Congress Cataloging in Publication Date
Alperovitz, Gar.
  Atomic diplomacy : Hiroshima and Potsdam / by Gar Alperovitz. –
2nd expanded ed.
    p.   cm.
  Includes bibliographical references and index.
  ISBN 0–7453–0948–8 (cloth)
  1. United States – Foreign relations – 1945–1953. 2. United States –
Foreign relations – Soviet Union. 3. Soviet Union – Foreign
relations – United States. I. Title.
E813.A75   1994
327.73047 – dc20   94–18542
                                                                        CIP

ISBN 0 7453 0948 8 hardback

Printed in the EC

FOR
MY DAUGHTER KARI
AND
MY SON DAVID

Let us re-examine our attitude toward the Cold War, remembering we are not engaged in a debate, seeking to pile up debating points. We are not here distributing blame or pointing the finger. We must deal with the world as it is . . .

—PRESIDENT JOHN F. KENNEDY
June 10, 1963

CONTENTS

ACKNOWLEDGMENTS

I wish to acknowledge and thank the following for the help they have given me, directly through advice, encouragement, material support, and the provision of information; and indirectly through their work: Emily and Julius Alperovitz, Oscar E. Anderson, P.M.S. Blackett, Sir Dennis Brogan, Michael Brower, Naomi Burns, E.H. Carr, Benjamin V. Cohen, Daniel S. Greenberg, Joseph C. Grew, Paul Y. Hammond, Elinor and Christopher Jencks, King's College (Cambridge University), Admiral William D. Leahy, Mrs Jacqueline Lushin, Archibald MacLeish, The Marshall Aid Commemoration Commission, George L. Mosse, Marcus G. Raskin, Joan V. Robinson, Alice Kimball Smith, The Henry L. Stimson Literary Trust, Arthur I. Waskow, William Appleman Williams.   G.A.

AUTHOR'S NOTE TO THE 1994 EDITION

THIS EDITION OF *Atomic Diplomacy* is being published in response to requests from professors, teachers of history, and religious educators – and to coincide with the fiftieth anniversary of the launching of the nuclear era. Although no changes have been made from the 1985 edition, three of the original Appendices have been deleted to make room for materials of particular interest to classes studying the decision to use the atomic bomb. Two are drawn from religious commentaries – the 1946 U.S. Federal Council of Churches report, "Atomic Warfare and the Christian Faith," and excerpts from the 1983 U.S. National Conference of Catholic Bishops' pastoral letter on war and peace, "The Challenge of Peace: God's Promise and Our Response". A third Appendix reprints excerpts from "Use of Atomic Bomb on Japan," written by the Intelligence Staff of the War Department, and given to the Chief of the Strategic Policy Section of the Operations Division on April 30, 1946. This official study came to light after 1985. It concludes that Japan would almost certainly have surrendered when the Soviet Union declared war in early August 1945, making even an initial November invasion landing on the island of Kyushu only a remote possibility.

AUTHOR'S NOTE TO THE 1985 EDITION

I HAVE BEEN ASKED to reissue *Atomic Diplomacy* in its original form to coincide with the fortieth anniversary of the bombing of Hiroshima. As I have indicated in the Introduction to the 1985 Edition, I believe that information which has become available since the work's first publication (August 1965) strengthens its major argument, and I have cited much of the new evidence, especially on the central role the impact of the atomic bomb on the Soviet Union played in U.S. thinking. Readers who have a specialized interest in particular aspects of the historical debate will find various secondary matters addressed in a new section, Appendix I, A Note on the Historical Debate Over Questions Concerning Truman's 1945 Strategy of Delay, and in the reference notes to the Introduction and to the Note (where I have also attempted to correct a few minor errors which have been brought to my attention).

I would like to express my thanks to Jon Mercer for his help in preparing this edition and the new Bibliography of Important Works, to Laura Gilliam for her assistance with the Bibliography, and to Kai Bird, Robert Borosage, Al Herrera, Max Holland, J.R. Parten, and the Reference Specialists in the Main Reading Room of the Library of Congress for their cooperation and help on a number of matters.

My deep appreciation to my wife, Sharon, for her ongoing warmth, support, and love cannot adequately be expressed in this brief word of acknowledgment.

Introduction to the 1985 Edition: The Bombing of Hiroshima and Nagasaki

It wasn't necessary to hit them with that awful thing.
—GENERAL DWIGHT D. EISENHOWER

WHEN *ATOMIC DIPLOMACY* WAS FIRST PUBLISHED twenty years ago, it focused attention on three controversial questions. Its primary argument was simply that the atomic bomb had a very significant influence on American views of diplomacy toward the Soviet Union well before it was used. The book explored the then rather new thesis that the weapon was inextricably bound up with President Harry S. Truman's strategy toward his Potsdam meeting with Stalin in July 1945, and that it was regarded at the time (in the words of Secretary of War Henry L. Stimson) as a "master card" of diplomacy.[1]

Atomic Diplomacy also argued that although as yet "no final conclusion [could] be reached" . . . "the evidence strongly suggest[ed]" that a major reason the bomb was used was "to make Russia more manageable. . . ." The phrase was atomic scientist Leo Szilard's description of views expressed by Truman's Secretary of State–designate, James F. Byrnes, in private conversations fully two months before Hiroshima and Nagasaki were destroyed. We shall return to this issue.

1

INTRODUCTION

The third important question touched upon was the impact of nuclear weapons on the beginning of the Cold War. In August 1945, Eisenhower felt that "before the atom bomb was used, I would have said yes, I was sure we could keep the peace with Russia. Now, I don't know. . . . People are frightened and disturbed all over. Everyone feels insecure again."[2] The book clearly suggested a new 1945 point of departure for interpretations of the rise of postwar hostility in Soviet-American relations, but it ended with the September 1945 meeting of the London Council of Foreign Ministers and recommended further research on precisely what role the bomb played in initiating the Cold War.

Atomic Diplomacy was originally a Cambridge University doctoral dissertation and Kings College Fellows' presentation. I had gotten involved in research on the atomic bomb quite by accident: As a young Ph.D. candidate in political economy, I was studying the development of American postwar economic strategy toward Europe, especially trade policy, and I could not understand the abrupt stops and starts in overall U.S. diplomacy (including commercial policy) toward Central and Eastern Europe in the period April–September 1945. Much to my surprise, my inquiry led to an investigation of a secret high-level U.S. policy debate about the relationship of the new weapon to all questions involving the Soviet Union at the time.

Though it was naive of me, I was also surprised that what was a rather scholarly and heavily documented work stirred so much public debate when it was published. The first wave of reaction, for instance, included a critical front page review in *The New York Times*. (The *Times* selected Senator Clinton Anderson, formerly a member of Truman's Cabinet and at the time a leading nuclear power advocate, to write about the issue.) On the other hand, a prominent nuclear scientist, Ralph Lapp, praised the book in a major *Life* magazine review.

There was also a rich and rather uneven range of academic comment. Some of it was fair: Were I to rewrite the book today, for instance, I would include in the body of the main text much more of the kind of detailed argumentation that I put in Appendix II twenty years ago. Though I believe the careful caveats and explorations presented are accurate, it is understandable that some authors may have been confused at one or two points.* (On the other hand, some of the academic comment over the two-decade period was—as one historian gently put it—"strained," to say the least.)[3,4]

THE HISTORICAL DEBATE

VIEWED IN THE BROADEST perspective, the most important and enduring response to *Atomic Diplomacy* has been an evolving reinterpretation of the early postwar period. I believe it fair to say, for instance, that the book's *fundamental* argument has been increasingly accepted (sometimes without apparent awareness of its source) in varying degrees in the years since it first appeared: Whereas previously there had been very little understanding that the atomic bomb played a significant role in American *diplomatic* calculations in 1945, even by the end of the 1960s a change in understanding was already well under way. It was perhaps best represented by revisions one highly respected student of the period, Herbert Feis, made in his *Japan Subdued.*

Feis had been a consultant to three Secretaries of War and had unusual access to the official documents and individuals involved. His initial 1961 position on the relationship of the atomic bomb to diplomacy had been:

> It *may* be also—*but this is only conjecture*—that Churchill and Truman and some of their colleagues conceived that besides bringing the war to a quick end, it would improve the chances of arranging a satisfactory peace. For would not the same dramatic proof of Western power that shocked Japan into surrender impress the Russians also?†[5]

In his revised edition in 1966, Feis concluded:

> It is *likely* that Churchill, and *probably also Truman,* conceived that besides bringing the war to a quick end, it would improve the chances of arranging a satisfactory peace both in Europe and in the Far East. *Stimson and Byrnes certainly had that thought in mind.* For would not the same dramatic proof of Western power that shocked Japan into surrender impress the Russians also?‡[6]

In the mid and late 1970s, several scholarly works extended this

---

* See also the new Appendix V, A Note on the Historical Debate Over Questions Concerning Truman's 1945 Strategy of Delay for additional argumentation related to such points.

† Emphasis added.
‡ Emphasis added.

general argument.[7] By the early 1980s, a well-respected study of James Byrnes's tenure as Secretary of State added the most recently available information to our picture of the bomb's early influence on diplomacy. Taking for granted an interpretation which had simply not been recognized two decades earlier, it included summary descriptions such as this:

> Truman, Byrnes, and virtually all the president's principal advisers on the bomb project were in agreement. The consensus of opinion among all those involved in integrating this revolutionary new force into American foreign policy was that the bomb promised to be, if not a total solution and the basis for a Pax Americana, at least a means for dealing with many of the problems of the postwar world.[8]

To be sure, many historians have not yet accepted the import of the evidence concerning the way the atomic bomb affected American leaders in 1945. Moreover, among those who have helped develop the new framework of understanding there has been considerable academic debate over precisely how the atomic bomb affected diplomacy and over important issues of emphasis (and such questions as exactly when within a particular three-week span certain decisions took place).* On the whole, however, and leaving aside academic dispute over secondary matters, I believe what is significant is that many authors have come to understand the book's most important broad contribution to our understanding of the early months of the Truman Administration, and to refine it with additional research.

The term "atomic diplomacy" itself is, in fact, increasingly used as a description of policy in studies of this period.[9] Moreover, information not available when *Atomic Diplomacy* first appeared has given additional support to a number of important points some writers previously challenged.† It is now beyond question that the bomb powerfully affected such top U.S. leaders as Secretary of War

---

* See below, Appendix V, pp. 343–49.

† For instance, Robert Messer's *The End of an Alliance* and Gregg Herken's *The Winning Weapon* confirm James F. Byrnes's influential role, and his reliance on the atomic bomb to bolster his Potsdam and post-Hiroshima diplomacy especially in connection with Eastern Europe and the Balkans.

Another widely discussed point concerned Truman's 1945 decision to send Harry Hopkins to meet with Stalin and Joseph Davies to meet with Churchill. During the 1970s, some historians argued the decision simply reflected Truman's vacillation and uncertainty at the outset of his Presidency and had nothing to do with considerations related to the atomic bomb. Newer information adds support to *Atomic Diplomacy*'s argument that the missions cannot be understood in isolation by confirming that the atomic bomb was discussed explicitly in

Henry L. Stimson, Secretary of State James F. Byrnes, and President Harry S. Truman. According to Truman, for instance, within a few days of Franklin Roosevelt's death on April 12, 1945, Byrnes told him the bomb would allow the United States "to dictate our own terms at the end of the war."[10] And on numerous occasions, Secretary of War Stimson advised the President of the significance of the weapon; his thinking during May (to choose only one illustration) was that "it may be necessary to have it out with Russia on her relations to Manchuria and Port Arthur and various other parts of North China, and also the relations of China to us. Over any such tangled weave of problems the S-1 [i.e., the atomic bomb] secret would be dominant. . . ."*[11]

The bulk of *Atomic Diplomacy* is a week by week review of diplomatic maneuvering in the summer of 1945 leading up to, during, and after the Potsdam Conference. The book reports on how the new weapon became involved in U.S. calculations in connection with disputes involving Poland, Bulgaria, Rumania, Manchuria, German reparations, etc. In brief, Truman had been advised by a majority of his top advisers to have an early diplomatic "showdown" (Secretary of the Navy Forrestal's term) with the Russians over a major symbolic issue then in contention (Poland)—*before U.S. troops were withdrawn from Europe to join the war in the Far East.* He initially followed this advice, but then reversed himself and put a number of matters off on the recommendation that "it was premature" to get into such negotiations until the bomb had been tested and demonstrated.

Stimson explained to Assistant Secretary of War John J. McCloy on May 14, 1945, his opinion

that the time now and the method now to deal with Russia was to

---

connection with both. The more recent evidence also shows that the dates the missions were decided upon ties in precisely with the very narrow period during which Truman made his fundamental strategic decision to delay a meeting with Stalin until the bomb had strengthened the U.S. hand, and that the decision to delay the meeting was discussed openly in connection with mission planning.

See Appendix V, A Note on the Historical Debate Over Questions Concerning Truman's 1945 Strategy of Delay, pp. 349–55, for a discussion of the missions and a review of the evidence concern-

ing how early the atomic bomb entered U.S. diplomatic planning. In Appendix V and in the references to it and to this Introduction, I have also taken up a number of specific smaller points in the literature ranging from the Balkans to Lend-Lease.

* Because of wartime security requirements, the weapon was usually referred to indirectly or by the code terms "Tube Alloy" and "S-1." Hereafter, the words "the atomic bomb" will be used within brackets in place of all indirect references in quoted text.

keep our mouths shut and let our actions speak for words. . . . We have coming into action a weapon which will be unique. Now the thing is not to get into unnecessary quarrels by talking too much and not to indicate any weakness by talking too much. . . .[12]

Truman postponed his Potsdam meeting in order to be sure that the weapon, still an untested scientists' theory, would actually work before negotiating with Stalin. The coincidence of the dates alone should have been enough to stimulate curiosity much earlier: The Alamogordo test was held on July 16, 1945; the Potsdam meeting began on July 17, 1945. *Atomic Diplomacy* relied primarily on the Stimson diary for documentation of the overall relationship between the new weapon and Truman's diplomacy, but very clear and explicit confirmation of the strategy is contained in the more recently opened papers of Ambassador Joseph Davies. In late May, Truman privately told the former Ambassador to Moscow the reason he had postponed the Potsdam meeting. In one version of his diary, Davies puts an asterisk in his text after Truman's comment that this had to do with the "budget," noting: "The atomic bomb. He told me then of the atomic bomb experiment in Nevada (*sic*). Charged me with utmost secrecy." In another version of his diary, Davies says in the text:

> To my surprise, he said he did not want it [the heads-of-government meeting] until July. The reason which I could assign was that he had his budget on his hands, and had to get that out. "But," he said, "I have another reason (*) which I have not told anybody."
> He told me of the atomic bomb. The final test had been set for June, but now had been postponed until July. I was startled, shocked and amazed.

Davies adds in the footnote referred to by the asterisk: "Uranium—for reason of security, I will have to fill this in later."*[13]

On the ship crossing the Atlantic to the Big Three meeting, Truman told an associate: "If it explodes, as I think it will, I'll certainly have a hammer on those boys."[14] Once the new weapon was success-

---

* Some observers doubted *Atomic Diplomacy*'s argument that the Potsdam meeting had been postponed for this reason. Averell Harriman, for instance, wrote: ". . . it is nonsense to believe—as some historians apparently do—that Truman post- poned the Potsdam Conference in order to have the bomb go off before the end of his meeting with Stalin. . . ." Harriman and Abel, *Special Envoy*, p. 490.

fully tested, close observers could not miss the effect. At Potsdam, Churchill told Stimson: "Now I know what happened to Truman yesterday. I couldn't understand it. When he got to the meeting after having read this report [of the successful test] he was a changed man. He told the Russians just where they got on and off and generally bossed the whole meeting." Churchill himself, according to Lord Alanbrooke,

> had absorbed all the minor American exaggerations and, as a result, was completely carried away. . . . We now had something in our hands which would redress the balance with the Russians . . . (pushing out his chin and scowling); now we could say, "If you insist on doing this or that, well . . ." And then where are the Russians![15]

The Potsdam Conference took place *after* the test of the first weapon but *before its demonstration to the world;* it was not yet the moment for a full-scale negotiation with the Soviets. The tactics of the meeting—with certain exceptions the United States stated its full demands, but, often preferring simply to wait, did not really negotiate on many issues—are reviewed in Chapters V and VI. Though the Potsdam record is clear, the discovery of Truman's personal diary in late 1978 adds a bit more confirming nuance to our understanding of the President's attitude: "Just spent a couple of hours with Stalin . . . ," Truman noted after a private meeting of July 17, 1945. "He said . . . he had some more questions to present. I told him to fire away. He did and it is dynamite—but I have some dynamite too *which I'm not exploding now.*"*[16]

The situation at Potsdam was odd: Truman had committed himself to meet with Stalin—and *until the bomb was proved,* he still believed he might need Stalin's help in the war against Japan. This was one of the primary reasons for going to Potsdam. But the new weapon had not yet been publicly displayed. The frustration of having discussions with Stalin at a time which from his point of view was still a few weeks too early I believe helps explain Truman's repeated complaint that he did not like having to travel all the way across the Atlantic (by ship) for the long meetings in Germany.

The first real negotiating showdown with the Soviets came at the

---

* Emphasis added. For a critique of other interpretations of Truman's mid-1945 policy, see Appendix II and the new Appendix V, A Note on the Historical Debate Over Questions Concerning Truman's 1945 Strategy of Delay.

London Council of Foreign Ministers a month after Hiroshima. John Foster Dulles (who was there) regarded the meeting—rightly, in my view—as the beginning of the Cold War. Secretary of State Byrnes later acknowledged that his first post-Hiroshima encounter with Molotov marked a major shift in U.S. policy—and he found the shock to the Soviets "understandable." (Secretary of War Stimson, talking with Byrnes at the White House just before the London conference, found him "very much against any attempt to cooperate with Russia. His mind is full of his problems with the coming meeting of the foreign ministers and he looks to having the presence of the bomb in his pocket, so to speak, as a great weapon to get through the thing. . . ."[17])

It was and is not my contention, incidentally, that the United States actually threatened the Soviets with the bomb at this time or any other during this period.[18] (It may or may not be that at a later point in the Cold War such a threat occurred.[19]) Nor do I believe American policy makers were malevolent men; they were trying to build a peaceful world and sought Soviet cooperation with their plans *as they conceived them*. In the process, however, we now know that the new weapon gave them sufficient confidence to attempt to reverse decisions on a number of key issues—in full awareness that in so doing they were unilaterally breaching specific understandings Roosevelt had reached with the Soviet leadership.[20] Nor was the policy of "atomic diplomacy" successful. Quite the contrary. If anything, it probably backfired—and by making the Soviets more wary it may well have prevented the subsequent settlement of several important matters. *

DIPLOMATIC CONSIDERATIONS AND THE USE OF THE ATOMIC BOMB

MOST OF THE CONTROVERSY caused by *Atomic Diplomacy* centered around the suggestion that diplomatic considerations *vis à vis* the Soviet Union played a role in the actual decision to bomb Hiroshima and Nagasaki. The argument was not the main point of the book, and was distinctly secondary to the bulk of its discussion of the

---

* See below, pp. 54–58; see also the new Appendix IV.

impact of the bomb on diplomacy. It was also stated very cautiously ("More research and more information are needed to reach a conclusive understanding of why the atomic bomb was used. . . . At present no final conclusion can be reached on this question . . . ," etc.). Nevertheless, many people were, not surprisingly, disturbed by the idea that other than purely military factors were involved.

Numerous authors took up the Hiroshima bombing question in the first decade after *Atomic Diplomacy*'s publication.* Though popular, public awareness has not yet caught up with the scholarly debate, here, too, major shifts in our detailed understanding of the decision have occurred. We have noted that Herbert Feis concluded that "probably" Truman and "certainly" Stimson and Byrnes also had the Russians in mind when the bomb was used. Historian Barton Bernstein, writing in the early 1970s, recognized that for "policy makers, the atomic weapons scheduled for combat use against Japan were intimately connected with the problem of Russia." Bernstein thought that the main reason the bomb was used was to end the war—and that its effect on the Soviet Union was a "bonus." However, he argued that "impressing the Soviet Union . . . did constitute a subtle deterrent to reconsidering combat use of the bomb and to searching for alternative means of ending the war." Bernstein also acknowledged that several of the questions related to the bomb "cannot be definitively answered on the basis of presently available evidence. . . ."[21]

Another serious scholar writing on the subject in the mid-1970s was historian Martin Sherwin, who came closer to the argument presented in *Atomic Diplomacy*. I had suggested that it appeared that U.S. officials had gotten so caught up in the idea that once demonstrated the bomb would be important in diplomacy toward Russia that when evidence of Japanese willingness to surrender came in, they could not or would not act upon it: "The issue is not why it was *decided* to use the bomb, but rather, how policy makers came to *assume* the bomb would be used, and why they never questioned this assumption. . . ."[22] Sherwin argued that probably the "principal motive" for using the bomb was to end the war, but he

---

* For a review of the enormous literature on the debate between traditionalists and revisionists, see Bernstein, "The Atomic Bomb and American Foreign Policy, 1941–1945."

recognized that "the expectation that its use would also inhibit Soviet diplomatic ambitions clearly discouraged any inclination to question that assumption." Sherwin, too, acknowledged the limitations of the available information, concluding: "Was an implicit warning to Moscow, then, the principal reason for deciding to use the atomic bomb against Japan? In light of the ambiguity of the available evidence the question defies an unequivocal answer."[23]

Subsequent research has both carried on the traditional argument and followed up leads developed in the initial so-called post-revisionist work. There have also been a number of serious but more popular accounts that bear on the question (John Toland's 1970 *The Rising Sun* and Peter Wyden's 1984 *Day One* are two of the most important). Finally, a good deal of work has been done on various individuals involved in diplomacy toward the Soviet Union during the period, and several diaries and personal memoirs have appeared which bear on the main issues in dispute.

On the basis of such research, inquiry into the Hiroshima decision can be taken a bit further than was possible twenty years ago. Perhaps at this point in history, discussion of the issues beyond narrowly scholarly circles can be carried on in a more thoughtful manner than when *Atomic Diplomacy* was first published.

It is important at the outset to define the question with some precision: If one asks *very generally,* "Why were the atomic bombs used at Hiroshima and Nagasaki?" it is obvious that one reason was to end the war against Japan, since that is what they accomplished (at least in part).* But this line of inquiry does not get us very far. To see why, it is necessary to ask several more narrowly focused questions. The first is: "From the *military* point of view, was the use of atomic weapons *necessary to end the war without an invasion?*" This is the justification President Truman repeatedly offered: "The dropping of the bombs stopped the war, saved millions of lives."[24]

Shortly after World War II ended, the official U.S. Strategic Bombing Survey concluded that

> certainly prior to 31 December 1945, and in all probability prior to 1 November 1945, Japan would have surrendered even if the atomic

---

* However, see below, p. 237*fn.*

bombs had not been dropped, even if Russia had not entered the war, and even if no invasion had been planned or contemplated.[25]

While this after-the-fact assessment cannot tell us what policy makers understood at the time, it does give a sense of how badly Japanese strength had deteriorated. It also brings into focus three crucial dates. Note carefully, first, that the invasion of Japan, which was estimated to cost between 500,000 and a million lives, was not scheduled until the spring of 1946, *roughly eight months after the Potsdam Conference and the bombing of Hiroshima on August 6.* As we shall see, there is little doubt that President Truman and his top advisers knew at the time that the full invasion of Japan was extremely unlikely. The real issue was whether the war could be ended before November 1, the date fixed for an initial preliminary landing on the island of Kyushu. Again, note carefully, this was scheduled to occur three full months after the meeting at Potsdam, and one week shy of three months after Hiroshima was bombed.

A specific question we need to answer is whether American policy makers understood that there were ways to end the war without using the atomic bombs and without either a landing or an invasion which would cost significant numbers of American lives. And this question itself needs to be refined. It is, for instance, clear from the record that *planning* for an invasion had to go forward whatever the top policy makers hoped for or believed; and, furthermore, troops in the field, the American public, and, above all, the Japanese, were given no inkling that an invasion might not be necessary. Marshall felt that "every individual moving to the Pacific should be indoctrinated with a firm determination to see it through."[26] (This understandably led many veterans to believe that had Hiroshima not been destroyed, they might have had to risk or lose their lives in an invasion.) However, it is *not* clear that the President believed the *planned* invasion would actually be launched; quite the contrary.

The Japanese code had been broken early in the war. Faint Japanese peace feelers appeared as early as September 1944.[27] In April 1945 top-level planning of the Joint Chiefs of Staff already included the possibility that a "threat [of a landing] in itself" might even bring about surrender.[28] On June 14, 1945, the Joint Chiefs of Staff asked the Pacific commanders to prepare for the possibility of a "sudden collapse or surrender . . ." (though they did not say this was imminent as yet).[29]

Until about mid-June it may still have been possible to believe an invasion was highly likely. At this time, however, six members of the Japanese Supreme War Council authorized Foreign Minister Togo to approach the Soviet Union "with a view to terminating the war if possible by September."[30] By July 13, 1945, Secretary of the Navy Forrestal described the latest intercepted cables as "real evidence of a Japanese desire to get out of the war. . . ." These included a message from Japanese Foreign Minister Togo to his Ambassador in Moscow instructing him to see Molotov if possible before the Potsdam Conference "to lay before him the Emperor's strong desire to secure a termination of the war." Forrestal notes: "Togo said further that the unconditional surrender terms of the Allies was (*sic*) about the only thing in the way of termination of the war. . . ."[31]

Various Japanese officials also tried the direct approach. Allen Dulles, overseeing secret OSS operations in Switzerland, had helped arrange the Italian surrender. Dulles reports that as early as April 1945, he and his associates were approached "by Japanese army and navy spokesmen there and also by some Japanese officials at the Bank for International Settlements in Basel. They wished to determine whether they could not also take advantage of [Dulles's] secret channels to Washington . . . to secure peace for Japan." After an active exchange of messages and a number of secret meetings, Dulles was ordered to report to Secretary Stimson at Potsdam "on what I had learned from Tokyo—they desired to surrender if they could retain the Emperor and the constitution as a basis for maintaining discipline and order in Japan after the devastating news of surrender became known to the Japanese people."[32]

Newly discovered documents confirm that information on the Dulles contacts and others reached Truman directly. Almost three months before Hiroshima, on May 12, 1945, William J. Donovan, Director of the Office of Strategic Services, sent a memorandum to the President which reported that a source

> talked with Shunichi Kase, the Japanese Minister to Switzerland. . . .
> Kase expressed a wish to help arrange for a cessation of hos-

tilities. . . . One of the few provisions the Japanese would insist upon would be the retention of the Emperor. . . .

On May 31, 1945, Donovan sent a further memorandum directly to the President reporting that on May 7, 1945, another source in Lisbon

> stated that he had been asked by Masutaro Inoue, Counsellor of the Japanese Legation in Portugal, to contact United States representatives. Source quoted Inoue as saying that the Japanese are ready to cease hostilities, provided they are allowed to retain possession of their home islands. . . .
> On 19 May, the OSS representative reported that Inoue again had repeated to source his desire to talk. . . .[33]

As important as these independent approaches were, they were far less significant than a major development which occurred within Japan during the summer—the highly unusual decision of the Emperor himself to become personally involved in the surrender process: The intercepted messages revealed the Emperor's urgent effort to open a direct negotiating channel through Moscow. During the last days of July, for instance, an intercepted cable instructed the Japanese Ambassador in Tokyo to arrange a Moscow visit for the Emperor's personal envoy, Prince Konoye:

> The mission . . . was to ask the Soviet Government to take part in mediation to end the present war and to transmit the complete Japanese case in this respect. . . . Prince Konoe (*sic*) was especially charged by His Majesty, the Emperor, to convey to the Soviet Government that it was exclusively the desire of His Majesty to avoid more bloodshed. . . . [34]

(The above message was given directly to President Truman by Stalin as well as intercepted directly. We have had access to some of the intercepted cables and other materials U.S. officials saw at the time only since 1979—some, but not *all* of them: Portions of documents at certain key points in the cable-related information at the National Archives are still not available to the public.[35])

Did Truman understand that he could in all likelihood end the war without using the atomic bombs and without resorting to an invasion? It is very difficult to believe he did not. We shall explore this question at length, but let us simply note at this point how two particularly important top officials about whom we have information understood what was happening at the time. Eisenhower was also at Potsdam. When Secretary of War Stimson told him atomic weapons were to be used against the Japanese, this was his reaction:

> During his recitation of the relevant facts, I had been conscious of a feeling of depression and so I voiced to him my grave misgivings, first on the basis of my belief that Japan was already defeated and that dropping the bomb was completely unnecessary, and secondly because I thought that our country should avoid shocking world opinion by the use of a weapon whose employment was, I thought, no longer mandatory as a measure to save American lives.

In Eisenhower's judgment, ". . . Japan was, at that very moment, seeking some way to surrender with a minimum loss of 'face.' . . ." The language he used on another occasion was more straightforward: " . . . it wasn't necessary to hit them with that awful thing. . . ."[36]

Until very recently we knew only that Eisenhower had expressed these views to Secretary of War Stimson. However, we now know that he also expressed them to the President in a meeting on July 20. General Omar Bradley confirms that, in his presence at lunch that day, when Truman said he was going to use the atomic weapons, Eisenhower challenged him directly.[*][37]

Truman also worked very closely with the highly regarded Chief of Staff he inherited from Roosevelt, Admiral William D. Leahy. There is no question about Leahy's view of the situation:

> It is my opinion that the use of this barbarous weapon at Hiroshima and Nagasaki was of no material assistance in our war against Japan. The Japanese were already defeated and ready to surrender because of the effective sea blockade and the successful bombing with conventional weapons. . . .
>
> My own feeling is that in being the first to use it, we had adopted an ethical standard common to the barbarians of the Dark Ages.

"I was not taught to make war in that fashion, and wars cannot be won by destroying women and children . . . ," Leahy later observed.[39]

---

[*] Eisenhower also reported to Forrestal after the war that he told the President "there was no question but that Japan was already thoroughly beaten . . . " when he talked to Truman at Potsdam.[38]

The forceful Admiral did not record specific diary entries on his conversations with Truman. Nevertheless, we know that the President's top military aide left no doubt as to his advice on the matter: "Naturally, I . . . acquainted President Truman with my own ideas about the best course to pursue in defeating Japan as fully as I had done with President Roosevelt."[40]

MORAL ISSUES

WE MUST PAUSE briefly to consider these statements. Many accounts of the Hiroshima decision neglect the fact that moral arguments were presented at the time. They tend to isolate the key decision makers from such concerns, as if they played no role in the thinking of men in positions of authority. Moreover, in recent years we have forgotten that the worries evident in the comments of Eisenhower and Leahy were not unique (though perhaps surprising to some, coming from military men). The idea that killing large numbers of civilians, of women and children, by indiscriminately destroying a whole city (even one like Hiroshima, which included modest military installations) was "barbarian" was common: Picasso's *Guernica* had symbolized the outrage of millions when Hitler helped Franco in the first bombing of cities during the Spanish Civil War; the Germans were denounced for the V-2 bombing of British civilian centers; the Japanese military were regarded as uncivilized in their bombing of urban populations in Manchuria.

While the United States used conventional bombs to destroy Japanese cities well before Hiroshima (the fire bombing of Tokyo on March 9–10, 1945, was particularly devastating), we can also regain some sense of how news of the first atomic bombs was received by recalling one or two commentaries directly concerned with the ethical issues. Here, for instance, was the response of the Catholic weekly *Commonweal* in an editorial entitled "Horror and Shame":

> We will not have to worry any more about keeping our victory clean. It is defiled. . . . The name Hiroshima, the name Nagasaki are names for American guilt and shame. . . . We have reached the point where we say that anything goes. That is what the Germans said at the beginning of the war. . . .

The Protestant journal *Christian Century* reported in an essay on "America's Moral Atrocity" that the magazine had been flooded with letters denouncing the use of "this incredibly inhuman instrument." "Our leaders seem not to have weighed the moral considerations involved. No sooner was the bomb ready than it was rushed to the front and dropped on two helpless cities, destroying more lives than the United States has lost in the entire war. . . ."[41]

VIEWS OF THE MILITARY

EISENHOWER AND LEAHY were not minor figures; they were, respectively, the triumphant Supreme Commander of the Allied Forces in Europe and one of Roosevelt's most respected advisers. Moreover, they were *military* men, individuals whose views on military matters could not easily be dismissed. Truman's regard for Eisenhower, and his recognition of the unique place the heroic Supreme Commander had already earned in American history, is also evident: It was, in fact, during a drive with Eisenhower shortly after the lunch at which he expressed his opposition to the bombing that Truman surprised him by saying: "General, there is nothing that you may want that I won't try to help you get. That definitely and specifically includes the presidency in 1948."[42]

As to Leahy: The five-star Admiral was the senior military officer of the United States as well as Chief of Staff to the President. He presided over all meetings of the Joint Chiefs of Staff, conveying the President's orders to it and bringing its recommendations to the President. (Leahy also presided over the Combined Chiefs of Staff when the U.S.–U.K. meetings took place in the United States.) The Joint Chiefs were responsible for the strategic and operational direction of all U.S. forces, and the then new institution was especially important for the Pacific war—a war not dominated by ground operations, but fought along vast distances by sea, air, and land and requiring much greater coordination. In countless photographs from the various Big Three meetings, you will find Leahy standing next to both Presidents Roosevelt and Truman; and in pictures from Potsdam of the Big Three and their three foreign ministers, you will often find Leahy an unexpected seventh figure next to Truman.[43]

I have cited Leahy's general comment above, made after the war, but here is how he recorded his views in his private diary as early as June 18, 1945:

> It is my opinion at the present time that a surrender of Japan can be arranged with terms that can be accepted by Japan and that will make fully satisfactory provision for America's defense against future trans-Pacific aggression.[44]

Recognition that the bomb was not essential to victory was not isolated. Top Navy officials were generally convinced that the sea blockade alone would force Japan to capitulate. Although the Army favored full preparations for an invasion, General Marshall, in an interview he gave on the subject before his death, commented that the bomb shortened the war only "by months."* The first reaction of the top British military figure, General Ismay, to the report that the atomic bomb was a success and could now be used, was one of "revulsion" ("For some time past it had been firmly fixed in my mind that the Japanese were tottering . . . ").[45]

Nor did Air Force leaders think the atomic bomb essential: General Curtis LeMay is reported to have felt that even without the atomic bomb and the Russian entry into the war, Japan would have surrendered in two weeks (the atomic bomb "had nothing to do with the end of the war"). As early as April, LeMay had argued the war could be ended by September or October without an invasion. When called back to Washington from Europe for consultations in June, representatives of the Strategic Bombing Survey also stressed that an invasion was unnecessary. The view that Japan would collapse in September or October seems to have been consistently held throughout the spring and summer. It was confirmed at Potsdam on July 16 when General Arnold made a specific point of reading into the record his judgment that Japan could be compelled to surrender without the bomb a month before the landing, i.e., in October:

> Japan, in fact, will become a nation without cities, with her transportation disrupted and will have tremendous difficulty in holding her

---

* We are attempting to get at the question of whether key military figures believed *in mid-July and early August* that the bomb was the only way to avoid an invasion. It is obvious that Marshall earlier had pressed planning for an invasion, even though (as we shall see) he told Truman on June 18—before the major intercepts came in—that the Russian declaration might lever Japan into surrender. His comment that the bomb only shortened the war "by months," though cryptic, is in line with Air Force and other estimates even before the July intercepts that the war would end in September or October without the bomb, the Russians, or, as we shall also see, a change in the surrender formula.

people together for continued resistance to our terms of unconditional surrender.[46]

Or, compare Churchill: "It would be a mistake to suppose that the fate of Japan was settled by the atomic bomb. Her defeat was certain before the first bomb fell. . . ."[47]

The fact that such judgments were offered at the time raises other important questions. For instance, precisely how and when did the President's Chief of Staff discuss the bomb with Truman? We know that the tough-minded Admiral made his views clear to the President, and he reports that Truman agreed with him about the central importance of seeking an end to the war which did not require an invasion.* However, we have almost no information on the discussions concerning the bomb itself between the two men.[48] It appears (as we shall see also in connection with James F. Byrnes) that either no notes were kept of the many secret private conversations the key individuals had, or that the records have been destroyed or lost. (Incidentally, Leahy was a very conservative anti-Russian adviser; his opposition to atomic weapons did not derive from his lack of concern for diplomatic objectives.)

Eisenhower also tells us that when he expressed his opposition to Stimson, "the Secretary was deeply perturbed by my attitude. . . ."[49] What was Truman's reaction when the Supreme Commander urged that atomic weapons not be used? We do not know.

Let us be quite clear: There is no doubt that the military figures approved *planning* for an invasion (although, of course, the invasion itself was never authorized). Their job was to be fully prepared to follow through on this option *if civilian authorities deemed it necessary*. It is also clear that they went along with the Presidential decision. But we are here after a different question: Did they think—and we must focus sharply on the last weeks of July and early August immediately before Hiroshima was destroyed, the period when the mounting evidence of Japan's deterioration poured in—that an invasion would be *necessary* if the new weapon was not used? What information we have (as we shall explore even more fully below)† makes it very difficult to believe that they did not

---

* See also below, pp. 29–30.
† See below, pp. 19–33.

understand that Japan was collapsing and that (in Eisenhower's words) "dropping the bomb was completely unnecessary" or (in Leahy's formulation) "the use of this barbarous weapon at Hiroshima and Nagasaki was of no material assistance in our war against Japan. The Japanese were already defeated and ready to surrender. . . ."

It is also important to remember that the military planning exercise went forward on the guidance in force at the moment—the then official, demanding assumption that "unconditional surrender" would be insisted upon.

OTHER OPTIONS

The uniformed military figures who felt the war could be ended without the use of atomic bombs were not alone. The Under Secretary of the Navy, Ralph Bard, was deeply disturbed at the prospect of the weapon's use. Bard had also become convinced that "the Japanese war was really won. . . ." As early as May 31, Bard, a member of the Interim Committee considering the new weapon, submitted a forty-two page memorandum on the subject. However, his views got little hearing in the Committee deliberations. On June 27 he submitted another top secret memorandum, this one registering his formal dissent from the Committee's recommendation that the bomb be used without specific warning.* Unwilling to let the matter drop, the Under Secretary secured a meeting with the President and pressed his case for warning the Japanese of the nature of the new weapon with Truman before he left for Potsdam. Bard got nowhere; he resigned his official post on July 1.[50]

Admiral Lewis L. Strauss, Special Assistant to Secretary of the Navy Forrestal, also believed that "the war was very nearly over. The Japanese were nearly ready to capitulate. . . ." Strauss (who replaced Bard on the Interim Committee after the latter's resignation) proposed to Secretary Forrestal that the bomb be demonstrated in a way which would not kill large numbers of civilians:

> . . . a satisfactory place for such a demonstration would be a large forest of cryptomeria trees not far from Tokyo. The cryptomeria tree

---

* See below, pp. 21, 44.

is the Japanese version of our redwood. It's a tree with a large bole . . . and very tall. I anticipated that a bomb detonated at a suitable height above such a forest . . . would lay the trees out in windrows from the center of the explosion in all directions as though they were matchsticks, and, of course, set them afire in the center. It seemed to me that a demonstration of this sort would prove to the Japanese that we could destroy any of their cities at will. . . .[51]

General Marshall also raised the idea early on that the bomb not be first used on a civilian area. After a meeting on May 29 with the Assistant Secretary of War, Marshall said (as McCloy recorded in a memorandum) that

he thought these weapons might first be used against straight military objectives such as a large naval installation and then if no complete result was derived from the effect of that, he thought we ought to designate a number of large manufacturing areas from which people would be warned to leave—telling the Japanese that we intend to destroy such centers. . . .

Again, note that it is a military leader who poses the moral question: "Every effort should be made to keep our record of warning clear. . . . We must offset by such warning methods the opprobrium which might follow from an ill-considered employment of such force."[52]

Marshall also proposed that instead of surprising the Russians with the combat use of the atomic bombs, they be invited to send observers to the Alamogordo test.[53]

Numerous scientists, of course, urged that a demonstration be arranged so the bomb's power would be clear to the Japanese before it was used against them. However, this much-written-about story is largely a side issue—a matter about which there is considerable confusion.

The Manhattan Project was originally begun because it was feared that Germany might produce and use atomic weapons. Once it was clear that Germany did not have such a capacity, and certainly after Germany's defeat, the initial reason many scientists agreed to work on the weapon disappeared. No one seriously thought Japan had the capacity to produce or deliver nuclear weapons.

Perhaps because so many scientists have recalled the commendable effort a vocal group among them made to forestall the use of atomic weapons after Germany's defeat, the literature on this subject is immense. *But the fact is, very little of the scientists' protest was considered seriously at the very highest decision-making levels.* To be sure, an advisory committee to an advisory committee considered their views (the Scientific Panel of the Interim Committee), but it functioned largely to water down urgings by disturbed scientists in the field. Peter Wyden's recent *Day One* gives a good account of the process by which the scientists were deflected (with the powerful help of J. Robert Oppenheimer and others), and puts their distinctly rearguard effort into perspective.

It is sometimes suggested that a demonstration bombing might not have worked, or that American prisoners might have been brought into the area. Again, perhaps there was no way to arrange a demonstration. But the overwhelming fact is that no one in high official position had any serious interest in attempting to devise a workable demonstration. Only a very few minutes were spent even discussing it—compared with the hours, weeks, even months of staff work that went into other important military projects.

(Incidentally, what fragments of evidence we have on Roosevelt's attitude suggest that he was not sure the bomb should be used against Japan. And if it were used, there are some indications that he believed a warning and possibly a demonstration in an area not inhabited by civilians would be appropriate.[54])

It is true that the scientists on the official advisory panel concurred in the recommendation that the atomic bomb be used, and, further, that to ensure the greatest shock, it be used against a civilian target. However, not only was this issue largely resolved before the mid-June Japanese drive to end the war was launched, but it was done in complete ignorance of the actual situation in the Pacific war. As Oppenheimer later put it, even the insiders among the scientists

> didn't know beans about the military situation in Japan. We didn't know whether they could be caused to surrender by other means or whether the invasion was really inevitable. But in the back of our minds was the notion that the invasion was inevitable because we had been told that. . . ."[55]

• • •

THE RUSSIAN OPTION

ANOTHER WAY to get at the question of whether during July and early August atomic weapons were still believed to be necessary to prevent an invasion is to attempt to define how, precisely, Truman and his top advisers viewed other options. The most important of these was a Russian declaration of war.

The United States recognized that since the focus of the Japanese diplomatic effort was the Soviet Union, a Soviet declaration of war had become extremely important—especially to the Japanese military, which held on to the hope that the one remaining major power might remain neutral. (As early as December 1944, for instance, Secretary of the Navy Forrestal noted: "Dispatches today from Japan indicate their awareness of increasing difficulty in their situation. Indications that they count on possible differences between Russia and Anglo-American interests to facilitate their position. . . ."[56]) For most of the war, U.S. diplomacy had made every effort to ensure that the Russians would enter the war, securing Stalin's pledge at Yalta to begin a Far Eastern campaign three months after Germany's surrender.

In early April the Soviet Union gave public notice of its intention to terminate its neutrality pact with Japan, and throughout May, June, and July the United States had no doubt that Russia intended to attack as promised. Japanese intelligence, as Stalin pointed out, could hardly miss the huge Soviet troop shipments to the Far East and the massing of the Red Army near the Manchurian border.

Churchill believed as early as September 1944 that the Japanese might well capitulate when the Russians entered the war.[57] U.S. officials knew that when the Red Army marched across the Manchurian border it would drive home (again, especially to the Japanese military) that Japan was defeated. On May 21, 1945, Secretary Stimson advised that "Russian entry will have a profound military effect . . ."[58]; and by early June the War Department Operations Division held that a Russian declaration of war might well produce surrender, either alone or in combination with a landing or "imminent threat of a landing."[59] In mid-June, General Marshall offered this advice directly to the President, stating:

... the impact of Russian entry on the already hopeless Japanese may well be the decisive action levering them into capitulation at that time or shortly thereafter *if* we land in Japan.*[60]

A point which has been missed in many studies of the Hiroshima decision is that the precise role a Russian declaration of war played in American thinking changed during the spring and summer of 1945. Up to mid-April, the Russians were regarded as important because their entry would pin down the Japanese in Manchuria, preventing them from reinforcing the mainland during an invasion. However, the U.S. Navy had achieved such command of the sea lanes that by April it had become impossible for Japan to withdraw its armies from Manchuria in any event.† Japanese morale and power had deteriorated to such an extent that the Russian declaration of war now came to be seen primarily in psychological terms—as a massive *shock,* which might in and of itself force Japan to capitulate.

There is in fact a precise parallel between the way U.S. leaders conceived of the Russian declaration of war and the atomic bombs: At first the bombs had also been expected to be used *in conjunction with an invasion.* But by the late spring and into the summer of 1945, Japan's situation had become so impossible that the weapons, too, were viewed in psychological terms—as a profound shock which was likely in and of itself to bring about surrender. The idea of using the limited number of bombs on essentially civilian targets—*rather than in direct support of the military landing*—would have been unthinkable a few months earlier.‡

Let us return to examine more closely the advice General Marshall gave the President on June 18. First note the word "if," which I have italicized; the landing was clearly not a certainty. Second, note several other terms: (1) "the already hopeless Japanese"; (2) Russian entry as "the decisive action"; (3) "levering them into capitulation." Third, note also Marshall's recognition that a *long* invasion

---

* Emphasis added.

† See below, pp. 77–81, 155–57. Numerous authors have either misinterpreted or mischaracterized the position taken in the book on this point. For instance, criticizing *Atomic Diplomacy* for (allegedly) contending that U.S. leaders did not want Soviet entry into the war, Daniel Yergin (*Shattered Peace*, p. 433) both misstates and misses the specific turns in policy delineated in the book,

namely: (1) The Russians were wanted *before April;* (2) in mid-May, Stimson told the State Department that "military considerations . . . [did] not preclude" raising troublesome political issues with the Soviets in the Far East; but (3) thereafter, U.S. leaders wanted to maintain the insurance of a Russian entry and looked to the Potsdam meeting with this in mind. See below, pp. 146–47; 156–58;174.

‡ See below, pp. 161–65.

involving massive casualties was no longer seriously contemplated at that time ("or shortly thereafter"). Fourth, remember this advice was given on the demanding assumption that the Presidential guidance concerning the "unconditional surrender" would remain in force. Fifth, and most important, note that the date was June 18, 1945—seven full weeks before Hiroshima. In the intervening period—almost two months—much stronger evidence of the deterioration of Japanese morale, and of their desire to end the war, poured in.

The argument that the atomic bomb had to be used to avoid an invasion turns in part on whether the Russian declaration of war was an available option—*and understood as such.* In attempting to clarify precisely what American decision makers understood, specific dates become very important—especially in establishing the attitude of the President himself. Though the official records tell us of his decisions, they do not fully illuminate how he understood the point about the Soviet Union. The 1978 discovery of Truman's private diary permits us to narrow the field initially to precisely one month—the time between June 17 and July 17. On the first date Truman records:

> I have to decide Japanese strategy—shall we invade Japan proper or shall we bomb and blockade? That is my hardest decision to date. But I'll make it when I have all the facts.[61]

(At the June 18 meeting Truman ordered the Joint Chiefs to go ahead with the Kyushu plan, saying they could "then decide as to the final action later."[62]) On the second date, July 17, Truman—after meeting with Stalin—entered two important observations in his diary. (This is after the initial sketchy reports of the successful atomic test had arrived, but before the full report from Alamogordo had been received.) The first diary entry concerns the timing of Soviet entrance into the war against Japan:

> He'll be in the Jap War on August 15th.

The second is Truman's confirmation of his understanding of the importance of a Soviet declaration of war:

> Fini Japs when that comes about.[63]

Clearly the Japanese were collapsing. The *coup de grâce* could be administered either by the shock of a Soviet declaration or by the atomic bomb. That by the end of July Truman preferred not to play the Soviet card is obvious; but that is not the issue. The question is whether top U.S. leaders *understood* that it was a very powerful card indeed. There is little doubt that they did; at the time they bombed Hiroshima they *chose* not to test whether their best intelligence estimates were correct—namely, that a Russian declaration of war seemed likely to precipitate a surrender without an invasion.

Indeed, although the United States had desperately wanted Russian participation in the war only a few weeks earlier, Japanese power had so deteriorated that U.S decision makers actively sought ways to avoid or slow down a Soviet declaration. The Russians had originally been included in the draft Potsdam Proclamation warning the Japanese to surrender—an inclusion which would have shown the unity of the Big Three and clearly indicated to the Japanese that any hope the Soviet Union would stay out of the war was an illusion. On Byrnes's recommendation, the Russians were cut out of the Proclamation. The fact that this statement was issued from the site of the Big Three meeting but *without* Stalin's signature, as might have been expected, gave rise to a vain hope within Japan that indeed the Russians might *not* enter the war.[64]

Churchill observed to Anthony Eden: "It is quite clear that the United States do not at the present time desire Russian participation in the war against Japan."[65] Secretary of the Navy Forrestal recorded in his diary on July 28, 1945: ". . . Byrnes said he was most anxious to get the Japanese affair over with before the Russians got in, with particular reference to [the Manchurian ports of] Dairen and Port Arthur. . . ."[66]

Soviet entry had been made contingent on the completion of negotiations with the Chinese over several issues concerning North China and Manchuria (mainly the return to Russia of areas and legal rights lost to Japan during the Russo-Japanese war of 1905). Although as Truman recorded, "most of the big points are settled,"[67] Truman and Byrnes cabled Chiang Kai-shek to keep negotiating but not to make any concessions. "I had some fear," Byrnes later reported, "that if they did not, Stalin might immediately enter the war. . . ."[68]

Not only did the United States no longer want Russian participation in the war, they made every effort to end the hostilities as fast as possible *before the Russians got in, or at least before they got very far into Manchuria.* Top American leaders were almost frantic. "Never have I known time to pass so slowly!" Byrnes later recalled.[69]

Indeed, even after the first intercepted Japanese message accepting the general terms of surrender came in, Truman ordered conventional military operations to continue full force. At the Cabinet meeting on August 10, 1945, Stimson "suggested . . . that it would be a humane thing . . . that might affect the settlement if we stopped the bombing. . . ." However, his view was "rejected on the ground that it couldn't be done at once because we had not yet received in official form the Japanese surrender. . . ." Stimson's diary entry continues: "This of course was a correct but narrow reason, for the Japanese had broadcast their offer of surrender through every country in the world." Forrestal's diary shows that Stimson also "cited the growing feeling of apprehension and misgiving as to the effect of the atomic bomb even in our own country," and that the Secretary of the Navy supported the advice that conventional bombing should cease.[70]

Truman refused to let up the pace even after the Japanese accepted the final American message which implicitly acknowledged the position of the Emperor. Well after Radio Tokyo had broadcast acceptance of the American terms (on August 14) but before the message had reached Washington through *official* channels, General Arnold (who wished to stage as big a *finale* as possible) was permitted to send 1,014 aircraft (approximately 800 B-29's and 200 fighters) to drop 6,000 tons of conventional explosives on Honshu.[71]

It is in the context of the tremendous rush to end the war *before the Russians got very far into Manchuria,* I believe, that we can understand how American leaders not only authorized the use of the second bomb against Nagasaki without, so far as we can tell, a moment's doubt—*but also seem to have had no inclination whatsoever to reconsider the attack once Hiroshima was destroyed.* One bomb alone sufficed, of course, to demonstrate the tremendous power of the new weapon in the American arsenal—both to the Russians and to the Japanese. Nor was there any longer any real question that the war would end without an invasion. The only important question was how *quickly* the war could be ended, a question which derived its particular urgency, *in August*, from American concern about the Soviet Union.

Again, the matter of dates should have been enough to stimulate obvious questions: The Russians were scheduled to enter the war three months after Germany's May 8 surrender—i.e., August 8 (amended, as we have seen, at Potsdam to August 15). Hiroshima was bombed on August 6 and Nagasaki was bombed on August 9.

"UNCONDITIONAL SURRENDER"

WHAT OF THE QUESTION of "unconditional surrender"? We are still attempting to discern whether Truman *understood* that he was almost certainly not going to have to invade Japan at the time he authorized the use of the atomic bombs. Historians have written at length about the surrender formula, ever since it was first revealed that the Acting Secretary of State during much of the period, Joseph Grew, advised Truman that a change in the unconditional surrender demand was likely to end the war. The most important point to focus on from our point of view is that the intercepted cables clearly showed that by June and July the only real sticking point in the Japanese position had indeed to do with the role of the Emperor. I have already quoted Forrestal's diary entry of July 13, 1945, but here is how one highly respected authority (Professor Robert Butow) has characterized the information: "It was all there, as clear as crystal: *Togo to Sato:'. . . Unconditional surrender is the only obstacle to peace. . . .'* "[72]

Did top American leaders *understand* that if they altered the surrender formula to assure the Japanese they could keep the Emperor there was a very high likelihood that the war would be ended long before a landing (to say nothing of an invasion)? We are not here interested in whether they *preferred* not to offer the Japanese assurances for the Emperor; we are trying to reconstruct their understanding of their options.

Some of the most powerful evidence we have on this point—from an "Estimate of the Enemy Situation" (as of July 6, 1945), prepared for the Combined Chiefs of Staff meetings at Potsdam—was fully declassified only in 1976. Here are some of its conclusions:

INTRODUCTION

We believe that a considerable portion of the Japanese population now consider absolute military defeat to be probable. The increasing effects of sea blockade and cumulative devastation wrought by strategic bombing, which has already rendered millions homeless and has destroyed from 25% to 50% of the built-up area of Japan's most important cities, should make this realization increasingly general. An entry of the Soviet Union into the war would finally convince the Japanese of the inevitability of complete defeat. Although individual Japanese willingly sacrifice themselves in the service of the nation, we doubt that the nation as a whole is predisposed toward national suicide.[73]

The document went on to emphasize that while an "unconditional surrender" was not imminent, "to insure the survival of the institution of the Emperor," the Japanese seemed likely to be willing to accept U.S. terms:

A conditional surrender by the Japanese Government . . . might be offered by them at any time from now until the time of the complete destruction of all Japanese power of resistance.[74]

In detailed support of this position, the Intelligence "Estimate" pointed out that the

Japanese ruling groups are aware of the desperate military situation and are increasingly desirous of a compromise peace, but still find "unconditional surrender" unacceptable. Indeed the formal acceptance of "unconditional surrender" by Japanese constituted authority must be deemed basically unlikely, since the term probably implies to the Japanese mind the overthrow of the Emperor and the position of the Imperial House, the extinction of the Japanese traditions and of the Japanese way of life, and the abolition of the Japanese constitution."[75]

The significance of this document goes beyond its recognition of the strategic importance of the Russians and of a change in the surrender terms; it is a formal warning both to top U.S. military and to top political leaders that if the formula is *not* changed, the war will continue in a costly, bitter, and bloody fashion for a long time.[76]

There is no doubt whatsoever that Truman was advised about the importance of changing the unconditional surrender formula by a number of the highest officials. We have already cited some of the OSS information presented to him by Donovan in the second week of May. Secretary Grew urged a change in the surrender terms in a meeting with Truman as early as May 28, 1945—more than two months before Hiroshima was destroyed.

Much more important from our point of view is the fact that there is abundant evidence that the President had no objection in principle to the change. According to Grew, for instance, at this meeting Truman "immediately said that his own thinking ran along the same lines as mine. . . ." Truman asked Grew to discuss the proposal with the Secretaries of War and Navy and the Chiefs of Staff. In a meeting the next day with Secretaries Stimson and Forrestal and General Marshall, these men also stated their agreement with the principle but "for certain military reasons, not divulged," it was felt that a statement giving some form of assurance to the Emperor *at that time* was not advisable.[77]

The undisclosed military reasons, of course, concerned the atomic bomb. At this meeting, Stimson also confirmed his understanding that Truman agreed in principle with the recommendation that the "unconditional surrender formula" be changed as proposed by Grew. Again, the main issue, as Forrestal noted, was that he did not want to proceed "at this moment. . . ." (Forrestal's account of this meeting, incidentally, is that "both Stimson and Grew most emphatically asserted that this move ought to be done . . ."—i.e., both the Secretary of War and the Acting Secretary of State were in strong agreement at a very early point on the matter.[78])

Another indication of the President's own view came in the June 18, 1945, White House military planning meeting. Here it was Admiral Leahy who raised the issue of altering the unconditional surrender formula, arguing that unless this was done it would make the Japanese desperate and increase American casualties. The official minutes of the meeting record:

> THE PRESIDENT stated that it was with that thought in mind that he had left the door open for Congress to take appropriate action with reference to unconditional surrender.*

Again, Truman indicated, however, that he did not wish to take action "at this time."[79] Leahy also recalls that in private discussions the President indicated his support for Leahy's argument for ending

---

* McCloy also proposed a warning and assurances for the Emperor at this time. For one description, see Hewlett and Anderson, *The New World*, p. 364.

the war without an invasion: "He was completely favorable toward defeating our Far Eastern enemy with the smallest possible loss of American lives. It wasn't a matter of dollars. It might require more time—and more dollars—if we did not invade Japan. But it would cost *fewer lives*."*[80]

Leahy's point is both correct and important: Truman did not regard a change of the surrender terms favoring the Emperor as of fundamental importance. After a meeting with him on July 18, Churchill also understood "there would be no rigid insistence upon 'unconditional surrender'. . . ."[81] *There is no question that the President was quite willing to offer such a change, even if it would take more time, if that would prevent an invasion:* On July 24, Truman told Stimson, too, that he would reassure the Japanese about the Emperor if (as Stimson put it) "they were hanging fire on that one point. . . ."[82]

The significance of the information we now have on the intercepted Japanese cables, on what top American intelligence believed, on what top diplomatic and military leaders recommended, and what Truman himself had concluded has not been fully appreciated:

It is very clear that well before atomic weapons were used, both the Japanese and U.S. governments had arrived at the same understanding of acceptable terms of surrender. Truman knew, moreover, that a change in the surrender terms in favor of the Emperor—on the best advice available at the time—was highly likely to end the war without an invasion.

Nor did the President have any fundamental objection to making this alteration: It is impossible to read the evidence of the time in a way that suggests Truman thought the "unconditional surrender formula" so important that he would stick to it to the end if this meant the United States would have to go through with an invasion.

Accordingly, at the time Truman permitted the Hiroshima and Nagasaki bombings he was aware—on the best advice available—that the war could in all likelihood be ended on terms which he had already deemed acceptable.

If this point were not clear from the documents of the time, we

---

* Emphasis in original.

need only recall that, in fact, Truman *did* alter the surrender terms to allow the Japanese to keep their Emperor. The "unconditional surrender" formula was simply adroitly abandoned when the time came. The Emperor is still there.

It is quite true, as many have pointed out (and as *Atomic Diplomacy* also showed), that there was a debate over whether it was best to offer Japan assurances about the Emperor before or after the atomic bombs were used. If he could, Truman apparently preferred to try to end the war *without* changing the surrender terms. *Given that he had decided to use the atomic bomb,* he also was advised (in the end especially by Byrnes[83]) that the best time to offer assurances to the Emperor was after its power had been demonstrated. It is, however, no longer possible to believe that the President was unaware that a change in this surrender formula alone seemed likely to end the war well before an invasion.

It is sometimes argued that the Japanese military would have fought to the death to avoid surrender. Perhaps. There are indeed some indications that *some* officers would have done so (although how widespread such actions might have been once the Emperor had intervened is questionable). But there are two difficulties with this line of argument: First, very often the wrong question is asked, for in most studies the argument is that the officer groups would have fought to the death to avoid *unconditional surrender*—i.e., to preserve the Emperor.

Much more important from the point of view of our immediate concern, the advice given to the President *at the time,* as we have seen, did not emphasize this as a determinative consideration. Indeed, there is very little evidence that American policy makers doubted that once the Emperor was guaranteed his position, he could settle whatever difficulties there were with challenges from officer groups. The Japanese Emperor was regarded as a living deity; as Acting Secretary of State Grew, an experienced former Ambassador to Japan, observed, top U.S. officials believed that if an "Imperial rescript" were issued a surrender could be arranged.[84] Or, as Admiral Leahy put it: "We were certain that the Mikado could stop the war with a royal word."[85]

Remember, we are not here focusing on the question often asked by writers considering this issue—namely, whether Truman "should have" changed the unconditional surrender formula—or the question of whether in fact this would have achieved the result his top advisers thought it would. Rather, we are attempting to get at a slightly different question, namely, *whether at the time he authorized the bombing of Hiroshima, Truman understood there were other options likely to end the war.* And we are particularly interested in the still more specific question of what he had to have understood in those last weeks of July and first days of August 1945. "Fini Japs when that comes about," he noted privately of the coming Soviet entry—and he must have understood (as indicated in the Intelligence "Estimate" prepared a month earlier, even before the most powerful Japanese cables came in) that the *combination* of the forthcoming Soviet declaration of war *with a change in the surrender terms* was all but certain to end the war without an invasion. To believe otherwise is to think the President incapable of comprehending the most obvious information presented to him at the time.

We need only add that if the President's priority was really *simply* to end the war before an invasion, there were fully three months before the planned landing on Kyushu, and eight months before the invasion. There was still plenty of time to use the atomic bombs if the combination of a Soviet declaration of war and a change in the unconditional surrender terms did not work. (And, as Admiral Leahy reminds us, if an invasion could be prevented, time was not an overriding issue to the President.)

Powerful additional insight into this question is given by the secret British report of the July 16, 1945, meeting of the U.S.–U.K. Combined Chiefs of Staff. This is *just before* the atomic bomb test was reported and is perhaps the last clear observation we have of how military leaders saw matters before everything changed. The U.S. Chiefs felt so strongly the unconditional surrender formula should be altered that they even attempted an "end run" indirect lobbying effort: They asked the *British military Chiefs* to see if they could get Churchill to raise the matter with Truman. As to how both the British and U.S. Chiefs understood the situation just before Alamogordo, here is the way General Ismay summarized the intelligence information of July 8 in his private report to Prime Minister Churchill:

The combined Chiefs of Staff at their first meeting had under consideration a paper prepared by the Combined Intelligence Staffs on the enemy situation, in which it was suggested that if and when Russia came into the war against Japan, the Japanese would probably wish to get out on almost any terms short of the dethronement of the Emperor.[86]

A suggestive entry in Truman's diary of July 18, 1945, also bears on this point. (The entry was written shortly after Stalin told the President about Japanese attempts to negotiate an end to the war and his planned response—which Truman termed "satisfactory.") First, as to Truman's understanding of what the Japanese were doing: The President describes the approach to Stalin as the "telegram from Jap Emperor asking for peace." He then goes on to note: "Believe Japs will fold up before Russia comes in. I am sure they will when Manhattan appears over their homeland."[87] The two-sentence sequence seems to indicate that the President believed the war would end ("fold up") *before* Russia entered even without the atomic bombs—and that he was *sure* it would once the fruit of the Manhattan Project was used. It is hard to tell for certain, but if this indeed was what he felt, it would accord with the view that he privately understood the situation in exactly the way Eisenhower did. For at the same time the Supreme Commander judged that "it wasn't necessary to hit them with that awful thing," he also believed the war could easily be ended without the Russians.[88] In any event, that the President was aware of the enormous deterioration of Japanese power is further documented by this entry.*

OTHER CONSIDERATIONS
RELATED TO THE SOVIET UNION

Such information makes it extremely difficult to believe that President Truman and his top advisers thought that unless they used atomic weapons against the Japanese they would have to undertake an invasion. By late July and early August—and probably earlier—the argument of "overriding military necessity" no longer held. It is

---

* Recall that Allen Dulles had been summoned to Potsdam. It may well be that the President had in mind arranging a quick "folding-up" through Dulles's Swiss negotiating channel.

clear that American leaders *preferred* the use of the new weapon over such other available options as the impending Russian declaration of war or a change in the surrender terms—but that is a different matter altogether.

Let us pause briefly to note one among the many elements of tragedy in the story we have so far reviewed: As we have seen, a major American concern was to end the war before the Russians got very far into Manchuria. *But, as Stimson, Marshall, and others recognized at the time,* the issues the President and Secretary of State were worried about in North China and Manchuria were all well within the military power of the Soviet Union to settle on their own terms in any event—whether or not the war ended a few weeks early.*

Before we can reach a full understanding of how American leaders came to use the first atomic bombs, we must explore one further aspect of their thinking—and we need to understand additional considerations related to the Soviet Union. This, however, involves a much more difficult task than our review of the more narrowly military related questions.

As I indicated at the outset, the information available twenty years ago was not conclusive on many points, and we still do not have all the facts. (Accounts that claim that we do, or that are written in an apparently authoritative manner which *suggests* we do, are simply wrong and are misleading.) There is, moreover, considerable evidence that at the time and subsequently a number of the people involved made efforts to keep their actions secret, and, in some cases, to distort the record.

This is true even among men of great personal integrity. For instance, we know without question that the President's Chief of Staff believed an invasion was totally unnecessary, and that he thought the use of the atomic bomb repugnant. We also know he made his views on the war clear to the President at the time. But out of respect for his confidential relationship, or for other reasons, Leahy apparently kept very few notes of his private discussion of these critical matters with the President, or if he did, he either destroyed them or they have yet to be discovered.

---

* See below, p.147.

Moreover, what notes Leahy did keep on the atomic bomb question are very circumspect. We know from other sources that at the June 18 military planning meeting, for instance, Assistant Secretary of War John F. McCloy raised the bomb question openly for discussion, but Leahy's diary does not mention it in his description of the same meeting. Again, on May 20, Leahy reports: "Discussed with Justice Byrnes the status and prospects of a new explosive that is in process of development 'Manhattan Project.' "

> Justice Byrnes has been directed by the President to make a study of this project on which some two billion dollars has already been spent. He, Byrnes, seems to be very favorably impressed with the possibilities of the new explosive. I still feel that the claims made by the scientists are at least extravagant.[89]

He also records on June 4:

> At 5:30 Mr. Justice Byrnes called at the house to discuss some results of his study of Dr. Busch's (*sic*) super explosive. He is more favorably impressed than I am with prospects of success in the final development and use of this new weapon.[90]

But these very brief entries are all we have. Leahy is known to have been skeptical of whether the new weapon would be all that its proponents claimed, but that is not the point at issue: During precisely these days Byrnes made no bones about his view that the bomb would give him enormous leverage *vis à vis* the Soviet Union, especially to insiders close to the President. We know also that he made a special visit to Leahy's home for this conversation. But Leahy's diary entry carries only the above, very brief mention.

A related problem is that the sheer mass of information on secondary matters has misled some writers. Large bureaucracies produce enormous amounts of paper—letters, memoranda, minutes of meetings, etc.—the stuff of day-to-day action, and of internal communication. There are documents containing the formal views of people at various levels of the State Department, the War Department, the separate military commands, and so on. We also know a great deal about the scientists' efforts to influence nuclear policy. Anyone who has any serious experience of Washington, however, knows that what appears on these documents is often quite different from what is going on at the highest level of decision making. (Having spent a number of the years since *Atomic Diplomacy* was written working in both Houses of Congress and at the policy level in the State Department, I now see this point even more clearly than I did in 1965.) In a sense we have been deluged with excessive information—about the wrong story.

Most accounts (including *Atomic Diplomacy*) have also relied heavily on the powerful and often moving diaries of Secretary of War Henry L. Stimson. Yet Stimson was a very old and sick man by the end of the war. Though he was formally Secretary of War, his influence with Truman was not great. He even had to ask special permission to go to Potsdam. Stimson was only sporadically consulted by Truman and his Secretary of State during the Big Three meeting; Byrnes had the ear of the President, and control of the major issues.

A further problem is the standard historian's difficulty with documents in general and diaries in particular: We know that the politicians involved often told people what they wanted to hear, and they very often did not tell them of other related, confidential matters. In some cases there is reason to believe the Secretary of State may have been currying favor with individuals who subsequently recorded their conversations, and that what was said was far different from what Byrnes believed.[91]

Compounding these difficulties is the basic fact that the bomb was shrouded in enormous secrecy—a secrecy which extended to the very highest government officials. When Secretary Stimson and General Groves first briefed Truman on the new weapon at his White House office on April 24, for instance, Groves was told to come in by the back door to avoid speculation. Truman refused even to keep Groves's secret report; he felt it was "not advisable."[92]

We know from Groves's cryptic memorandum summarizing the meeting that during the discussion "a great deal of emphasis was placed on foreign relations and particularly on the Russian situation."[93] And we know that Stimson asked for the meeting the day after Truman's angry April 23 meeting with Molotov, urging

> it is very important that I should have a talk with you as soon as possible on a highly secret matter . . . [which] has such a bearing on our present foreign relations and has such an important effect upon

all my thinking in this field that I think you ought to know about it without much further delay.*

Truman reports that Stimson told him "the atomic bomb would be certain to have a decisive influence on our relations with other countries." We also know Stimson's formal views as outlined in a written memorandum, and we know *something* about the discussion from Stimson's diary and Groves's memorandum. It is clear, however, that there is much we do not know.[94]

How cautious top officials were in handling matters related to the bomb and diplomacy is also indicated in other ways. For instance, we have noted that at the meeting during which Stimson told Acting Secretary of State Grew he agreed that the unconditional surrender formula should be modified, the Secretary of War also told Grew that the time was not yet appropriate. "Since some of those present were not supposed to know about the atomic bomb," the official history of the Atomic Energy Commission summarizes, "Stimson could not reveal the real reason he considered the timing wrong."[95] Again, at the June 18 White House meeting discussing plans for military operations against Japan, at the last minute Truman asked Assistant Secretary of War John J. McCloy for his opinion. McCloy thought the idea of an invasion fantastic in view of the atomic bomb's imminent availability. But when he brought up the subject, as the same official study put it, McCloy "sensed the chills that ran up and down the spines assembled there," for the bomb had not been discussed so openly even in official circles.[96]

A further illustration: When Truman asked Ambassador Joseph Davies to undertake his mission to see Churchill, as we have seen, he told him very privately that the reason he was delaying a meeting with Stalin was that he wanted to wait until the atomic bomb had been tested. Davies recorded in his diary: "Charged me with utmost secrecy. . . ."[97] Again, as one high-level Potsdam participant has recalled, the U.S. delegation was bolstered when news of the successful test strengthened their negotiating hand *vis à vis* the Russians, but the whole matter was "hush-hush."[98]

---

* See below, p. 61. Only a very few historians seem to have recognized that the subject of the atomic bomb was brought to the President's atten- tion in the specific context of the confrontation with Molotov over Poland.

SPECIAL PROBLEMS
IN CONNECTION WITH BYRNES

EXTREME SECRECY is only one of the difficulties facing anyone who seeks to reconstruct how American policy makers thought about the atomic bomb at this time. The best scholarly studies we have are intelligent interpretations of what is contained in the main papers currently available. But if one reads them very closely, something appears to be missing at regular and crucial points.

The story of Hiroshima and Potsdam involves above all the person of James F. Byrnes, and there are special problems with information related to the President's chief adviser. A large part of what appears to be missing in even the best accounts relates to Byrnes's activities and advice during the crucial weeks from the death of Roosevelt in mid-April to the end of June 1945.

We are beginning to know Byrnes better each day, thanks in large part to the work of scholars who have in the last decade combed his personal papers and the diaries and papers of his closest associates. Robert Messer's *The End of an Alliance* is particularly useful, but there have also been several other important works.[99] These studies make it abundantly clear that Truman's Secretary of State and his personal representative on the Interim Committee, the man closest to him on matters related both to the atomic bomb and diplomacy toward the Soviet Union, was an exceedingly complex, secretive, and even devious politician.

Truman himself privately referred to Byrnes on several occasions as his "conniving Secretary of State." While initially the President regarded him highly (he was to change his opinion), even at the outset of his Administration he was quite clear about his character. "All country politicians are alike," Truman confided to his diary about Byrnes. "They are sure all other politicians are circuitous in their dealings. When they are told the straight truth, unvarnished, it is never believed—an asset *sometimes*."*[100]

The closest student of Byrnes in these years (Messer) offers us these additional insights: ". . . Byrnes was congenitally uncandid. . . ." ". . . Byrnes' constant sensitivity to the public, political

---

* Emphasis in original.

implications of virtually everything he said or did is evident. . . ."
Byrnes went to inordinate lengths to control information related to
his activities as Secretary of State:

> Byrnes' efforts at manipulating history include his deliberate edit-
> ing, altering and at times even fabricating evidence of his past as it
> is recorded in the documents and other manuscript sources. . . .
> Byrnes' manipulation of his personal papers goes beyond the nor-
> mal limits of genteel dishonesty. Extensive research of these archi-
> val records leads unavoidably to the conclusion that they have
> been systematically doctored. . . .

For instance:

> Correspondence that for years was meticulously collated and pre-
> served with an attached carbon copy of Byrnes' response suddenly
> begins to include incoming letters and memoranda on sensitive sub-
> jects from which Byrnes' reply has been detached. . . .

And:

> In 1954 the persistent scholars at the Department of State ap-
> proached Byrnes' former associates . . . for any records they might
> have relating to the Potsdam Conference of July, 1945. One such
> associate was Walter Brown, Byrnes' long time friend. . . . Byrnes
> did not know that during the conference Brown had kept a detailed
> daily journal recording Byrnes' activities and his private utterances
> concerning the negotiations. . . . Byrnes was at first furious when he
> learned of the existence of such a diary. However, Byrnes' initial
> anger soon subsided and he eventually turned this record, too, to-
> ward his own uses. . . .
>
> The edited "excerpts" of Brown's diary entries for July 1945 that
> Byrnes eventually sent the State Department alter the meaning and
> substantially destroy the significance of Brown's diary. . . . The al-
> terations and deletions, indicated in Byrnes' own hand throughout
> the copy of the diary sent him by Brown, distort and at times totally
> reverse the meaning of the actual contemporary record.

"Having made certain that the State Department would no longer
trouble with the Brown diary," Messer observes,

> Byrnes sent what he titled "Excerpts From Notes of Walter Brown"
> to the State Department with his "best wishes . . . ," and the rewrit-
> ten diary became part of the record relied on by the State Depart-
> ment and by many historians. When asked directly by individual
> private scholars for information on some of the same subjects for
> which he had sent the State Department his own manipulated evi-

dence, Byrnes with the straightest of faces politely referred the inquiring historian to the official State Department record.[101]

Many of Byrnes's after-the-fact changes in the record seem to have been especially designed to protect him from conservative attack in the years after he left office, but Truman's Secretary of State was extremely secretive throughout his lifetime as a public official. Byrnes used a private stenographic code to keep notes on key subjects, a code that still is not decipherable. He conducted the greater part of his business in one-to-one sessions or on the telephone in the era before sound-actuated recording devices and self-imposed telephone taps had become standard procedure for government officials. Byrnes greatly feared "leaks" from the bureaucracy, and operated as much as possible at arm's length from the State Department, both before and after his formal appointment as Secretary. "God Almighty, I might tell the President sometime what happened," Byrnes told close associates at the London Council of Foreign Ministers, "but I'm never going to tell those little bastards at the State Department anything about it."[102]

BYRNES'S ROLE

THOUGH IT SEEMS difficult to believe, there is evidence that during the summer of 1945 Byrnes was even more secretive than his normal pattern: Not even his closest associates, men who were usually kept abreast of his dealings, were informed of work he had undertaken for Truman in connection with diplomatic matters, to say nothing of the atomic bomb.[103] For this reason, it is necessary to spend a bit more time than usual piecing together what we know about the man and his relationship to the President.

Truman placed a great deal of trust in Byrnes when he chose him as his first Secretary of State: With no Vice-President in office after Truman succeeded Roosevelt, Byrnes became next in the line of succession. (In 1945, moreover, before the modern institution of the National Security Adviser, the position of Secretary of State carried much greater weight than it does today.) Byrnes had been a Governor, a Senator, a Supreme Court Justice, Roosevelt's "Assistant President," and a major contender for the Vice-Presidency. He was also a person to whom Truman felt politically obligated: Roosevelt had picked Truman over Byrnes in a surprise decision in 1944. Truman had in fact indicated that he would nominate Byrnes at the Chicago convention.

There were other reasons for Byrnes's special position of influence: When Truman had first come to the Senate, Byrnes had taken him under his wing and made the young Missouri Senator something of a protégé. Truman accepted his old mentor as an equal at the outset of his Administration, agreeing (before Byrnes would accept the nomination) to give him a high degree of autonomy in the management of foreign affairs. Byrnes was regarded as uniquely influential, combining the personal access to the President of a Hopkins with highly independent authority to speak on foreign relations.[104]

Well before he formally took office, Byrnes played a powerful role in privately advising Truman—from the very first days of his Administration. "Immediately upon becoming President, I sent for him because I wanted his assistance," Truman later recalled.[105] On the first full day of his Presidency, April 13, Truman met with Byrnes for a half hour and discussed "the current political-military situation." The next morning, Byrnes, along with Secretary of Commerce Henry Wallace, accompanied the President to Union Station to meet the train carrying Roosevelt's body from Georgia. Byrnes then rode with Truman and Wallace in the President's limousine in the funeral procession up Pennsylvania Avenue to the White House. In the afternoon of the same day, Byrnes met again with Truman and White House Chief of Staff Leahy for nearly two hours until they finally adjourned to attend the funeral services in the East Room. The following day Byrnes traveled with Truman by special train to Hyde Park for Roosevelt's burial. En route, Byrnes and Truman had "intense" private talks. The next day, the 16th, Byrnes met again alone with Truman for nearly three hours.[106]

No one during the crucial first days of Truman's Administration had more direct, private contact with the new President. Presidential Counselor Samuel Rosenman believed that "by the day the President took office, on April 12, 1945, he had already decided upon Byrnes becoming Secretary of State." This view was echoed in the contemporary press. As early as April 15, Washington correspondents began describing Byrnes as "personal adviser to Mr. Truman."[107]

INTRODUCTION

At the moment of Roosevelt's death the existing Secretary of State, Edward Stettinius, was involved in preparations for the San Francisco founding meeting of the United Nations. To avoid any awkwardness, Truman and Byrnes agreed that for the time being Byrnes would adopt as low a public profile as possible. Evidence of their private contact, however, reveals that Byrnes's public remoteness from Truman during the period before he took the oath as Secretary was a ruse used until Stettinius finished his official participation in the San Francisco Conference. On April 17, for instance, when the White House released the list of the President's Official Appointments, Byrnes's name was not mentioned, though it had been prominent on the unpublished list for the 13th to the 16th. Byrnes, by prearrangement with Truman, informed the press that he was returning to South Carolina "to rest."[108]

Between April 16 and the time he was officially sworn in on July 3, Byrnes's activities were carried on in great secrecy. He shuttled back and forth between South Carolina and Washington, time and again, quietly slipping into the capital to attend high-level policy discussions at the White House. We know very little about these meetings (except that they occurred), and even less about his private, personal discussions with the President. However, we do know two fundamental facts: Truman had determined that Byrnes would be Secretary of State, and he decided also (on May 3) that the man in charge of foreign affairs would also be the man to represent him on the Interim Committee considering policy toward the atomic bomb. The choice of a person connected first and foremost with diplomacy, and particularly diplomacy toward the Soviet Union, for this job—and not, for instance, a military specialist—highlights the early and deep connection of the bomb with foreign affairs.

We also know that Byrnes was a highly ambitious politician—and that the forthcoming meeting with Stalin was to be one of the most momentous events in his tenure as Secretary of State.

BYRNES'S VIEW OF THE ATOMIC BOMB

WE ARE ATTEMPTING to gain a deeper understanding of how top American officials came to use atomic weapons against Japan and, specifically, how they understood the relationship of the new weapon to other foreign policy objectives. In the case of the President's chief adviser, given his extraordinary secrecy, and given the difficulties with what evidence we do have, it is necessary to approach the matter somewhat indirectly. Nevertheless, by combining different people's observations of Byrnes during the period between Roosevelt's death and the Potsdam Conference, it is possible to develop a coherent picture of how the Secretary of State viewed the most important issues.

We have already noted Truman's report that at one of their very first meetings Byrnes told him that "in his belief the atomic bomb might well put us in a position to dictate our own terms at the end of the war. . . ."[109] And we have cited a brief excerpt from atomic scientist Leo Szilard's report of a meeting in May 1945. Byrnes "did not argue that it was necessary to use the bomb against the cities of Japan in order to win the war," Szilard noted. "Mr. Byrnes' view [was] that our possessing and demonstrating the bomb would make Russia more manageable in Europe. . . ."[110]

We know, further, that at virtually every opportunity on the Interim Committee considering the matter, Byrnes (representing the President) took a tough line against any attempt to seek international control of the new weaponry. Very early on, Byrnes saw the atomic bomb as important bargaining leverage, potentially useful in all manner of international negotiations.

The Secretary of State–designate was also intensely interested in how long the U.S. monopoly would last, probing scientists on the question in meetings of the Interim Committee's Scientific Panel on May 31. Byrnes repeatedly stressed the need for the United States to maintain its nuclear monopoly as long as possible, and to accelerate research in order to stay ahead. On the same day Byrnes intervened forcefully in opposition to General Marshall and others to argue against the possibility the Russians would be told of the bomb's existence before it was used against Japan.[111] Byrnes's opposition to prior disclosure reversed the tenor of the committee's discussion, and the members agreed that the Soviet Union should not be approached before a public demonstration of the bomb against Japan.* The decision was, in fact, Byrnes's: Speaking as the Presi-

---

* For the subsequent slight modification of this decision, see below, pp. 202–4.

dent's personal representative, he virtually imposed the recommendation on the committee.[112]

Again, after a very brief discussion with the scientists on whether a technical demonstration might be feasible, we also know that it was Byrnes (following an earlier suggestion by James Conant) who proposed that the bomb be used as soon as possible and without warning against a target centering on a Japanese war plant surrounded by civilian housing.[113]

To the above information we may add several direct observations of Byrnes's attitude. From another report by Szilard of his May 28, 1945, meeting with Byrnes (which appeared after *Atomic Diplomacy* was first published):

> Byrnes . . . was concerned about Russia's postwar behavior. Russian troops had moved into Hungary and Rumania; Byrnes thought it would be very difficult to persuade Russia to withdraw her troops from these countries, and that Russia might be more manageable if impressed by American military might. I shared Byrnes's concern about Russia's throwing around her weight in the postwar period, but I was completely flabbergasted by the assumption that rattling the bomb might make Russia more manageable. . . .
>
> I was concerned at this point that by demonstrating the bomb and using it in the war against Japan, we might start an atomic arms race between America and Russia which might end with the destruction of both countries. . . .
>
> I was rarely as depressed as when we left Byrnes's house and walked toward the station.[114]

From the original, undoctored version of the diary of his assistant, Walter Brown:

> [July 17, 1945:] JFB had hoped Russian declaration of war against Japan would come out of this conference. Now he thinks United States and United Kingdom will have to issue joint statements giving Japs two weeks to surrender or face destruction (secret weapon will be ready by that time).[115]

> [July 20, 1945:] JFB determined to outmaneuver Stalin on China. Hopes [Chinese Foreign Minister] Soong will stand firm and then Russians will not go in war.[116]

> [July 24, 1945:] [Byrnes was] still hoping for time, believing that after [the] atomic bomb Japan will surrender and Russia will not get in so

much on the kill, thereby being in a position to press for claims against China.[117]

From Ambassador Joseph Davies' diaries:

[July 28, 1945:] [Byrnes] was having a hard time with reparations . . . , [but the] details as to the success of the atomic bomb, which he had just received, gave him confidence that the Soviets would agree as to these difficulties. . . . Byrnes' attitude that the atomic bomb assured ultimate success in negotiations disturbed me more than his description of its success amazed me. . . . I told him the threat wouldn't work, and might do irreparable harm.[118]

[July 29, 1945:] Because of the New Mexico development, [Byrnes] felt secure anyway. He elaborated on the extent of the power of the atomic bomb. . . . SECRETARY BYRNES suggested that the New Mexico situation had given us great power, and that in the last analysis it would control. . . .[119]

From Stimson's diary, reporting on a meeting with Assistant Secretary of War John J. McCloy in early September:

[Byrnes] was on the point of departing for the Foreign Ministers' meeting and wished to have the implied threat of the bomb in his pocket during the conference. . . .[120]

From Stimson's diary, September 4, 1945:

Jim Byrnes had not yet gone abroad and I had a very good talk with him afterward sitting in the White House hall. . . . I took up the question which I had been working at with McCloy up in St. Huberts, namely how to handle Russia with the big bomb. I found that Byrnes was very much against any attempt to cooperate with Russia. His mind is full of his problems with the coming meeting of foreign ministers and he looks to having the presence of the bomb in his pocket, so to speak, as a great weapon to get through the thing. . . . [121]

YALTA AND EASTERN EUROPE

THE RELATIONSHIP of the atomic bomb to diplomacy in Byrnes's thinking cannot be fully grasped without recalling that Byrnes was identified in American politics as the foremost spokesman and representative of the Yalta agreement: Roosevelt had selected Byrnes as the authorized interpreter of the agreements both to the American public and to the Congressional leadership. Byrnes had also personally had a major hand in drafting the famous "Declaration on Liberated Europe," which vaguely promised consultation on how to achieve free elections in Eastern Europe in the future, but (with the understanding of all parties) specifically eliminated any definition of precisely what was intended when, and contained no enforcement procedures.

At Yalta, Byrnes, a onetime court stenographer, had taken shorthand notes of a number of key discussions—virtually the only detailed record of several of them. Truman later said that he called upon Byrnes precisely because he wanted "to get his firsthand account of what had gone on. . . ."[122] Byrnes used his position, and the fact that he had the only direct, verbatim account of several secret Yalta conversations, to cement his relationship as chief adviser to Truman on foreign policy. However, his situation was not without difficulties: One of the reasons for Byrnes's extreme secrecy was that his private notes revealed that Roosevelt had indeed made major concessions to Stalin on Eastern Europe—a fact which directly contradicted what Byrnes had been proclaiming in public and to key members of Congress.

"When you read this you will immediately see reasons why it should be kept under lock and key," Byrnes told Truman in a covering note transmitting his stenographic record. "Should it fall into the hand of anyone close to the columnists, it could start a war on several fronts."[123]

(That Truman also felt constrained not to admit concessions had been made to Stalin is evidenced by his direct denial to his own Cabinet on August 10, 1945, of the fact that there had been an understanding reached at Yalta about Far Eastern matters.[124])

The recent scholarship on Byrnes demonstrates that given the rather compromised position he was in, the Secretary of State–designate followed a very complex strategy during the spring and summer of 1945. *Publicly,* he repeatedly gave assurances that Roosevelt had not made major concessions to Stalin, particularly in connection with Eastern Europe—*and was personally and politically identified with this position.* Privately, however, he acknowledged *to a very few key people* that his public position was quite different from the specific understandings he knew Roosevelt had reached. *At the very same time,* he was preparing recommendations to the President for the forthcoming Potsdam Conference which urged a tough line toward the Soviets that was consistent with his public posture and a direct contradiction of his private awareness.[125]

Byrnes was also—*at the same time*—trying to impress upon influential columnists (like Walter Lippmann) and other important public figures (like former Ambassador Joseph Davies) who were worried about the deterioration of relations with the Soviet Union that his attitude toward the Russians was one of cooperation. It was, indeed, as Robert Messer has observed, an "elaborate international masquerade"—even more involved in its details than this summary can suggest.[126] We can understand why Byrnes was anxious that his notes on Yalta not "fall into the hands of the columnists"—as well as why Truman privately judged Byrnes to be "conniving."

One or two early critics of *Atomic Diplomacy* felt the book presented too devious a picture of American policy makers. The new evidence suggests that the story it tells is, if anything, probably a less than adequate account of the inordinately complex manner in which Truman's Secretary of State actually operated. The most important point from the standpoint of the question we are now investigating, however, is that Byrnes had a very powerful stake in maintaining his publicly proclaimed position—namely, that the United States had not and would not concede Soviet domination of Eastern Europe. As the man who had first interpreted the Yalta agreement to the American people, assuring them that no concessions had been made, Byrnes knew his own political standing was also directly linked to his capacity to make good on this promise.

U.S. STRATEGY, APRIL TO JULY 1945

ATOMIC DIPLOMACY WAS WRITTEN without benefit of the new material on Byrnes. If there is one significant aspect of the argument that may require modification, it has to do with Byrnes's role in providing advice to Truman on the Russian situation. In his recent *Day One,* Peter Wyden suggests that Byrnes's confidence in the atomic bomb's decisive diplomatic importance and his early advice to the President account for the tough stance Truman took in his famous April 23 first meeting with Molotov. The meeting centered on the Polish problem—a problem regarded at the time as symbolic of the understandings that had been reached on Eastern Europe in general.[127]

Wyden is probably partly correct, though there is no way (as yet) to know for sure. The fact that most of his other advisers, as *Atomic Diplomacy* demonstrated, also urged an immediate showdown over Poland, makes it impossible to sort out the precise lines of influence with currently available information. It is a matter of record, however, that in consultations with his advisers on the Polish question, Truman made a number of statements indicating that he personally had already decided upon a tough stance—and it is also a fact that prior to this time he had had several conversations with Byrnes both about the atomic bomb and about the Yalta understandings.

It is also difficult to know precisely when and how Byrnes (as opposed to Stimson) was involved in the decision to delay major negotiations with Stalin until after the new atomic weapons technology had been demonstrated. The record shows that Stimson urged this course, and that Truman postponed the Potsdam meeting until the test could take place. But it is clear that the President was also consulting with Byrnes. For instance, when on June 6 Stimson reported to him on the Interim Committee deliberations (and said the "greatest complication" would occur if the bomb had not been proven before the Big Three meeting), Truman said that Byrnes had already told him of the Interim Committee decisions.[128] Truman also had important atomic scientists report to Byrnes at this time (and not, for instance, to Stimson, who chaired the Interim Committee); and he had men like Ambassador Joseph Davies report to Byrnes. Given the importance of the forthcoming meeting with Stalin and Churchill, there is little doubt that Truman and Byrnes discussed major issues related to it well before Byrnes was formally sworn in.* And considering what we know of Byrnes's general attitude, it is very difficult to believe that Truman did not have very clear (and tough) advice from him on strategy concerning the bomb and the Russians during the summer months.

---

* See below, pp. 357–59, for additional information on this point.

Nonetheless, we do not have clear documentation of what went on between the two men. What we know is that sometime between April 25 and May 16 Truman decided to delay negotiations with Stalin until the atomic bomb could strengthen his hand. We can also reconstruct the general strategic conception: The overall approach was probably best described by Stimson in two conversations he had in mid-May 1945. The first concerned whether to attempt to renegotiate the Yalta accord on the Far East. Stimson noted that the "questions cut very deep . . . [and were] powerfully connected with our success with [the atomic bomb]. . . ."[129] He urged delay, summarizing the reasons as follows:

> I tried to point out the difficulties which existed and I thought it was premature to ask those questions; at least we were not yet in a position to answer them. . . . It may be necessary to have it out with Russia on her relations to Manchuria and Port Arthur and various other parts of North China, and also the relations of China to us. Over any such tangled weave of problems [the atomic bomb] secret would be dominant and yet we will not know until after that time, probably . . . whether this is a weapon in our hands or not. We think it will be shortly afterwards, but it seems a terrible thing to gamble with such big stakes in diplomacy without having your master card in your hand.[130]

The argument for delay was also described in this mid-May diary report on a conversation with McCloy:*

> The time now and the method now to deal with Russia was to keep our mouths shut and let our actions speak for words. The Russians will understand them better than anything else. It is a case where we have got to regain the lead and perhaps do it in a pretty rough and realistic way. . . . This [is] a place where we really held all the cards. I called it a royal straight flush and we mustn't be a fool about the way we play it. They can't get along without our help and industries and we have coming into action a weapon which will be unique.
>
> Now the thing is not to get into unnecessary quarrels by talking too much and not to indicate any weakness by talking too much; let our actions speak for themselves.[131]

Atomic Diplomacy explored a number of aspects of this strategy. Utilizing the Stimson diary and other sources, it attempted to show

---

* This quotation is the fuller version of the diary entry I cited briefly at the outset.

how the bomb affected U.S. thinking on Poland, Manchuria, the Balkans, Central Europe, and other areas where U.S.-Soviet interests were in conflict. The new information discovered since 1965 powerfully reinforces the by now overwhelming case that top U.S. policy makers saw the bomb as an extraordinarily important weapon not only in their military but in their diplomatic arsenal. It underscores, too, that not only Truman and Stimson, but especially Byrnes, was waiting expectantly for it to strengthen the U.S. hand against Stalin. While we do not know Byrnes's precise role in connection with advice to Truman on the value of delay—or on several diplomatic issues which were put off until the bomb could be tested—everything we know of his attitude, of his relationship to the President, and of his central role as the man preparing the U.S. position for the forthcoming Potsdam meeting makes it highly unlikely that the strategy could have been adopted without his full involvement and agreement.*

One day we may have more details, but on the fundamental issue there is no doubt at all: It is in fact clearer with Byrnes than with any other top U.S. official that the bomb played a *central* strategic role in his conception of how to deal with the Russians.

THE BOMBING OF HIROSHIMA AND NAGASAKI

WE ARE NOW in position to return to the question of how atomic bombs came to be used at Hiroshima and Nagasaki.

Had James F. Byrnes kept a diary as voluminous as that of Secretary Stimson, our understanding of the history of 1945 would probably be somewhat different from what it currently is. Nevertheless, the information we have gives us a rather clear (if as yet not entirely complete) picture of what happened.

The more one learns about events surrounding the atomic bomb, it is increasingly obvious that there were only two real insiders: Truman and his Secretary of State. Despite the records we have of Stimson's thinking, Truman did not share a close relationship with the ailing Secretary of War. Many of the most important strategy sessions probably occurred between Byrnes and Truman in the pri-

---

* For other evidence that Byrnes and Truman privately developed strategy toward Stalin together *before* Byrnes became Secretary of State on July 3, see Byrnes, *Speaking Frankly*, p. 71, and Davies diary, June 5, 1945.

vacy of the Oval Office and during the long conversations on the ship going to Potsdam. (After one such shipboard talk Truman noted in his diary of his old Senate teacher: "My but he has a keen mind!"[132])

Truman left Washington on July 7 and spent the entire month leading up to Hiroshima working intimately with Byrnes isolated from normal White House pressures. It is clear that of the two, the man with the lead on foreign policy was Byrnes. Moreover, Byrnes, a first-rate bureaucratic in-fighter, was very good at limiting the access of others to the President. At Potsdam, Stimson, for instance, complained that Byrnes was "hugging matters pretty close to his bosom." Harriman, too, was cut out and never fully forgave Byrnes. ("Stimson [also] . . . had plenty of free time," Harriman recalled, "so we sat in the sun together outside his villa talking. . . ."[133]) During the time they were away from Washington, Truman left little doubt about how he saw this matter; he was, he wrote from Potsdam, "backing up Jim Byrnes to the limits."[134]

I have cited the newer information on Byrnes's character, on his general role, on the evidence we have of his many private meetings with Truman, on his stance as interpreter of Roosevelt's last understandings with Stalin, and on his overall view of the significance of the atomic bomb. Byrnes was a man who during the period we are considering at the outset of his tenure as Secretary of State believed it important to attempt to force the Russians to concede major points at issue in North China, Manchuria, and Central and Eastern Europe.* At the time, given his public position as the person who had conveyed to the American people the promise that no major concessions had been made to Stalin, Byrnes had made Eastern Europe a high priority. Finally, Byrnes had the narrowest view of the atomic bomb—as an implied threat which would help achieve his diplomatic goals.

"The historic fact remains, and must be judged in the aftertime," Winston Churchill observed after the war, "that the decision whether or not to use the atomic bomb . . . was never even an issue." Before his death President Truman also confirmed: "The

* Byrnes's views were later to change substantially. On the twists and turns in Byrnes's subsequent policies, and on his political vulnerability see especially Herken, *The Winning Weapon,* and Messer, *The End of an Alliance.*

atom bomb was no 'great decision.' That was not any decision that you had to worry about."[135]

How could this be?

Atomic Diplomacy traced the ins and outs of U.S. diplomacy leading up to Potsdam and proposed a tentative explanation suggesting the following sequence of events: (1) It appeared, *first,* that in the early spring of 1945 (up to April at least) no one doubted that the atomic bomb, like any military weapon, would be used when it was ready. (2) Thereafter, and quite naturally, assuming that the bomb would be used, top U.S. officials began to realize it could strengthen their hand diplomatically against the Soviet Union—and they developed their strategy on the basis of this calculation, postponing major negotiations, and the Potsdam meeting itself, until the bomb could be tested. *However,* (3) by mid-summer (especially in late June and July) the military reasons for using the weapon began to disappear as the intercepted cables demonstrating Japan's rapid deterioration flowed in. A number of the most important military officials clearly understood what was happening, and they recognized that from a strictly military point of view the bomb was not necessary to prevent an invasion.

The difficulty lay primarily with those who were deeply involved with diplomacy—for they had embraced the assumption the bomb would be used, and indeed, developed an overall theory that it would be critical to their diplomacy *vis à vis* the Soviet Union. The detailed story of how this idea came to be deeply intertwined with diplomacy over the summer of 1945 (and not specifically the question of how the bomb came to be used) is the core of the material presented in *Atomic Diplomacy.* It is not so much that top decision makers calculatedly decided to use the weapon, but, rather, that it became central to their thinking, probably in ways they did not fully understand themselves. It appears that some of them came to be so bound up in the idea the bomb would be the "master card" against the Russians that they simply could not grasp the implications of the evidence that Japan could be forced to surrender without the new weapon.[136] Or possibly, as suggested by Leo Szilard's report on his conversation with Byrnes, at least some of the major figures seemed to know that the war was over but wanted to use the bomb anyway. In either interpretation the Russian factor—*implicitly or explicitly*—is the key to the puzzle.

The belief of top U.S. officials that the bomb would help them achieve diplomatic objectives is very clear in connection with the Manchurian problem, but it is also obvious that they saw it as important to overall diplomacy in Europe. The Stimson diary documented the general influence of the new weapon twenty years ago, and the newer information helps fill out the basic story. What we have learned in the last two decades strongly suggests the above explanation roughly describes what probably happened—especially the information on what the key military figures believed, and on Byrnes's early and deep involvement in advising the President both on nuclear questions and Yalta-related issues after Roosevelt died.

We still do not have answers to all the questions, of course, and it is *possible* that the President and Byrnes believed they were simply carrying out traditional policies and got so carried away with their desire to end the war that they didn't stop to think. But it is hard to sustain this interpretation in the face of the evidence of Japan's attempt to surrender, of U.S. intelligence reports on that attempt, of the direct advice of men like Leahy, Eisenhower, Arnold, and others that the war could be ended without an invasion (and that the bomb was not militarily necessary), of the repeated advice that a Russian declaration of war and/or a change in the surrender terms would end the fighting, and, finally, of Truman's acknowledgment that a change in the unconditional surrender formula was not a matter of principle, and that he planned to exploit all other available opportunities, even if it cost more time and money, to forestall an invasion.

A case could always be made, of course, that the bomb would help the war effort. (How could such a case *not* be made?) But reflecting especially upon the difference between those deeply involved in diplomacy toward Russia, and the various military figures who were not so involved, it is clear that military factors alone—and especially Truman's oft-repeated argument that the bomb was necessary to avoid an invasion—simply cannot explain the choices made during the final two months of the summer.

Nor can Byrnes especially—who knew exactly what he was doing—be easily interpreted as simply carrying out traditional policies. I would add that at Potsdam American officials became very excited by the news from Alamogordo, enthusiastic even, in their estimation of how much the atomic bomb would help them with the

Russians. Whatever doubts they might have had probably disappeared in the heady atmosphere. A recent report by one high-ranking member of the delegation is that even on the basis of the first skimpy news of the successful New Mexico test, Truman told reparations chief Edwin Pauley that the bomb "would keep the Russians straight." According to Pauley's deputy, J. R. Parten, "everyone was pretty high. . . ."[137]

Finally, it is simply a fact of history that neither President Truman nor Secretary Byrnes appears to have experienced the moral difficulties with killing large numbers of civilians that so disturbed men like Eisenhower and Leahy.*

BEGINNING OF THE COLD WAR

LET THERE BE NO MISTAKE: We still do not have all the facts about the atomic bomb story; there is plenty of digging for young historians to do. However, the focal point for further research is clear, and perhaps future scholarship will give greater precision to what we know about the relationship of the destruction of Hiroshima and Nagasaki to the views top American leaders held about the weapon and diplomacy toward the Soviet Union.

Space does not permit a full treatment of the final question posed by *Atomic Diplomacy*—the role the atomic bomb played in initiating the Cold War. The book was in fact only one of a number which raised serious questions about this period, and despite continuing scholarship by many authors, many issues remain unresolved. A vast literature on the Cold War has been produced in the last two decades, and many revisionists and nonrevisionists have contributed to it.[139]

Nor did the original book do more than suggest a point of departure for inquiry into the overall problem. Nonetheless, the fact that the major questions in dispute primarily concerned *Eastern and Central Europe* in 1945—and not Russian expansion threatening *Western Europe* in 1947—obviously suggested a reconsideration of

---

* Except (for Truman, at least) *after* the evidence of the enormous destruction came in and the President decided not to press forward with a third attack. "The thought of wiping out another 100,000 people was too horrible," he remarked at a Cabinet meeting on August 10. Secretary of Commerce Wallace's diary continues: "He didn't like the idea of killing, as he said, 'all those kids.' "[138]

the dynamics of the very earliest Cold War years.* Let me make only one or two observations about such issues at this point.

First, recent research on U.S. diplomacy during the early fall of 1945 has confirmed and reinforced *Atomic Diplomacy*'s argument that after the demonstration of the new weapon at Hiroshima and Nagasaki a diplomatic offensive was launched to reduce Soviet influence in Eastern Europe—and that confidence to undertake so difficult a task did in fact derive in large part from the atomic bomb. We have already cited the Stimson diary references to Byrnes's desire to have the bomb "in his pocket" to back up demands for changes in Bulgaria and Rumania at the September 1945 London Council of Foreign Ministers. The work of historians Gregg Herken and Robert Messer has provided additional documentation of the very clear linkage in Byrnes's strategy between the bomb and his approach to Eastern Europe at his first post-Hiroshima encounter with the Russians.[140]

Second, one source of confusion about this period stems from the fact that Byrnes's policy failed miserably. Some writers have pointed out that no significant change was achieved—and then attempted to argue *as if this were evidence that U.S. policy did not have major change as its objective.* Others have noted that there were twists and turns in U.S. policy both during and after the period covered by *Atomic Diplomacy*.[141] But the fact is (failure or not, and with all its convolutions, in part the result of Byrnes's political problems), one of the Secretary of State's most important objectives nonetheless remained forcing the Russians to reduce their hold on Eastern Europe. Moreover, Byrnes continued to believe the atomic bomb would ultimately give the United States sufficient power to accomplish this objective: He left office complaining the Russians "don't scare"—and went on to write a book urging that the U.S. *demand* that the Soviet Union sign a German peace treaty and withdraw from Central and Eastern Europe. ". . . I do not believe it is wise to suggest a course of action unless one is willing to carry it

---

* On Truman's roll-back intentions, see also Yergin, *Shattered Peace*, p. 105; and pp. 109–32 on the U.S. focus on the Balkans during and after Potsdam through the London Conference. On Truman's specific reversals of Roosevelt's policies, and on the belief that the tough line would achieve cooperation *as U.S. policy makers defined cooperation*, see below, pp. 71, 76, 76*fn*, 83–88, 139–74, 178, 185, 205–24, 231–35, 278. Also see Messer, *The End of an Alliance*, and Herken, *The Winning Weapon*, on the Potsdam and London meetings.

through . . . ," Byrnes observed. "We should not start something we are not prepared to finish." If the Russians refused to cooperate with his approach, Byrnes proposed the United States should then use "measures of the last resort" to compel them to comply.[142] It is often forgotten that James F. Byrnes was one of the most highly placed of those who recommended a "preventive war" during the period when the United States had a nuclear monopoly if this were the only way to achieve diplomatic objectives it deemed important.

But this takes us well beyond September 1945, the point at which *Atomic Diplomacy* ends. Nevertheless, in a very fundamental sense, the impact of the basic conceptions which informed policy in the early postwar months did not disappear. As Walter Lippmann observed in 1947, U.S. diplomacy "became confused, lost sight of the primary and essential objective" when it "became entangled in all manner of secondary issues and disputes in the Russian borderlands."[143]

Lippmann's early postwar analysis (published initially as articles responding to the famous "Mr. X" containment thesis) still offers a fruitful way to approach a number of problems which have their origins in the early 1945 period. Lippmann's overall argument did not concern malevolence or evil intention. It focused instead on the *situational logic* of American-Soviet relations in Europe. One of Lippmann's fundamental criticisms of U.S. policy was that in 1945 and 1946 it attempted to force the Soviets to relax their grip on Eastern Europe *before there was agreement on what to do about postwar Germany.* To the degree the United States tried to resolve Eastern European matters while fears about Germany were still unsettled, Lippmann suggested, the Russians were bound to tighten their hold. Conversely, if there was ever to be a chance of gaining a more flexible Soviet policy in Eastern Europe, the German question had to be resolved first.

I believe the most important effect of the atomic bomb on major European issues was that *from the very start* it altered four aspects of American diplomatic-strategic thinking:

First, the new weapon gave U.S. policy makers confidence that the United States alone had full power to handle postwar Germany: *From the American point of view,* Germany seemed unlikely ever again to be a threat. Instantaneously, the Russians were no longer required to deal with what had until then been the single most important problem worrying American policy makers. As Joseph Davies noted at Potsdam, "because of the New Mexico development [Byrnes] felt secure anyway."*[144]

This is perhaps the least recognized shift in strategy brought about by the new technology. Perhaps it is understandable: Things changed so quickly!

American leaders had anticipated the public would likely require the withdrawal of most U.S. troops from the Continent after the war—and until the atomic bomb was proved, the Russians were needed, for better or worse, to a greater or lesser extent to jointly insure against a renewed German threat. Policy makers *may have wanted to* challenge the understandings which Roosevelt had reached with Stalin, but there were limits to the extent to which this could be done.

From the Russian point of view, if the potential German threat were resolved in cooperation with the United States, as Lippmann believed (correctly in my judgment), there were reasons, including possible postwar assistance, for them to try to work out the difficulties which existed. This is not to say there would not have been difficulties with the Soviet Union, or that everything would have worked out well. But it is also not reasonable to assume that the sterility of the Cold War as we know it was an absolute historical inevitability. Austria and Finland, in different ways, offer suggestive illustrations of other possibilities.

Second, from the American point of view, Germany could even be built up, partly to solve obvious economic problems, partly as a counterweight to the Soviets. There simply was no need to worry. Slowly at first, then faster, U.S. policy rebuilt the economic and then the military power of Germany—a move which, whatever its motivations, nonetheless threatened the Russians, who did not have atomic weapons to protect them.

Third, as we have seen, the atomic bomb gave American policy makers confidence they had sufficient power to attempt to undo the Yalta understandings. Byrnes was quite aware that Roosevelt had conceded substantial control of Eastern Europe to the Soviets, whatever some U.S. policy makers might have wished. Nevertheless,

---

* On this point, see below, pp. 205–24.

Byrnes's strategy was to press for implementation of the vague Declaration on Liberated Europe, which generally promised democratic elections, *even though he understood this to be a contravention of the more specific understandings.* In so doing, U.S. policy created fears that the Soviet Union would be weakened in an area vital to its security at the same time it simultaneously began to rebuild Germany.*

Finally, of course, the bomb itself was a threat. Immediately after the failure of Byrnes's policy at the London Council of Foreign Ministers, Truman announced that the United States was not interested in serious efforts to achieve international control of nuclear weapons. At Reelfoot Lake in Tennessee the President called a press conference just after the meeting's close to state pointedly that if other nations were to "catch up" with the United States, "they [would] have to do it on their own hook, just as we did."[145]

A few days later in a private conversation with a lifelong Missouri friend, Truman acknowledged full awareness of the implications of his decision. He agreed, he said, with his friend's comment: "Then Mister President, what it amounts to is this. That the armaments race is on. . . ."†

Any serious analysis of the beginnings of the Cold War, I believe, requires an assessment of these factors—none of which is comprehensible without recognition of the dramatic impact the atomic bomb had on American policy makers.

THE RELEVANCE OF HIROSHIMA TODAY

ATOMIC DIPLOMACY IS A study of a very limited period, a brief six months in the summer and early fall of 1945. It is an incision into the fabric of ongoing history which illuminated attitudes and policies

---

* Martin Herz's book, *Beginnings of the Cold War*, usefully reviews this period and, especially, the much neglected armistice agreements which were in force at the time. See Appendix IV for my review-essay on the 1945–47 period of the Cold War.

† See Herken, *The Winning Weapon*, p. 39. A wide range of historical research has demonstrated that subsequent U.S. proposals for international control of atomic weapons during the 1946 period were put forward with full awareness that they were constructed in a way that made them all but impossible for the Russians to accept: They guaranteed a U.S. monopoly for many years until (*if* everything went well) sufficiently satisfactory control and inspection procedures were in place. Herken also provides a useful review of U.S. atomic policy, and its limitations, from 1945 to 1950. Also see Messer, *The End of an Alliance*, for the early period, and especially the restrictive form in which U.S. proposals, such as the Baruch plan, were put forward.

at a particularly important moment, but does not attempt to do more.*

It is forty years since Hiroshima and Potsdam. Both the United States and the Soviet Union now have massive arsenals of nuclear weapons. Is there a way forward to a less threatening international environment?

In connection with several important issues, reflection on 1945 helps clarify a logic which still dominates major power relations. In Europe the security problem is similar in many respects to what it was forty years ago—except that it has been escalated a hundred-fold: There is unlikely to be any serious relaxation of Soviet domination of Eastern Europe so long as Germany is a potential threat. Conversely, strategies which reduce tensions in Central Europe may help open the way (if anything can) to change in Eastern Europe.

The Polish problem dominated the very first days of the 1945 conflict between the United States and the Soviet Union. It has become a larger, not smaller issue. If it is ever to be resolved peacefully, a much deeper structure of Central European security—whether through nuclear-free zones or disengagement plans—is a primary requirement.

In connection with the problem of nuclear weapons itself, the arms race can only be moderated by a decision *to make this a priority,* and by direct negotiations. And both of these are likely to occur only to the extent ordinary citizens press top officials to consider the larger issues at stake. The Hiroshima story teaches how easy it is for decision makers to lose sight of deeper questions of ethical and global significance in the absence of express public concern and clear citizen constraint.

Perhaps two personal comments may be in order in this connection during this fortieth anniversary year of the bombing of Hiroshima:

For most Americans, Hiroshima is an abstraction; it represents either a gigantic mushroom cloud, or a symbol of massive death and destruction. Even the numbers are beyond ordinary comprehen-

---

* In this connection the reader may perhaps find my essay "The United States, the Revolutions, and the Cold War: Perspective and Prospect"—on long-term trends in U.S. interventionism—of interest (in my *Cold War Essays*). To gain a deeper understanding, the modern period must be located in the history of America's conception of its role in the world. William Appelman Williams' work on the origins of American expansionism, economic and other, is relevant here. See especially Williams' *The Tragedy of American Diplomacy,* and his recent *Empire as a Way of Life.*

sion: roughly 200,000 deaths in the final reckoning. We need to shake the hold of both conceptions; I believe that only thereafter can we return to the larger implications with an adequate awareness of the true stakes.

John Hersey got it right in his book *Hiroshima:* The atomic bomb was first of all an intimate, personal, highly individual experience. To walk the streets of Hiroshima today is to be forced to recognize the obvious: A young housewife passes, walking arm in arm with an elderly woman, perhaps her mother-in-law; three school children, maybe nine years old, scamper up the road; a tired, aged garbage collector makes his rounds. Such people today remind us that such people then, individuals, were the ones who felt the experience of Hiroshima; and it was a very, very direct one indeed.

Reflect for a moment on the death of a loved one, perhaps a father or mother; reflect on a moment of personal illness. There is no way to grasp the meaning of Hiroshima, ultimately, to 200,000 *individuals*. In the attempt, however, it may be possible to begin to break loose from the abstractions to know what nuclear warfare meant, really, to fellow human beings.

"I was not taught to make war in that fashion . . . ," Admiral Leahy observed. "Wars cannot be won by destroying women and children. . . ." Eisenhower was "conscious of a feeling of depression. . . . It wasn't necessary to hit them with that awful thing. . . ." Why is it that some men were able to preserve their hold on ethical standards? And some were not? What stands out from the record, no matter how the remaining questions are finally resolved, is that most American leaders were *not* guided by the same ethical considerations that an Eisenhower or a Leahy felt in their approach to Hiroshima.

Pope Paul VI called Hiroshima an act of "butchery of untold magnitude."[146] What does it take, ultimately, for a society to teach its members "not to make war on women and children"? Increasing numbers of people, from men like George F. Kennan to the American Catholic bishops to countless individuals who have chosen in some way to break their silence on the problem posed by the nuclear arms race, are asking this question. We can do nothing today about Hiroshima; we can only look to ourselves, to our actions or our inactions, to whether we contribute by deed or by silence to fostering an environment which restrains or allows or promotes the next Hiroshima.

Preface

Dear Mr. President,
I think it is very important that I should have a talk with you as soon
as possible on a highly secret matter. I mentioned it to you shortly
after you took office, but have not urged it since on account of the
pressure you have been under. It, however, has such a bearing on our
present foreign relations and has such an important effect upon all my
thinking in this field that I think you ought to know about it without
much further delay.

> —*Secretary of War Henry L. Stimson*
> *to President Harry S. Truman,*
> *April 24, 1945*

THIS NOTE WAS WRITTEN twelve days after Franklin Delano Roosevelt's death and two weeks before World War II ended in Europe.[1]
The following day Secretary Stimson advised President Truman that
the "highly secret matter" would have a "decisive" effect upon America's postwar foreign policy. Stimson then outlined the role the atomic
bomb would play in America's relations with other countries.[2] In
diplomacy, he confided to his diary, the weapon would be a "master
card."[3]

This book begins in the spring of 1945, a time when postwar problems unfolded as rapidly as the Allied armies converged in Central
Europe. During the fighting which preceded Nazi surrender the Red
Army conquered a great belt of territory bordering the Soviet Union.
Debating the consequences of this fact, American policy makers defined a series of interrelated problems: What political and economic
pattern was likely to emerge in Eastern and Central Europe? Would
Soviet influence predominate? Most important, what power—if any—
did the United States have to effect the ultimate settlement on the very
borders of Russia?

Roosevelt, Churchill, and Stalin had attempted to resolve these issues of East-West influence at the February 1945 Yalta Conference.

With the Red Army clearly in control, the West was in a weak bargaining position. It was important to reach an understanding with Stalin before American troops began their planned withdrawal from the Continent. Poland, the first major country intensely discussed by the Big Three, took on unusual significance; the balance of influence struck between Soviet-oriented and Western-oriented politicians in the government of this one country could set a pattern for big-power relationships in the rest of Eastern Europe.

Although the Yalta Conference ended with a signed accord covering Poland, within a few weeks it was clear that Allied understanding was more apparent than real. None of the heads of government interpreted the somewhat vague agreement in the same way. Churchill began to press for more Western influence; Stalin urged less. True to his well-known policy of cooperation and conciliation, Roosevelt attempted to achieve a more definite understanding for Poland and a pattern for East-West relations in Europe. Caught for much of the last of his life between the determination of Churchill and the stubbornness of Stalin, Roosevelt at times fired off angry cables to Moscow, and at others warned London against an "attempt to evade the fact that we placed, as clearly shown in the agreement, somewhat more emphasis . . . [on Soviet-oriented Polish politicians in the government]."*

Roosevelt died on April 12, 1945, only two months after Yalta. When Truman met with Secretary Stimson to discuss the "bearing" of the atomic bomb upon foreign relations, the powers were deeply ensnarled in a tense public struggle over the meaning of the Yalta agreement. Poland had come to symbolize *all* East-West relations. Truman was forced to pick up the tangled threads of policy with little knowledge of the broader, more complex issues involved. How the new President faced this challenge, and how he approached the fundamental problem of postwar American-Soviet relations, are primarily themes of this book.

Herbert Feis, a noted expert on the period, has written that "Truman made up his mind that he would not depart from Roosevelt's course or renounce his ways."[4] Others have argued that "we tried to

---

* See Appendix I for a detailed review of
the Polish problem.

work out the problems of the peace in close cooperation with the Russians."[5] It is often believed that American policy followed a conciliatory course, changing—in reaction to Soviet intransigence—only in 1947 with the Truman Doctrine and the Marshall Plan. My own belief is somewhat different. It derives from the comment of Truman's Secretary of State that by early autumn of 1945 it was "understandable" that Soviet leaders should feel American policy had shifted radically after Roosevelt's death:[6] It is now evident that, far from following his predecessor's policy of cooperation, shortly after taking office Truman launched a powerful foreign policy initiative aimed at reducing or eliminating Soviet influence from Europe. Much of the material in the following pages attempts to illuminate this conclusion.

The ultimate point of this study is not, however, that America's approach to Russia changed after Roosevelt. Rather it is that the atomic bomb played a role in the formulation of policy, particularly in connection with Truman's only meeting with Stalin, the Potsdam Conference of late July and early August 1945. Again, my judgment differs from Feis's conclusion that "the light of the explosion 'brighter than a thousand suns' filtered into the conference rooms at Potsdam only as a distant gleam."[7] I believe new evidence proves not only that the atomic bomb influenced diplomacy, but that it determined much of Truman's shift to a tough policy aimed at forcing Soviet acquiescence to American plans for Eastern and Central Europe. The weapon "gave him an entirely new feeling of confidence," the President told his Secretary of War.[8] By the time of Potsdam Truman had been advised on the role of the atomic bomb by both Secretary Stimson and Secretary of State Byrnes. Though the two men differed as to tactics, each urged a tough line. Part of the book attempts to define how closely Truman followed a subtle policy outlined by Stimson, and to what extent he followed the straightforward advice of Byrnes that the bomb (in Truman's words) "put us in a position to dictate our own terms at the end of the war."[9]

A study of American policy in the very early days of the Cold War must inevitably deal with Soviet actions and reactions. I wish to stress that this book is basically an analysis of *American* policy; it is not an attempt to offer a detailed review of *Soviet* policy. Stalin's approach seems to have been cautiously moderate during the brief few months here described. It is perhaps symbolized by the Soviet-sponsored free elections which routed the Communist Party in Hungary in the autumn of 1945. The book does not attempt to interpret this moderation, nor to explain how or why Soviet policy changed to the harsh totalitarian controls characteristic of the period after 1946.

The judgment that Truman radically altered Roosevelt's policy in mid-1945 nevertheless obviously suggests a new point of departure for interpretations of the Cold War. In late 1945 General Eisenhower observed in Moscow that "before the atom bomb was used, I would have said, yes, I was sure we could keep the peace with Russia. Now I don't know . . . People are frightened and disturbed all over. Everyone feels insecure again."[10] To what extent did postwar Soviet policies derive from insecurity based upon a fear of America's atom bomb and changed policy? The book stops short of this fundamental question, concluding that further research is needed to test Secretary Stimson's judgment that "the problem of our satisfactory relations with Russia [was] not merely connected with but [was] virtually dominated by the problem of the atomic bomb."[11]

Similarly, I believe more research and more information are needed to reach a conclusive understanding of why the atomic bomb was used. The common belief is that the question is closed, and that President Truman's explanation is correct: "The dropping of the bombs stopped the war, saved millions of lives."[12] My own view is that presently available evidence shows the atomic bomb was not needed to end the war or to save lives—and that this was understood by American leaders at the time. General Eisenhower has recently recalled that in mid-1945 he expressed a similar opinion to the Secretary of War: "I told him I was against it on two counts. First, the Japanese were ready to surrender and it wasn't necessary to hit them with that awful thing. Second, I hated to see our country be the first to use such a weapon . . ."[13] To go beyond the limited conclusion that the bomb was unnecessary is not possible at present. However, I have attempted to define the remaining questions with some precision. The issue is not why it was *decided* to use the bomb, but rather, how policy makers came to *assume* the bomb would be used, and why they never questioned this assumption as Eisenhower did.

The information and views here presented challenge many common opinions. I have made no attempt, however, to take up the various arguments offered by the great number of writers, both serious and casual, who have touched upon the subject. At certain points I have presented the ideas of one or two representative authors for comparison with new information. But so far as possible I have eschewed contention, and reduced debate and controversy to a minimum.

Looking back to the views I held when I began this study six years ago, I am deeply aware of how much my own understanding of the period has changed, and how my original ideas have been challenged by new facts. In the course of my research I have often been reminded of a comment made by the economist John Maynard Keynes. My experience has matched his insight, and Keynes's point may be useful as a word of introduction for others: "The difficulty lies, not in the new ideas, but in escaping from the old ones, which ramify, for those brought up as most of us have been, into every corner of our minds."[14]

G. A.

Washington, D.C., 1964

CHAPTER I

The Strategy of an Immediate Showdown

It was now or never. . . .
—PRESIDENT HARRY S. TRUMAN
April 23, 1945

IT WAS A SHORT TWO WEEKS before the combined strength of Britain, the United States, and the Soviet Union forced the collapse of Nazi power and the end of the Second World War. Only eleven days had passed since the death of Franklin Delano Roosevelt. The new President of the United States prepared for his first meeting with a representative of the Soviet Union. Rehearsing his views on the subject of the negotiation—a reorganization of the Polish government—Truman declared that if the Russians did not care to cooperate, "they could go to hell."* A few hours later the President expressed the same view to Soviet Foreign Minister V. M. Molotov in language which, according to the President's Chief of Staff, was "not at all diplomatic."[1]

THE FIRM APPROACH

ALTHOUGH THIS ENCOUNTER is often overlooked by those who stress Truman's desire to continue his predecessor's policy of "cooperation with the Russians," the fiery and blunt language was not the result of a moment's flash of temper.[2] The new President had care-

---

* This is taken from Bohlen's notes. (Forrestal, *Diaries*, p. 50; see also Truman, *Year of Decisions*, p. 77.)

fully considered his approach to Molotov. By the third week of April 1945 he and most of his senior advisers had agreed that Roosevelt's policy of "cooperation" had to be reconsidered and that it would now be wise strategy to face the Russians with a firm negotiating position and strong language.

The immediate problem concerned a reorganization of the Polish government established under Soviet auspices as the Red Army drove the Germans to the banks of the Oder. Both Roosevelt and Churchill had promised support for a government "friendly" to the Soviet Union, one which would not open the way to a future German attack.[3] At Yalta it had been agreed that the Soviet-backed Warsaw government "now functioning in Poland" would be "reorganized" to form a "new" government by the addition of Western-oriented Polish political leaders.[4] After a considerable debate over a number of lesser points, following Yalta the "Polish question" had reduced to a three-way struggle over the allocation of power in the new government.[*] Each of the Big Three promoted his favored Poles. As Admiral Leahy put it, the power struggle was now "the nub of the issue."[5]

Just before Truman took office, Stalin attempted to define the problem more precisely by suggesting that the Yugoslav precedent be "more or less" followed in Poland—that is, that the Warsaw government be expanded by adding approximately one new minister for each four already in the Cabinet, to achieve a power ratio of one in five.[†] This would give the more Soviet-oriented Poles predominant influence. Almost immediately upon taking office, Truman rejected Stalin's proposal. Churchill thought it "remarkable" that the new President "felt able so promptly to commit himself" to a position totally opposed to the Russian view and very close to the Prime Minister's own stand.[6] Neither Truman nor Churchill wished to commit himself

---

[*] See Appendix I for a detailed discussion of the post-Yalta negotiations.

[†] The actual precedent depends upon how one evaluates the political coloration of various Yugoslav Cabinet members. No attempt at such an independent assessment is made. The ratio 1 of 5 (20%) is taken from Churchill and Truman. It is possible to find various estimates of the ratio: Lane gives 1 of 5 (20%) (*I Saw Freedom Betrayed*, p. 65); Churchill gives 1 of 5 (20%) in one place, but 6 of 31 (19%), elsewhere (*Stalin's Correspondence*, I, pp. 340, 343); Truman endorsed both of these figures contained in Churchill's messages (*Stalin's Correspondence*, II, p. 224), Truman gives 6 of 31 (19%) elsewhere (*Year of Decisions*, p. 109); Stalin gives 4 of 18 or 20 (22% or 20%) (Sherwood, *Roosevelt and Hopkins*, p. 901); Feis gives 6 of 27 (22%) (*Churchill, Roosevelt, Stalin*, p. 576); Woodward gives 5 of 28, or 3 of 28 (18% or 11%) (*British Foreign Policy*, p. 507*fn.*); Mikolajczyk even gives 50% (*The Pattern of Soviet Domination*, p. 132).

to terms for the reorganization of the government and, in a joint message to Stalin on April 18, they urged that the Warsaw government meet on an equal basis with the group of Western-oriented Polish political leaders.[7] Such a meeting would give the same status to the Warsaw government and to the group of nongovernmental political figures. It would implicitly reject the Russian demand that the Warsaw government be recognized as the "core" of the reorganized government.

The struggle over power in the new Polish government stemmed in great part from the vagueness of the Yalta agreement itself. The Soviet interpretation could be sustained by certain sections of the protocol, the Anglo-American by others. The language was imprecise. The President's Chief of Staff, Admiral Leahy (who had opposed the Soviet view at Yalta), believed the agreed formula gave the Russians what they asked; it could be stretched "all the way from Yalta to Washington without ever technically breaking it." Roosevelt had agreed with this view.[8] In fact, the language was sufficiently favorable to Stalin's view so that, just before his death, Roosevelt felt it necessary to caution Churchill against attempting to "evade" the fact that "we placed, as clearly shown in the agreement, somewhat more emphasis" on the Warsaw government than on the Western-oriented political leaders.[9]

Despite the general thrust of this message, Roosevelt did not accept Stalin's view that the Warsaw government should hold four out of five posts in the new government. Unfortunately he did not have time to give more precision to American policy before his death. In mid-April between Stalin and Churchill there was a great and seemingly unbridgeable difference of views; between Stalin and Roosevelt, a lesser, but ill-defined difference.

When Truman took office he was fully aware of the limitations of the Yalta language. He complained to his Secretary of State that the vague wording did not give him firm footing in his stand against the Russians.[10] Thus, it was in spite of his understanding and in spite of Roosevelt's attempt to restrain Churchill, that Truman accepted the advice of the State Department and sided with Churchill in the dispute over the Polish government.

The importance of the Polish issue lies not so much in the details of the diplomatic dispute, however. The long war with Germany was in its final phase, and "in its larger aspects," as Truman stated at the time, the Polish question had become "a symbol of the future development of our international relations."[11] The matter had an importance which transcended the specific points at issue. It must be understood as a basic question involving primary matters of American policy and—as the President and his advisers believed—the fundamental structure of American-Soviet relations. Behind the firm approach Truman took to the Polish question was a new estimate of the requirements of diplomacy toward the Soviet Union: all of the President's important advisers, save two, felt it necessary to have a symbolic showdown with Russia which would clarify relationships and force the Russians to cooperate with American principles throughout Eastern and Central Europe. Thus, the Polish issue was seen as symbolic, not merely as another in a series of seemingly infinite negotiations. The reasoning which underlay this view can best be understood by reviewing the arguments presented to the President by his ambassador to the Soviet Union, W. Averell Harriman.[12] On April 20, eight days after Roosevelt's death, Harriman explained his belief that the leaders of the Soviet Union were following two policies at the same time. One was a policy of cooperation with the United States and Great Britain, the second a policy of extension of Soviet control over neighboring states by independent action. In Harriman's view, certain elements around Stalin had misinterpreted American generosity—especially in the matter of Lend-Lease aid—and America's desire for cooperation, as indications of "softness." They believed the Soviet government could "do as it pleased" in Eastern Europe without risking challenge from the United States.[13]

Harriman argued that Soviet domination in Eastern Europe was intolerable. He believed that the United States was faced with "a barbarian invasion of Europe." He was convinced that Soviet control over any country meant not only that its influence would be paramount in the country's foreign relations, but also that the Soviet system with its secret police and its extinction of freedom of speech would prevail. Faced with these "unpleasant facts," Harriman believed it was necessary to decide what America's attitude should be. He argued that a reconsideration of Roosevelt's policy was necessary. It was essential to abandon the illusion that the Soviet government was likely to act in accordance with the principles which the rest of the world held in international affairs.[14]

Earlier, Harriman had urged that the United States select "one or two cases" where Soviet actions were intolerable and "make them realize that they cannot continue their present attitude except at great cost to themselves."[15] Now he took up the Polish case with the President. He argued that a firm American line had to be taken in this instance in order to establish all relations with Russia on a new basis. A firm approach was the only way to achieve practical cooperation. Harriman told the President he believed Stalin had discovered that an honest execution of the Yalta decision would mean the end of the Warsaw government, and that he had therefore abandoned the Yalta agreement. Harriman did not feel that two interpretations of the Yalta decision were possible and urged support for his view in the Polish dispute. He admitted that a firm approach might possibly jeopardize the Charter meeting of the United Nations, set for April 25 at San Francisco.[16]

"I am . . . a most earnest advocate of the closest possible understanding with the Soviet Union," Harriman had commented a few days earlier, "so that what I am saying relates only to how best to attain such understanding."[17] Harriman was extremely confident that a strong stand would not precipitate a break with the Soviet Union. It is this confidence which is the most striking feature of the American attitude, for not only Harriman but almost every senior government official shared the same sense of the power relationships. Harriman and others judged that the United States had sufficient power to demand acceptance of its terms for Eastern Europe.

This estimate of the relative strengths derived primarily from a judgment regarding the economic positions of the two countries. Harriman, who had spent much of his time in Moscow dealing with the Lend-Lease program, had often advised of the "enormous" requirements of the invasion-devastated Russian economy. The Russians had already requested a large postwar credit, which Harriman estimated would amount to six billion dollars.[18] He now argued forcefully that the Soviet government would yield to the American position "because they needed our help in their reconstruction program." For this reason, the United States could "stand firm" on important issues "without running serious risks."[19]

Harriman reported that some quarters in Moscow believed it was a matter of life and death to American business to increase exports to Russia. He said that, of course, this was untrue, but that a number of Russian officials nevertheless believed it. A firm approach would dispel this illusion. Once more Harriman repeated that he was not pessimistic about the outcome of a confrontation based upon a firm stand. In fact, not only was there little to fear, but such an approach was the one way to arrive at a new "workable basis with the Russians."[20]

The strategy Harriman offered can be summarized in a few sentences: Soviet actions in Eastern Europe had to be opposed by the United States. Since America had overwhelming economic power, and the Soviet Union enormous reconstruction requirements, the United States was in an extremely favorable bargaining position. A reconsideration of Roosevelt's policy was necessary. A firm stand and an immediate symbolic showdown would make the Russians realize that they could continue their domination of Eastern Europe only at "great cost to themselves." Since American economic aid was so important to the Russians, the showdown was likely to bring favorable results and cooperation with American principles. There was only the slightest chance of failure and a break in relations.

STRONG WORDS ON A STRONG POSITION

THIS FIRST LONG MEETING between the President and Harriman—one of many similar high-level discussions of diplomatic strategy in mid-April 1945—exhibits four basic assumptions of policy. The first was opposition in principle to Soviet desires in Eastern Europe and disgust at Soviet actions in the area. Most key American policy makers feared Soviet domination, the imposition of totalitarian governments, and the breakdown of economic interchange between Eastern and Western Europe.* Disturbed by their judgment of Soviet intentions, most American advisers agreed that the United States would have to take a more active role in demanding that the Soviet Union accept democratic-capitalistic governments in Eastern Europe. A favorable organization of the Polish government was the immediate

---

* See below, pp. 100–2, 125–28.

point at issue, but this was regarded only as a prerequisite to early elections which would establish democratically based authority in the country.[21] In fact, the single most important requirement of policy for each country in Eastern Europe, in the American view, was an early free election.*

A second point to remember is that in early 1945 American policy makers were thinking primarily about Eastern Europe. The fear of subversion in Western Europe was not great—Communist parties were not only cooperating with, but actively supporting, conservative regimes in Italy, France, and Belgium.† Nor were policy makers much worried about the possibility of military aggression in Western Europe; the immediate issue was the organization of Europe behind Red Army lines. Anxiety about this question reveals other assumptions common in policy-making circles in April 1945. One was a belief that America's own interest required active influence in Eastern Europe. What went on in the liberated areas had already been defined as "of urgent importance to the U.S." by the time Truman took office.[22] Though often overlooked, such interest in Eastern Europe was an abandonment in principle of the ideal of isolation.

Finally, another assumption was that the United States had sufficient economic and military power to persuade or force the Soviet Union out of the area, or at the very least, to achieve cooperation with American policies and a substantial reduction in Soviet influence. Since this goal was accepted by almost all major advisers, the most important questions were those of strategy; the focal point of policy was the judgment of the relative bargaining power available to each side in any confrontation over Eastern Europe. It is to this question that Harriman had addressed himself, urging that American economic power was so great that a symbolic diplomatic showdown would force the Russians to yield to the American position. "Russia is really afraid of our power or at least respects it," he told Secretary of War Stimson,

---

* See below, pp. 179–80, 196, 259–64.

† See below, pp. 179–80, for a discussion of this point. It is true, of course, that there was some fear of Communist subversion in Western Europe. Harriman warned of this at times. (*Forrestal Diaries*, pp. 39–40.) There was also a brief flurry of concern in the State Department associated with the "Duclos letter." (See *Conference of Berlin*, I, pp. 267–80.) However the immediate points at issue were all in Eastern Europe and by and large policy makers assumed they could control the situation in Western Europe. (See, for example, Truman, *Year of Decisions*, pp. 236–37.)

and he confidently asserted that although Russia might "try to ride roughshod" over her neighbors, "she really [is] afraid of us."[23]

The Ambassador was not alone in this judgment. His position has been delineated in some detail not only because of the obvious importance of arguments presented by an experienced ambassador to the Soviet Union, but precisely because Harriman's well-articulated view was supported in essentials by almost every important adviser consulted by the President.* In addition to Harriman the chief figures involved were Acting Secretary of State Joseph C. Grew, Secretary of State Edward Stettinius, Chief of Staff to the President Admiral William D. Leahy, Secretary of War Henry L. Stimson, and Secretary of the Navy James V. Forrestal.

In a round of talks during April, Harriman discussed basic strategy with each of the above men. His consultations with the State Department were, of course, a matter of normal procedure. He found that the chief officials in the Department were in agreement that economic aid could and should be used to bring the Russians into line in Eastern Europe.[24] Admiral Leahy was also "canvassed" (to use his term) by Harriman on April 21. The Ambassador found Leahy sympathetic to his basic views and in agreement that economic aid to Russia now should be "limited exclusively to material that would assist in the common war effort."[25] Secretary of War Stimson also agreed with the concept of the strategy; his only objections—important ones—concerned the *timing* and method to be employed. Finally the day before he saw Truman, Harriman spoke at length with Secretary of the Navy Forrestal. He urged "much greater firmness" toward the Russians. Forrestal was enthusiastically in favor of the firm approach and, in fact, had long maintained contact with Harriman in Moscow; his private diaries were filled with Harriman's cables and his own favorable comments.[26]

Of course, Harriman's most important allies were in the State Department. Roosevelt often ignored the advice of the Department during his lifetime.[27] (He had not even bothered to read the briefs prepared for his use before the Yalta Conference.)[28] However, in the last weeks of Roosevelt's life, with his chief aide, Harry L. Hopkins,

---

* See below, pp. 99. 108–9. for disagreement by Stimson and Marshall over timing.

hospitalized and out of government, and the President's own health failing, the Department was increasingly called upon to take responsibility for policy decisions of ever greater importance.*[29] When Roosevelt was replaced by Truman—who admittedly knew very little about foreign affairs—officials in the Department of State were asked to join in making decisions of the highest importance. Joseph C. Grew was a key figure, for the Acting Secretary of State saw Truman regularly to brief him on diplomatic questions.[30] Secretary Stettinius was out of Washington for most of the remainder of his term of office, and Grew was the chief official of the Department.

The Acting Secretary was an extremely conservative State Department representative. Grew not only doubted the possibility of cooperation with the Russians (and was personally opposed to men like Hopkins), but was *already* convinced that "a future war with Soviet Russia is as certain as anything in this world can be certain."[31] It is a sign of the policy-making atmosphere in Washington after Roosevelt's death that Grew, who had formerly rarely reached the ear of the President with his firm advice, was able to write to a friend three weeks after Truman took office: "If I could talk to you about the new President you would hear nothing but the most favorable reaction. . . . He certainly won't stand for any pussyfooting in our foreign relations and policy. . . . You can imagine what a joy it is to deal with a man like that."[32]

When Harriman returned to Washington for consultations after Roosevelt's death, he found that Grew and others near to Truman were far more sympathetic to his strategy for dealing with Russia than Roosevelt and his chief aides had been. Harriman seems to have sensed the opportunity this gave him, for he undertook his round of policy discussions with great energy. Convinced that only a firm line could establish relations on a sound basis, the Ambassador pressed his case with vigor and intelligence. It is not accurate, however, to say that Harriman's efforts changed policy. As early as April 3, Secretary Stimson noted in his diary that "there has been growing quite a strain of irritating feeling between our government and the Russians"; and almost all the men Harriman spoke with in mid-April had come in-

---

* See Appendix I.

dependently to the conclusion that a firm line with Russia was necessary.[33] It is, therefore, more to the point to note that Harriman's presence and activities in Washington during the first weeks of the new Truman administration served to focus attention on the Soviet problem, and to stimulate a new consensus on a precise strategy for treating with Russia.

Thus, Harriman's fast-moving series of Washington discussions set the stage for a new policy based upon already well-developed views. The actual decision was taken just before Molotov's meeting with the President on April 23. A few hours before receiving the Soviet Foreign Minister, Truman called in his senior advisers for a final review of strategy. There was a short dispute over the meaning of the Yalta agreement on Poland. Admiral Leahy held that the language "was susceptible of two interpretations."[34] Although he opposed the Soviet position on Poland, he believed the Russians were within the terms of the Yalta agreement.* However, Secretary Stettinius argued that only the view urged by the State Department was possible. More important than the details of the discussion, however, was the general view accepted by the meeting. All of the senior advisers, with two important exceptions, agreed with the President and Ambassador Harriman on strategy. As Secretary Forrestal put it, "This difficulty over Poland could not be treated as an isolated incident."[35] The matter had to be seen in terms of the larger perspective. It was a symbolic issue. "For some time the Russians had considered that we would not object if they took over all of Eastern Europe."[36] Forrestal argued: "We had better have a showdown with them now rather than later."[37] As Admiral Leahy summarized, "The consensus . . . was that the time had arrived to take a strong American attitude toward the Soviet Union . . ."[38]

The agreement that a symbolic showdown would be wise and expedient was almost unanimous. Only Stimson, who agreed with the principle of such a showdown, but opposed immediate action, noted that when Harriman and others "moved for strong words by the President on a strong position," there was only one person besides himself

---

* Leahy's position is curious. It appears that he judged a showdown to be so important—it "would have a beneficial effect upon the Soviet outlook"—that he was prepared to ignore his own belief that the Russians were advocating a legitimate interpretation of Yalta. (*I Was There*, p. 352; Diary, April 23, 1945, p. 63.)

prepared to offer a different view.[39] The solid consensus derived not only from the preparatory work done by Harriman and the attitudes already accepted by the senior advisers; equally important, the new President had made it abundantly clear from almost the first days of his administration that he personally believed a "firm" line necessary. Even before his April 20 interview with Harriman, when Truman had heard of a new Soviet-Polish treaty he had decided to "lay it on the line" with Molotov.[40] At the long discussion of strategy with Harriman, the President had interrupted his ambassador before he got to the heart of his proposal to say that he "was not afraid of the Russians" and that he "intended to be firm." He reiterated this view at three separate points during the discussion.[41] Like Harriman and the others, Truman believed a showdown would risk very little. It was his opinion that "the Russians needed us more than we needed them."[42] Truman would make "no concessions" from American principles. He was quite aware of the strength economic aid gave to America's bargaining position, and he believed there was not much danger of a break. He planned to let Molotov know his feelings "in words of one syllable."[43]

Thus, Truman was in accord with his advisers, and, indeed, was enthusiastically in favor of a firm line. In fact, at the April 23 meeting, he did not wait to hear the consensus before offering his own view. Instead, he initiated the discussion by declaring that "our agreements with the Soviet Union so far had been a one-way street and that he could not continue." He believed it was necessary to set relations on a new basis; "it was now or never. . . ."[44]

REMOVING THE LAST OBSTACLE TO THE SHOWDOWN STRATEGY

AT FIRST READING, the showdown strategy appears as an inexplicable reversal of the policy that was being followed by Roosevelt only a few weeks earlier. American economic power was as great when Roosevelt lived as it was in the first weeks of the Truman administration; the leverage this fact gave to diplomacy was no less powerful. To understand fully the changes in American policy in mid-April, it is necessary to go beyond the discussion thus far presented. During the war three major obstacles had blocked those advisers who urged a firm line toward the Russians. The first—Roosevelt's strong belief that cooperation was possible—died with the President. Truman was personally far less sympathetic to the Russians and, indeed, at a time when Roosevelt was begging for support for Lend-Lease aid to the Russians in 1941, then Senator Truman was suggesting: "If we see that Germany is winning the war we ought to help Russia and if Russia is winning we ought to help Germany and that way let them kill as many as possible. . . ."[45]

The second obstacle to a firm line was a fear that American-Soviet cooperation might be destroyed and that a separate peace between Germany and the Soviet Union might be signed.[46] This objection was obviated by the collapse of German power. But there had been a third obstacle to the firm line: the fear that a showdown and tough approach might lose Soviet help in the war against Japan.[47] At the time of Roosevelt's death, this argument had lost none of its force in policy-making circles.

The need for Soviet help in the Japanese war had disturbed no individual more than General John R. Deane, Chief of the United States Military Mission in Moscow. Like Harriman, Deane had long been urging a tougher policy with the Russians;[48] and, like Harriman, he believed that American economic aid could be used to force the Russians to accept American policies, in both the military and the political fields.[49] Both Deane and Harriman had suffered innumerable personal frustrations in dealing with the suspicious Russians.[50] Deane reported to General Marshall at the end of 1944 that he had "become gradually nauseated by Russian food, vodka, and protestations of friendship."[51] Deane emphasized the great value of American aid to the war-torn Soviet Union, and he complained of the lack of cooperation on numerous minor requests. "We are in the position of being at the same time the givers and the suppliants," he wrote. "This is neither dignified nor healthy for U.S. prestige."[52] Deane joined his friend and colleague Harriman in the effort to convince Washington to adopt a much greater degree of firmness. "I feel certain we must be tougher," he wrote to Marshall.[53]

Despite his repeated urging, however, during Roosevelt's lifetime, Deane had met with as little success as Harriman.[54] The Joint Chiefs of Staff to whom he reported were even more concerned than the

President with the need for Soviet help against Japan. They wished to do nothing that might jeopardize future relations.[55] Frustrated by this unanswerable argument against the firm approach, Deane spent the winter months of early 1945 trying to find a way to reduce American dependence on Soviet help in the Far East.[56] In cooperation with General Frank N. Roberts, Deane produced a series of studies which showed that air bases in Siberia, sought by the United States for B-29 bombing operations against Japan, would actually be of little value; they would increase the total bomb tonnage delivered on Japan by only 1.39 per cent over what might be achieved by using available Pacific bases; the Siberian bases would certainly not be worth the logistical effort needed to establish and supply them.[57] Deane was also able to show that sufficient supplies could be delivered to meet all the requirements of Soviet participation in the Japanese war without having to clear a Pacific supply route.[58]

After the death of Roosevelt, Deane returned with Harriman to Washington for consultations. He took along his studies "to help sell my ideas to the Chiefs of Staff."[59] He urged that the United States "withdraw from all cooperative ventures that were not essential to winning the war and . . . stop pushing our proposals on the Russians and force them to come to us."[60] Thus, while Harriman urged Washington political advisers to adopt a tougher approach, Deane worked hard to convince the military authorities that Soviet help was less essential than had previously been thought. The advice from the two Moscow colleagues was completely complementary, and, at the same time that Harriman won approval for his showdown strategy, Deane was able to prove his case. On April 24 the Joint Chiefs canceled plans for B-29 bases in Siberia and put aside plans for clearing a Pacific supply route to the Soviet Union.[61]

It had also been thought that Soviet troops would be needed to hold down the Japanese Kwantung army so as to prevent reinforcement of the main islands during the actual invasion.[62] However, by mid-April the Joint Chiefs found they could accomplish this objective by other means. American control of the Japanese seas was now so well established that the movement of Japanese forces from the China mainland to the home islands could be prevented.[63] To be sure, Soviet participation in the war against Japan would be useful—especially the shock value of a declaration of war by the third major power—but, by

April 24, the Joint Staff planners advised the Joint Chiefs of Staff: "Early Russian entry into the war against Japan is no longer necessary to make the invasion feasible."[64] There was no objection to this report, and it was officially adopted by the Joint Chiefs on May 10.[65]

Deane was "elated" by these decisions: "As far as military collaboration was concerned, they cleared the decks of any dependence we were placing on Russian generosity."[66] At the April 23 meeting with the President, Deane was thus able to second Harriman's firm strategy with few qualms that the formerly unanswerable objection would be raised. Deane felt "we were in a position to be tough and indifferent," and he told Truman that in Moscow he had learned that "if we were afraid of the Russians we would get nowhere."[67] He concluded: "We should be firm."[68] Consequently, the summary consensus of the meeting, written by Admiral Leahy, which began, "The time had come to take a strong American attitude toward the Soviet Union," ended with the judgment, "No particular harm could be done to our war prospects if Russia should slow down or even stop its war effort in Europe and Asia."*[69]

Thus the President and most of his chief advisers were convinced that an immediate symbolic showdown would risk very little. It would make the Russians understand that they could not continue their policies in Eastern Europe "except at great cost to themselves" and would establish cooperation on a "realistic basis." When Truman met with Molotov, a few hours after the discussion with his advisers, he "went straight to the point."[70] The President indicated that the Soviet Union could not expect American economic assistance unless the Polish discussions continued on the basis of the American proposals. Truman pointedly remarked that the issue had become a matter of public concern and that it would not be possible to get congressional approval

---

* At the April 23, 1945, meeting two further arguments supplemented Deane's major point. Harriman noted that a year had passed since the Russians had agreed to start collaboration in the Far East, but none of the agreements had been carried out. Hence, the United States could not count on a Soviet commitment to enter the war. Deane also argued that "regardless of what happened" the Russians would enter the Pacific war as soon as they could because they had interests in the Far East and could not risk a letdown by their war-weary population. (Truman, *Year of Decisions*, p. 79.) Though these arguments conflicted in their estimate of Soviet intentions, they pointed to the same conclusion: a firm stand would not have major implications for the war against Japan. Despite the argument Harriman made at the April 23 meeting, his own views seem to have been more consistently in line with those of Deane. On other occasions he "was satisfied [the Russians] were determined to come in" the Japanese war because of their requirements in the Far East. (Forrestal, *Diaries*, p. 55; Leahy Diary, April 19, 1945, p. 82.)

for economic-assistance measures without public support. The Soviet government would do well to "keep these factors in mind" when considering the American proposals on Poland.[71]

Although he understood that the Yalta agreement was vague, Truman told Molotov that the American interpretation was the only one possible.[72] "All we were asking was that the Soviet Government carry out the Crimea decision," he declared. Molotov said that the Soviet government believed the remaining difficulties could easily be overcome, and he began to discuss the general problem of Allied cooperation. Truman responded "sharply" that an agreement had been reached on Poland and that "there was only one thing to do, and that was for Marshal Stalin to carry out that agreement."[73]

Molotov said that Stalin had offered his view of the agreement in previous messages, and he added that he personally could not understand why, if the three governments could reach an agreement on the composition of the Yugoslav government, the same formula could not be applied in the case of Poland.[74]

Once more Truman replied "sharply" that "an agreement had been reached. . . . It was only required to be carried out by the Soviet Government." Molotov again began to explain that he could not accept the view that the Yalta agreement had been broken. Again Truman declared that the United States asked only that the Soviet Union carry out its agreements. Molotov should clearly understand that American cooperation could be had only on this basis, not "on the basis of a one-way street."

"I have never been talked to like that in my life," Molotov declared.

"Carry out your agreements and you won't get talked to like that," Truman responded.[75]

AMERICA'S ECONOMIC LEVERAGE

TRUMAN'S DECISION to force the Polish issue to a showdown "was more than pleasing" to his Chief of Staff. Admiral Leahy believed that the blunt language "would have a beneficial effect on the Soviet outlook."[76] Along with the President and his other senior advisers, Leahy judged that "the Russians had always known that we had the power," and they should "know after this conversation that we had the determination. . . ."[77] The matter was one of basic principle; Leahy concluded that "the President's strong American stand at this meeting . . . leaves to the Soviet only two courses of action: either to approach more closely to our expressed policy to Poland, or to drop out of the Association of Nations."[78]

Despite Leahy's confident estimate of the force of the showdown, the Soviet Union did not choose either alternative. Within twenty-four hours parallel messages reached Truman and Churchill from Moscow. Stalin commented that "one cannot but recognize as unusual a situation in which two governments—those of the United States and Great Britain—reach agreement beforehand on Poland, a country in which the U.S.S.R. is interested first of all and most of all, and place its representatives in an intolerable position, trying to dictate to it." The Soviet Premier emphasized the importance of Poland to Soviet security: "You evidently do not agree that the Soviet Union is entitled to seek in Poland a government that would be friendly to it. . . . This is rendered imperative . . . by the Soviet people's blood freely shed on the fields of Poland. . . ." Stalin remarked that by "turning down the Yugoslav example as a model for Poland, you confirm that the [Warsaw] Provisional Government cannot be regarded as a basis for, and the core of, a future Government . . ." This meant there could be no progress. Stalin concluded that there was "only one way out of the present situation and that is to accept the Yugoslav precedent."[79]

Thus, the first response to the showdown strategy did not justify the hopes of the President and his advisers. Nevertheless, on the same day that Stalin's reply came in, Secretary of State Stettinius made another effort to make Molotov understand the stakes involved. In a discussion held at San Francisco, Stettinius once more affirmed the American position and emphasized that future economic aid would depend entirely upon the mood and conscience of the American people. He advised Molotov that he would have his last opportunity to prove that Russia deserved economic assistance.[80] Stettinius' efforts met with no success and on April 29 he reported to Truman that the Polish issue had reached an impasse.[81]

The crisis over Poland deepened when in the first week of May information reached Washington that the Warsaw government had already begun to administer territory taken from Germany on the Polish western border.[82] Though this had been accepted in principle at Yalta, no final settlement had been made; and the action indicated Russian determination to support the Warsaw government's claim to legitimacy and its right to a predominant role in a reorganized government.[83] Molotov also renewed an earlier request that the Warsaw government be represented at San Francisco,[84] and he confirmed reports that sixteen Polish underground leaders—some of them political figures—had been arrested on charges of obstructing the Red Army.[85] Although the American and British governments believed the extremely anti-Russian Poles could well have given cause for the Soviet charges, there was little information available, and the arrests seemed aimed at predetermining Polish political issues.[86] Much disturbed by the Soviet attitude, on May 5 the American and British governments jointly announced they would not continue discussions of the Polish issue until a full explanation of the arrests had been given.[87]

Thus the firm line of policy was maintained, as was the parallel position of the United States and Britain. The real issue, of course, still centered on the "Yugoslav precedent," and Truman cabled Stalin on May 4 to say that he supported a long message of Churchill's which had simultaneously rejected the Yugoslav precedent and urged a number of points of procedure.[88] The President said there could be no question of the Warsaw government coming to San Francisco and told Stalin that the American viewpoint had not changed.[89] However, again the President was unsuccessful. On May 7, the State Department reported the latest Russian response on the Polish question. "It was a turndown in every respect," Acting Secretary Grew told Admiral Leahy, "both as to setting up the government and also with regard to the sixteen Polish leaders . . ."[90]

It now was obvious that the showdown strategy had failed. Faced with a setback, Truman's advisers decided it was necessary to further emphasize and dramatize American determination. As early as April 11, Ambassador Harriman and the Department of State were in agreement that the United States "should retain current control of . . . credits [to the Russians] in order to be in a position to protect American vital interests in the formulative period immediately following the war."[91] Lend-Lease aid during the war had been provided according to Soviet requests and American resources, with very little question raised about supporting evidence for Soviet requirements.[92] Harriman believed that Lend-Lease shipments should now be limited exclusively to materials that could be directly related to the common war effort.[93] General Deane had urged the same policy upon the Joint Chiefs of Staff.[94] Any Soviet request which might extend beyond the war period could then be processed in connection with arrangements for a large-scale Soviet credit which had been discussed at Yalta and which still figured in the administration's strategy.[95] Indeed, a limitation on Lend-Lease followed logically from the view that American diplomacy could gain if the Soviet Union were more dependent upon economic assistance. This would increase America's economic leverage and would "make the Soviet authorities come to us," as Deane had phrased it.[96]

Harriman had also pressed this view during his April round of consultations. By early May, Secretaries Stimson and Forrestal, Acting Secretary Grew, Admiral Leahy, and the Joint Chiefs of Staff had endorsed the strategy.[97] On May 8, the day of the German surrender and a day after the report of Stalin's rejection of the President's stand on the Polish issue, Acting Secretary Grew decided to move from consensus to action. Together with Assistant Secretary of State William L. Clayton and Lend-Lease Administrator Leo T. Crowley, he brought the President a draft order authorizing an immediate cutback of Lend-Lease shipments now that the war in Europe was over.[98] Truman agreed with the strategy and signed the order. Almost immediately ships on the high seas bound for the Soviet Union were ordered to turn back, instructions were given to discontinue the loading of ships in port, and goods already aboard ships in American harbors were unloaded.[99] The harshness of this action stirred considerable public protest, and on May 11 the President substituted a slightly modified instruction which allowed ships already at sea to continue and permitted the completion of loading operations already under way.[100] Despite this modification, however, Truman did not change the substance of the order.*

---

* Truman later disclaimed responsibility for the abrupt "*manner* in which the [cutback] order was executed," saying that he had not read the paper he signed. This seems dubious, since there was a great effort by at least four advisers to make sure the President understood what he was doing. But even if one accepts the President's report, the fact remains that Truman immediately substituted a slightly modified order which accomplished substantially the same purpose. The President, of course, has never disclaimed responsibility for this action. As to the harsh execution of the first order, even Harriman was taken aback by the thoroughness with which lower officials acted upon orders from above. (*Year of Decisions*, p. 228; Daniels, *The Man of Independence*, p. 271; Feis, *Between War and Peace*, p. 27*fn.*) On another occasion, Truman offered what, as will be shown, is probably the most accurate recollection; namely that the timing, but not the substance of the action, was a "mistake." (*New York Times*, Feb. 15, 1950.) See below, pp. 271–72.

The abrupt Lend-Lease cutback put great pressure on the Russians, especially as no warning had been given for an action which was bound to disrupt the careful plans of a scarcity wartime economy.[101] As is evident, the timing of the cutback—in the midst of the deadlock after the initial Polish showdown—was certain to be interpreted as economic pressure aimed at forcing the Russians to yield in the diplomatic confrontation. The full story of the Lend-Lease cutback has not been made public. Hitherto it has not been possible to demonstrate conclusively that the Lend-Lease cutback was designed primarily to put pressure on the Russians. However, fresh evidence on this matter indicates that the advisers who urged the action did so precisely for this reason. Moreover they understood their actions would be interpreted as pressure. That the President was fully informed of the strategy and party to it is also shown by reports of discussions among his top advisers.

Truman received complementary advice on the matter from two distinct sources. The State Department, in consultation with Harriman, had long been agreed upon the strategic value of close controls over aid to the Soviet Union.[102] Immediately before the final order was given, however, Lend-Lease Administrator Crowley telephoned Acting Secretary Grew to confirm his understanding of, and agreement with, the action. He particularly wanted the President to understand the implications of the cutback, and asked to accompany Grew when the order was explained to Truman; he wanted "to be sure the President thoroughly understands the situation and that he will back us up and will keep everyone else out of it." Crowley foresaw that "we would be having difficulty with the Russians, and he did not want them to be running all over town looking for help."[103]

At the same time that Crowley and Grew were preparing to explain the Lend-Lease order to the President, Secretary Stimson was at the White House. Stimson too wanted to be certain that the President fully understood the Lend-Lease problem; he had asked for an interview for the single purpose of advising "the necessity of a more realistic policy in regard to the Russians and the use of Lend-Lease towards them." Stimson thought the best approach would be to eliminate the Lend-Lease protocol. He found that the President agreed and, indeed, was "vigorously enthusiastic" in support of his viewpoint. Truman said it was "right down his alley." After his interview Stimson telephoned Grew to report on his conversation. The Acting Secretary was

"very much pleased" at the President's attitude.[104] Two days later
Stimson discussed strategy with Assistant Secretary of War John J.
McCloy, explaining that the Russians had "rather taken [the lead]
away from us because we have talked too much and been too lavish
with our beneficencies." However, the Secretary of War was confident that America's power would bring the Russians into line: "They
can't get along without our help and industries. . . ."[105]

After Truman endorsed the memorandum, Ambassador Harriman
telephoned Grew to report that "the Lend-Lease thing was settled."
Like Crowley, Harriman had few doubts about the effect of the order.
He predicted that "we would be getting a good 'tough slash-back' from
the Russians but that we have to face it."[106] For this reason, Crowley
was asked to work out a statement to give to the press. On May 12,
Crowley telephoned Grew to ask his opinion of a draft which read:

> In view of the end of hostilities in Europe a careful re-examination is
> being made of Lend-Lease programs with a view to allocating ma-
> terials to theaters where they are most needed.

Grew approved the draft. He noted that "the statement did not
seem to bring the Russians in directly," and commented approvingly:
"That was good. . . ." Grew wanted to be sure the Russians were not
named, "since this whole thing is full of dynamite. . . ." Crowley
suggested that "it would be a good idea when the Russians came to us
just to say to them that we were going to reconsider their request
because we have to use some of these materials in other theaters." He
remarked that "what had disturbed the White House apparently was
that War Shipping felt that when the men quit loading ships for Russia, they would immediately start to talk and they felt that a statement
should be made." Crowley explained that his draft "was as little as we
could say. . . ."[107]

As these conversations show, there can be no doubt that the abrupt
Lend-Lease cutoff was designed primarily with the Russians in mind.
To be sure, the action was in accord with the terms of the law requiring an end to the program in Europe after Germany's defeat.[108] But
this was not an overriding consideration, for the law allowed Lend-
Lease aid for those assisting in the war against Japan and admitted of a
wide range of interpretations for use in Europe even after the German
surrender. The cutoff did not, in fact, eliminate the flow of goods

specifically related to Soviet participation in the war against Japan, although there was now a more careful screening of requests.* The law also allowed a generous interpretation which provided supplies to British forces in Europe after the German surrender on the grounds that these forces freed other resources for Japan. A parallel interpretation, though equally justifiable under the law, was not applied to Soviet forces in Europe or elsewhere.[109] Thus, contrary to a commonly held opinion, the law did not require an immediate halt of Lend-Lease shipments to the Soviet Union after the defeat of Germany. As has been indicated, the primary motivation for the timing of the Lend-Lease cutback is to be found in the prevailing concepts which guided the showdown strategy.†

Despite the increased economic pressure which the Lend-Lease cutback created, and despite Stettinius' warning to Molotov, the Russians did not yield in the diplomatic confrontation. A brief message from Stalin on May 10 responded to Truman's last communication and noted that the American note still refused to accept the Warsaw government as the "basis" for the reorganized Polish government. The Soviet Premier concluded: "I am obliged to say that this attitude rules out an agreed decision on the Polish question."[110]

Once again the showdown strategy had failed to bring the promised results. Again there was a direct challenge to the theory that economic pressure would bring the Russians into line with American views. Most American policy makers responded to the challenge, not by reconsidering the assumptions of the strategy, but by following the pattern they had established after the initial setback: They decided that the showdown had to be continued and that the pressure on the Russians had to be increased. Truman's advisers converged upon him with the suggestion that the American position be reaffirmed and emphasized at the highest level, in a face-to-face confrontation with Stalin. On May 14 Admiral Leahy advised the President that an early meeting with Churchill and Stalin was an absolute necessity—"The

---

* After the order, Soviet requests were reduced by 50 per cent in many categories, the first time such screening had been applied since the initiation of the Lend-Lease program. (Feis, *Between War and Peace*, pp. 329–33; U.S. Defense Dept., "Entry of the Soviet Union into the War Against Japan," p. 75.)

† Feis attempts to argue that the provisions of the law were the main reason for this action (*Churchill, Roosevelt, Stalin*, p. 647). For further information on how little Truman felt himself restricted by the law, however, see *Conference of Berlin*, I, pp. 805–20 (especially p. 819), and II, pp. 341, 1184–85.

Polish issue had become a symbol of the deterioration of our relations with the Russians."[111] The next day Acting Secretary of State Grew and Ambassador Harriman emphasized the same point. Grew told Truman that "we all felt in the Department of State that it was of the utmost importance that the Big Three meeting should take place as soon as possible." Harriman then explained that Russia was "the number one problem affecting the future of the world and the fact was that at the present moment we were getting farther and farther apart. . . ." Harriman said that he felt the "establishment of a basis for future relations with Russia and the settlement of those immediate issues could only be done at a tripartite meeting, that the longer the meeting was delayed the worse the situation would get, and that while he assumed . . . that we were not prepared to use our troops in Europe for political bargaining, nevertheless, if the meeting could take place before we were in a large measure out of Europe he felt the atmosphere of the meeting would be more favorable and the chances of success increased. . . ."[112]

Similar views prevailed in London. Eden reported the breakdown of the Polish negotiations to Churchill and urged that the Soviet Union now had to be "brought up sharply against realities."[113] Churchill agreed, responding that the relationship with the Russians could now "only be founded upon their recognition of Anglo-American strength."[114] The Prime Minister believed that "the decisive, practical points of strategy" involved *"above all* that a settlement must be reached on all major issues . . . *before the armies of democracy melted* . . ."[115] On May 6 he proposed an immediate heads-of-government meeting to the President. On May 11 and May 12 he sent further pleas to Truman: "Surely it is vital now to come to an understanding with Russia . . . before we weaken our armies mortally . . ."[116] To Eden, he confidentially advised: "It is to this early and speedy show-down and settlement with Russia that we must now turn our hopes."[117] On May 14 Eden told Truman that "no solution of the [Polish] problem could be expected until there could be a meeting between the President, the Prime Minister and Stalin."[118]

CHAPTER II

The Strategy of a Delayed Showdown

We shall probably hold more cards in our hands later than now.

—SECRETARY OF WAR
HENRY L. STIMSON
May 16, 1945

ALTHOUGH HIS DECISION to force a showdown with Russia had been taken with regard to the specific issue of Poland, Truman's resolve was not limited solely to this dispute. In fact, Poland had been chosen as a *symbolic* issue; the implications of the showdown were expected to affect the whole structure of Soviet-American relations.* It is not surprising, therefore, that in the last week of April Truman also decided to take a strong line on diplomatic problems in Central Europe. Here, however, it was not American economic aid which was central to the tough strategy, but the advantageous position of American troops in Germany.

Soviet-American disputes in Central Europe arose out of the special circumstances of German collapse. The Allies had hoped to avoid the bitter territorial struggle that had occurred in the last days of the First World War and by the late autumn of 1944 had prudently negotiated an agreement delineating zones of occupation to be established in Germany after the fighting.[1] However, the military situation had changed considerably after the agreements were signed. Apparently realizing the inevitable outcome of the war, Hitler reduced resistance

---

* See above, pp. 69–70.

to the Anglo-American advance in the west while he concentrated forces against the Russians in the east. He seemed to hope at least to give over more of Germany to troops whose homes had not been devastated by the Nazi invasion, and at most to sow suspicion and encourage a struggle for the control of German territory.[2]

As a consequence, the western armies found themselves deep within the Soviet zone of Germany, much farther to the east than had originally been expected. As a matter of course, early in April Eisenhower proposed a simple arrangement which would have allowed military commanders in Germany to arrange withdrawals to the agreed zones.[3] Eisenhower's suggestion was immediately opposed by Churchill. On April 5, the Prime Minister cabled Roosevelt urging a "stand fast" order. He noted that final agreement on occupation zones for Austria had not yet been negotiated and, since Russia would very likely occupy almost the whole of the country, he thought it might "be prudent for us to hold as much as possible in the north."[4] At the same time, Churchill directed General Ismay to oppose any major troop movements and to refer any suggested withdrawal to the President and himself.[5]

Churchill's strategy was not very complicated. Despite the existing protocol, which specifically required troop withdrawals after German capitulation, he believed it might be possible to obtain additional concessions from the Russians if he could maintain the extended troop positions. Realizing the relative weakness of the British bargaining position, he counted heavily on the value of the troop withdrawals in the next round of negotiations.[6] Although in communication with Roosevelt he linked the withdrawal only to the relatively minor unsettled Austrian zonal questions,* privately he informed Ismay that his purpose was far more general—before the armies were withdrawn, "political issues operative at that time should be discussed between the heads of Governments, and in particular . . . the situation should be viewed as a whole and in regard to the relations between the Soviet, American and British Governments."[7]

Churchill's approach to Roosevelt was made well in advance of the

---

* For more information on this dispute, see
Feis, *Between War and Peace*, pp. 65–69,
149–51.

war's end, before the time when large-scale troop movements would have to be made. In a parallel action, the British Chiefs of Staff proposed a temporary "stand fast" order. This was accepted by the Joint Chiefs of Staff, so that while the matter was being discussed between London and Washington, Eisenhower was directed to maintain the troop positions.[8] The temporary directive was issued on the day Roosevelt died (April 12), and Churchill moved immediately to exploit his advantage. On April 14 he reaffirmed the substance of his earlier instruction to Ismay,[9] and on April 18 he took the matter up with Roosevelt's successor. To achieve his end, the Prime Minister was now prepared to utilize whatever argument he thought most persuasive. Undoubtedly aware of American concern over the developing problems of scarcity in Central Europe, he abandoned the attempt to link the withdrawal to the Austrian zonal dispute and switched the basis of his attack.* "The Russian occupational zone has the smallest proportion of people and grows by far the largest proportion of food . . ." he cabled Truman. "Before we move from the tactical positions we have at present achieved," the Russians should be forced to agree that "the feeding of the German population must be treated as a whole and that the available supplies must be divided *pro rata* between the occupational zones."[10]

When this suggestion reached Washington, Truman referred the matter to the Joint Chiefs of Staff for advice.[11] He found them unwilling to use the troop positions for political purposes.[12] From London, Ambassador John G. Winant advised that an attempt to bargain the troop positions for better food distribution might jeopardize cooperative-control arrangements for Germany.[13] Unwilling to alter the direction of Roosevelt's policy less than a week after his death, the new President deferred to his advisers (as he tended to do on decisions involving military matters) and on April 21 responded to Churchill: "The fact that the Russian zone contained the greater portion of German food-producing areas . . . was well known" before agreement was reached on the zones. Acceptance of the agreement "was in no way made contingent upon the conclusion of satisfactory arrangements for an equitable distribution of German food resources." Truman suggested that Eisenhower be given discretion to make troop

---

* See below, pp. 100–2, 125–28.

adjustments, but that where time permitted, he should refer major movements to the Combined Chiefs of Staff.*

While Truman and Churchill debated a course of action, a further temporary directive was issued which continued to withhold discretion to make troop withdrawals.[14] With the movements still held up, Churchill returned to the struggle. Ignoring Truman's argument that food could not be bargained for, the Prime Minister once more switched his ground, reverted to the issue raised earlier with Roosevelt, and continued to urge his main point upon the President. On April 24 he noted that "all questions of our spheres in Vienna or arrangements for triple occupation of Berlin remain unsettled." He begged that the troops be held in place until the issues had been satisfactorily resolved.[15]

At about the time this message went out, Eisenhower wrote Marshall: "I do not quite understand why the Prime Minister has been so determined to intermingle political and military considerations in attempting to establish a procedure for the conduct of our own and Russian troops when a meeting takes place. My original recommendation . . . was a simple one. . . . One of my concerns was the possibility that the Russians might arrive in the Danish peninsula before we could fight our way across the Elbe and I wanted a formula that would take them out of that region at my request. . . . I really do not anticipate that the Russians will be arbitrary in demanding an instant withdrawal. . . ."[16]

THE FIRM APPROACH IN CENTRAL EUROPE

THE MESSAGES FROM Churchill and Eisenhower reached Washington shortly after Truman's April 23 confrontation with Molotov. Although Poland was the question the President discussed with the Soviet Foreign Minister on that date, the decision to force a showdown with Russia involved a fundamental change of course. Despite his earlier willingness to follow the advice of the Joint Chiefs, Truman

---

* This quotation is Leahy's paraphrase of Truman's message. (*I Was There*, p. 350.) There is disagreement on the date of this message. Leahy, Mosely, Feis, and Wilmot say April 21, 1945. (*I Was There*, p. 349; "The Occupation of Germany," p. 602; *Churchill, Roosevelt, Stalin*, p. 609; *The Struggle for Europe*, p. 795.) Churchill indicates it was between April 21 and April 24, 1945. (*Triumph and Tragedy*, p. 516.) Truman says April 23. (*Year of Decisions*, p. 214.)

now committed himself to the tough approach; he decided to maintain the American troop positions in the Soviet zone of Germany. Reversing himself completely, Truman rejected Eisenhower's view and accepted Churchill's. In a cable to the Prime Minister on April 26, he pointed out that even under the existing directives the Russians could not require a troop withdrawal without the approval of the heads of government.[17] The President suggested a joint message to Stalin which linked the troop withdrawals to a satisfactory solution of the remaining Austrian issues. Delighted at Truman's agreement with his firm strategy, Churchill approved the draft and parallel messages went American stand against Russia.†

Thus, despite the fact that he recognized "the Russians were in a strong position," Truman followed the showdown on Poland with a firm approach to the problem of cooperation in Central Europe.[18] He wanted acceptance of his proposals for the administration of Austria and believed that by refusing to fulfill the previous understanding on Germany he could force Stalin's acquiescence. His joint action with Churchill once more stressed his willingness to present a united Anglo-American stand against Russia.*

Again, various military authorities believed this handling of the troop issue would bring negative results. The Joint Chiefs of Staff had already raised their objections. In Britain, General Ismay, the chief of the Imperial General Staff, felt that "considering that we have already agreed with the Russians as to the Zones of Occupation in Germany, I consider Winston is fundamentally wrong in using this as a bargaining

---

* Truman obscures this point in his memoirs so as to make it appear that he refused to follow Churchill's approach. He does not quote the April 27, 1945, message, which quite clearly shows his change of position. Thus three extraneous issues were injected into the dispute: Truman made it clear that the troops would not be withdrawn from the Soviet zone of Germany until the Russians yielded on the delineation of the Austrian zones of occupation, the apportionment of zones and facilities in Vienna, and the establishment of a satisfactory Allied Control Council for Austria. In fact, the Churchill-Truman tactic utilized a heavy hammer to attempt to drive a small nail, for on none of these questions were there major differences. For this reason one wonders whether Truman, like Churchill, might not have been trying to use the Austrian issues as an excuse to keep the troops in place until *all* political issues had been resolved with the Russians. (For Truman's recollection of what happened, see *Year of Decisions*, pp. 62, 214–16, 303–4; but also see Churchill, *Triumph and Tragedy*, p. 517; *Stalin's Correspondence*, I, pp. 337–38; II, p. 224; Ehrman, *Grand Strategy*, pp. 154–55. For more information on the disputed points, see Feis, *Churchill, Roosevelt, Stalin*, p. 622; *Between War and Peace*, p. 66.)

† This is another place where those who stress Truman's willingness to follow Roosevelt's policies miss the change in strategy after April 23, 1945. It is simply an error to say, as Feis does, that "Truman carefully carried out all the agreements which Roosevelt had entered." (*Churchill, Roosevelt, Stalin*, p. 600; see also p. 636, and Woodward, *British Foreign Policy*, p. 518*fn*.)

counter."[19] In Germany, Eisenhower believed it "indefensible" to use the troops to gain advantage on the Austrian issues. He was certain that "to start off our first direct association with Russia on the basis of refusing to carry out an arrangement in which the good faith of our government was involved would wreck the whole cooperative attempt at its very beginning."[20]

It appears that these judgments were correct, for immediately difficulties arose in Austria, where Soviet troops held a position almost as advantageous as the Anglo-American position in Germany. The Russians had already shown awareness of their own bargaining strength; on the day after Truman's showdown with Molotov, Andrey Y. Vyshinsky had informed American and British representatives that Karl Renner, a former Socialist chancellor of the Austrian Republic, had presented a plan for creating a provisional government. Vyshinsky had indicated that the Soviet government would favor such a development.[21] Shortly after linking the troop question to the Austrian issues, the British and American governments had responded that they wished to be consulted on the establishment of a new government. They had urged the Soviet Union to defer recognition of Renner. But the Russians showed little interest in this proposal, Renner proclaimed the establishment of a provisional government, and on April 29 Radio Moscow announced that the Soviet commander in Austria had recognized the new government.*[22]

The Russian armies were clearly in a position to determine the course of events in Austria, and this initial response to Truman's firm line was hardly encouraging. Although Renner's government appeared to represent all Austrian political elements, its establishment without Western consultation sidestepped the question of Allied administration and cooperative control of the country.[23] Truman had the American embassy file a protest emphasizing the need for joint responsibility: "We assume that it remains the intention of the Soviet Government that supreme authority in Austria will be exercised by the four powers acting jointly on a basis of equality . . . until the establishment of an Austrian government recognized by the four powers."[24]

---

* This indicated a practical working arrangement with the military. Moscow did not grant diplomatic recognition at this time. (*Conference of Berlin*, I, p. 334.)

Truman did not accompany this message with a suggestion that the Western troops might withdraw to the agreed zones so that the unresolved Austrian issues could be considered independently. Instead, he continued to hold to the American demand on the points at issue. Stalin's response was equally firm. Now he refused to allow Western representatives to enter Vienna until a satisfactory solution of the zonal questions had been achieved. He also indicated that Allied control of Austria would not be established until the Anglo-American tactic was abandoned.*[25]

Thus, by the first week of May there were grave doubts that the American plan for cooperative control of Austria would be fulfilled. Despite renewed protests from London and Washington, a stalemate had been reached and it appeared that Stalin would not yield to a firm approach in Central Europe any more than he was yielding to a similar approach regarding Poland.[26] Churchill's reaction was typical; he urged that the Anglo-American troops be held in position *even if* the Western position were accepted on the Austrian problems. Moreover, he was certain that an immediate confrontation with Stalin was essential. On May 4 the Prime Minister wrote to Eden: "The Allies ought not to retreat from their present positions to the occupational line until we are satisfied about Poland, and also about the temporary character of Russian occupation of Germany, and the conditions to be established in the Russianized or Russian-controlled countries in the Danube valley, particularly Austria and Czechoslovakia, and the Balkans."[27] Churchill followed this statement of intent with a series of messages to Truman. The Polish and Central European stalemates were now bound up together in an over-all crisis of confidence between the powers. Thus, in the same May 6 message in which he demanded an immediate meeting with Stalin, Churchill urged: "We should hold firmly to the existing position obtained or being obtained by our armies."[28]

Truman responded that he would "stand firmly on our present announced attitude toward all the questions at issue."[29] Although this reaffirmed the President's earlier message linking the troop withdrawal

---

* Apparently Stalin was more disturbed by the tactic of linking the troop withdrawal to the political issues than he was with the American position on the points in dispute. As will be seen, after the troops were withdrawn, he quite readily agreed to a satisfactory solution of all of the political problems. See below, pp. 131–32.

to the Austrian question, Churchill tried to get a commitment to his more general view that the troops be held in position until *all* issues were settled in a meeting with Stalin. On May 11, he cabled: "I earnestly hope that the American front will not recede."[30] On May 12 he appealed to the President again, reiterating the argument that it was essential to come to an understanding with Russia "before we . . . retire to the zones of occupation."[31] Truman's reply on May 14 neither refused nor accepted the general "stand still" order *and the President continued to maintain troops in position on the previous basis.**

This situation immediately had repercussions throughout the heart of Europe. In fact, Truman had tied his own hands. By making withdrawal from the Soviet zone in Germany dependent upon the resolution of the Austrian issues, he lost all initiative; the Russians rejected his stand on the points in dispute, and the troops held their positions. With the West refusing to fulfill the previous agreements for withdrawal, Stalin refused to establish joint control arrangements. It seemed that Truman's own strategy also prevented cooperative control of Germany.

Additional complications now arose. At Churchill's insistence, at the last minute a brief military-surrender document had been substituted for the longer surrender instrument which had previously been drawn up by the powers.† Consequently, no formal basis for establishing the Allied Control Council existed, nor were the principles of Allied administration embodied in the surrender agreement as had originally been planned.[32] On May 16 Eisenhower reported that Churchill refused to establish joint control procedures for Germany because this would offer an occasion for the Russians to demand that the troops be withdrawn to the agreed zones.[33] Eisenhower said he

---

* This has been emphasized because various accounts make it appear that because he refused a general "stand still" order Truman wished to withdraw American troops to their zones. In fact, there was no substantive change in the situation. (See Churchill, *Triumph and Tragedy*, p. 557; Feis, *Churchill, Roosevelt, Stalin*, p. 637; Truman, *Year of Decisions*, p. 248; *Conference of Berlin*, I, p. 11.)

† The reason for this substitution has never been adequately explained. Churchill's overriding interest at this time was to forestall

troop withdrawals from the Soviet zone. It is probable that Churchill objected to the long surrender document because—as he explained to Eisenhower when the terms of the document had been written in declaration form— he feared the provisions establishing joint control would give Stalin a basis for demanding that the Anglo-American troops be removed to the agreed zones. (See Feis, *Between War and Peace*, pp. 76–77; Mosely, "Dismemberment of Germany," p. 497; Smith, *My Three Years in Moscow*, p. 20.)

was finding it difficult to carry out his orders without agreement on joint control. A week later he told Washington his mission could not be carried out unless the terms of surrender were made public and the Allied Control Council was proclaimed.[34]

Thus, by mid-May, Truman was faced with a direct challenge to the plan for cooperative control of Central Europe. There were no signs that Allied Control Councils would be established in either Austria or Germany. The President was forced to consider his future course of action.

SECRETARY STIMSON AND THE IMMEDIATE SHOWDOWN

To THOSE ADVISERS who had urged a firm line on all issues in dispute between Russia and the United States, there seemed no way out of the mid-May stalemate except an immediate face-to-face meeting with Stalin. Truman had now been urged to hold such a confrontation by Churchill and almost every important American adviser concerned with policy making. However, official opinion was not unanimous on the point. One influential member of the Cabinet not only opposed an early meeting but also objected on more fundamental grounds to the line of action being taken regarding Poland and Central Europe.

Almost alone among the presidential advisers at the April 23 discussion (at which a decision had been made to take a firm stand with Molotov), Secretary of War Stimson had argued against an immediate showdown over the Polish issue. Although Stimson believed in a "more realistic policy" utilizing Lend-Lease aid "toward" the Russians, he had not agreed with the group decision. He objected to the timing, the method, and the issue chosen for the symbolic confrontation. One reason for this was Stimson's belief that the Russians were not likely to yield on the specific point at issue. More important, however, was his conviction that much could be gained by delaying all diplomatic disputes.

At the April 23 meeting Stimson had presented a series of arguments to convince the President that a showdown over Poland had to be avoided. He thought it important "to find out what the Russians were driving at" in their interpretation of the Yalta agreement. He pointed out that "in the big military matters" the Soviet government had kept its word, and the military authorities of the United States had come to count on it. "In fact, they had often done better than they had promised." On that account, he believed it was important to find out what motive they had in connection with these border countries and what their ideas of independence and democracy were in the areas they regarded as vital to the Soviet Union.[35]

Stimson was a leading American conservative. He had established a brilliant record as a Wall Street lawyer, had served as Secretary of War under President William Howard Taft, had acted as Secretary of State under President Herbert Hoover, and though an eminent Republican, had agreed to join President Franklin Roosevelt's war Cabinet.[36] His caution derived from no sympathy for the Soviet system. Rather, he prided himself on a realistic approach to world affairs, and he had long ago acknowledged the Soviet "claim that, in the light of her bitter experience with Germany, her own self-defense . . . will depend on relations with buffer countries like Poland, Bulgaria, and Rumania." Stimson understood that these relations would be "quite different from complete independence on the part of those countries,"[37] but he had come to the conclusion that facts had to be faced.

"The Russians perhaps were being more realistic than we were in regard to their own security," he told Truman at the April 23 meeting.[38] "We had to remember that the Russian conception of freedom, democracy, and independent voting was quite different from ours or the British."[39] When he returned from the discussion, Stimson dictated a caustic diary entry attacking an overly legalistic interpretation of the Yalta agreement: "Although at Yalta [Russia] apparently agreed to a free and independent ballot for the ultimate choice of the representatives of Poland, yet I know very well . . . that there are no nations in the world except the U.S. and U.K. which have a real idea of what an independent free ballot is."[40]

The essence of Stimson's view was a conservative belief that the postwar power structure in Europe had to be acknowledged so that a *modus vivendi* could be established with Russia. Although he wished to preserve American economic interests in Eastern Europe, he took for granted Soviet special interests in the border countries just as he accepted American special interests in Latin America—the two areas were "our respective orbits."[41] If the parallel Soviet interest in Eastern Europe were understood, Stimson believed "our position in the western hemisphere and Russia's in the eastern hemisphere could be adjusted without too much friction."[42] He believed this would require a fair acceptance of Soviet claims. He was critical of some policy makers who were "anxious to hang on to exaggerated views of the Monroe Doctrine and at the same time butt into every question that comes up in Central Europe."[43]

Stimson did not dwell on this point with Truman. He admitted that the Russians had made a good deal of trouble on minor military matters and that it had sometimes been necessary to "teach them manners." However, on the greater matter of the Polish question, he believed that without fully understanding how seriously the Russians felt we might be "heading into very dangerous waters." He noted that the Russian viewpoint was undoubtedly influenced by the fact that before World War I most of Poland had been controlled by Russia. Stimson said he would like to know how far the Russian reaction to a strong position on Poland would go. It was his opinion that the Russians would not yield. He urged that the President "go slowly and avoid an open break."[44]

Stimson knew that Truman had rejected his advice at the April 23 meeting. He confided to his diary that "nobody backed me up until it came round to Marshall."[45] The General still thought Soviet help might be of some use in the Japanese war, but this was not the only reason he had come to Stimson's defense on the Polish issue.[46] Two weeks before Roosevelt's death Stimson had sensed the increasingly tough view a number of advisers were taking toward Russia. As early as April 2 he thought this "a very serious matter, for we simply cannot allow a rift to come between the two nations without endangering the entire peace of the world."[47] Expecting trouble, Stimson had summoned Marshall so as to keep "close with him in order to have my power in my elbow for the conference that may come up."[48] With Marshall as an ally, Stimson had been prepared to enter the policy conflict over Poland. It was time, he noted in his diary, "for me to use all the restraint I can on these other people who have been apparently getting a little more irritated."[49]

Although he had prepared for the fight, after the meeting with the President, Stimson was aware that Harriman and Deane had outmaneuvered him. He attributed their energetic activities to the fact that they had "been suffering personally from the Russians' behavior on minor matters for a long time." He was disturbed that "they were evidently influenced by their past bad treatment," for he believed that the victory of the tough line set the stage for a severe test of Soviet-American relations.[50] "It was one of the most difficult situations I have ever had since I have been here. . . . We are at loggerheads with Russia on an issue which in my opinion is very dangerous and one which she is not likely to yield on in substance. . . . In my opinion we ought to be very careful and see whether we couldn't get ironed out on the situation without getting into a head-on collision."[51]

EUROPEAN STABILITY AND AMERICAN SECURITY

THE REASON STIMSON felt so strongly about this point was not, as is often supposed, that he feared the tough line would lose Soviet help in the Japanese war. Though this had indeed been an important point at an earlier stage, strategic plans no longer required Soviet assistance. To be sure, some military leaders still felt that an early Russian entry into the war would be of general value, but Stimson himself does not seem to have been particularly concerned about the point at this time, and, in fact, he had reasons for wishing to end the war before the Russians entered it.* The main reason Stimson believed a rift between the two nations would endanger the "entire peace of the world" was his conviction that cooperation with Russia was absolutely essential to the postwar stability of Europe; if the European economy collapsed, Stimson believed, chaos, revolution, and war would result. "All of this is a tough problem requiring coordination between the Anglo-American allies and Russia," he confided to his diary; "Russia will occupy most of the good food lands of Central Europe. . . . We must find some way of persuading Russia to play ball."[52]

Thus, Stimson's awareness of Soviet security interests was bolstered by his strong desire for Soviet cooperation in postwar Europe. He believed American interests were already involved, for Stimson had come to define American security as dependent upon European stabil-

---

* Stimson was worried that Soviet entry would mean Soviet domination of Manchuria. For the relationship between his fears and his strategy for ending the war, see Chapter IV.

ity.[53] The Secretary's reasoning was natural for a man who had been deeply involved in public affairs at the Cabinet level since 1911. Having lived through two European wars which had involved the United States, he concluded that world peace was "indivisible."[54] To avoid a future war it was necessary to lay the basis for a lasting European peace.* Stimson feared the disease and starvation in Central Europe which might be "followed by political revolution and communistic infiltration." He felt it "vital" to keep Western Europe "from being driven to revolution or communism by famine,"[55] and he concluded that "an economically stable Europe . . . is one of the greatest assurances of security and continued peace we [the United States] can hope to obtain."[56]

Stimson also wanted the "restoration of stable conditions in Europe" because he believed that "only thus can concepts of individual liberty, free thought and free speech be nurtured."[57] Despite his concern with the possibility of revolution, the Secretary was not pessimistic about the future. He believed wise policy could persuade the Russians to establish arrangements in Europe which would also redound to their benefit. Consequently, Stimson focused his attention on ways to promote cooperation in the heart of the Continent—Germany and Austria.

Throughout the war, Stimson had stressed the need for sound economic conditions in Central Europe.[58] He had led the fight against Secretary of the Treasury Henry Morgenthau's plan for destroying great sectors of German industry. He feared the consequences of eliminating such an important factor in the European economy. To accept Morgenthau's advice, he reasoned, would involve "poisoning the springs out of which we hope that the future peace of the world can be maintained." He urged that methods of "economic oppression . . . do not prevent war; they tend to breed war."[59] Instead of following such a plan it would be wise to restore German industry under careful controls.[60] "We should not remove [German] capacity for

---

* See also Byrnes's 1945 argument, "Two wars in one generation have convinced the American people that they have a very vital interest in the maintenance of peace in Europe." (Senate Committee on Foreign Relations, *A Decade of American Foreign Policy*, p. 55.) Again, Stimson's 1945 declaration that "the worst thing we did to break the chance of peace after the last war, and to tempt willful nations toward aggression, was to keep out." (*On Active Service*, p. 599.)

aiding in the restoration of stable conditions in Europe and the world."[61]

Stimson viewed the problems of Germany and Austria in exactly the same way as he saw the broader issues of the Continent. Since Soviet troops would be in control of the good food lands, cooperation would be essential to economic stability. As early as October 1943, Stimson stressed the need for open trading arrangements: "Central Europe after the war has got to eat. She has got to be free from tariffs in order to eat." Policy makers who did not understand this did not have "any grasp apparently of the underlying need of proper economic arrangements to make the peace stick."[62]

The problem was as important to the Secretary in 1945 as it was in 1943, but now the issue was more urgent. In mid-April, Assistant Secretary of War John J. McCloy returned from an inspection of Europe reporting "complete economic, social and political collapse" in both Germany and Austria.[63] Stimson summarized the situation to the Cabinet on April 20 as "chaos" and "near anarchy."[64] On May 16 he pressed Truman on the matter, strongly urging American efforts to create stability. "The eighty million Germans and Austrians in Central Europe necessarily swing the balance of that continent," he argued. "A solution must be found."[65]

Leaving aside all other considerations, it is fair to say that by mid-April, when tension between America and Russia began to mount, Secretary Stimson believed it wise to yield to considerable Soviet political influence in Poland in the interest of a solution to European economic problems. To attempt to press the Polish issue to a showdown he believed both futile and dangerous; the Russians would not yield, and a break would destroy the possibility of cooperation. On the other hand, Stimson felt that the record of military cooperation offered reason for hope of a successful postwar relationship. While other advisers urged a showdown with Russia, Stimson tried to "hang onto" the fact that Russia and the United States had "always gotten along for a hundred and fifty years' history, with Russia friendly and helpful." "Our respective orbits do not clash geographically and I think that on the whole we can probably keep out of clashes in the future," he noted.[66] But he reminded himself that this would "require the greatest care and the greatest patience and the greatest thoughtfulness."[67]

In this spirit the Secretary of War also opposed the tough approach to German problems. He advised against pressing the attempt to use the German troop positions to achieve political objectives in Austria.[68] Instead, he urged a policy of cooperation with Russia which would treat Germany "as an economic unit."[69] More generally, he urged that the United States dissociate its policy from British diplomacy. He believed that "Churchill, now that Mr. Roosevelt was dead, was seeking to take a more active part in the direction of matters of grand policy in Central Europe." At the end of April he suggested to Marshall that they "ought to be alert now that a new man was at the helm in the Presidency to see that he was advised as to the background of the past differences between Britain and America on these matters."[70]

Thus, on the specific diplomatic issues in question, and on the general issue of American collaboration with Britain, Stimson was opposed to the advisers who urged an immediate showdown with Russia. His policy, however, was not so simple and straightforward as the above analysis at first suggests. On May 14, Stimson told Assistant Secretary McCloy that "the time now and the method now to deal with Russia was to keep our mouths shut."[71] The word "now" must be carefully noted, for it is essential to remember that Stimson's recommendations were forged in the heat of an intense policy-making debate and were designed to counter the pressure for an immediate showdown with Russia. To understand his longer-term policy, it is necessary to consider the Secretary's thinking on matters of great strategic importance.*

THE STRATEGY OF A DELAYED SHOWDOWN

ON APRIL 24, the day after Truman's showdown with Molotov, Stimson wrote to the President: "I think it is very important that I should have a talk with you as soon as possible. . . . [The atomic bomb]† has such a bearing on our present foreign relations and such

---

* For a detailed exposition of Stimson's views on the need to treat the German and Continental economies as a unit, see *Conference of Berlin*, II, pp. 754–57, 808–9.

† Because of wartime security requirements, the weapon was usually referred to indirectly or by the code terms "Tube Alloys" and "S-1." Hereafter the words "the atomic bomb" will be used within brackets in place of all indirect references in quoted text.

an important effect upon all my thinking in this field that I think you should know about it without much further delay."[72]

The President agreed to see Stimson immediately, and on April 25 Truman was briefed at length on the nuclear development program. The Secretary presented a memorandum which began: "Within four months we shall in all probability have completed the most terrible weapon ever known in human history. . . ."[73] Stimson was extremely confident of success.*[74] He said that a "gun-type" bomb would be ready about August 1. For this weapon no test would be necessary. A second would be available before the end of the year. Early in July a test of an implosion weapon would be held in New Mexico. Another trial could be held before the first of August if necessary. Less than a month after the successful test a "Fat Man" weapon would be ready for combat.[75]

For three quarters of an hour Stimson discussed the atomic bomb with the President. It was *assumed*—not decided—that the bomb would be used.† Stimson told Truman that for some time Japan had been the target of the weapon development program. A special Twentieth Air Force group was about to leave for its overseas base. Stimson expressed confidence that the bomb would shorten the war.[76] However, the use of the bomb against Japan was not the main subject the Secretary wanted to discuss.

Although shortly after Roosevelt's death Stimson had casually mentioned to Truman that an "immense project . . . was under way—a project looking to the development of a new explosive of almost unbelievable destructive power," he had felt no compelling reason to discuss the matter fully with the new President at that time.[77] It was only after the showdown with Molotov that he asked for a special interview with the President. He was prompted to do so not because of the weapon's potential effect on the Japanese war, but primarily be-

---

* A diary entry notes "success is 99% assured." (Stimson Diary, April 11, 1945.) On April 23, British representatives reported to London that it was "as certain as such things can be" that the first bomb would be ready in late summer. (Ehrman, *Grand Strategy*, p. 275.)

† Stimson later noted, "*At no time* from 1941 to 1945 did I ever hear it suggested by the President or any other responsible member of the government that atomic energy should not be used in the war." (*On Active Service*, p. 613.) A few days after Stimson's talk with the President, Field Marshal Wilson, the British representative on the Combined Policy Committee (which discussed nuclear developments) informed Sir John Anderson that the Americans had *already* proposed "to drop a bomb sometime in August." (Ehrman, *Grand Strategy*, p. 276.) *See also* Gowing, *Britain and Atomic Energy*, p. 372.

cause it had "such a bearing on our present foreign relations and such an important effect upon all my thinking in this field."[78]

Although we do not have full information on Stimson's discussion with the President, it is important to understand the Secretary's conception of the atomic bomb's role in diplomacy. On April 25 he told Truman the bomb was "certain" to have a "decisive" influence on relations with other countries. Truman reports that the discussion centered "specifically" on "the effect the atomic bomb might likely have on our future foreign relations," but summarizes the forty-five-minute conversation in only three short paragraphs. Consequently, one must go beyond this information to understand the general line of strategy Stimson advocated.[79]

The key to the Secretary's view was a consistent judgment—held from at least mid-March 1945—that the atomic bomb would add great power to American diplomacy once it was developed.[80] He considered that no major issue could be realistically discussed without an estimate of the bomb's role.[81] He believed it "premature" for the United States to raise diplomatic issues in the Far East until the bomb had been tested.[82] Similarly, he believed it essential that the discussion of European issues be postponed; he told the President on May 16, "We shall probably hold more cards in our hands later than now."[83]

As Secretary of War, Stimson was the most important man in government with full information on the highly secret nuclear program. Urging his strategy of delay among the very small circle of advisers privy to the secret, he had to impress his colleagues with the incredible powers likely to be released by the still-untested weapon. The Secretaries of State and the Navy, and Ambassador Harriman, wanted not only an immediate showdown in Europe but also an immediate confrontation on certain Far Eastern diplomatic issues. Stimson records that he had "a pretty red-hot session" urging postponement of a meeting on the latter questions—"Over any such tangled weave of problems, [the atomic-bomb] secret would be dominant, and yet we will not know until after that time probably, until after that meeting, whether this is a weapon in our hands or not. We think it will be shortly afterward, but it seems a terrible thing to gamble with such big stakes in diplomacy without having your master card in your hand."[84]

Stimson urged that we take "time to think over these things a little bit harder."[85] He also took Harriman into his confidence and "talked over very confidentially our problem connected with [the atomic bomb]" and its relation to European matters.[86] At the same time, he discussed the role of the bomb and European diplomacy with British Foreign Secretary Anthony Eden, outlining "to him the progress which we have made and the timetable as it stood now, and . . . its bearing upon our present problems of an international character."[87] In general, the point the Secretary of War repeatedly emphasized was the need to postpone any confrontation with the Russians until the atomic bomb had been proved and demonstrated.

Despite his emphasis on the weapon's value for diplomacy, Stimson did not believe the new power could be used to *force* the Russians to accept American terms on diplomatic issues. He thought such a course would inevitably lead to an arms race.[88] Stimson knew, as he told Truman, that it was "practically certain" that the United States could not maintain a monopoly of the bomb for very long.[89] He explained that "the future may see a time when such a weapon may be constructed in secret and used suddenly and effectively with devastating power by a willful nation or group against an unsuspecting nation or group."[90] For these reasons, Stimson believed that some form of international control of the new development was absolutely essential. If control were not achieved, the results could be disastrous. "In other words," he told Truman, "modern civilization might be completely destroyed."[91]

Thus, Stimson's view that the atomic bomb would be "decisive" in diplomacy did not depend upon its use as a threat. Caught between the desire to use the bomb as an instrument of diplomacy and the knowledge that its use as a threat would lead to a "disaster to civilization," Stimson resolved his dilemma by urging that the secret of the weapon be offered as a bargaining counter in negotiations to establish a peace settlement.[92] As early as December 1944, the Secretary searched for diplomatic *"quid pro quos"* which might be asked of Russia in exchange for information on nuclear energy and participation in a system of international control.[93] Two months before Roosevelt's death, he raised the same question with subordinates.[94] Discussing the problem with Truman at the April 25 interview, he declared: "The question of sharing [the atomic bomb] . . . and . . . upon what terms, becomes a primary question of our foreign relations."[95]

Stimson suggested that the President appoint a special "Interim Committee" to advise him on the method to use the bomb against Japan and the political implications of the new force.[96] Following the April 25 interview, the Secretary and Truman discussed problems connected with the bomb on several occasions, at least on May 1, 2, 3, and 4.* Stimson suggested that the President have a close confidant and personal representative on the Interim Committee.[97] It was clear that the most important problems would relate to the role of the bomb in diplomacy, and the obvious choice in Stimson's view was James F. Byrnes, the man Truman had privately designated to become his new Secretary of State.[98]

Although the diplomatic implications of the atomic bomb dominated private discussions between Stimson and Truman during the last week of April and the first week of May, we do not have precise information on the exact date on which Stimson advised the President to postpone diplomatic confrontations with the Russians. From available information, there can be no doubt that the Secretary urged this general view during the last week of April, probably at the April 25 meeting.† But in the tense atmosphere of the showdown over Poland and the developing stalemate in Central Europe, Stimson's general point soon reduced to a more specific recommendation—the Secretary advised that a heads-of-government meeting be delayed until the atomic bomb had been tested early in July. He felt that "the greatest complication was what might happen at the meeting of the Big Three" if the tests had not been completed.[99]

In urging this line of advice, Stimson came into direct conflict with those policy makers who wanted to maintain the firm line. They feared that unless there was an immediate showdown—before American troops were substantially withdrawn from Europe—the Soviet Premier would not yield. Forced to acknowledge the crucial role of the troops—and, indeed, as aware of their importance as the other advisers and Churchill—Stimson offered specialized military information to support his strategy of delay. In company with General

---

* There probably were other discussions not recorded in the documents.　† See Appendix II for a detailed examination of the probable date.

Marshall, on May 14 he explained the role of the atomic bomb to Anthony Eden. He assured the Foreign Secretary that there was no reason to fear delay, since the actual figures for troop withdrawals for the rest of the summer would not reach 50,000 per month out of a total of three million.[100] Stimson explained to the President two days later: "The work of redeploying our forces from Europe to the Pacific will necessarily take so long that there will be more time for your necessary diplomacy with the other large allies than some of our hasty friends realize."[101]

With this reassurance, Stimson's strategy of a delayed showdown was fully developed. Though at first glance it appeared that Stimson was prepared to concede Soviet political domination in Poland, in fact, the Secretary had a far more subtle strategy in mind. He was opposed to an *immediate* showdown on the Polish issue, for he believed the Russians would not yield on a matter so vital to their security. This would be especially true if the atomic test failed and, as expected, American troops were eventually withdrawn from the Continent. But while he opposed a strong immediate stand on the Polish issue, he did not give up hope of influencing affairs in Poland and elsewhere in Eastern Europe. At the very least, the atomic bomb would seal whatever cooperative arrangements cautious diplomacy could negotiate, and it was likely to be much more effective; two months before the bomb was to be used, he looked to the future, confiding to his diary a brief sketch of the *"quid pro quos* which should be established in consideration for our taking [the Russians] into partnership" for control of the new force. Among the Soviet concessions he sought were a satisfactory "settlement of the Polish, Rumanian, Yugoslavian, and Manchurian problems."[102] Thus, though he was more restrained in approach, Stimson's ultimate aims were not substantially different from those of Truman's other advisers.

Nor, indeed, did he differ on the need for a showdown, for Stimson did not think the Russians would be brought into line without a show of American determination. "It is a case where we have got to regain the lead," he told McCloy, "and perhaps do it in a pretty rough and realistic way." There would probably have to be a forceful confrontation of some kind, and Stimson had few doubts about the ultimate outcome—it "was a place where we really held all of the cards." Success depended only upon prudence, subtlety, and delay. He told

McCloy that the American bargaining position was like "a royal straight flush and we mustn't be a fool about the way we play it. . . . We have coming into action a weapon which will be unique. Now the thing is not to get into unnecessary quarrels by talking too much and not to indicate any weakness by talking too much; let our actions speak for themselves."[103]

CHAPTER III

The Decision to Postpone a Confrontation with Stalin

If we ever compromise with principle, such compromise is only a temporary measure in order the better to attain our main objective in the end.

—ACTING SECRETARY OF STATE
JOSEPH C. GREW
June 4, 1945

IMMEDIATELY AFTER his April 25 talk with Stimson, President Truman began to respond to the broad line of advice offered by his Secretary of War. Within a few days even British representatives knew a committee would be set up "to consider the whole range of political issues which will arise in connection" with the atomic bomb.[1] On May 2, Truman authorized arrangements for the Interim Committee and accepted Stimson's suggested list of members. On May 4, formal invitations for the first meeting of the Committee were issued.[2]

At the same time he approved this proposal, Truman also named a personal representative to the Committee. Evidently agreeing that the atomic bomb would have decisive implications for diplomacy, Truman followed the suggestion that the man designated to be Secretary of State represent the President. On May 3, James F. Byrnes's agreement to serve on the Interim Committee was secured.[3] Shortly thereafter the President also asked Byrnes to make an independent study of the bomb's potentialities.[4]

There is very little direct evidence available regarding Truman's personal view of the atomic bomb during April and May.* It may therefore be important to note that in choosing Byrnes, the President put his confidence in a man who took an extremely tough-minded view of the weapon's role in diplomacy. From the very first, Byrnes seems to have exaggerated the power of the development. It was Byrnes, not Stimson, who first told the President the key facts about the atomic project. When he did, on the day after Roosevelt's death, he declared "with great solemnity" that the United States was "perfecting an explosive great enough to destroy the whole world."[5] Byrnes believed that a nuclear monopoly could be maintained for seven to ten years.[6] Hence he did not fear an arms race as did Stimson. Nor did he search for diplomatic *quid pro quos* the Russians might offer for admittance to an international control scheme. Instead, Byrnes felt that during the monopoly period the Russians would be forced to agree to an American plan for lasting world peace. Once established, the new regime of peace would obviate possible conflicts in the postmonopoly period.† In mid-April, Byrnes told the President that in his belief the atomic bomb would "put us in a position to dictate our own terms at the end of the war."[7]

Truman's choice of Byrnes to become his Secretary of State and personal representative for atomic matters is only indirect evidence of the President's sympathy with Byrnes's general approach.‡ As we shall see, in the following months, as each crucial decision regarding the atomic bomb and diplomatic strategy arose, when there was a choice between the views offered by Stimson and by Byrnes, the President almost invariably followed the advice of his Secretary of State. However, in April and May, when the atomic bomb was still only an expectation, the President did not often have to choose between the two men. In fact, from his point of view the only important question

---

* There is a great deal known about the President's view for each of the following months of 1945. This will be discussed in due course.

† See Hewlett and Anderson, *The New World*, pp. 354–57. Also below, pp. 244–46.

‡ Byrnes, who had taken his own short-hand notes at Yalta, also briefed Truman on the meaning of the agreements. Byrnes was deeply concerned about Eastern Europe and, in fact, was personally responsible for bringing a reluctant Roosevelt to propose those sections of the Yalta protocol which later committed the United States to a direct interest in the area. It may, therefore, be extremely significant that at the time Truman decided upon a firm showdown approach over Poland, the only person to have advised him on the role of the atomic bomb in diplomacy, problems of Eastern Europe, and the relationship between the two questions, was the tough-minded man he had chosen to become his Secretary of State. (Truman, *Year of Decisions*, pp. 11, 22, 87; Byrnes, *Speaking Frankly*, pp. 32–33.)

Truman had to decide at this time was whether or not to postpone diplomatic issues until the bomb was tested. Decisions as to methods of utilizing the new power could be made after it had been proved.

As we have seen, by the last week of April the President was committed to the immediate showdown strategy on the Polish issue, and he had adopted a correspondingly tough attitude toward American troop positions in the Soviet zone of Germany. Early in May he had cut Lend-Lease shipments to emphasize American determination. However, the President's general line of policy had achieved very little success. In fact, the immediate showdown strategy had reached an impasse; the Russians had not yielded on the problem of Poland and there was no sign that an Allied Control Council would be established in Germany. With Stalin failing to respond to increased pressure, American policy makers had to consider their course of action.

The deadlock over the symbolic Polish issue was a direct personal challenge to those who had urged a firm line. To retreat not only would involve a loss of face, but would defeat the fundamental purpose of a showdown designed to structure Soviet-American relations on a new basis. Hence, only three months after Yalta, there seemed no suitable course but another heads-of-government meeting and an immediate confrontation with the Soviet Premier. At such a meeting all matters in dispute could be discussed and the full range of American bargaining counters could be brought into play. Churchill argued the same point to Eden: "The Polish problem may be easier to settle when set in relation to the now numerous outstanding questions of the utmost gravity which require urgent settlement with the Russians. . . ."[8]

At precisely the same time these views were being pressed, Secretary Stimson began intensive policy discussions in preparation for the coming atomic test. In fact, the Polish issue and the atomic bomb now became inextricably bound together as Stimson discussed the implications of the weapon with the President almost every day of the tense first week of May. Stimson had already urged Truman to avoid a break over the Polish problem.[9] After the showdown with Molotov, he had urgently sought an interview because of the atomic bomb's bearing on the current crisis.[10] He told Truman that, once tested, the weapon would be decisive in all matters of foreign relations.[11] And it is undoubtedly at this time that he first introduced the idea that a basic confrontation should be delayed until the new power had been demonstrated.

Thus, Truman found himself at the focal point of two contradictory streams of policy advice. It was now impossible to continue the existing course without a new show of determination or a radical change; by the end of the first week of May Stalin had shown he would not yield unless something more was done. Indeed, the Soviet Premier had already taken unilateral action by recognizing the Warsaw government, by concluding with them a bilateral treaty, by transferring German territories to Polish administration, and by announcing the arrest of Western-oriented Polish underground leaders. If Truman failed to act, it was obvious that new *faits accomplis* would eliminate all hope of Western influence and democracy in Poland. The President's policy had to go forward; it could not stand still.

Truman sympathized with the arguments of his "firm" advisers, and he shared Churchill's general conception of the Polish dispute.[12] Temperamentally suited to straightforward actions, he had initially adopted the showdown strategy not only with little hesitation but with much enthusiasm. His convictions and the commitment of his prestige argued powerfully for a continuation of the strategy to its logical conclusion and an early meeting with Stalin. Standing firmly in the path of these considerations, however, was new information of what Truman termed "the almost incredible developments that were under way and the awful power that might soon be placed in our hands."[13] Could a delay be endured? The President now had to choose between the strategy of an immediate showdown and the only other alternative offered—the strategy of a delayed showdown.

Truman's crucial decision came in an early-May response to a cable from Churchill. The President stated that he agreed a tripartite meeting was necessary, but that he could not leave Washington for another two months![14] Truman's enthusiasm for an immediate showdown had disappeared. He would not be able to come to a meeting until early July, the time when the first atomic test would be held.* A

---

* The atomic test was later delayed for technical reasons and, accordingly, Truman later delayed the meeting again. (See below, pp. 148–49.) Available records establish that Truman postponed the Potsdam meeting because he wished to wait for the atomic test. Unfortunately, however, they do not disclose the precise date of discussions leading to this decision. See Appendix II for a review of available information bearing on the matter.

few days later he discussed the matter in great secrecy with Secretary Stimson. The full records of this conversation are not available, but there is no question about the main point at issue. Truman told Stimson his strategy concerning the timing of the tripartite meeting. Stimson left the meeting completely satisfied, and in a "skeleton outline" circumspectly summarizing the discussion, he commented that he agreed with the President that there was much to gain and little to lose by delay. Then, writing the same phrases he habitually used to refer to the secret project, Stimson added: "Therefore I believe that good and not harm would be done by the policy toward your coming meeting which you mentioned to me. We shall probably hold more cards in our hands later than now."[15]

Thus, by the second week of May, Truman had accepted the fundamental point of Stimson's strategy—a confrontation with Stalin would be delayed. Truman's decision came as a shock to most of the advisers who felt that a meeting with Stalin had to be held at the earliest possible time. If the meeting was delayed, the showdown might take place after large numbers of troops had been redeployed to the Pacific. Doubts would be cast upon America's determination. Besides, what could be gained by waiting?* Grew, Harriman, and Leahy found Truman's decision all but incomprehensible; until this time the President had not only accepted each logical step in the firm line of policy, but had taken the lead in establishing the American position. His advisers begged him to reconsider his decision. Ambassador Harriman warned the President he "would be confronted with a much more difficult situation two months from now than he would if the meeting could be arranged within the next few weeks."[16]

Similarly, Churchill expressed great disappointment at the late date—"every minute counts." He proposed that the two heads of government take the initiative by inviting Stalin to a meeting, and pleaded that American troop positions be held.[17] At the same time, the Prime Minister urgently instructed Ismay: "All reduction of Bomber Command is to be stopped."[18] And he asked Eisenhower not to destroy

---

* Outside the inner circles of the atomic-development project very few had Stimson's faith in the power of the new weapon. As Stimson has written, that the atomic bomb might "be a lemon" was an "opinion common among those not fully informed." Admiral Leahy was certain the atomic bomb would not work. Although Harriman knew of the project, he conceived of it only as a possibility pending actual test. (Stimson, *On Active Service*, p. 615; Leahy, *I Was There*, pp. 265, 440; Truman, *Year of Decisions*, p. 11; Feis, *Between War and Peace*, p. 97*fn.*)

captured German aircraft—"We may have great need of these some day."[19] On May 12 he cabled Truman again: "I am profoundly concerned about the European situation. . . . Anyone can see that in a very short space of time our armed power on the Continent will have vanished. . . . This issue of a settlement with Russia before our strength has gone seems to me to dwarf all others."[20]

But Truman would yield neither to the pleas of his advisers nor to the logic of Churchill.* Responding to Harriman, Grew, and Bohlen, he was firm: he could not leave Washington because he had to prepare a "budget message."[21] On May 14 he told Churchill that while he agreed that an early tripartite meeting was essential, he could not yet suggest a date for the meeting.[22]

In reality, of course, Truman's mention of a "budget message" was an impossibly weak excuse and was evidently given only to those (like Bohlen) who were not privy to the atomic secret. Everyone agreed upon the overriding importance of the issues in dispute, and there was overwhelming logic in maintaining the diplomatic pressure by an immediate meeting. Once troop withdrawals began Stalin would understand, as Churchill pointed out, "time is on his side if he digs in while we melt away."[23] A "budget message" could not explain Truman's rejection of such considerations and it appears that on May 10 and May 14 Stimson confidentially delineated the more sophisticated strategy to Harriman and Eden.[24]

In delaying a confrontation with Stalin, Truman relaxed pressure on the Russians and thereby cast doubt upon America's determination to force matters to a showdown. However, he did not give up all diplomatic leverage; the main objection to delay was fear that American troops would actually be withdrawn. Churchill consistently stressed the inevitable weakening effect upon the Western negotiating position, Eden raised the matter with Stimson on May 14, and Harriman urged it upon the President on May 15.[25] Truman fully agreed on the importance of the troops[26] and, in fact, spent the first week of May studying the redeployment timing.[27] As we have seen, when he

---

* Eden was informed of the atomic bomb's role in diplomatic strategy on May 14, 1945. It is probable that Churchill received a briefing on the matter from Harriman when they dined together privately on May 22. Thus, it appears that Churchill, like the American advisers, pressed for an early meeting despite his awareness of the strategy. It is probable that he was simply unwilling to gamble such important European diplomatic stakes on the outcome of the atomic test. (Stimson Diary, May 14, 1945; *Conference of Berlin*, I, p. 20.)

decided to delay a meeting with Stalin, he did so on Stimson's specific assurance that "the work of redeploying our forces from Europe to the Pacific will necessarily take so long that there will be more time for your necessary diplomacy with the other large allies than some of our hasty friends realize."[28]

TRUMAN'S SYMBOLIC REVERSAL

TRUMAN'S POSTPONEMENT of a confrontation with Stalin was the crucial decision of the spring of 1945. Once he made up his mind, Truman was forced to consider his course on all major issues in dispute with Russia. He knew it was futile to continue his firm line without an immediate face-to-face meeting. On the other hand, the President did not want to yield the points at issue. In this situation, necessity was the mother of invention; the President had to devise a method which would reduce tensions, forestall a unilateral Soviet solution to the Polish problem, and keep the door open to Western influence.* In short, he needed to gain time. These points, of course, followed the general logic of Stimson's delayed showdown strategy, but Truman's method—an ingenious one—was apparently his own creation; he decided upon symbolic missions to Moscow and London which would dramatize America's desire to break with the firm Churchillian policy and would explore ways to re-establish—at least temporarily—the Rooseveltian policy of cooperation.

Information on the decisions of early May is extremely sketchy. Although Truman made no change in his public stand until late in May, it appears that he began to prepare a conciliatory course even before his cable telling Churchill that a meeting had to be delayed. On May 4 Truman asked Roosevelt's old aide Harry Hopkins, who was at that time terribly ill, if he would be able to serve as his personal representative to Stalin.[29] When Truman finally committed himself to the Hopkins mission two weeks later—at the height of the tense atmosphere emanating from the deadlock over Poland and Central Europe—his decision had powerful overtones. As Halifax pointed out, Hopkins was "the most eminent living repository of Mr. Roose-

---

* Compare also Admiral Leahy's early view that the Polish matter should "be put to the Russians in such a way as not to close the door to subsequent accommodation." (Forrestal, *Diaries*, p. 50.)

velt's policy."[30] The mission, according to Secretary Stettinius, was designed to "assure Stalin that the death of Mr. Roosevelt would not alter the United States' policy of co-operating with the Soviet Union."[31] But this is an understatement, for the mission signaled a fundamental break with the firm line—the decision to send a negotiator to Moscow blatantly reversed the British-American declaration that the Polish question could not even be discussed until satisfactory information had been given about the arrests of the Polish underground leaders.*

Although the Secretary of the Navy was told that Hopkins was going to Moscow only to get "an evaluation" of the Russian attitude on questions "on which at the present time there seems a danger of a sharp and substantial division," it was clear that a special representative would not be going to Moscow unless Truman had decided to make some concessions.[32] For this reason, when the State Department was consulted—at the last minute—it strongly opposed the trip.[33] So did Byrnes, who had personally briefed Truman on the Yalta argeements.[34] Arthur Bliss Lane, the man who would go to Warsaw as American ambassador, was "filled with misgivings" and threatened to resign.[35]

Truman's decision to break with the firm line of policy was underscored by a second aspect of the Hopkins mission: the President did not tell Churchill of his plans until after the mission was publicly disclosed.[36] He also refused to agree to Churchill's urgent request that Hopkins visit London as well as Moscow.[37] Instead, Truman asked Joseph E. Davies to visit Churchill.[38] This move was dramatic and ironic notice of Truman's new line of action, for Davies, a former ambassador to the Soviet Union, was personally opposed to the tough Churchillian approach and was a well-known advocate of Soviet-American cooperation.[39] The purpose of the Davies mission was equally symbolic: the Ambassador was to tell Churchill that Truman wished to meet with Stalin *alone* before the Big Three Conference.†[40]

There could be no better way to emphasize America's desire to dissociate policy from Churchill's influence. The mission was a com-

---

* See above, p. 83.

† Truman later tried to minimize this point, but there is no doubt about his intentions at the time. See Truman, *Year of De-* cisions, p. 260; Churchill, *Triumph and Tragedy*, p. 577; Feis, *Churchill, Roosevelt, Stalin*, p. 650; *Between War and Peace*, pp. 124–25; *Conference of Berlin*, I, pp. 67–85; Woodward, *British Foreign Policy*, p. 521*fn.*

plete reversal of attitude. From the very first days of his administration Truman had indicated a strong desire to work closely with Churchill and to meet with him at the earliest possible time.[41] The President had suggested a Washington meeting at the time of Roosevelt's funeral[42] and, on April 22, had urged Churchill to come to the United States during the San Francisco United Nations Conference.[43] Plans had been set for a visit by Churchill at the end of May.[44] A visit by Truman to Churchill had also been discussed and the President had been more than willing to go to London.[45] But with the Davies mission all these plans were abruptly abandoned. Truman now told his advisers that a meeting with Churchill might "give the Russians the impression we were ganging up on them," he cabled the same point to the Prime Minister, and he asked Davies to convey the message directly.[46] Thus, instead of a symbolic meeting with Churchill, there was to be a somewhat ostentatious change of plans: a private presidential meeting with Stalin!

Although the Davies and Hopkins missions were not announced until the end of May, as we have seen, Truman had begun to consider this course of action even before he announced the decision to delay a confrontation with Stalin. Stimson spoke with Truman about the atomic bomb on April 25, two days after the showdown with Molotov. Almost immediately Truman contacted Davies and Hopkins. He held his first meetings with them on April 30 and May 4 respectively.[47] Thus, he had begun to prepare his alternative policy even as he continued to adhere publicly to the firm line. Evidently sustaining the hope, as late as May 12, that Stalin might yield, Truman took his first irrevocable steps away from the immediate-showdown strategy almost a month after summoning the two men.[48] Only on May 19 and May 22—after it was unquestionably clear that Stalin would not back down—did Truman dispatch short messages to Moscow and London suggesting the trips.*[49]

Truman was extremely secretive about preparations for the two missions. He did not consult the Secretary of State, the Acting Secretary of State, the Polish experts in the Department of State, or Admiral Leahy, until the very eve of the trips, a month after he had

---

* The origin of the Hopkins mission is one of the most closely guarded government secrets. Despite repeated attempts, the State Department has refused my requests for further information. A report on additional details must await the opening of the presently closed archives.

initially contacted Davies and Hopkins.[50] The Secretary of the Navy did not learn of the trips until May 20.[51] As Arthur Bliss Lane, the designated ambassador to Poland, has written, all that was known in the Department of State was that "suddenly and secretly, in the last days of May, Harry Hopkins" left for Moscow.[52] Thus, almost all of the advisers who wanted an "immediate showdown" were unaware of the alternative approach the President was preparing.* Moreover, the President ordered that Hopkins's cables be shown only to a limited few of the senior advisers who customarily had access to such information.[53] This unusual secrecy is further indirect evidence of the relationship of the trips to the secret atomic project; it would have been inconceivable, except in extraordinary circumstances, for Truman to send Hopkins to discuss the most important outstanding diplomatic questions without consulting, or at least notifying, the Secretary of State.†

FORESTALLING A SOVIET SOLUTION IN POLAND

THUS, HAVING DECIDED to postpone a confrontation with Stalin, Truman dispatched his special envoys to repair damage done during the showdown crisis.[54] The general problem was to reduce tensions, but Hopkins had more specific tasks; he sought to forestall a unilateral Soviet solution of the Polish problem, to get consultations for reorganization of the Warsaw government started, and to keep the way open to as much Western influence in the country as possible.

Hopkins's first meeting with Stalin took place on May 26. Immediately he declared his purpose: "He wished to tell the Marshal of the real reason why the President had asked him to come, and that was the question of the fundamental relationship between the United States and the Soviet Union."[55] He said he "wished to state as frankly and forcibly as he knew how to Marshal Stalin the importance that he,

---

* It is true that in mid-April, Harriman suggested Hopkins might be a good man for a mission to Moscow. However, it is not clear from the available evidence whether Harriman made this suggestion in a. general sense or in connection with Stimson's strategy. It appears that the former was the case, for Harriman disagreed with the strategy even after he learned of it on May 10. (Truman, *Year of Decisions*, pp. 257–58; Stimson Diary, May 10.) As is obvious, Sherwood's report that Harriman suggested the trip in mid-May is simply in error. (*Roosevelt and Hopkins*, pp. 885–87.)

† See Appendix II for a critique of other interpretations of the Hopkins mission.

personally, attached to the present trend of events and that he felt that the situation would get rapidly worse unless we could clear up the Polish matter."[56]

It had been clear from the beginning—and had been a chief policy consideration—that the Polish question would have implications for basic Soviet-American relations. On a number of occasions in his discussions with Stalin, Hopkins underscored this point, emphasizing that the problem "had become a symbol."[57] He said that although there were a number of other matters he wished to discuss, the Polish impasse was the primary problem.*[58] He told Stalin the President had decided upon a special mission because he felt great anxiety over the situation and because he wished to find some way out of the difficulty so as to continue Roosevelt's policy of cooperation.[59]

Harriman, who accompanied Hopkins, also stressed the importance of the point. He observed that in selecting Mr. Hopkins the President "had chosen a man who, as the Marshal knew, not only had been very close to President Roosevelt, but personally was one of the leading proponents of the policy of cooperation with the Soviet Union." He noted that the United States had "very intimate relations with Great Britain," but nevertheless felt it "desirable that the United States and the Soviet Union should talk alone on matters of special interest to them and that that was also one of the reasons for Mr. Hopkins's visit."[60]

At first these gestures of conciliation must have seemed a suspicious change from the firm line American policy had taken until this time. Stalin commented only that "the reason for the failure on the Polish question was that the Soviet Union desired to have a friendly Poland, but that Great Britain wanted to revive the system of *cordon sanitaire* on the Soviet borders."[61] When Hopkins replied that the United States did not have such intentions, Stalin said "if that be so we can easily come to terms in regard to Poland."[62]

The next day, May 27, Hopkins asked Stalin for comments on questions worrying him. The Soviet Premier immediately listed a number of issues where "recent moves on the part of the United States Government" had caused "a certain alarm." He said Soviet government circles had the "impression that the American attitude toward

---

* See below, pp. 128, 149–50.

the Soviet Union had perceptibly cooled once it became obvious that Germany was defeated, and that it was as though the Americans were saying that the Russians were no longer needed."[63] Of the issues Stalin raised, the two most important touched directly on the strategy of an immediate showdown. He was bitter over the American position on the Polish question, and he disliked the methods used by American diplomacy.

"At Yalta it had been agreed that the existing government was to be reconstructed and . . . anyone with common sense could see that this meant that the present government was to form the basis of the new," Stalin declared. "No other understanding of the Yalta Agreement was possible. Despite the fact that they were simple people, the Russians should not be regarded as fools . . . nor were they blind and they could quite well see what was going on before their eyes."[64]

Stalin then criticized the manner in which Lend-Lease had been curtailed: "If the refusal to continue Lend-Lease was designed as pressure on the Russians in order to soften them up, then it was a fundamental mistake. He said he must tell Mr. Hopkins frankly that if the Russians were approached frankly on a friendly basis much could be done but that reprisals in any form would bring about the exact opposite effect."[65]

This brought the main problems out into the open and a good deal of the second meeting was devoted to Hopkins's attempt to explain the American position on all of the points at issue.[66] After considerable discussion, Hopkins reverted to the fundamental problem—the United States wished to find a way to end the Polish stalemate and begin consultations for the government reorganization. While he hoped a way to begin could be found, "he had no thought or indeed any right to attempt to settle the Polish problem during his visit."[67] Later, focusing on specifics, Hopkins stressed the substantive requirements of American policy for Poland; there would have to be assurances that early elections would be held and that they would take place in a free atmosphere. There must be freedom of speech, right of assembly, right of movement. All political parties except the fascist should be permitted free use of press, radio, meetings, and other facilities of political expression. All citizens should have the right of public trial, defense by their own counsel, and the right of habeas corpus. "If we could find a meeting of minds in regard to these general principles which would be the basis for future free elections then he was sure we could find ways and means to agree on procedures. . . ."[68]

Stalin replied that "these principles of democracy are well known and would find no objection on the part of the Soviet Government." He assured Hopkins the Polish government would welcome the principles. He had reservations on only two points: in time of war the freedoms could not be enjoyed to the full extent; and they could not be applied fully to fascist parties trying to overthrow the government.[69]

Having reached agreement on the requirements for free elections, the two men took up the points at issue in the deadlock. Early in the talks Stalin had emphasized the need to recognize the Warsaw government as the "basis" of the new government. He had again urged the Yugoslav precedent be followed: one Polish leader should be admitted to the government for each four existing Cabinet members. This would provide four new posts out of a total of eighteen or twenty, and was precisely the same view Stalin had urged throughout the spring.[70]

Until this time the United States had rejected the Soviet position, and the stalemate had begun with Stalin's subsequent refusal to summon the Polish leaders for consultations to reorganize the government.[71] However, at the time he decided to send Hopkins, it appears that Truman also decided to concede the major point at issue; now, on May 30, Hopkins declared the President "anticipated that the members of the present Warsaw regime would constitute a majority of the new Polish Provisional Government."[72] This broke the log jam, for it committed American policy to the existing government as the "basis" of the new government. Hopkins cabled the President: "The conference tonight was encouraging. It looks as though Stalin is prepared to . . . permit a representative group of Poles to come to Moscow to consult with the Commission."[73]

The precise discussion of how great a majority the Warsaw government would have in the reorganized government is not available, but the American commitment went beyond Hopkins's general statement. Stalin proposed a list of candidates for inclusion in the government and after discussion Hopkins cabled that the United States would have to accept the Soviet view if any progress was to be made. Truman approved this recommendation.[74] It appears that after considerable haggling, Stalin and Hopkins split the difference between the original American view that Warsaw should have about half the seats in the new Cabinet and the Russian view that they should have about four fifths: when the Polish political leaders finally reached Moscow for discussions, they met a united stand of the three powers and were told that the Warsaw government would have the main part of the government.[75] Thereafter two thirds of the Cabinet was assumed to be Warsaw's share.*[76]

Once Warsaw's role as the "basis" of the new government had been recognized, Stalin was quite willing to invite the Poles to Moscow for consultations. In fact, as Hopkins noted in another context, Stalin seemed inclined "to make it easy for Churchill to get out of a bad situation."[77] Originally, Truman and Churchill had suggested that eight Poles be invited to Moscow for the reorganization talks. They had suggested four from the Warsaw government, one independent from Poland, and three from the London Polish groups.[78] (This would give Warsaw half of the delegation and accorded with the idea that the Warsaw government might have half the seats in the new Cabinet.) However, after Stalin and Hopkins had completed their discussions, it was agreed that a total of twelve Poles would be invited to Moscow: only four from the Warsaw government, five indepen-

---

* The available documents on the Hopkins-Stalin talks omit the key paragraphs on this point, and my requests for further information have been refused. However, there is enough other evidence to leave little doubt about the commitment: Feis reports Hopkins agreed to a "dominant" role for the Warsaw government. (*Between War and Peace*, p. 107.) That this probably meant the two-thirds figure seems clear since (1) Stettinius and Harriman broached this figure to Eden early in May; (2) on his way to Moscow, Harriman raised the power ratio with Mikolajczyk; (3) the Polish talks began on the two-thirds basis with no American objection; (4) after the completion of the talks Harriman again reported his opinion that two thirds was the best figure possible. (Woodward, *British Foreign Policy*, p. 510; Rozek, *Allied Wartime Diplomacy*, pp. 379–80, 395–98; Mikolajczyk, *The Pattern of Soviet Domination*, p. 143; *Conference of Berlin*, I, p. 727.) The American Ambassador to Poland, Arthur Bliss Lane, reports that Hopkins agreed to a ratio which would deprive the independent Poles of majority control. For this reason he believed the reorganization talks would fail, asked to see the Presi-

dent to protest the "Yugoslav precedent," and considered resignation. (*I Saw Freedom Betrayed*, pp. 70–71, 73, 75.) Supplementary evidence comes from the British side. Churchill vaguely indicated to Mikolajczyk that the British and American ambassadors were instructed to agree *both* to the Yugoslav precedent and a 50–50 ratio! (Rozek, *Allied Wartime Diplomacy*, p. 390.) Churchill actually instructed Clark Kerr, in part, that "the settlement will inevitably be 'based upon' the present Warsaw Government." He warned that "so far as public appearances are concerned" it had to look like the Poles reached this conclusion themselves. (Feis, *Between War and Peace*, p. 204.) The American position is also indirectly indicated by Harriman's complaint that Clark Kerr's instructions did not allow him to make the British commitment sufficiently clear. Also note Molotov's unchallenged remark at the first Commission meeting that there was no need to direct the Poles since the powers were already agreed that the Warsaw government would be the "basis" or "nucleus" of the new government. (Feis, *Between War and Peace*, p. 207.)

dents from Poland, and three from London.[79] Thus, from the point of view of public appearances, Stalin accorded the Warsaw government a far smaller role in the consultations than had originally been proposed by Truman and Churchill.*

With this successful compromise, the chief purpose of Hopkins's mission to Moscow had been accomplished. A unilateral Soviet solution to the Polish problem had been avoided, the negotiations to reorganize the government would soon be resumed, and the door had been kept open to Western influence in the country. With the deadlock broken, there remained only two tasks. First, the actual reorganization of the government would have to take place. Second, the pledge of free elections would have to be fulfilled. Both of these problems would be taken up later, but before leaving Moscow, Hopkins attempted to clear up one final aspect of the Polish dispute. He asked that the sixteen arrested Polish underground leaders be released "so that we could clear the atmosphere."[80] Stalin refused this request, but promised lenient treatment.†[81]

On June 15, a week after Hopkins completed his work, the various Polish leaders arrived in Moscow for consultations to reorganize the provisional government.[82] There were no divisions within the three-power Commission, and by June 22 agreement had been reached granting fourteen of twenty-one seats in the new Cabinet to the Warsaw government.‡[83] Harriman gave his government's approval to the understanding, and on July 5 Truman accorded the government diplomatic recognition.[84] The President also reported: "The new Polish Provisional Government of National Unity has informed me in a written communication that it has recognized in their entirety the

---

* It is interesting to note that Admiral Leahy, who believed the Yalta language sustained Stalin's interpretation, had predicted this result from the very first: "I did not believe that the dominating Soviet influence could be excluded from Poland, but I did think it was possible to give to the reorganized Polish Government an external appearance of independence." (*I Was There*, p. 352.) Much later Mikolajczyk claimed that "three or four" of the five Poles chosen from within Poland were biased in favor of the Warsaw government. However, at the time he was highly pleased with the list. He noted that Stalin had agreed to name three honorable but nonparty people from within Poland. The remaining two had been named not by Stalin but by Truman. (*The Pattern of Soviet Domination*, p. 128; Rozek, *Allied Wartime Diplomacy*, pp. 384–86; *Stalin's Correspondence*, II, p. 216.)

† He made good on this promise. Four of the sixteen were not tried, the remainder received light prison sentences, and all were released in 1946. (Lane, *I Saw Freedom Betrayed*, p. 75fn.)

‡ After the agreement the figure was changed to sixteen of twenty-one. (*Conference of Berlin*, pp. 716–17, 727.) Unaccountably Woodward gives fourteen of twenty. (*British Foreign Policy*, p. 514.)

decisions of the Crimea Conference. . . . The new Government has thereby confirmed its intention to carry out the provisions of the Crimea decision with respect to the holding of elections. . . ."[85]

RE-ESTABLISHING COOPERATION IN CENTRAL EUROPE

WITH THIS DECLARATION, Stimson's original point—that a tension-reducing compromise would have to be found in Poland—was implemented as policy. As will be shown, the President had reason to believe that early free elections would establish a democratic Poland organized along Western lines.* Truman's mid-May objectives were not restricted to the negative goal of preventing a Polish *fait accompli,* however. Once the heads-of-government meeting had been delayed, the President was confronted with the immediate need to establish at least temporary working arrangements to prevent a breakdown of the European economy.

Each day in the spring of 1945 dramatized the importance of a cooperative relationship with the Russians. From all sides came reports of danger. As early as April 13—the first full day of his Presidency—Truman received an urgent State Department memorandum declaring: "Political stability and the maintenance of democratic governments which can withstand the pressures of extremist groups depend on the restoration of a minimum of economic stability."[86] Two days later the same point was made personally by the Secretary of State—the success of the United Nations would "be seriously jeopardized, if not defeated, by internal chaos in the liberated countries."[87]

On April 20 Secretary Stimson told the Cabinet that Assistant Secretary of War McCloy had "found conditions of chaos and in some cases of near anarchy in Germany."[88] On April 26, McCloy reported directly to the President: "There is complete economic, social and political collapse in Central Europe . . ." The Assistant Secretary emphasized the imperative need for food, fuel, and transportation in Germany. He advised: "We are going to have to work out a practical relationship with the Russians. It will require the highest talents, tolerance and wisdom to accomplish our aims."[89]

---

* See below, pp. 135–38.

On April 27, Oliver Lyttelton, British Minister of Production, informed the President that not only the liberated countries but Britain faced a serious shortage of food and other materials.[90] Truman's assistant, Judge Samuel I. Rosenman, returned from an extensive inspection of economic and food problems in Western Europe reporting a "critical" food situation and "desperate" conditions requiring American help.[91] A week after the collapse of German resistance, Secretary Stimson warned of the "strong probability of pestilence and famine in Central Europe."[92]

Although the President had initially differed with Stimson on the Polish question, he had always shared the Secretary's fundamental concern about general European problems; both men believed European stability absolutely essential to world peace. Truman regarded the chaotic economic situation in liberated Europe as "one of the most urgent" crises he had to resolve.[93] He saw a "grave danger of such political and economic chaos as to . . . jeopardize . . . economic stability which is the necessary basis for a firm and just peace."[94]

Like Stimson, the President viewed European problems with an eye to American national interest. Truman also saw that two European wars had inevitably drawn the United States into conflict. From this experience Stimson had generalized that peace was "indivisible." Similarly, Truman held that "a breach of peace anywhere in the world threatens the peace of the entire world."[95] He later wrote that "the one purpose that dominated me in everything I thought and did was to prevent a third world war."[96] Because he wanted "a peace settlement that would be lasting," the President believed it necessary to organize European economic conditions so as to prevent "another Hitler['s] rise to power."[97] To Truman it was the "literal truth" that "if we let Europe go cold and hungry," the United States would lose "the foundations of order on which the hope for world-wide peace must rest."[*][98]

Having defined world peace as dependent upon European stability, and American security as dependent upon world peace, Truman concluded: "The reconstruction of Europe was a matter that directly

---

[*] The British ambassador, sensing this deep concern, cabled Churchill: "I should also expect the Americans in dealing with us to be more responsive to arguments based upon the danger of economic chaos in European countries than to the balder pleas about the risks of extreme Left Governments or of the spread of Communism." (Churchill, *Triumph and Tragedy*, p. 611.)

concerned us, and we could not turn our back on it without jeopardizing our own national interests."[99] In the first week of June 1945—two full years before the Marshall Plan—Truman told his advisers: "We were committed to the rehabilitation of Europe, and there was to be no abandonment this time."[100]

In general, Truman also agreed with Stimson that it was vital to bring together the Eastern and Western halves of the European economic unit. Food was the critical problem, and supplies from Eastern Europe were essential. Even before taking over the Presidency, Truman had given the problem considerable thought. In a May 16 discussion with the Secretary of War, he recalled at great length talks he used to have with his friend Senator Elbert Thomas of Utah—"I would point to a map of Europe and trace its breadbasket, with Hungary a cattle country and Rumania and the Ukraine as the wheat area. Up to the northwest lay Western Germany, Northern France, Belgium and Britain with their coal, iron, and big industries. The problem . . . was to help unify Europe by linking up the breadbasket with the industrial centers."*[101]

Truman also shared Stimson's conviction that a strong German economy was essential to European stability. Unlike Roosevelt, "at no time" did Truman believe Germany should be dismembered.[102] As a Senator, he had opposed the Morgenthau plan, and as President he felt even more strongly about the issue.[103] On May 10, Truman approved a new directive for the administration of Germany—JCS 1067/8—which considerably modified the tough economic terms Roosevelt's earlier directive had imposed.[104] Moreover, although he endorsed almost all of Roosevelt's other appointments, Truman replaced Roosevelt's reparations representative with his own man.[105] Roosevelt had named a Jew, Dr. Isador Lubin, who could be expected to show little sympathy to the Germans. Truman chose Edwin W. Pauley precisely because he did not wish to weaken the German economy and he knew Pauley would be "tough" in the reparations talks with Molotov.[106] Indeed, Truman was completely in accord with Stimson's basic recommendations on Germany. The Secretary of War

---

* Truman seems to have taken an especially deep interest in this problem. Other visitors also found he would pull out a map of Europe to explain his profound conviction that a way had to be found to link the trade of Eastern and Western Europe. (See Smith, *My Three Years in Moscow*, p. 27.)

confided to his diary: "The President . . . has been very receptive to all my efforts in these directions."[107]

Thus, in all essential respects Truman understood the problems of European stability in much the same way as his Secretary of War. It was necessary both to strengthen the European economy and to work out a way to link the food-producing areas with the industrial zones. From such premises, it was immediately evident that the crucial problem was administration in the heart of Central Europe, primarily in Germany. But Red Army occupation of the eastern part of that country presented the same problem, on a smaller scale, which persisted in the larger unit of the Continent: there could be no economic stability without Soviet cooperation. "There was danger of complete economic and social collapse," Truman reasoned. "Therefore, it was imperative that there be established at the earliest possible moment a council to make policy for Germany as a whole."[108]

It is important to recognize that, despite appearances, Truman's April 23 showdown with Molotov was in complete accord with the fundamental objective of achieving Soviet cooperation. Indeed, it was a means to that end. Truman had initially judged that a symbolic showdown and strong language would force the Russians to cooperate not only in Eastern Europe but in their general relations with the United States. He had not envisioned a tense stalemate, but a blunt clarification of attitudes which would clear the way for cooperation on a self-consciously realistic basis. In initially rejecting Stimson's conciliatory advice, he had differed primarily on tactics, not on objectives. Similarly, in maintaining American troops in the Soviet zone of Germany he had expected not Soviet intransigence, but a realistic trading of advantage which would secure American political objectives in Austria.

But by mid-May, in Germany, as in Poland, there was no sign that Stalin would yield to the firm approach. As we have seen, one group of advisers felt that an immediate meeting with Stalin was the only possible course of action; Churchill continued to urge that American armies hold their positions in the Soviet zone. However, the implications of Truman's decision to postpone a meeting with Stalin were as clear for his German policy as for his Polish policy. The moment the President decided to delay a Big Three meeting until the atomic bomb was tested, he was forced to devise a new course of action. The Secretaries of State, War, and the Navy all advised that a declaration of principles for Allied administration of Germany be issued and that the Allied Control Council be promptly activated.[109] As in the Polish case, Truman had to find a formula which would elicit Soviet cooperation and yield as little advantage as possible.

Establishing an administrative council was the heart of the matter, and although the Polish impasse was the primary cause of the Hopkins mission, Truman set his representative an important secondary task: he was to try to secure Stalin's agreement to the German Control Council.[110] Following the President's instructions, Hopkins raised the issue early in his talks with the Soviet Premier. He noted that Eisenhower had already been named American representative for the Council and asked that Marshal Zhukov be designated Soviet representative.[111]

Initially, Stalin replied that he had not heard of Eisenhower's appointment, but would designate Zhukov in the near future.[112] A day passed, and Hopkins pressed the point again: "It would be most desirable if Marshal Stalin could announce publicly as soon as possible the appointment of Marshal Zhukov . . . so that that body could start its work as soon as possible."[113] At the same time Hopkins raised the matter in Moscow, instructions were sent to the American representative at the European Advisory Commission in London; he was to propose that an Allied declaration of principles for the administration of Germany be signed and issued by June 1.[114]

Hopkins reported that Stalin seemed quite willing to designate Zhukov and that he agreed "on the necessity of having a unified policy towards Germany . . . ; otherwise he said the Germans would attempt to play one off against the other."[115] This confirmed reports from London and Frankfurt of a strong Soviet desire for joint administration of the country.[116] From the Soviet point of view, cooperative administration would provide badly needed industrial materials from the western zones in exchange for food from the eastern zones.[117] It also appeared that cooperative control of Germany was a key point in Soviet plans for postwar security. Stalin told Hopkins: "Not only this war but the previous war had shown that without United States intervention Germany could not have been defeated and that all the events and developments of the last thirty years had confirmed this."[118]

Despite Soviet interest in cooperative administration, it was doubtful that the Control Council could be established so long as Truman maintained American troops in the Soviet zone of occupation. Eisenhower sensed this clearly, and at the same time Hopkins was discussing the appointment of Zhukov, the American Commander asked the Combined Chiefs of Staff for instructions on the troop positions. He said he anticipated one question the Russians would raise when the declaration of principles was signed would be the date on which American forces would withdraw from the Russian zone. "It is possible that Russians may establish such withdrawal as a corollary to the establishment of Control Council on a functioning basis," he noted. "Any cause for delay in . . . withdrawal would be attributed to us and might well develop strong public reaction."[119]

A week before Hopkins left for Moscow Truman had told Churchill he preferred to wait to see what happened before deciding either to withdraw the troops or hold them in place until a Big Three meeting.[120] For the next three weeks—throughout the period of the Hopkins mission—Truman maintained this position. On the President's instructions, the Joint Chiefs of Staff refused Eisenhower permission to withdraw the troops as a condition of the establishment of the Control Council.[121]

But this decision was very soon challenged. Hopkins secured Stalin's agreement to designate Zhukov as Eisenhower's counterpart.[122] When the two military leaders met in Berlin on June 5 to sign the Four Power Declaration for Germany, American troops were still deep in the Soviet zone of occupation. It was now a month after the German surrender, and Zhukov immediately made it clear that the agreement to establish the Control Council would not be implemented until American troops were withdrawn to the agreed occupation zones.[123]

Initially, Truman had linked the troop withdrawals with the unresolved Austrian zonal problems. By the first week of June, however, these issues (which, in any case, had never been of great importance) were all but resolved. The only question in dispute concerned the disposition of airports in Vienna.[124] Thus, Truman had to decide whether to maintain the American troop positions despite the all but completed accord in Austria.

Churchill cabled that he viewed "with profound misgivings the retreat of the American army to our line of occupation in the Central Sector, thus bringing Soviet power into the heart of Western Europe."[125] He said he hoped "that this retreat, if it has to be made, would be accompanied by the settlement of many great things."[126] Privately he told the Foreign Office: "I am still hoping that the retreat of the American centre to the occupation line can be staved off till 'the Three' meet . . ."[127]

However, from Germany three separate and dissenting appreciations were sent to Washington. Eisenhower again advised that the troops should be withdrawn.[128] Robert Murphy, Eisenhower's political adviser, cabled a similar view, adding that he saw no grounds for discouragement about the prospects of Soviet cooperation—"On the contrary I find that definite progress has been made. I am convinced that the Russians believe the Control Council necessary. . . ."[129] Finally, Harry Hopkins, returning from Moscow via Germany, cabled that the "present indeterminate status of the date for withdrawal of Allied Troops from area assigned to the Russians is certain to be misunderstood by Russians as well as at home."[130]

Truman's decision came in the second week of June. Hopkins's successful resolution of the Polish issue undoubtedly helped convince the President he could deal with Stalin. With the Potsdam Conference more than a month away, he decided that the price of Soviet cooperation in Germany was withdrawal of American troops.[131] On June 12, he cabled Churchill: "In consideration of the tripartite agreement . . . I am unable to delay the withdrawal of American troops from the Soviet zone in order to use pressure in the settlement of other problems . . . I am advised that it would be highly disadvantageous to our relations with the Soviet to postpone action in this matter. . . ."[132] After incorporating a modification suggested by Churchill, on June 14 Truman proposed to Stalin that orders be given for simultaneous troop withdrawals in Germany and Austria.[133]

This settled the matter in all essential respects. The firm line taken at the end of April was repealed. Although there was a slight delay connected with the final determination of zones in Vienna and Berlin, the American troop withdrawal took place in the first days of July.[134] At about the same time, final agreement on the Austrian zonal problem was reached.[135] Soviet troops were withdrawn from the western zones in Austria on July 22,[136] and by the end of the month the

Allied Control Council was functioning in Germany.[187] As in Poland, Truman's new diplomacy achieved its basic aims. The crisis in Allied relations had been resolved and the way was clear for cooperative administration in the heart of Germany. A second major point of Stimson's recommendation had been implemented.

THE HOPE OF THE STRATEGY OF DELAY

ON JUNE 6, 1945, Acting Secretary of State Grew sent a short but emphatic cable to Hopkins, who was preparing to leave Moscow: "The President, the Secretary and I send you heartiest congratulations and appreciation."[138] At about the same time, Assistant Secretary of War McCloy commented to the Secretary of the Navy that "Harry's visit had largely dispelled the growing suspicion of Stalin and Molotov."[139] To a Cabinet meeting, Acting Secretary Grew proudly reported: "I don't believe as a rule in crowing before the sun is really up, but I may say that the international scene is a great deal brighter. . . . "[140] And Admiral Leahy noted in his diary that both he and the President "felt that Hopkins had been very successful in allaying some of the suspicions that the Russians had about our motives."[141]

To the many who have interpreted the Hopkins mission as a victory for Stalin's policy in Poland and Germany, it is very difficult to explain why official Washington considered the mission a great success.* After all, the President had yielded basic points of a policy he had adamantly pressed only a few weeks earlier. The key to understanding, of course, is not difficult to find when one looks beyond the views of the Polish exiles and Churchill—who regarded any compromise as a defeat—to the views of the President *after* he had agreed to Secretary Stimson's strategy. Once the President had decided to wait for the atomic bomb, his main objectives were to avoid a Soviet *fait accompli* in Poland, and to establish a practical cooperative relationship in Germany. Both objectives required, as Leahy neatly summed it up, that the suspicions of Stalin be allayed.

In fact, Hopkins's mission perfectly implemented the strategy of a delayed showdown offered by Secretary Stimson. As we have seen, the

---

* See, for example, Churchill's comment that the Russians "had gained their object by delay." (*Triumph and Tragedy*, p. 583.)

Secretary had defined a number of actions necessary to establish proper relationships in Europe. First, he recommended that a confrontation on major issues be postponed until the atomic test. Second, he counseled that much of the Russian position on Poland would have to be accepted—at least temporarily. Third, he argued that United States policy had to be dissociated from the principles and person of Churchill. Finally, he urged that some way be devised to "persuade Russia to play ball" in Central Europe.

In every respect, Truman's use of the Hopkins mission fulfilled these objectives. In fact, Hopkins did even better than hoped, for on the spur of the moment he was able to resolve a major conflict over voting procedure for the Security Council of the United Nations.[142] Joseph Davies's mission to Churchill simultaneously underscored America's intention to break symbolically with Churchill. In this, its major objective was accomplished, and despite the fact that Churchill refused to agree to a preliminary private meeting of Truman and Stalin, the Prime Minister could do little about the President's refusal to meet privately with him in Britain.[143] As Truman had promised, there was to be no "ganging up."

In the spirit of this broad strategy, Truman also reversed himself on other points. His original blunt cutoff of Lend-Lease was now modified in two respects: on the day Hopkins left for Moscow, Truman told a press conference all materials provided for in existing Lend-Lease agreements would be delivered. He explained that the original cutoff order was not so much a cancellation of shipments as a gradual readjustment to conditions following the collapse of Germany.[144] Four days later, in Moscow, Ambassador Harriman amiably offered to review the whole Lend-Lease situation with Molotov.[145] In succeeding discussions, American aid was once more provided on the basis of usefulness to the prosecution of the war, rather than as a diplomatic weapon of pressure in the Polish conflict.[146]

Similarly, the firm line yielded on a second economic point. At Yalta it had been agreed that a commission made up of the three powers would meet to determine German reparations. However, after the Yalta Conference, the United States and Britain had urged that France be added to the commission. The Soviet Union refused to go beyond the Yalta agreement, and the Western powers, quite aware of the intense Soviet desire for industrial reparations, refused to allow the commission to meet unless the French were accepted.[147] The Western effort followed the same logic of economic pressure which figured in the initial Polish showdown. As late as the first week of May the United States had refused Soviet requests to begin the commission talks,[148] but when Hopkins arrived in Moscow he informed Stalin that the American reparations representative would come to Moscow—without the French.[149]

A similar change occurred in regard to the captured German fleet. On May 23 Stalin cabled Truman noting that the German Navy had refused to surrender to the Soviet Union.[150] In this message, and three days later in a talk with Hopkins, Stalin recalled the agreement that the Allies would require German forces to surrender to the forces they had fought. He pointed out that when German troops who fought Russia tried to surrender to the West, Eisenhower had promptly turned them over to the Soviet commander. He asked that, as in Italy, a fair share (one third) of the German fleet be turned over to the Soviet Union.[151] Again Truman's reply was conciliatory. Hopkins was allowed to say that the United States had no objections to such sharing.[152] Eisenhower proposed that a naval commission be established to arrange for the dispositions.[153] And the President cabled he was sure a solution could be reached which would be "fully acceptable to all of us."[154]

Despite Truman's relaxation of pressure in connection with these three issues, in reality, the President yielded very little. The Lend-Lease talks were restricted to deliveries for a six-month period, and subsequently less than half of the new Soviet requests were granted.[155] The Moscow Reparations Commission met for the first time on June 21 (four months after it had been authorized at Yalta), failed to resolve basic reparations issues, and merely delayed the problem until the Big Three met in mid-July.[156] Similarly, although Truman's response on the German fleet question was sympathetic, there was no action on the Soviet request after May 30 and the matter was also held over for the Big Three.[157]

It is not surprising that Truman chose to maintain control over final disposition of these economically important matters. From the beginning, the President had recognized the huge requirements of the war-ravaged Soviet economy and had sought to capitalize on this weakness by using American economic resources to achieve diplomatic objectives. There is no evidence that Truman ever abandoned this basic approach.* Indeed, as he prepared for his coming meeting with Stalin, he asked Congress for authority to increase the Export-Import Bank's lending capacity to $3,500,000,000. This would make an additional $2,800,000,000 available for loans during the coming year.[158] Of this amount, approximately one billion dollars was to be earmarked for a Soviet loan.[159] Accordingly, the first item on the suggested agenda for the talks with Stalin was: "Credits to the U.S.-S.R."[160]

Thus, Truman looked to the future expecting American economic power would still be of great value in dealing with Russia. His satisfaction with Hopkins's mission reflected this confidence, for he felt the door had been kept open to the future exercise of that power. He was not thinking only of the Soviet Union, however. The President believed American economic assistance would be effective in persuading the newly organized Polish provisional government to hold early elections. Such elections, he believed, would produce a democratic Poland governed along Western lines and amenable to American influence.

It will be recalled that Truman had directed Hopkins to obtain guarantees for a number of specific democratic principles for the new Poland. On recognizing the new provisional government, the President had underscored its pledge of support for all aspects of the Yalta agreement, including the provisions for early free elections. To the President, the pledge for free elections was not merely a slogan of idealistic intent; shortly after Hopkins finished his talks with Stalin, Harriman began to discuss the conditions of American economic aid to the ravaged country. He made it clear that free elections, and nondiscriminatory treatment of American investments and trade, would insure a friendly American attitude.[161]

Within policy-making circles there was no attempt to disguise this strategy. As final negotiations on the composition of the Polish government neared completion, Harriman cabled that it was "of inestimable importance from a political standpoint to begin negotiations

---

* As late as a December 1946 Cabinet discussion, "the President mentioned the reports in the morning's newspapers of the deficiencies in the grain crop in Russia. . . . He said he believed . . . that it must have become clear to them by now that they, as well as others, would have to look to the United States as the sole source of relief on the question of food." (Forrestal, *Diaries*, p. 234.)

at once with a view of granting promptly a small credit," and that this "will have a far-reaching and permanent effect on the influence of the U.S. in the political scene in Poland and particularly on our influence in connection with the carrying out of the final step in the Crimea decision, namely, the holding of truly free elections."[162] Harriman also reported the new government had agreed to allow American representatives to travel freely in the country and to admit American news correspondents.[163] He had great hopes that the elections, when held, would be fully observed.

Harriman's recommendation for an immediate small loan was well received in Washington. Although legal restrictions prohibited a credit, the American ambassador was authorized to promise economic assistance from a number of other available sources.[164] As the State Department looked to the future, it delineated its plans in explicit terms: "In order to implement our policy of establishing a truly independent democratic Polish state, we should be prepared . . . to assist through credits or otherwise in the reconstruction of Polish agriculture and industry."[165] Furthermore, in assisting "through credits and otherwise . . . we should insist on the acceptance by Poland of a policy of equal opportunity for us in trade, investments, and access to sources of information."[166]

In reality, a strategy based on the vigorous use of American economic aid to obtain political objectives in Eastern Europe was nothing more than a continuation of the broad line of policy laid down in the April showdown with Molotov. However, by late May, Truman and his advisers had come to believe that economic aid was only one weapon—and perhaps the least effective—in the American diplomatic arsenal. The belief that the atomic bomb would add great power to American diplomacy now dominated the thinking of the most important American policy makers. On May 28—the day Hopkins held his third talk with Stalin—designated Secretary of State Byrnes told one of the nuclear scientists that America, by possessing and demonstrating the atomic bomb, would make Russia more manageable in Eastern Europe.[167] On June 4, Byrnes expressed great confidence in the atomic bomb to Admiral Leahy.[168] On June 6—the last day of the Hopkins-Stalin talks—Secretary Stimson confided to his diary his belief that a satisfactory solution for the Polish problem would be arranged in exchange for allowing the Russians to participate in a system of international control of atomic energy.[169] On the same day—before Stimson could express these thoughts—President Truman told the Secretary of War that the bomb would be the crucial factor in achieving a favorable resolution of not only the Polish issue, but of problems in Rumania, Yugoslavia, and Manchuria.[170] Thus, while Hopkins negotiated an agreement which kept the door open to future American influence, Byrnes, Stimson, and Truman all waited expectantly for the atomic bomb. They were confident that once it was available it would strengthen the American hand; it would provide sanctions for the pledge of free elections and would be useful in securing other objectives in Poland and elsewhere in Eastern Europe.

For all these reasons Truman looked to the future with immense confidence. He did not regard Hopkins's negotiation as a defeat, but as a subtle success which kept the way clear for further diplomacy; he viewed the Polish agreement as "only a beginning."[171] The new American ambassador to Poland, Arthur Bliss Lane, not knowing of the atomic bomb, could not understand why Truman had postponed a meeting and had apparently yielded so much to Stalin. At the time Hopkins was completing his talks with Stalin, Lane complained to the President that "our attitude toward Soviet Russia in connection with the Polish issue should be integrated with the many other issues in Central Europe, particularly the Soviet blackouts in the Balkan states and the states of Central Europe." Truman told Lane there was nothing to fear. He said "that he had precisely the same opinion and that this would be the fundamental subject which he intended to discuss at the Big Three meeting." However, he would not force the issue to a showdown now. The President explained that while Hopkins was negotiating "it would be desirable not to exert too much pressure." Nonetheless, as Acting Secretary of State Grew minuted, the President left *"no doubt as to his intention to insist on the eventual removal of the Soviet blackout in the countries mentioned. . . ."*[172]

In sum, the President and his advisers regarded Hopkins's diplomacy as a delaying action, not a defeat. It matters little that the strategy eventually failed. What is important is that in the thinking of American policy makers final determination of the Polish issue and of other problems in Eastern and Central Europe depended upon the results of the atomic test. An early showdown had failed, but a later one—if necessary—would probably succeed. In this spirit, Ambassador Harriman cabled his feeling that "the stage is set as well as can be done at the present time."[173] And, confidently writing to a friend, Acting Secretary of State Grew declared: "If we ever compromise with principle, such compromise is only a temporary measure in order the better to attain our main objectives in the end."[174]

CHAPTER IV

The Far East and Two Faces of the Strategy of Delay

It may be necessary to have it out with Russia on her relations to Manchuria and Port Arthur and various other parts of North China, and also the relations of China to us. Over any such tangled weave of problems [the atomic-bomb] secret would be dominant . . .

—SECRETARY OF WAR
HENRY L. STIMSON
May 15, 1945

ALTHOUGH THE POLISH PROBLEM and the rumblings of dispute in Central Europe dominated official Soviet-American relations during the spring of 1945, within policy-making circles the urge to alter America's approach to Russia had not been limited to European matters. At the same time the President's advisers recommended a showdown on Poland, they also advocated that Truman reconsider American policy toward the Far East.

At Yalta, when Soviet help had been thought essential to the invasion of Japan, Roosevelt had pledged American support for certain Soviet Asian objectives, primarily in Manchuria and North China. In exchange he had received Stalin's promise to enter the war two to three months after Germany's collapse and his pledge to support Chiang Kai-shek's Nationalist Government in China. The Red Army would enter the war on condition that "the former rights of Russia violated by the treacherous attack of Japan in 1904" were restored. Specifically, the southern half of Sakhalin Island would be returned to the Soviet Union; the Manchurian port of Dairen would be internationalized ("the pre-eminent interests of the Soviet Union in this port being safeguarded"); Port Arthur would be leased to the Soviet Union as a naval base; and the Chinese Eastern and the South Manchurian railroads, "which provide an outlet to Dairen," would be operated by a Soviet-Chinese company ("it being understood that the pre-eminent interests of the Soviet Union shall be safeguarded . . ."). Additionally, Roosevelt promised American support to preserve the *status quo* in Outer Mongolia. Finally, the Kurile Islands would be handed over to the Soviet Union.[1]

The Manchurian railroads and ports were of considerable importance to the Russians because they provided a warm-water outlet for the Trans-Siberian Railroad.[2] Since it was understood that the agreement concerning these matters (and Outer Mongolia) would require the concurrence of Chiang Kai-shek, Roosevelt agreed to "take measures" on "advice from Marshal Stalin" to obtain Chiang's approval so that the claims of the Soviet Union would be "unquestionably fulfilled" after the defeat of Japan.[3]

Roosevelt's endorsement of this accord was given with little hesitation. He regarded the concessions as extremely reasonable—they constituted little more than the restoration of Russia's pre-1905 rights in the area.[4] Ambassador Harriman felt that the Yalta agreement usefully defined and limited Soviet claims: "It would have been a simple matter for the Soviets to give expression to popular demand by establishing People's Republics of Manchuria and Inner Mongolia."[5] Since the area had not been controlled by Chiang Kai-shek for many years Admiral Leahy believed that in exchange for Soviet support in the war, Stalin had received only "misnamed" concessions.[6]

Indeed, the agreement seemed quite advantageous to the United States. Besides the then vital promise of an early Soviet declaration of war, Stalin's support for Chiang Kai-shek was regarded as extremely important. China was in many ways a mirror image of Poland; in both countries if the great powers chose to support their own dissident political groups, the result was likely to be civil strife and international tension. Stalin needed Western support for the Soviet-oriented Warsaw government and Roosevelt needed Stalin's support for Chiang's Nationalist regime. After Yalta, American policy makers felt there was a good chance that—as in 1927—the Soviet Union would support Chiang Kai-shek in his struggle against the Communists.[7] The American ambassador to China, convinced that the Soviet Union controlled the Chinese Communists,[8] was delighted when they agreed to take a subordinate role in Chiang's official delegation to the San Francisco United Nations Conference.[9] Stalin made no effort to raise the status of the Communists, although at precisely the same time he was trying (unsuccessfully) to get Western recognition of the Warsaw government's right to represent Poland at San Francisco.[10]

Stalin also showed every sign of following through on the pledge to enter the Japanese war. On April 5 the Soviet Union publicly declared its intention to denounce the Soviet-Japanese nonaggression pact.[11] Even the most casual observers recognized, as the *New York Herald Tribune* commented, "Russia is preparing to enter the war in the Far East."[12] Ten days later Stalin reaffirmed the Soviet commitment to become a belligerent in a conversation with General Patrick J. Hurley, the American Special Representative and Ambassador to China. The Soviet Premier underscored both his intention to support Chiang and his plan to enter the war two to three months after the defeat of Germany. (This was the length of time it would take to transport sufficient supplies and troops from Europe across the Trans-Siberian Railroad.)[13] Although it was necessary to maintain secrecy to prevent Japanese intelligence from learning of the Soviet plan, Stalin and Hurley delineated a specific understanding to implement the accord. It was agreed that the President would arrange to have the Chinese Foreign Minister, T. V. Soong, come to Moscow by June 15. At that time treaties embodying Stalin's pledge of support for Chiang, and Chiang's approval of the Yalta arrangements for Outer Mongolia and Manchuria would be negotiated. Then Stalin would declare war.[14]

In the first days of his Presidency, Truman did nothing to alter Roosevelt's commitments. On April 19, a week after taking office, he told T. V. Soong that he should go to Moscow "as soon as he could, so that relations between China and Russia could be established on a firmer basis."[15] Three days later the President reaffirmed Roosevelt's Far Eastern pledges in a discussion with Molotov. He "intended to carry out all the agreements made by President Roosevelt."[16]

Even as Truman was making these pledges, however, American specialists on Soviet affairs began to argue the need for a "reconsideration" of Roosevelt's agreement. On April 19, Harriman told the State

Department he believed Hurley's judgment of Stalin was "too optimistic." Harriman believed Stalin would eventually support the Communists against Chiang.[17] Similarly, General Deane persuaded the Joint Chiefs of Staff that Russian aid for an invasion of Japan was no longer needed and that it would involve political problems.* By April 24 the Joint Staff Planners had gone so far as to advise: "If Russia enters the war her forces will probably be the first into Manchuria. This will raise the question of introducing at least token U.S. forces into Asia."[18] Finally, George F. Kennan, the chargé d'affaires in Moscow, and a good friend of Harriman and Deane, cabled a powerful argument in support of a new firm approach. His position was delineated in a State Department summary presented to the President on April 24:

> Kennan . . . calls attention to the fact that words have a different meaning to the Russians. Stalin is prepared to accept the principle of unification of Chinese armed forces and the principle of a united China, since he knows that these conditions are feasible only on terms acceptable to the Chinese Communists. Stalin is also prepared to accept the idea of a free and democratic China, since a free China means to him a China in which there is a minimum of foreign influence other than Russian. Kennan is convinced that Soviet policy will remain a policy aimed at the achievement of maximum power with minimum responsibility and will involve the exertion of pressure in various areas. He recommends that we study with clinical objectivity the real character and implications of Russian Far Eastern aims. . . .

The chargé's final argument dovetailed with the advice of Harriman and Deane: "It would be tragic if our anxiety for Russian support in the Far East were to lead us into an undue reliance on Russian aid."[19]

These views reached the President at precisely the same time he chose to force a showdown on the Polish issue. He was warned of the politically disadvantageous consequences of Soviet military operations on the China mainland at the same time that he was told that Soviet entry into the war was no longer essential for an invasion. Immediately the President was faced with a twofold question: Should the United States encourage Russia to declare war, or would it be better to procrasti-

---

* See above, p. 79.

nate, refusing to fulfill the Yalta understanding? Such a course might discourage Soviet entry indefinitely—or at least until Stalin had given specific assurances that he would respect Nationalist sovereignty in Manchuria and North China.

A May 10 cable from General Hurley precipitated a major discussion of the issue. Hurley reported that he had discussed the general Far Eastern situation with Chiang Kai-shek. He believed Chiang knew most of the terms of the Yalta accord and was certain that the Chinese leader would agree in substance to all of its provisions. There might only be problems about the use of words such as "pre-eminent" and "lease," which had especially unfavorable connotations in China. Hurley said that Chiang had already received reports of large-scale Soviet troop movements across the Trans-Siberian Railroad. With speculation rife in Chungking, he advised that it was time for Truman to allow him to reveal the Yalta agreement.[20]

Hurley's cable required a decision as to whether the Soviet Union should be encouraged to enter the war. Harriman, about to return to Moscow, argued that the United States should not fulfill the Yalta agreement—or at least not until new Russian pledges had been obtained. On May 11 he told a meeting in the Secretary of the Navy's office that "it was time to come to a conclusion about the necessity for the early entrance of Russia into the Japanese war." Deeply pessimistic in his view of Soviet intentions, he told Forrestal that once the Red Army entered the war "Russian influence would move in quickly and toward ultimate domination . . . There could be no illusion about anything such as a 'free China' once the Russians got in . . . The two or three hundred millions in that country would march when the Kremlin ordered."[21] Later the same day, Harriman told Admiral Leahy that Russia would enter the war "and will in the end exercise control over whatever government may be established in Manchuria and Outer Mongolia."[22]

The next day Harriman argued his case at the State Department. Before going back to Moscow he wished to have a precise definition of the American view of Soviet entry into the war. He posed these questions: "(1) The Yalta Agreement: Should it be re-examined? . . . (2) How urgent is the necessity for quick Russian participation in the war? . . ." Harriman also wanted to know whether Soviet occupation of Japan would be accepted, what arrangements would be made for a trusteeship in Korea, and how the United States wished to handle a number of other minor Far Eastern questions.[23]

The meeting agreed that Harriman's points should be formulated precisely "for discussion with the President."[24] Working in great haste to prepare for Harriman's return to Moscow, on the same day Acting Secretary of State Grew produced a formal exposition of the problem. In parallel letters to the Secretaries of War and the Navy, Grew stated that before fulfilling the Yalta agreement, the State Department thought it "desirable" to obtain additional commitments and clarifications from Stalin; the Soviet government should agree not only to support Chiang Kai-shek, but also to influence the Chinese Communists to yield to the Nationalist government; the Soviet government should reaffirm support for Chinese sovereignty in Manchuria and for a four-power trusteeship for Korea; the Soviet government should also agree to grant emergency landing rights for commercial planes in the Kurile Islands.

Grew declared that the State Department wished to withhold fulfillment of the existing Yalta accord as a bargaining tactic to obtain the new commitments. Aware that this would be breaking Roosevelt's agreement, Grew wanted to know whether there were military objections to such an approach: "Is the entry of the Soviet Union . . . of such vital interest to the United States as to preclude any attempt . . . to obtain Soviet agreement to certain desirable political objectives? . . . Should the Yalta decision in regard to Soviet political desires in the Far East be reconsidered, or carried into effect in whole, or in part?" Finally, should a Soviet demand for participation in the Japanese occupation be granted?*[25]

Truman did not wait for a judgment as to the military value of Soviet entry into the war. Sympathetic to Harriman and others who predicted the consequences of Soviet military operations on the China mainland, Truman did not wish to encourage Soviet entry if he could help it.†[26] On May 12 he cabled Hurley that it was not "appropriate at the present time" to fulfill the agreement.[27] On May 14, in a talk with

---

* On May 19, 1945, Acting Secretary Grew passed a sleepless night and, mulling over the international situation, confided his private fears to paper: "Once Russia is in the war against Japan, then Mongolia, Manchuria, and Korea will gradually slip into Russia's orbit, to be followed in due course by China and eventually Japan. . . ." (Grew, *Turbulent Era*, II, pp. 1445–46.)

† Later his view changed slightly. See below, p. 168.

T. V. Soong, the President held back information on the Yalta accord and refused to respond to questions regarding the role of the Soviet Union in the Far East. Soong, anxious for Stalin's help against the Communists, told the President he thought it very important that he should "proceed to Moscow to discuss this situation with the Soviet authorities . . ." But now Truman's earlier advice that Soong should leave "as soon as he could" had been revised. At the suggestion of Grew, it was decided to postpone consideration of his trip. As the Acting Secretary summarized the discussion, "this matter was left open."[28]

Thus, Harriman had achieved his primary objective: he had blocked immediate fulfillment of the Yalta agreement. While senior officials debated a further course, the United States would not give up the bargaining counters it held by virtue of its influential position with the Chinese government. Moreover, the President's decision, like his decision in favor of a showdown over Poland, certainly showed that he was not anxious to encourage Soviet participation in the war. There was a good chance that he might be persuaded to continue to refuse instructions to complete America's half of the Yalta bargain.

Inevitably, Truman's May 14 decision to postpone fulfillment of the Far Eastern agreement also opened the way for the Secretary of War's strategy of delay. When Stimson received the State Department inquiry, his response was instantaneous: "The questions cut very deep. . . . In my opinion [they] are powerfully connected with our success with [the atomic bomb]."[29] His reasoning followed his earlier advice on the Polish question: It would be wise to delay all negotiations until the atomic bomb added its power to the American bargaining position. Now it was time, as he told McCloy on May 14, "to keep our mouths shut."[30] The next day, discussing the "questions which Grew had propounded to us in relation to the Yalta Conference and our relations with Russia," Stimson tried desperately to convince Harriman, McCloy, Forrestal, and Grew of the need for delay. He summarized his argument in a long diary entry:

> I tried to point out the difficulties which existed and I thought it was premature to ask those questions; at least we were not yet in a position to answer them. The trouble is that the President has now promised apparently to meet Stalin and Churchill on the first of July and at that

time these questions will become burning and it may be necessary to have it out with Russia on her relations to Manchuria and Port Arthur and various other parts of North China, and also the relations of China to us. Over any such tangled weave of problems [the atomic-bomb] secret would be dominant and yet we will not know until after that time probably, until after that meeting, whether this is a weapon in our hands or not. We think it will be, shortly afterwards, but it seems a terrible thing to gamble with such big stakes in diplomacy without having your master card in your hand. The best we could do today was to persuade Harriman not to go back until we had had time to think over these things a little bit harder.[31]

POSTPONING A RECONSIDERATION OF FAR EASTERN ISSUES

ONCE MORE the same question had been posed: Should the United States raise delicate political problems for negotiation now, or later? Although the still-untested weapon might add great power to the American bargaining position, the State Department felt the only absolutely certain bargaining counters derived from American influence with Chiang Kai-shek. Negotiations should take place before Russia entered the war. The War Department, on the other hand, argued the wisdom of waiting until the "master card" was available before attempting to "have it out with Russia."

Contrary to a commonly held opinion,* the War Department did not object to raising the political questions because it feared this might jeopardize Soviet assistance in the war against Japan. Although some military leaders still wished for an early Russian declaration of war, at the end of April Truman's handling of the Polish issue had established a new principle: American political objectives were worth more than Soviet help for the invasion strategy. This judgment was reaffirmed when the Secretary of War answered Grew's questions with the declaration: "Military considerations . . . do not preclude an attempt by the United States Government to obtain Soviet agreement to desirable political objectives in the Far East."[32] Stimson's official War Department assessment was supported by General Marshall, Secretary Forrestal, and Assistant Secretary of War McCloy.[33]

---

* See Feis, *Churchill, Roosevelt, Stalin*, p. 637.

For this reason, Stimson bolstered his argument for delay not with dire warnings about the consequences of losing Soviet help in the war, but with the argument that America was in a relatively weak diplomatic bargaining position at the present juncture. He made it clear that without the strength of the new weapon, the power relationships in the Far East were much more favorable to Russia than to the United States: "The concessions . . . are generally matters which are within the military power of Russia to obtain regardless of U.S. military action short of war." His official conclusion was a study in understatement: "It is not believed that much good will come of a rediscussion at this time."[34]

Although a "rediscussion" raising the threat of a refusal to fulfill the Yalta agreement seemed futile, Stimson had no objection to beginning an exploration of the Soviet position. He concurred in the desirability of obtaining the commitments and clarifications, but argued against pressing the American position too far. Finally, of course, Stimson pointed out that it was much too early to raise the question of Soviet occupation of Japan.[35]

With the State Department urging an immediate reconsideration and the War Deparment counseling delay, the decision was now brought directly to the President. Each side pressed its case once again; Harriman, about to leave for Moscow, told Truman on May 15 that he felt it important to have an understanding of the American position before he met with the Russians. Truman agreed in general terms, but took no stand on the matters in dispute.[36] The next day Stimson met with the President to discuss diplomatic timing.[37] There is little doubt that it was also at this meeting that he expressed the deep concern of his previous night's diary entry—his awareness that a heads-of-government meeting in the first week of July would occur a few weeks too early to know the atomic-test results.[38]

Presently available records do not show to what extent the Secretary of War voiced his view that it would be "a terrible thing to gamble with such big stakes in diplomacy without having your master card in your hand"[39]—that is, to what extent he urged not only the general principle of delay, but specifically that the meeting be postponed beyond the end of June. They do show, however, that by the end of his conversation with the President, all of the Secretary of War's fears had been dispelled.[40] When he left Truman, he was satisfied that the President fully agreed with him as to strategy, and in a memorandum written later the same day he expressed his approval of Truman's approach.[41] Truman's subsequent actions show both that, as in the Polish case, the President chose Stimson's advice over Harriman's, and that Truman agreed to an additional postponement.*

There was very little Truman had to do to implement the strategy of delay in the Far East; the essence of Stimson's view was to do nothing until after the atomic test. Earlier, when Truman had agreed to reverse his initial decision on Poland, it had been necessary to send a mission of conciliation to allay the suspicions caused by the premature showdown. Now, however, Stimson asked only that "we keep our mouths shut"—that is, that the President stall. Thus, on the one hand, Truman had only to continue to withhold instructions to fulfill the Yalta conditions of Soviet entry into the war, and on the other, he had only to continue to refuse the State Department's suggestion that the threat of a "rediscussion" be used to obtain new Soviet concessions.

Following Stimson's advice with great precision, the President did absolutely nothing. Hurley received no instructions to inform Chiang Kai-shek of the Yalta agreement, and the State Department was not allowed to initiate a new *démarche*. Two and a half weeks after Truman began to procrastinate, he once more reviewed strategy with the Secretary of War. Meeting with Stimson on June 6, the President reaffirmed his agreement that the issues would not be settled until after the atomic bomb had been demonstrated, saying he hoped that at that time the Russians would offer cooperation in Manchuria as one of a number of diplomatic *quid pro quos* for taking them into partnership to control the new atomic force.[42]

During the weeks Truman was holding off Ambassador Hurley and the State Department, Stimson tried to speed up the tempo of work on the atomic bomb at the Los Alamos Laboratories.[43] "We were under

---

* From Stimson's May 15, 1945, diary entry (quoted on p. 145) it is clear that he was under the impression that Truman had definitely committed himself to a meeting on July 1. As has been shown, the President had only suggested an indefinite date after June 30. In the previous chapter I have described some of the conversation between Stimson and Truman reviewed in this paragraph, to show how the President pleased the Secretary of War by accepting his general strategy toward the meeting. Here, I wish to stress that in the same conversation Stimson's specific worry about whether the meeting was definitely fixed for July 1 was also dispelled.

incredible pressure to get it done before the Potsdam meeting," J. Robert Oppenheimer, director of the Laboratory, has testified.[44] For his part, the President tried to postpone his meeting with Stalin once again. Altering his earlier suggestion that the heads of government might meet any time after June 30, he cabled Churchill in the third week of May to state that he could not yet name a date for the meeting but that "I may, within the next two weeks, have more information bearing on a date."[45] The contractors supplying firing circuits and molds for casting the nuclear explosive had fallen two weeks behind in deliveries; thus, the test would take place two weeks later than originally expected.[46] With the latest information available, on May 28 Truman instructed Hopkins to suggest that the Big Three meet on July 15.[47] Thus, when a week later Stimson warned of the "greatest complication" if the bomb had not been "laid on" Japan by the time of the meeting, Truman reassured him that he "had postponed that until the 15th of July on purpose to give us more time."[48]

This new delay of the Potsdam meeting enraged Churchill. The Prime Minister had never understood why the President wished to hold off so long and now—still wishing to maintain pressure on the Russians—he was furious. Churchill cabled both Truman and Stalin, urging that the meeting be held "in the very near future . . . about the middle of June."[49] On May 30, Stalin replied that it was Truman, not he, who had suggested the July 15 date. Churchill's reply was filled with urgency: "I consider that July 15th, repeat July, the month after June, is much too late. . . . I have proposed June 15th, repeat June, the month before July, but if that is not possible, why not July 1st, July 2nd, or July 3rd?" Stalin's response was brief: "I should like to tell you again that July 15 was suggested by President Truman . . . ." It was only when faced with the united stand of Truman and Stalin that Churchill yielded to the frustrating and seemingly inexplicable dictates of the strategy of delay.[50]

A WAY TO PREVENT RED ARMY CONTROL OF MANCHURIA

ALTHOUGH STIMSON had opposed a "rediscussion" based on a threat to withhold completion of the Yalta understanding, he had raised no objection to an *exploration* of the Soviet position vis-à-vis the Far

East. With no fundamental disagreement between the State and War Departments on this narrow point, Truman instructed Hopkins to undertake a third task while in Moscow—on May 28 he and Harriman sought a clarification of the Soviet attitude on the future treatment of China, Manchuria, and Korea.[51] Hopkins's report to the President summarized the favorable results of the discussion:

> Stalin made categorical statement that he would do everything he could to promote unification of China under the leadership of Chiang Kai-shek. . . . He specifically stated no Communist leader was strong enough to unify China. . . . He repeated all his statements made at Yalta, that he wanted a unified and stable China . . . to control all of Manchuria. . . . He stated categorically that he had no territorial claims against China and mentioned specifically Manchuria and Sinkiang and that he would respect Chinese sovereignty in all the areas his troops entered. . . . Stalin stated that he would *welcome representatives of the Generalissimo to be with his troops entering Manchuria* in order to facilitate the organization of Chinese administration in Manchuria. . . . Stalin agreed with America's "open door" policy and went out of his way to indicate that the United States was the only power with the resources to aid China economically after the war. He observed that Russia would have all it could do to provide for the internal economy of the Soviet Union. . . . Stalin agreed that there should be a trusteeship for Korea. . . .* [52]

These assurances were all that could be asked. The exploratory talks had obtained the objectives sought and even from the State Department's point of view had rendered an immediate "rediscussion" of the Yalta agreement unnecessary. On purely diplomatic grounds there was now far less reason to consider withholding fulfillment of the Yalta accord.† Although it was impossible to know whether Stalin would honor his pledges, both Hopkins and Harriman were optimistic. "We were very encouraged by conference on the Far East," Hopkins cabled; and Harriman added, "The talks . . . were of real value, particularly Stalin's agreement to take up . . . the political matters

---

* The emphasized sentence was thought to be the most important point, for it would mean a dominant role for the Nationalist Government rather than the Communist Chinese. (*Conference of Berlin*, I, p. 62.)

† For this reason it is not possible to know for certain whether Truman might have changed his position and permitted the State Department to threaten a breach of the Yalta agreement. Even while Hopkins and Harriman were in Moscow, the State and War Departments struggled over the issue. (Feis, *China Tangle*, p. 308*fn*.) More light may be shed on this point when access to all the relevant documents is allowed.

affecting China . . . and also his agreement to allow the Generalissimo's representatives to go into Manchuria with the Russian troops. . . ."[53]

Even though he felt the ultimate settlement of the Manchurian issues could not be completed until the atomic bomb had been demonstrated, Truman was delighted with these reports. In a diary entry at this time Stimson records: "[The President] asked me if I had heard of the accomplishment which Harry Hopkins had made in Moscow and when I said I had not he told me there was a promise in writing . . . that Manchuria should remain fully Chinese except for a ninety-nine-year lease of Port Arthur and the settlement of Dairen which we had hold of. . . ."[*54]

At the same time Hopkins pleased the President with his report on the Far East he also cabled that Stalin had repeated the pledge that the Red Army would be prepared to march by August 8, but that no troops would be committed until agreement on the basis of the Yalta accord had been reached with China. Stalin suggested that T. V. Soong come to Moscow as soon as possible. Hopkins advised: "This procedure seems most desirable from our point of view. . . . He left no doubt in our mind that he intends to attack during August. It is therefore important that Soong come here not later than July 1st."[55]

Truman agreed to send Soong to Moscow to begin discussions with Stalin before the beginning of July.[56] Despite this decision, however, *he did not decide to fulfill Roosevelt's Yalta pledges.*† On June 4 he informed Hurley in general terms that a number of problems relating to the maintenance of a democratic government in China would be dealt with *when the heads of government met.*[57] And, as we shall see, he continued to follow the strategy of delay, refusing to settle the final negotiations until the atomic bomb had been shown.‡ Although this decision initially followed the rather simple logic that the new weapon would be a "master card" in the ultimate diplomacy, there was now a second reason for wishing to delay the negotiations. If a Soviet declaration of war could be postponed, it now became obvious that the atomic

---

* This is apparently an exaggeration. No record of a written agreement has been found, nor does such an agreement reappear in later negotiations on these points.

† I have emphasized this point because some have thought that because Truman agreed to send Soong, he also agreed to fulfill the Yalta accord. As will be shown, the deduction does not follow from the fact. (See Feis's error, *Between War and Peace*, pp. 113–14.)

‡ See below, pp. 240–42.

bomb might end the war before the Red Army crossed the Manchurian border. Thus, not only would the bomb influence the negotiations, but—far more important—it might provide a way to prevent Soviet military control of the area.

In fact, the Soong mission now became intimately bound up with the use of the atomic bomb and the desire to prevent the Red Army from entering Manchuria. This subtle and complex question will be taken up in due course. But, for a proper understanding of American strategy, it must first be understood that, contrary to the opinion of some writers,* the President's seemingly conciliatory decision to send Soong to Moscow (and his subsequent attitude toward the mission) did not derive primarily from a feeling that great care had to be taken for fear that Stalin might delay his entry into the war. On the contrary, by mid-May this fear (which had indeed troubled Washington at an earlier date) had all but disappeared. In its place there was now almost unanimous agreement that the Red Army would attack in mid-August.

Ironically, Truman's showdown over Poland had provided the best test of Soviet intentions in the Far East: although General Marshall had warned that a tough approach might jeopardize an early declaration of war against Japan, in fact, his judgment had been proven wrong.† Even at the height of the tensions over Poland, there was every sign that Russia would enter the war as soon as sufficient numbers of troops had been transported across the Trans-Siberian Railroad. Before Hopkins left for Moscow, and before there was any break in the tense atmosphere, Stimson noted in his diary (on May 15) that there was no longer much doubt about Stalin's plan to enter the war at an early date.[58]

---

* Feis consistently presents the unsupported opinion that "the surviving wish to have Russian cooperation in the war continued to constrain American officials in their differences with the Soviet Union over various European situations." This is a vital point in one accepted interpretation of this period; those who have not taken proper account of the atomic bomb's role in the diplomacy of delay must explain why Truman adopted a conciliatory attitude during May and June. The easiest, but incorrect, explanation is the one offered by Feis: Truman did not want to lose Russian help in the war against Japan. As will be shown, however, not only was there no longer a fear that Russian help would be lost by political action, but Truman hoped to *delay* Russian entry. Thus, as explained, the Hopkins mission and Truman's conciliatory approach derived not from military considerations, but from the desire to delay a diplomatic confrontation with Stalin until the atomic bomb had been shown. (Feis, *Churchill, Roosevelt, Stalin*, pp. 599–600; *Japan Subdued*, p. 14; Ehrman, *Grand Strategy*, p. 294. See also my Appendix II.)

† See above, p. 99.

Indeed, for some time Marshall seems to have been almost alone in his cautious estimate of Stalin's intentions; his was the conservative Army view (as Admiral Leahy has observed), which carefully and skeptically examined every form of assistance which could be added to the invasion strategy.[59] But both before and after the showdown, the fear that Stalin might delay his entry into the war does not seem to have dominated the thinking of other senior policy makers. Throughout the last half of the war, at Teheran, at Moscow, at Yalta, Stalin had promised to join the fight against Japan two to three months after the defeat of Germany.[60] After October 1944 Churchill had "no doubt whatever" that Stalin would declare war as soon as Germany was beaten.[61] And Roosevelt told Harriman, "I have at no time entertained any doubts whatever" as to Stalin's intentions.[62]

Even those who did have doubts were greatly reassured by the April Soviet notice of intention to denounce the nonaggression pact with Japan.[63] As we have seen, in mid-April Stalin explicitly reaffirmed his plan to declare war two to three months after German surrender.[64] On April 22 Molotov made it clear to Truman that Russia had lost no interest in the Yalta understanding.[65] The two American representatives in Moscow, Ambassador Harriman and General Deane, repeatedly counseled that Russia would enter the war at an early date because of its own interests in the Far East.[66] Secretary Forrestal, Acting Secretary of State Grew, Secretary Stimson, all agreed with this estimate.[67] There were continuous reports of Soviet troop movements to the Far East and by mid-May even Marshall seems to have been won over. After a talk with the cautious General, Stimson recorded that "we" now think Russia will enter the war at an early date.[68] A week later Marshall endorsed Stimson's assurance that there was no danger that raising the political issues would jeopardize a Russian declaration of war.[69] Hence, Hopkins's May 28 report that Stalin "left no doubt in our mind that he intends to attack during August" only confirmed the existing consensus.*[70]

Thus, it is clear that after mid-June the American approach to the question of Soviet entry into the Japanese war was no longer domi-

---

* Note also the phrasing of Grew's May 12 letter: " . . . In connection with the political effects of the *expected Soviet entry* . . . " (Department of Defense, "Entry of the Soviet Union into the War against Ja- pan," p. 69.) Compare Churchill's May 14 message to Halifax: "Having regard to their [Russia's] own great interests in the Far East, they will not need to be begged . . . " (Churchill, *Triumph and Tragedy*, p. 576.)

nated by a fear that Stalin might delay until all of the "dirty work" had been done, as Marshall had once feared. Secretary of the Navy Forrestal was probably closer to the truth when he later commented that "fifty divisions could not have kept them *out.*"[71] The real question was whether the war could be ended before the Red Army—and, inevitably, Soviet influence—flowed from Siberia across the Manchurian border. As they pondered this question, American policy makers had to consider Japan's capacity to sustain the hostilities and to decide whether or not the United States could afford to dispense with a Soviet declaration of war.

From any rational military point of view, Japan was already defeated. By early summer the better part of the Imperial Navy had been sunk and the Imperial Air Force had been reduced to the impotence of sporadic kamikaze attacks.[72] B-29 bombers met only limited resistance as they struck at targets of choice. Between March 9 and June 15 almost seven thousand bomber missions were dispatched for urban incendiary attacks; losses amounted to only 136 planes, an average of a mere 1.9 per cent of the sorties.[73] Japanese morale slumped after repeated poundings, in the course of which the greatest single man-made disaster in history was recorded: the March 10 raid on Tokyo resulted in 124,000 casualties.[74] General Curtis E. LeMay's grisly boast was only a slight exaggeration: the bombing raids were "driving them back to the stone age . . ."[75] But this was only the beginning. With the capitulation of Germany, it was clear that the full force of American and British power would be focused on only one target.[76] Now Japan, with a productive capacity only 10 per cent as large as America's, would bear the brunt of the best military resources accumulated during the European war.[77] Clearly, defeat was inevitable. In fact, Japanese leaders had already reached this conclusion; their main reason for continuing the struggle was a desire to try to modify the rigid unconditional-surrender formula. They hoped that by purchasing the good offices of the Soviet Union with Japanese-controlled concessions on the China mainland they might improve the surrender terms.[78] But here too there were ominous signs; Soviet denunciation of the nonaggression pact raised grave doubts that this frail hope could be fulfilled.[79]

In this situation American policy makers recognized the crucial role a declaration of war by Russia would play. It would close the one remaining loophole which allowed Japanese leaders to find hope in a continuation of the war. Indeed, with Japanese power and morale crumbling, the continued though fading Soviet neutrality was the proverbial straw to the drowning man; *both* Japanese military *and* political leaders, for different reasons, rested their hopes and their strategies on the next move of the Soviet Union. The military thought possibly that Russia might be persuaded to join with Japan, but, more realistically, they hoped for Soviet neutrality. The political leaders thought possibly that Russian neutrality might be maintained, and hoped that Russian mediation might end the war with less stringent surrender terms.[80]

Although Japanese peace feelers had been sent out as early as September 1944[81] (and Chiang Kai-shek had been approached regarding surrender possibilities in December 1944),[82] the real effort to end the war began in the spring of 1945. This effort stressed the role of the Soviet Union. In April a new Japanese government headed by the moderate Admiral Suzuki was formed. The man chosen to be foreign minister—Shigenori Togo—was carefully selected; he was well known for his opposition to the war and his friendliness toward the Soviet Union (he was a former ambassador to Moscow). Togo accepted the post on the understanding that he would be free to try to end the war,[83] and immediately the new government initiated a major diplomatic *démarche* which, subtly straddling the narrow agreement between the various Japanese political and military groups, delicately carried Japan's last hope forward in exploratory talks with Russia.[84]

It is not the purpose of this essay to analyze the various Japanese maneuvers based on the hope of Russian help.* These continued from April until the end of the war,[85] and since the United States had broken the Japanese codes much earlier in the war, they were known to the highest American authorities.[86] The important point for our purposes is that the increasing dependence of Japan upon the attitude of the Soviet Union had major implications for American policy. Although the April 24 report that Soviet help was no longer needed *for*

---

* For more information on these matters, see Butow, *Japan's Decision to Surrender;* Kase, *Journey to the Missouri;* Togo, *The Cause of Japan;* F. C. Jones, *et. al., The Far East 1942–46;* Zacharias, *Secret Mis-* sions. Note especially Butow, pp. 60, 61, 65, 66, 67, 71, 72, 78–80, 83–91, 110, 123; Kase p. 84; Jones, pp. 126–32; Zacharias, pp. 359–60.

an invasion was endorsed by the Joint Chiefs on May 10,[87] it now appeared that a Soviet declaration in and of itself might shock Japan into surrender long *before* an invasion would have to be launched.

The political and psychological value—as distinct from the purely military value—of Russian entry into the war had long been acknowledged by Churchill. As early as September 1944 the Prime Minister had argued that Japan would surrender once faced by the combined strength of the three powers.*[88] However, American policy makers had been reluctant to rely upon the shock value of Russian entry. For months, as they cautiously plotted an invasion, they had refrained from overly optimistic assessments of the possibility of surrender.[89] But by the late spring of 1945, it was impossible to overlook this opportunity to end the war without an invasion.

In mid-April the Joint Intelligence Committee reported that Japanese leaders were looking for a way to modify the surrender terms to end the war.[90] The State Department was convinced the Emperor was actively seeking a way to stop the fighting.[91] By April 24 the Joint Staff Planners cautiously suggested that an invasion *"threat in itself"* might bring *unconditional* surrender.[92] The War Department too was impressed by the changed Japanese attitude.[93] In late April the chief United States Army planners initiated studies on "what we do if Japan decides to surrender on V-E Day."[94] Admiral Leahy was convinced the war could be ended long before an invasion would have to be launched.[95] Secretary Forrestal and Acting Secretary Grew believed that a statement reassuring the Japanese that "unconditional surrender" did not mean dethronement of the Emperor would probably bring an end to the war.[96] Secretary Stimson thought that even a powerful *warning* by itself might bring capitulation. He added that guarantees for the Emperor would make the prospect for quick surrender much better.[97]

Within Japan, the destruction of the last of Japanese naval power and the loss of Okinawa—the first major island of the home chain—strengthened the hand of the moderates urging peace.[98] By mid-June six members of the Supreme War Council had secretly entrusted For-

---

* The judgment was held consistently for almost a year; on July 17, 1945, General Ismay reported a Combined Intelligence Staff estimate to Churchill that "when Russia came into the war against Japan, the Japanese would probably wish to get out on almost any terms short of the dethronement of the Emperor." (Quoted in Ehrman, *Grand Strategy*, p. 291.)

eign Minister Togo with the task of approaching the Soviet Union "with a view to terminating the war if possible by September."[99] By early July the United States had intercepted messages from Togo to the Japanese ambassador in Moscow which showed that the Emperor himself had now taken a personal hand in the matter and had directed that the Soviet Union be asked to help end the war.*[100] The Emperor's intervention confirmed earlier intelligence estimates, and it unquestionably signaled Japan's willingness to surrender. Forrestal termed the telegrams "real evidence of a Japanese desire to get out of the war."[101] Grew has confirmed the importance of the Emperor's intervention; for American leaders, as Leahy put it, "were certain that the Mikado could stop the war with a royal word."[102]

As the Japanese position deteriorated, on May 21, Secretary Stimson advised that a Russian declaration of war would have a "profound military effect." He ordered further studies of the problem. As these were being prepared, Stalin reported to Hopkins that there were renewed Japanese feelers aimed at securing Soviet help to end the war.[103] In early June, Stimson received a report from the War Department's Operations Division which concluded:

> Like [that of] the Germans, [Japanese] protracted resistance is based upon the hope of achieving a conditional surrender. . . . Probably it will take Russian entry into the war, coupled with a landing, *or imminent threat* of landing . . . to convince them of the hopelessness of their position.[104]

By mid-June even the extremely cautious General Marshall advised the President that "the impact of Russian entry on the already hopeless Japanese may well be the decisive action levering them into capitulation at that time or shortly thereafter if we land in Japan."[105] In early July the Combined Intelligence Committee was even more definite—"An entry of the Soviet Union into the war would finally convince the Japanese of the inevitability of complete defeat."†[106]

---

* Truman's recent declaration that he knew of these approaches removes former doubts as to whether the intelligence information reached the highest officials. (*Conference of Berlin*, I, p. 873.)

† The complicated and continuously changing military picture has been misunderstood by almost every important observer. Ehrman's analysis, which recognizes that American policy makers were not overly anxious for Russian help, is the best. However, Ehrman misses the two radical shifts in American military thinking; he fails to give proper weight to the April 24 judgment that Russia (*Continued on next page*)

The various assessments of the shock value of a Russian declaration of war were based, of course, upon the assumption that the Japanese would be forced to accept "unconditional surrender." However, by the end of May, every important senior American policy maker, including the President, had decided that, if necessary, the rigid surrender formula would be substantially modified to assure the Japanese that the Emperor would retain his throne.[107] As Acting Secretary of State Grew noted on May 29, it was only "the question of timing [that] was the nub of the whole matter."[108] As early as April 18 the Joint Planners had reported that a clarification of the surrender terms in itself might be all that was needed to achieve surrender.[109] Throughout May this judgment was continuously reinforced so that by June it was clear to American leaders that either a Russian declaration of war or a change in the surrender terms was likely to bring capitulation.[110] Almost certainly a combination of the two measures would stop the fighting immediately.

(It is not my purpose to argue whether either or both of these measures would, in fact, have ended the war. What I wish to show is that American leaders *believed* such a result was likely. Hence, their decision to use the atomic bomb was made at a time when the best intelligence and military advice indicated there were other ways to end the war without an invasion. As will be shown, the bomb was used not because there were no alternatives, but precisely because American policy makers wished to avoid the political consequences of these alternatives.)

Thus, as each day of the spring passed, it became more and more doubtful that an invasion would be needed to force Japanese capitulation. To be sure, it was important to go forward with planning for an invasion, especially since General Marshall did not wish to weaken morale by raising possibly false hopes, but such planning now took on a contingency aspect; it was necessary to be prepared, but actual

---

(*Continued from preceding page*)
was no longer needed *for an invasion,* and he misses the mid-June judgment that a Russian declaration of war could make an invasion unnecessary. (Ehrman, *Grand Strategy,* pp. 292–95.) Feis's failure to distinguish results is the other possible error; he thinks American policy makers always wanted Russian help. He mentions, but does not realize the importance of the April 24 judgment and completely misses the mid-June assessment. Typically he fogs the argument by mixing up early-April judgments with late-April opinions and with general comments from different periods throughout the summer. (Feis, *Japan Subdued,* p. 13.) Hewlett and Anderson make the same mistakes, confusing different assessments made at different times throughout the summer. (*The New World,* p. 349.)

operations would be launched only if all other methods to end the war failed.[111] Thus, as Admiral Leahy has stressed, *"The invasion itself was never authorized."*[112] Prudence, not necessity, dictated military thinking. Advance preparations for an invasion which would not in any event begin until November 1 (three months after Russia was expected to declare war) followed the logic of Admiral Ernest J. King's advice to the President:

> So far as preparation was concerned, we must aim now for Tokyo Plain; otherwise we will never be able to accomplish it. If preparations do not go forward now, they cannot be arranged for later. Once started, however, they can always be stopped if desired.[113]

In this spirit, when Truman approved the plans outlined by the Joint Chiefs on June 18, he made it absolutely clear that he would "decide as to the final action later."[114] As Assistant Secretary of War McCloy has emphasized, the President let it be known that he would withhold his final decision until the time "beyond which there would not be further opportunity for a free choice."*[115]

While American military planners outlined alternatives for all eventualities, the President and his senior civilian advisers focused their attention on more immediate matters; every important American policy maker, including the President, had grave reservations about Russian military operations in Manchuria. Some, of course, like Admiral Leahy (who took a "jaundiced view" of Russian domination of the area) had never believed a Russian declaration of war should be encouraged.[116] But if it could be arranged, Harriman, McCloy, Grew, Forrestal, Stimson, Byrnes, and Truman, all preferred to end the war without Russia, or at least before the Red Army had gotten very far into Manchuria.†[117] Thus, they no longer directed their efforts to forcing capitulation before the November 1 target date for an invasion, but before the August 8 target date for Soviet entry. "I

---

* This point is often overlooked. For instance, R. C. Batchelder's recent *The Irreversible Decision* (p. 119) still argues that an invasion was taken for granted.

† Even Leahy's published memoirs hint at this purpose. Note his discreet understatement: "Some of us indulged in a hope that Japan might get out of the war before the Soviet Government came in." (Leahy, *I Was There*, p. 419.) See also Eisenhower's report of a discussion with Truman in mid-July: "I told him that since reports indicated the imminence of Japan's collapse I deprecated the Red Army's engaging in that war." (Eisenhower, *Crusade in Europe*, pp. 441–42; Forrestal, *Diaries*, pp. 78–79.)

must frankly admit . . . I would have been satisfied had the Russians determined not to enter the war," Secretary of State Byrnes cautiously hinted in 1947. "I believed the atomic bomb would be successful and would force the Japanese to accept surrender on our terms."[118]

But the fact that all eyes were on the August 8 target date, rather than the November 1 invasion date, has been affirmed and reaffirmed in much more explicit terms: "Though there was an understanding that the Soviets would enter the war three months after Germany surrendered," Byrnes has more recently testified, "the President and I hoped that Japan would surrender before *then*."[119] And still more explicitly: "We wanted to get through with the Japanese phase of the war before the Russians came in."*[120]

A War Department report made to Stimson at the time stated the crucial consideration in more general terms:

> [An early] Japanese surrender would be advantageous to the U.S., both because of the enormous reduction in the cost of the war and because it would give us a better chance to settle the affairs of the Western Pacific *before too many of our allies are committed there and have made substantial contributions to the defeat of Japan.* . . .[121]

Byrnes has also stated specifically that he wished to end the war before Russia entered, because "I feared what would happen when the Red Army entered Manchuria."[122] This statement deserves close attention, because it underscores the important point that Japan was so weakened and Russia had so little capacity to undertake an amphibious invasion that there was never any danger of Soviet operations in the Japanese home islands.† Thus, the desire to end the war before Russia entered was not based primarily, as is sometimes thought, on a

---

* This fact also undoubtedly accounts for Byrnes's use of the conjunction "and" instead of the preposition "to" in a key statement in his memoirs; he writes that it was "essential to end the war as soon as possible *and* avoid the invasion." The two goals, of course, were not the same. Elsewhere Byrnes has admitted that from among the alternative ways to end the Japanese war before an invasion the atomic bomb was chosen so as to avoid Russian entry. (Byrnes, *All in One Lifetime,* pp. 286, 300, 308.)

† Max Beloff has noted this point, but misunderstood its significance. Attempting to confute P. M. S. Blackett's argument that the atomic bomb was used to end the war before the Russians reached Japan, he rightly notes that there was never any chance that the Russians would get that far. However, he overlooks the more fundamental point that American policy makers saw the bomb as a way to keep the Russians out of Manchuria. Thus Blackett's argument, though wrong in detail, is right in substance. (Beloff, *Soviet Policy,* p. 106; Blackett, *Military and Political Consequences,* pp. 116–30. See also U.S. Senate, *Hearings: Military Situation in the Far East,* p. 6.)

wish to prevent Soviet occupation of Japan.* Rather, American policy makers, aware that Russia could conquer the Japanese armies on the China mainland in less than two months,[123] desperately hoped to end the hostilities before Soviet military operations paved the way for Soviet domination of Manchuria and North China.

It was with this diplomatic objective in mind that American policy makers once again considered the political value of the atomic bomb. Despite their subsequent assertions, they were no longer primarily worried about having to undertake a costly invasion of Japan.[124] They believed a Russian declaration of war in itself would probably end the war quickly if necessary. They were also prepared to moderate the surrender terms to end the war before an invasion.† Consequently, the fundamental objective was no longer military, but political—could the war be ended before August 8?

Truman had already decided (or assumed) that the bomb would be used in Japan. Even in his April 24 discussion with Stimson, there had never been any question about whether the new weapon would be employed when it was ready.‡ At the end of April, General Marshall gave Field Marshal Wilson information on the operational use of the new bomb and told him it would be used sometime in August.[125] Indeed, the President has emphasized: "Let there be no mistake about it. I regarded the bomb as a military weapon and never had any doubt that it should be used."[126]

Thus the only question was how, not whether, the atomic bomb would be employed. Originally, at about the time of the Yalta Conference, the bomb had been regarded as a new tactical weapon of unusual force; Marshall planned to use it *in conjunction with an invasion*.[127] A total of nine bombs were to have been dropped as three

---

* Later, Stimson argued that an end to the war before Russian operations had begun in Manchuria would also obviate Soviet claims to help occupy Japan. See below, p. 238.

† This fact also allows us to delineate American priorities with some precision. The most important objective was to end the war without an invasion. Since there seemed little problem about this, the dominant questions were: Could the war be ended before Russia entered? And could the unconditional-surrender formula be maintained? It is easy to show that if forced to choose between Russian entry and modifications of the surrender formula, American leaders preferred to relax the surrender terms offered to the Emperor. But, as Byrnes has written, a further political value of the bomb was that it seemed to obviate such a choice—"I believed the atomic bomb would . . . force the Japanese to accept surrender *on our terms*." (Knebel and Bailey, *No High Ground*, p. 36; Stimson, *On Active Service*, p. 621; Grew, *Turbulent Era*, II, p. 1450; Byrnes, *Speaking Frankly*, p. 208.)

‡ See above, p. 104.

armies assaulted the island of Kyushu from different directions. Two bombs would have supported each attack, and in each case a third would have been brought into operation against Japanese reserves.[128] From this point of view, the idea that the few available bombs might be squandered on civilian or quasi-military targets would have seemed a waste of irreplaceable resources needed for the invasion. However, the deterioration of Japanese power and morale permitted a reconsideration of these plans.

In fact, American policy makers now saw a Russian declaration of war and the atomic bomb as military and psychological equivalents. Originally, they had regarded Russian entry as important mainly because of its value to the invasion strategy. Shortly after they revised this assessment, however, they saw that a Russian declaration of war in and of itself might be enough to shock Japan into surrender. Similarly, although they had first regarded the atomic bomb as a supporting weapon, to be used tactically in the actual invasion, they now came to see that it might be powerful enough in and of itself to shock Japan into surrender. Thus, by the end of May the President's special representative, Byrnes, "was confident that, when developed, it would bring a speedy end to the war in the Pacific."[129]

It was for this reason that the Interim Committee seriously considered neither whether to use the atomic bomb, nor whether to use it in support of an invasion. Japan was in such dire straits that American leaders felt it wise to approach the bomb as a weapon of terror. Hence, when the Interim Committee met on May 31 to consider the problem, the only important question was how the bomb could be used to end the war quickly, that is, how it could be used with the greatest psychological effect.[130] As Stimson was later to write, to edge the faltering Japanese into capitulation, all that was needed was "a tremendous shock,"[131] or, in General Marshall's words, "a terrific shock."[132]

The Interim Committee considered the matter first in a joint meeting with its scientific panel. As Arthur H. Compton, a member of the panel, has written, "It seemed a foregone conclusion that the bomb would be used. It was regarding only the details of strategy and tactics that different views were expressed."[133] In fact, the Committee was not given much information about the relationship of the bomb to the war. There was little discussion of alternative methods to end the war.

Although Hopkins had just reported that there was "no doubt" Stalin would enter the war in August, apparently nothing was said about awaiting the results of the Russian declaration of war or about using the bomb in conjunction with the Russian declaration.[184] J. Robert Oppenheimer has testified: "We didn't know beans about the military situation in Japan. We didn't know whether they could be caused to surrender by other means . . ."[135] The only question was the best way to use the bomb so as to create a dramatic and shocking effect.[*][136]

First, the President's special representative asked one scientist about a suggestion that the Japanese be given some striking but harmless demonstration of the bomb's power before using it in a manner that would cause great loss of life. For about ten minutes the proposition was the subject of general discussion. Oppenheimer could think of no demonstration sufficiently dramatic to convince the Japanese that further resistance was futile. Others objected that the bomb might not explode, or that the Japanese might shoot down the delivery plane or bring American prisoners into the test area. If the demonstration failed to bring surrender, the chance of administering the maximum surprise shock would be lost.[137]

After some discussion, Stimson offered a conclusion which commanded general agreement: there would be greater shock value if the bomb was dropped without advance warning. While it would be unwise to aim only for a civilian area, it would be best to make as profound a psychological impression on as many of the inhabitants as possible. James B. Conant suggested, and Stimson agreed, that the best target would be a vital war plant employing a large number of workers closely surrounded by workers' houses. The next day, when the Interim Committee met in executive session, Byrnes formally proposed the Committee recommend that the bomb be used as soon as possible and without warning against a Japanese war plant surrounded by workers' homes. The Committee adopted the suggestion.[†]

---

[*] I have seen no evidence for Ehrman's assumption that "the Interim Committee made its recommendations with full knowledge of the strategy for the Pacific." (*Grand Strategy*, p. 279.)

[†] The preceding paragraphs rely heavily upon Hewlett and Anderson, *The New World*, pp. 358–60.

I have not dealt with the important story of the attempt by a group of scientists to prevent use of the atomic bomb against a civilian target. On June 16 the Scientific Panel, reviewing suggestions made by a number of scientists, reported to the Interim Committee that they could propose no (*Continued on next page*)

At the same time the Interim Committee was reaching this conclusion Secretary Stimson and General Marshall discussed the best method to employ the new weapon.[138] Of course, the Secretary of War bore ultimate responsibility for recommendations as to the use of the weapon, but there was little difference between his view and that of the Committee. The objective was the most dramatic and shocking disclosure of the new force, and Stimson and the Committee agreed that an unannounced strike upon a large city was the best approach[139]—"Any other course . . . involved serious danger to the major objective of obtaining a *prompt* surrender from the Japanese."[140]

Stimson took every precaution to ensure that the attack would make the greatest impression. Fearing that the B-29 raids might bomb out Japan so thoroughly that the atomic weapon would not have a fair background against which to show its strength, Stimson spoke to both the President and Army Air Forces Chief, General Henry H. Arnold, about the matter. It was agreed that orders would be issued not to bomb a number of cities, so that unblemished targets would be available when the bomb was ready.[141]

On June 1 Byrnes reported the recommendation of the Interim Committee to the President.[142] Since Truman had already assumed use of the weapon, and since he already saw it primarily as a way to end the war before Russia entered, the only real point he had to approve was whether the Committee's approach would produce the greatest shock effect. He told Byrnes that, regrettable as it might be, so far as he could see, the only reasonable conclusion was to use the bomb.[143] He told Stimson the bomb "should be dropped as nearly as possible upon a war production center."[144] He approved the Committee's recommendation,[145] and early in June the commander of the special B-29 group stationed in the Pacific was informed that one atomic bomb would be available for use against the enemy on August 6, 1945.[146]

(*Continued from preceding page*)
technical demonstration likely to bring an end to the war. This recommendation was based on two assumptions: (1) that the bomb was needed to avoid an invasion; (2) that the war had to be ended very quickly. Since neither the panel nor the Committee discussed alternative ways to end the war without an invasion, it is not surprising that this recommendation was produced. Note that even this evaluation came two weeks *after* the Interim Committee had reported the best method to use the bomb to the President, and two months after Truman had assumed its use in the war. The views of the scientists never reached the President. (Feis, *Japan Subdued*, p. 43; Hewlett and Anderson, *The New World*, pp. 369–70;

A SUBTLE PROBLEM OF THE STRATEGY OF DELAY

THUS STIMSON'S JUDGMENT that the atomic bomb would be dominant over the "tangled weave" of political problems in the Far East became a major feature of American policy. When Stimson first offered his strategy of delay, he had stressed mainly that the bomb would eventually strengthen the American diplomatic hand. However, now a second aspect of the policy had emerged: the atomic bomb could pay political dividends by ending the Japanese war before Russia entered. Obviously, this would preclude Russian domination of Manchuria, but there were also important implications for European political problems: a quick end to the war would allow the President to maintain large concentrations of troops in Europe during the initial postwar negotiations.

Indeed, Truman felt it politically so important to have a major force in Europe that on June 6 (a month *after* German surrender) he told his staff he "would withdraw only the troops we could *spare from Europe* for our war in the Pacific."[147] In reality, however, by now he hoped the bomb would allow him to end the war not only before an invasion had begun, but many months before—that is, before massive troop transfers, which could take from four to six months to complete, had progressed very far.[148] The thought "uppermost" in his mind was "how soon we could wind up the war."[149] Thus, in a talk with Stimson concerning the atomic bomb, he "stressed the need for speed in the Pacific" at the same time he argued the necessity of maintaining troops in Europe for political purposes.[150]

Although Stimson had successfully urged the political value of the atomic bomb's capacity to end the war quickly, there was a major

---

Knebel and Bailey, "The Fight over the A-Bomb"; see also Alice K. Smith, "Behind the Decision to Use the Atomic Bomb.")

One member of the Interim Committee, Under Secretary of the Navy Ralph A. Bard, later changed his mind. His June 27 dissent stressed a combination of three alternative ways to end the war without the use of the bomb: "Emissaries from this country could contact representatives from Japan . . . and make representations with regard to *Russia's position* and at the same time give them some *information* regarding the proposed use of *atomic power*, together with whatever *assurances* the President might care to make *with regard to the Emperor* of Japan. . . . It seems quite possible to me that this presents the opportunity which the Japanese are looking for. I don't see that we have anything in particular to lose . . . The only way to find out is to try. . . ." (Quoted in Knebel and Bailey, *No High Ground*, pp. 109–10.) Emphasis supplied.

problem which prevented straightforward execution of the strategy of delay. As Stimson had noted on May 15, one of the "great uncertainties" was "when and how the [atomic bomb] will resolve itself."[151] This point was also raised at Truman's June 18 discussion of military strategy. Until this time all conventional military planning by the Joint Chiefs had been kept quite separate from discussions of the atomic bomb.[152] At this meeting, however, Assistant Secretary of War McCloy found the invasion plan fantastic; he was sure the bomb would end the war. As he later told Secretary Forrestal, he argued that the bomb "was pertinent not merely to the question of the invasion of the Japanese mainland but also to the question of whether we needed to get Russia in to help us defeat Japan."[153] Although the President welcomed McCloy's arguments, the meeting went forward with its plans because it was agreed that no one could be absolutely sure the bomb would work. The President would make his final decision later.[154]

Despite the great confidence of Stimson and the others, American policy makers were still dealing with an untested weapon; simple prudence required that they not rely entirely upon the unknown quantity. It was undoubtedly for this reason that, as we shall see, despite his desire to end the war before the Red Army crossed into Manchuria, Truman did not yet wish to abandon a Russian declaration of war as an alternative way to prevent an invasion. In fact, Truman told his military advisers that firmly securing the declaration was a major objective of his trip to Potsdam.[155]

Indeed, if the bomb should fail, he would lose nothing by encouraging early Russian entry, for without the new force the United States would hardly be in a position to oppose Stalin's political objectives in Asia. As Stimson had pointed out, the Russians could choose to "await the time when U.S. efforts will have practically completed the destruction of Japanese military power and can then seize the objectives they desire at a cost to them relatively much less than would be occasioned by their entry into the war at an early date."[156]

Since an early declaration might still be useful, there was every reason to hold on to the option of a Russian shock ending to the war. Yet Truman's problem was extremely subtle; for, if the bomb should work as expected, he did not want, as we have seen, to encourage Stalin to launch his Manchurian offensive. Truman's late-May decision to send Soong to Moscow forced him to consider his course with some care. When Soong arrived at the end of June, he would be asked to affirm the Yalta accord as a condition for Russian entry into the war. Should the United States fulfill Roosevelt's pledge to "take measures" to ensure that Russia's claims would "unquestionably" be met?

Weighing all considerations, on June 13, the Joint Chiefs of Staff recommended that a Soviet declaration of war was just valuable enough to warrant fulfillment of the Yalta accord.[157] Now that the shock value of Soviet entry had replaced the minimal value of the Red Army's usefulness to an invasion, the Joint Chiefs reversed the April 24 decision that no Pacific supply route would be cleared "until the Soviets on their own initiative so request."*[158] They now also discarded the judgment that "only such contributing operations as are essential to establish conditions prerequisite to invasion" should be conducted.[159] Instead, on June 29 they directed that new plans be prepared for keeping open a sea route to Russian Pacific ports.[160] General Deane was instructed to tell the Russian military that the Joint Chiefs would like to discuss coordination of efforts for the war, and *for the first time* the scope of the Potsdam Conference was broadened to include a discussion of military cooperation in the Japanese war.†[161] Nevertheless, the Joint Chiefs (with the exception of Marshall) were restrained in their enthusiasm for Soviet help. At the military discussion of June 18 the President was left with this statement of the military position:

> Admiral King said he wished to emphasize the point that, regardless of the desirability of the Russians entering the war, they were not indispensable, and he did not think we should go so far as to beg them to come in. While the cost of defeating Japan would be greater, there was no question in his mind but that we could handle it alone. He thought that the realization of this fact should greatly strengthen the President's hand in the forthcoming conference.‡ [162]

---

* See above, p. 79.

† I have not been able to find the precise date of the decision to broaden the Conference agenda. Available evidence shows that it was after Stalin agreed to the Potsdam meeting at the end of May. The decision probably was taken on June 13, together with the recommendation that Russia be encouraged to declare war. (Department of Defense, "Entry of the Soviet Union into the War against Japan," p. 72.)

‡ In fact, of the professional military leaders Marshall, still taking the Army view that Russian help would be valuable, was the only positive force in favor of encouraging Russia. King's view is given above, Leahy had never wanted the Russians to enter the war, and the following day General Arnold presented the view that the Air Force could finish the war alone. (Craven (*Continued on next page*)

Despite its qualifications, the mild recommendation that the Yalta conditions for Soviet entry be met was at odds with Stimson's argument that the Far Eastern negotiations should be delayed. Truman's decision was once again in favor of the Secretary of War. Although he had to send Soong to Moscow or risk revealing that he might not fulfill Roosevelt's Yalta pledge, Truman now decided that the Chinese Foreign Minister would not be allowed to complete his negotiations with Stalin.[163] As Byrnes has subsequently revealed, the President's execution of the strategy of delay was extremely subtle:

> Our purpose was . . . to encourage the Chinese to continue negotiations. . . . If Stalin and Chiang were still negotiating, it might delay Soviet entrance and the Japanese might surrender. The President was in accord with that view.* [164]

Thus, Truman continued to straddle two policies at once. He continued to attempt to delay a Soviet attack, hoping that the war could be ended quickly by the atomic bomb;[165] and on the other hand, until he was sure of his course, he avoided any action which might lose the insurance of a Russian declaration of war should the atomic test fail.[166]

Probably because of the notorious inability of the Chinese to maintain secrecy, Truman did not reveal his strategy to Soong. Instead, he let it be known in various indirect ways that he wished the Sino-Soviet negotiations to drag out at least until mid-July and probably longer. Meeting with T. V. Soong on June 9, Truman revealed the Yalta agreement and indicated generally that he would continue Roosevelt's commitment.[167] However, when Soong met with Grew two days later to discuss details, the Acting Secretary of State refused to give a precise definition of the American position. Soong wanted to know what was meant by the pledge to support the *"status quo"* in Outer Mongolia, and the "pre-eminent interests" of Russia in Dairen and the

---

(*Continued from preceding page*) and Cate, *Air Forces in World War II*, V, pp. 711, 741.)

Compare General Ismay's comment that Soviet help was "worthless from the military point of view." Also Churchill's remark: "We are in a good position there. We don't care if [Stalin] comes into the war against the Japanese or not. We don't need him now." (Ismay, *Memoirs*, p. 403;

Mikolajczyk, *The Pattern of Soviet Domination*, pp. 133–35.)

* Although this statement was made with respect to a specific cable sent to Soong after his arrival at Moscow, I have placed it here at the outset of the argument as it is my purpose to show that this course was followed from the end of June, with slight variations, until the middle of August.

Manchurian Railroad.[168] Grew's vague responses brought Soong at one point to ask just what the United States had supported. Grew would give no definite answers. Instead, he said he assumed no final agreement could be reached until the Big Three considered the problem at Potsdam.[169]

Such a statement from the Acting Secretary of State spoke volumes; the United States had no interest in an early conclusion of the Sino-Soviet negotiations. However, Soong still wished for more details, and unable to get them from Grew, he asked to see the President again.[170] On June 14 he probed Truman's stand, trying to get a more definite assessment, but he found that the President would not be pinned down.[171] He stated only that he wanted to get early Russian help in the war, but that he "wished to assure Dr. Soong that he would do nothing which would harm the interests of China, since China was a friend of the United States in the Far East."[172] Two days later, on June 16, Grew and Truman privately agreed that certain portions of the Yalta accord could not be settled until the Big Three met.[173] Shortly thereafter Grew included Far Eastern problems on the recommended agenda for Potsdam.[174]

At the same time that the President met with Soong he instructed General Hurley to inform Chiang Kai-shek of the Yalta commitment.[175] Hurley found that Chiang had already been told of the understanding by the Soviet ambassador.[176] He reported that the Chinese leader was pleased with Soviet assurances of support for Chinese territorial integrity and political independence under Nationalist sovereignty.[177] Since Chiang counted heavily upon Stalin's help against the Communists, and since China had no control over the areas in which Russia sought concessions, Hurley was certain there would be no difficulty in fulfilling the Yalta accord—"I am convinced that the Soviet Union and China will be able to reach an agreement quickly."*[178]

Thus, when Soong reached Moscow in an American Army plane at the end of June a curious reversal of roles had occurred.[179] The United States, which had originally agreed to press Chiang to accept

---

* General Wedemeyer later attempted to argue that Chiang was disappointed at the Yalta terms, and General Hurley later contended that he was trying to modify the Yalta terms, but these claims are not borne out by the 1945 documents. (See U.S. Senate, *Military Situation Far East*, pp. 2417, 2432, 2885–89.)

the Yalta terms, had now lost interest in completing the Sino-Soviet negotiations. In fact, Truman clearly wished to delay a settlement and was in no hurry to fulfill the conditions of Soviet entry into the war. On the other hand, Chiang Kai-shek greatly valued an agreement with Stalin which would redound to his benefit in the struggle against the Chinese Communists. He was only too happy to pay the Yalta price in an area where Chinese authority had not been exercised for years.[180] He had nothing to lose, for once the Red Army crossed the Manchurian border there would be little he could do to eliminate Soviet influence. Consequently, as Harriman has testified, when Soong reached Moscow, the Chinese Foreign Minister "made it clear to me that his Government was anxious to reach an agreement with the Soviet Union, and to this end he was prepared to make concessions which *we* considered went beyond the Yalta understanding."[181] Indeed, as soon as the negotiations began, the American ambassador found that instead of having to "take measures" to see that the Chinese agreed to Stalin's claims, he had to hold Soong back at a number of steps along the way.[182]

Stalin offered a four-piece package: a treaty of friendship and alliance which explicitly and publicly conveyed Soviet support to Chiang instead of the Communists; an agreement to recognize the independence of Outer Mongolia; an agreement regarding the Manchurian ports of Dairen and Port Arthur; and an agreement covering the Manchurian railroads.[183] The points where differences might arise were not of great importance. They inevitably involved the interpretation of the Yalta pledge to preserve the *status quo* in Outer Mongolia and to safeguard the "pre-eminent interests" of the Soviet Union in the Manchurian ports and railroads.[184]

China had not exercised control over Outer Mongolia since 1911, and Stalin interpreted the phrases to require *de jure* Chinese recognition of the country's acknowledged *de facto* independence.* He also argued that Soviet "pre-eminent interests" required Soviet administrative control over an internationalized regime in the port of Dairen; and joint Sino-Soviet ownership of railroads, with Soviet manage-

---

* The situation was anomalous in that both the Soviet Union and China paid lip service to Chinese sovereignty in the area, while the Mongolian government entered into independent relations with foreign powers. (*Conference of Berlin,* I, pp. 865–67.)

ment.*[185] These claims were far less than the pre-1905 rights Roosevelt had promised to support, and Chiang had no important objections to the substance of the Yalta accord.[186] Initially, however, he wished to avoid the politically difficult recognition of Outer Mongolian independence.[187] He also preferred Chinese administration over Dairen, and Chinese ownership of the railroads, with joint Sino-Soviet control and mixed management.[188]

As can be seen, none of these were important points of disagreement. The differences were trivial compared with Stalin's pledge to support Chiang materially and morally against the Communists, to withdraw Soviet troops from Manchuria after the fighting and, above all, to take Chiang's administrators with the Red Army into the Soviet zone of combat.[189] As Stalin and Soong began to bring their initial negotiating positions closer together, however, the United States intervened decisively. Despite the State Department's recommendation that Chiang "would be well advised" to recognize the independence of Outer Mongolia,[190] on July 4 Truman instructed Harriman to "informally" tell Soong that he did not believe the Yalta agreement necessitated recognition of the Mongolian government.[191] Byrnes, who had just taken office as Secretary of State, "was afraid Soong would . . . make additional concessions if he were in doubt about our attitude."[192] Hence, a further message was sent to Chungking urging Chiang not to go beyond the American interpretation of Yalta.[193]

Truman later characterized these efforts as "strong diplomatic support to China while T. V. Soong negotiated . . . in Moscow," but this description is misleading.[194] In fact, Truman attempted not to support Chiang, but to *restrain* him.† By now it was clear that the talks could be stretched out until the atomic test and the Potsdam Conference.[195] Thus, on July 6—the day Truman sailed for Potsdam— Harriman received a further instruction: he was now to tell the Rus-

---

* Later it was claimed that Stalin's demands went "substantially beyond the Yalta understanding." At the time, however, the State Department advised that Stalin's claims were "clearly more advantageous to China" than the terms calling for the complete restoration of the rights possessed by Russia prior to the Russo-Japanese War to which Roosevelt had agreed. (*Congressional Record*, Aug. 27, 1951, p. A5415; *Conference of Berlin*, I, pp. 864–72.) The State Department has also advanced the dubious argument that the general agreement to recognize Chinese sovereignty in Manchuria should have taken precedence over the specific terms regarding the restoration of previous rights. (*Ibid.*, p. 870.)

† This is sometimes obscured, because despite *Chiang's* desire for agreement, *Soong* did not wish to be personally responsible for yielding on the politically touchy issues. (*Conference of Berlin*, II, pp. 1245–46.)

sians and Chinese that the United States wanted no final agreement to be concluded until the American government had been fully consulted. At an "appropriate time" the United States would also like to make certain that the treaties provided for nondiscriminatory treatment against third parties in the operation of the ports, railroads, and trading arrangements in the area.[196] This would ensure that America's traditional "Open Door" policy would be protected. Finally, Harriman was told that the United States could not accept Stalin's interpretation of the "pre-eminent" Soviet interests in the ports and railroads.[197] Following these instructions, the American ambassador secured Soong's promise that no agreement would be concluded until Truman had been consulted.[198] Harriman then advised Soong to break off his negotiations with Stalin.[199]

As these diplomatic efforts went forward, military planning placed less and less reliance on the Soviet Union. On July 3, the Joint Chiefs instructed General Arnold to reserve four cities for attack by the atomic bomb.[200] On July 4 the British formally approved the use of the new weapon against Japan.[201] On July 11, the Joint Chiefs recommended that only after other competing demands had been met should Russia be sent Lend-Lease equipment for possible use in the Japanese war.[202] And on the eve of the Potsdam Conference Admiral Leahy rejected the suggestion that he "take up with the President as soon as possible the question of Lend-Lease to Russia." He felt the matter "was involved with the date that Russia might enter the war against Japan and that the date might not be determined at this conference, since it might depend upon agreement between Russia and China."[203]

While the American government laid its plans on the assumption that Sino-Soviet agreement would not be reached, however, Chiang Kai-shek and T. V. Soong made renewed efforts to conclude the negotiations. "The fact is that in spite of the position I took Soong gave in on several points to achieve his objectives," Harriman later testified.[204] Chiang sent Soong new instructions: he was now to yield to the Soviet position regarding Outer Mongolia. Soong was instructed to suggest that a plebiscite be held and to promise that China would accord *de jure* recognition to a new independent status at the war's end. In exchange for this concession, Chiang asked for specific pledges of Soviet help against the Communists.[205]

Stalin too was anxious to complete the negotiations. On July 10 he accepted Chiang's offer. He "stated categorically that he would support only the National government in China and that all the military forces in China must come under the control of the government."[206] Now the only points in dispute concerned the minor questions of control and management for Dairen and the Manchurian railroads.[207]

At this juncture, Harriman and T. V. Soong considered their next step. The Chinese Foreign Minister had already agreed not to complete the negotiations until Truman had been consulted.[208] With the Big Three Conference (and the atomic test) less than a week off, Harriman reported that if the United States held to its interpretation of the Yalta agreement, the negotiations would be delayed at least that long.[209] Truman and Byrnes, now in mid-Atlantic aboard the cruiser *Augusta*, radioed back instructing Harriman to say that although the United States did not want to act as interpreter, they believed the Chinese should not meet the Russian position regarding the port of Dairen and the railroads. Harriman was also told to reaffirm the American demand that no final agreement be concluded until the United States had been consulted.[210] This message, together with Soong's previous assurances, precluded final agreement. The Chinese Foreign Minister now followed Harriman's advice and, despite Stalin's protests, broke off the talks and left for Chungking on July 14.[211] Harriman reported that Soong was willing to leave the final negotiations in Truman's hands.*[212]

Thus, the strategy of delay had been fully implemented. Truman looked forward with great optimism as he considered the leverage the July 16 atomic test might give to two faces of his diplomacy[213]—now the Manchurian negotiations would be completed only after the "master card" had been demonstrated; and, with luck, the war might be dramatically ended with the Red Army still stalled on the far side of the Manchurian border.†

---

* For more information on these discussions see Feis, *China Tangle*, pp. 315–21; *Japan Subdued*, pp. 60–61; *Between War and Peace*, pp. 113–14; Truman, *Year of Decisions*, pp. 315–21; Byrnes, *Speaking Frankly*, p. 205; *All in One Lifetime*, pp. 290–91; U.S. Dept. of State, *Relations with China*, pp. 114–25; *Congressional Record*, Aug. 27, 1951, pp. A5410–16.

† Ehrman, misunderstanding this subtle point, thinks the United States "did not intend to seek actively to prevent Russia from declaring war. . . . " (*Grand Strategy*, p. 292.)

Under the influence of the new strategy, American military policy had gone through radical reversals in the few months of Truman's Presidency. From the early judgment that Russian entry was "a prerequisite to a landing in the Japanese homeland," it had shifted to the late-April decision that "early Russian entry . . . is no longer necessary." Finally, Truman's ultimate conclusion had been reached: *"If the test should fail, then it would be even more important to us to bring about a surrender before we had to make a physical conquest. . . ."*[214]

American diplomacy had followed suit. At Yalta, Roosevelt had promised to "take measures" on "advice from Marshal Stalin" to arrange Chiang Kai-shek's concurrence in the conditions for Soviet entry into the war. The American ambassador had received a stern directive: "We should not permit the Chinese Government to gain the impression that we are prepared to assume responsibility as 'adviser' to it in its relations with the U.S.S.R."[215] Truman, however, had reconsidered Roosevelt's arrangements and in the middle of May had decided to postpone fulfillment of his predecessor's pledges. By mid-June his policy had come full circle; the American ambassador now coached the Chinese Foreign Minister in his every move. And the Soong mission, originally designed to induce an early Soviet declaration of war, now served quite another purpose. Contesting minor railroad and port issues, American diplomacy utilized the mission to execute a carefully articulated stalling action; as the President and his advisers waited for the atomic bomb, the Soong negotiations were carefully set in the path of the Red Army poised for its assault across the Manchurian border.

CHAPTER V

The Tactics of the Potsdam Conference (I)*

The President was tremendously pepped up by [the report of the successful atomic test] and spoke to me of it again and again when I saw him. He said it gave him an entirely new feeling of confidence and he thanked me for having come to the Conference and being present to help him in this way.

—Secretary of War
Henry L. Stimson
July 21, 1945

A face-to-face meeting with Stalin had originally played no part in President Truman's approach to Manchuria and the intimately related question of Soviet participation in the Japanese war. Despite the President's June comment that it was important to meet with the Soviet Premier in order to insure an early Russian declaration of war, the decision to hold a heads-of-government meeting so soon after Yalta had initially derived from entirely different considerations. The original motivation had been a desire to maintain the pressure of the immediate showdown approach; and the chief concern had been to

---

*I have chosen the word "tactics" for the title of this and the next chapter to emphasize that in no way can the essay be considered a history of the Potsdam negotiations. Many complicated and important questions are treated only briefly. Other questions are not dealt with at all. I have, however, taken up the substantive issues Truman and Byrnes felt to be most important (Byrnes, *Speaking Frankly*, pp. 67–68), and the reader is referred to *Conference of Berlin*, I and II, for a detailed record of the meeting.

reduce or eliminate Soviet influence in Eastern and Central Europe.*

The President's decision to delay a confrontation with Stalin implied no abandonment of this fundamental approach. Although Truman's conciliatory attitude during May and June has led many observers to believe that Truman was determined to follow Roosevelt's broadly cooperative approach, in fact, the firm line of policy initiated in April had been set aside only as a temporary tactical maneuver as the President awaited the outcome of the atomic test. Hopkins's resolution of the Polish issue only removed the chosen symbol of the President's policy; but there was no change in the fundamental objective. The Polish issue had taken on special significance mainly because it had seemed to afford an opportunity to establish precedents for all of the liberated countries† and now the basic question once more came to the fore.

Thus, even as Hopkins negotiated in Moscow, the President and his advisers laid plans to renew the firm approach to political and economic problems in Eastern and Central Europe. Truman told Grew this would be the "fundamental subject" of his meeting with Stalin.[1] And on June 15, the President directed Admiral Leahy to prepare an agenda for the Conference. The restrained approach could now be abandoned. It was time, he stated, "to take the offensive."[2]

Originally, three powerful considerations had given Truman confidence that his firm approach to the Soviet Union might succeed. Not only had it been decided that Soviet help was no longer needed *for an invasion* of Japan, but the American Army had been at its greatest strength in Europe; and the leverage of American economic power had seemed irresistible at a time when the Soviet government was beginning to consider its vast postwar reconstruction requirements.‡ These fundamental considerations did not change during the two summer months of conciliation and delay.

Despite Churchill's earlier fears, Stimson's promise that redeployment would not materially weaken American strength on the Conti-

---

* See above, pp. 87–88. This of course, continued to be the primary motivation. See, for example, Byrnes's statement: "We anticipated little discussion at Potsdam about the Japanese phase of the war. . . . [In preparation] we concentrated on the sub-

jects incident to winding up the European conflict. . . . " (Strauss, *Men and Decisions,* p. 437.)

† See above, pp. 70–71.

‡ See Chapter I.

nent was fulfilled; as Potsdam approached there were still more than three million American and British troops in Europe.* Prospects for the future also looked bright; the Joint Chiefs of Staff reported there would be excess troops on the Continent well into 1946.[3] And on July 5, the day before Truman embarked for the Conference, the House Select Committee on Post-War Military Policy gave approval to proposals for a peacetime military conscription and training program, an action which stimulated hope that American conventional power would not be dissipated immediately after hostilities.[4] Secretary of State Byrnes—acting less than twenty-four hours after taking office on July 3—reminded the President that American troops in Europe would be of primary importance "from the political aspect."[5] Byrnes thereby officially affirmed his support for the consensus that, as Grew put it, without adequate power "our diplomacy becomes weak and ineffective."[6]

Similarly, as Potsdam approached, there was no diminution in American economic bargaining strength, and, indeed, the President's advantage in this respect had considerably increased. Truman intended to offer economic aid to Stalin, and as we have seen, the first item on his agenda was "Credits to the U.S.S.R."[7] But whereas in April the President had only been able to speak of his hope that Congress would make this source of negotiating power available to his administration, now he was in a far stronger position. As the President left for his meeting with Stalin, both the Senate and House committees considering postwar financing gave an extremely friendly reception to Lend-Lease Administrator Leo T. Crowley as he presented the administration's official proposals. Crowley encountered few objections to legislation to increase the lending authority of the Export-Import Bank from $700 million to a full $3.5 billion in the first year of peace. Even the eminently conservative Senator Robert A. Taft agreed with Crowley's suggestion that Russia could receive a first-year credit of approximately one billion dollars.[8] Taft thought this a "fair amount."[9]

Such support undoubtedly added to Truman's confidence that he would be able to dispose of large-scale credits in his bargaining with

---

* Information provided by the U.S. Department of Defense. Estimated world-wide strength of American (excluding British) forces on August 31, 1945: 11,913,639; esti-mated total for USSR on the same date: 10,600,000. See also Eisenhower, *Crusade in Europe*, p. 429.

Stalin. Additionally, however, the President knew he would have control over other resources certain to be of great importance to the Soviet government. Stalin had already pressed his strong interest in German industrial reparations and in a division of the German fleet—and control over both of these was largely in Western hands. Moreover, there were other bargaining counters available, for it was known that Stalin would seek Anglo-American agreement to a revision of the Montreux Convention governing the Dardanelles, to Soviet participation in a trusteeship over former Italian colonies, and to recognition of the governments established under Soviet auspices in the Balkans.[10]

But more important than any of these considerations, of course, was Truman's belief that the atomic bomb would almost certainly lend great power to his diplomacy. Indeed, the need to wait until the new force had been tested and demonstrated before discussing diplomatic issues with Stalin had been a controlling factor throughout the summer. The Potsdam meeting itself had been twice postponed for this reason. Now, in early July, as Truman has written, "Preparations were being rushed for the test atomic explosion in Alamogordo, New Mexico, at the time I had to leave for Europe, and on the voyage over I had been anxiously awaiting word on the results."[11] On the eve of his first meeting with the Soviet delegation, the President confidently told an associate: "If it explodes, as I think it will, I'll certainly have a hammer on those boys!"[12]

With such an array of diplomatic power at his disposal the President was evidently quite hopeful that although his initial showdown had been frustrated, a new "offensive" might succeed. The primary objective remained the promotion of economic and political stability throughout Europe—a goal regarded as the *sine qua non* both of world peace and of American security.* For one thing, this meant a commitment to a strong Continental economy which had powerful implications for the American approach to Germany.† But in Eastern Europe, "if the political situation . . . could be adjusted so that Hungary, Yugoslavia, Rumania, and Bulgaria, as well as Poland and Aus-

---

* See above, pp. 100–3, 125–26.   † See below, pp. 209–21.

tria, could all have governments of their own people's choosing," Truman believed, "this would help us in our plans for peace."[18]

Thus, as in Poland, although American diplomats were concerned with possible restrictions on free trading arrangements,[14] the first objective was to secure reasonably representative and Western-oriented governments which would promote democracy through free elections.[15] As in Poland, as Crowley told Congress, economic leverage would provide one source of strength in the attempt to achieve this objective in each country.[16] But, first it would be necessary to reduce or eliminate dominant Soviet influence. It was the hope of American diplomacy that the Soviet Union would agree to establish representative governments throughout its zone of military control. And it was the belief of American diplomats that early free elections would dissipate whatever remained of the substantial Soviet wartime authority in the area.[17]

At this late date in the Cold War it is extremely difficult to recapture the assumptions and conceptions of American diplomacy in 1945. It must therefore be emphasized that at the time the optimistic American appraisal was not simply wishful thinking. Stalin's December 1944 abandonment of the Greek Communists seemed very real evidence of his willingness to cooperate. In France, Italy, and Belgium, the Communist parties, at the height of their influence because of their predominance in the resistance movements, meekly yielded much authority to Western-oriented governments.[18] In Finland, where Soviet influence was great, free elections had already taken place (in March).[19] In Austria, the Renner government established with Soviet support met the State Department's criterion as "representative."[20] In Czechoslovakia, President Eduard Benes reported no Soviet interference in political matters, American reporters were given free rein and the United States maintained satisfactory diplomatic relations.[21]

Even in Poland, the hope that early free elections would be held as pledged was strengthened when visiting Western correspondents were permitted unrestricted freedom and when wartime political controls restraining the Western-oriented groups were relaxed.*[22] To be sure,

---

* The political situation in Poland presented a mixed picture. However, American hopes were reinforced by reports, such as the one from the Western-oriented former premier, Mikolajczyk, that he was "hopeful that through the strength of the Peasant party a reasonable degree of freedom and (Continued on next page)

there were disturbing events at this time,[23] and at a later date the entire atmosphere was to change, but one cannot understand American strategy without recognizing that in the late summer of 1945 there seemed reasons to believe that Stalin might be prepared to work with the West: The actions of the Communist parties in France, Greece, and Italy, and Soviet support for democratic governments in Finland, Czechoslovakia, and Austria were of very real political significance: They yielded power to anti-Communist groups in the crucial formative period of postwar politics. For the Communists to attempt later to regain the lead would not be easy.*

Thus, though their hopes were later to be disappointed, as American diplomats surveyed the problems of Europe in the late summer of 1945, they were not deeply worried about problems in the West,[24] and they had considerable confidence that their plans for democratic governments might be implemented almost everywhere on the Continent.† Their confidence, however, did not easily extend to Southeastern Europe. For here, despite the fact that Communist armies found themselves supporting monarchies,[25] Stalin did not show the same attitude he exhibited elsewhere. And for this reason, the real focus of American attention was in the Balkans.‡

The immediate issues arose because the conduct of the war had given the Soviet Union predominant political power in Hungary, Bulgaria, and Rumania. American policy makers acknowledged, as the Acting Secretary of State advised the President on June 28, that "spheres of influence do in fact exist, and will probably continue to do so for some time to come."[26] Grew went on to comment: "In view of the actual Eastern European sphere and the Western Hemisphere bloc

---

(*Continued from preceding page*)
independence can be preserved now and that in time, after conditions in Europe become more stable and Russia turns her attention to her internal development, controls will be relaxed and Poland will be able to gain for herself her independence of life as a nation. . . . " (*Conference of Berlin*, I, p. 728.)

* For an illuminating account of how this policy appeared from the point of view of the more militant and independent Communists, see Djilas, *Conversations with Stalin*, especially pp. 12–13. Regarding the Soviet abandonment of the Greek Communists, see below, p. 182.

† Byrnes did not lose this confidence for a very long time. In July 1947—exactly two years after Potsdam—he was still convinced that there was no immediate danger of Communist revolution in Western Europe and his interest was still focused on Eastern Europe. If the other powers would "hold firm," he was certain that the Soviets would "retire in a very decent manner." (*Speaking Frankly*, pp. 294–95.)

‡ The term "the Balkans" does not properly include Hungary. However, the State Department regarded the problems of Hungary, Bulgaria, and Rumania as the same, and it is therefore convenient to use "the Balkans" in the loose sense common in many documents. This is also Churchill's usage. (*Triumph and Tragedy*, p. 227.)

. . . we are hardly in a position to frown upon the establishment of measures designed to strengthen the security of nations in other areas of the world . . ."[27] Despite this judgment, however, Grew and others did not hesitate to urge an active initiative to promote American policy objectives throughout the Soviet-controlled areas.[28]

The problems of implementing a policy designed to establish a new political and economic order within the Soviet area were considerable. American awareness that spheres of influence existed reflected not only the obvious fact that the Red Army occupied the entire region; equally important was the fact that the Soviet political position in each country had been acknowledged—and indeed, endorsed—by the United States and Britain in three separate agreements negotiated during the last months of the war.

The first was the famous arrangement initiated by Churchill and concluded between the Soviet Union and Britain after discussions lasting from May to October 1944. "Let us settle our affairs in the Balkans," Churchill had proposed to Stalin, and the two had agreed to acknowledge "90 per cent" Soviet influence in Rumania in exchange for "90 per cent" British influence in Greece. Additionally, Soviet influence was defined as "80 per cent" in Bulgaria, "80 per cent" in Hungary, and "50 per cent" in Yugoslavia.* Churchill had thus recognized varying degrees of Soviet predominance in three Balkan countries in exchange for a free hand in Greece and joint responsibility in Yugoslavia. In his report to the Cabinet on this accord, Churchill stressed the need to respect Soviet security requirements: "Thus it is seen that quite naturally Soviet Russia has vital interests in the countries bordering on the Black Sea, by one of whom, Rumania, she has been most wantonly attacked with twenty-six divisions, and with the other of whom, Bulgaria, she has ancient ties."[29]

Roosevelt had initially accepted the Churchill-Stalin arrangement for only a three-month trial period.[30] There is no doubt that the President had qualms about the idea of a division of responsibilities, but there was little he could do about it.[31] He allowed his ambassador to "observe" the negotiations between Churchill and Stalin, and although Harriman could not commit the President, neither did Roose-

---

* These final agreed percentages are taken from Woodward, *British Foreign Policy*, p. 308. Churchill's report (*Triumph and Trag-* *edy*, p. 227) gives only the initial British bid and neglects to discuss subsequent negotiation between Molotov and Eden.

velt instruct him to raise any objections.[32] Indeed, by mid-October Roosevelt had cabled Churchill and Stalin: "I am most pleased that you are reaching a meeting of your two minds. . . ."[33] More important than this general message of approval, however, was the fact that by early 1945 Roosevelt, fully aware of the meaning of his action,[34] had explicitly endorsed the general understanding when it was "translated"[35] into the terms of the armistice agreements for Hungary, Bulgaria, and Rumania.[36]

These second Balkan agreements granted the Soviet commander (who was also chairman of the Allied Control Commission in each instance) the same almost unlimited authority which the earlier Italian armistice had granted to the West.[37] In Rumania, Soviet authority was to continue without diminution until a peace treaty had been signed.[38] Reflecting the reduced percentages (as was explicitly understood),[39] the Bulgarian and Hungarian armistice terms vaguely allowed that Western representation on the Allied Control Commissions in the two countries might be increased in the "second phase" beginning after German capitulation and extending until the peace treaties had been signed.*

The Churchill-Stalin arrangements were tested in December 1944, when British troops were used to establish order in Greece.[40] "Stalin . . . adhered strictly and faithfully to our agreement of October," Churchill has written, "and during all the long weeks of fighting the Communists in the streets of Athens, not one word of reproach came from *Pravda* or *Izvestia*."[41] As Churchill was to point out, Stalin's respect for British predominance in Greece, "in spite of the fact that all this was most disagreeable to him . . ."[42] reaffirmed the validity of the basic accord and underscored the reciprocal obligations-toward the Soviet sphere undertaken by the West.[43]

The Churchill-Stalin arrangement, the armistice agreements, and the Greek incident established the framework for the early 1945 discussions at Yalta. Here the third agreement covering the Balkans was negotiated. Before the Conference, the State Department—which had

---

* It is quite surprising that scholars have paid so little attention to the only detailed agreements relating to Southeastern Europe. The armistice texts are readily available. (See Senate Committee on Foreign Relations, *A Decade of American Foreign Policy,* 1941–49, pp. 455, 482, 487, 494.)

objected to Roosevelt's acknowledgment of the first informal Churchill-Stalin accord and his endorsement of the armistices[44]—tried to convince the President that his position had to be reconsidered.[45] On the eve of the Conference, the State Department argued that Western influence in the area could be re-established only if democratic governments were promoted and free elections were held. In addition to a general "Declaration" of intent, the Department urged the President to propose a new consultative agency with real power to assist the countries "in setting up governmental authorities broadly representative of all democratic elements in the population."[46]

Roosevelt, however, was not prepared to challenge the Soviet prerogatives he had so recently endorsed. Byrnes reports that he "did not like" the State Department's proposal.[47] And shortly before the Conference, Stettinius told Eden of Roosevelt's "misgivings."[48] Under considerable pressure from his own delegation (among them Byrnes, who was "greatly impressed" with the proposal), during the Yalta meeting Roosevelt reluctantly agreed to propose a considerably modified version of the Declaration.[49] This pledged the powers to consult "where in their judgment conditions require" assistance to establish democratic governments.[50] The requirement of unanimity even before consultations could begin, of course, acknowledged Soviet authority and veto rights in the area. But Roosevelt gave further and more specific definition to his understanding of the spheres-of-influence arrangement. Without hesitation, the President rejected the heart of the State Department proposal, excising the provisions which would have established an agency with power to implement the broad ideals. Moreover, Secretary of State Stettinius was authorized to remove even the few phrases of the general Declaration which pledged the powers to "establish appropriate machinery for the carrying out of the joint responsibility set forth in this Declaration."*[51]

Similarly, at Yalta Roosevelt made no attempt to reconsider the specific conditions of the armistice agreements he had signed, and it is apparent from discussions before and during the Conference that the President regarded the broadly phrased Declaration primarily as a device to offset domestic criticism of the *de facto* spheres-of-influence

---

* It is difficult to understand how Feis can characterize these as "some minor changes of language." (*Churchill, Roosevelt, Stalin*, p. 550.)

understanding.* Truman's special representative for the Balkans later commented: "The facile use without any definition of such controversial terms [as 'democratic elements,' 'free elections,' et cetera] would alone be sufficient reason to doubt the soundness of the document as a basis for joint action."[52]

Indeed, two weeks after Yalta, when the Soviet government exercised its prerogatives under the armistice agreement by intervening in Rumania to establish a new government under Petru Groza, Roosevelt (like Churchill), refusing to make more than a mild gesture on the basis of the Declaration, suggested only that consultations might be in order.[53] When the Soviet government rejected this suggestion by pointing out that their actions were within the terms of the armistice agreement,[54] much to the dismay of the State Department, Roosevelt refused to pursue the matter.† American representatives remained at their posts in Rumania, and the President told associates that the situation could not be considered a "test case" of relations with Russia.‡[55]

---

* The Secretary of State's special assistant supported the Declaration as "the most powerful antidote that we can devise for the rapidly crystallizing opposition in this country" to the United Nations idea. Stettinius himself offered it to Roosevelt because something was needed "to reassure public opinion in the United States and elsewhere." (*Conferences at Malta and Yalta,* pp. 98, 101.)

† Molotov's rejection argued that even the mild American *démarche* "envisaged a broader interpretation of the Crimea decisions . . . than corresponds with the facts. The declaration in question . . . is based upon the presence . . . of Allied Control Commissions." (See *Conference of Berlin,* I, p. 398.)

‡ Churchill later wrote: "If I pressed [Stalin] too much he might say, 'I did not interfere with your action in Greece; why do you not give me the same latitude in Rumania?' . . . I was sure it would be a mistake to embark on such an argument." (*Triumph and Tragedy,* p. 420–21.) It is often claimed that the Churchill-Stalin deal was meant to last only until the end of the war, and that Soviet unilateral actions in the liberated countries violated the Yalta agreement. (Churchill, *Triumph and Tragedy,* p. 227; Byrnes, *Speaking Frankly,* p. 73.) Neither claim stands up to careful examination.

Although Churchill initially tried to secure Roosevelt's and the Cabinet's agreement to his arrangements with the argument that they would last only for the duration of the war, and although in 1953 he was to make the same claim, there is no evidence that Churchill ever reached such an understanding *with Stalin.* On the contrary, it was only too obvious that the agreement would have lasting influence, and it was precisely for this reason—to protect the British position in Greece—that Churchill promoted it. Furthermore, *after* German capitulation, in correspondence and talks with Stalin, Churchill explicitly acknowledged the continuing obligations of the arrangement. (*Triumph and Tragedy,* pp. 74, 75, 77–78, 227, 560, 636; Woodward, *British Foreign Policy,* pp. 307–08.)

More important, however, is the fact that the agreement was directly translated into the armistice terms, which specifically endorsed Soviet predominant influence. Again, though the West hoped to improve its status after the war, the agreements make no provision for this. As Lord Strang has stated, the result of even the more moderate Bulgarian armistice terms "was to open the way for exclusive Soviet influence." (Strang, *At Home and Abroad,* p. 225.) And indeed, before Roosevelt agreed to the terms of the armistices, Harriman carefully and explicitly warned him that they acknowledged Soviet control over internal politics. (Feis, *Churchill, Roosevelt, Stalin,* pp. 415–16, 448–57.)

Finally, besides the fact that the broadly

A REVERSAL OF VIEWPOINT

WITH THE DEATH of Roosevelt, however, the State Department found itself with a second opportunity to press the case for an active American interest in the Soviet sphere of influence. It now seemed possible that actions to implement the broad ideals of the Yalta Declaration might be taken. By May 10, Secretary Stimson, sensing a State Department campaign to commit the new President, and fearing the consequences of a new initiative, noted that it was "time to take precautions against a stampede into a dangerous reversal of our viewpoint . . . namely, not to get mixed up in a Balkan row."[56] On the same day, he advised Truman: "We have made up our minds on the broad policy that it was wise not to get into the Balkan mess even if the thing seemed to be disruptive of policies which the State Department thought were wise." He reminded the new President that "we have taken that policy right from the beginning, Mr. Roosevelt having done it himself or having been a party to it himself."[57]

At first, Truman seemed briefly to accept Stimson's advice.[58] But during the period immediately preceding Hopkins's mission, true to his basic view that the United States had a vital interest in the problems of the entire Continent, the President accepted the strong views of the State Department by committing himself to an active policy of intervention in an area controlled by Yugoslavia.[59] By the end of May, Truman had moved five divisions to the Brenner Pass and had shifted part of the Adriatic fleet north in a show of power which forced Tito to accept Western control of the important port of Trieste.*[60]

---

phrased Yalta Declaration in no way affected the armistice terms, as has been shown, Roosevelt quickly agreed to strike all of the operative clauses from the State Department's proposal. The Declaration does indeed proclaim the ideal of "concerting the policies of the three Powers," but after Roosevelt's alterations, what was left was an agreement to consult *only* "when, in the opinion of the three governments, conditions . . . make such action necessary." (*Conferences at Malta and Yalta*, p. 972.) Hence, the Russians were accorded full power to veto even the suggestion of consultations. Though the Secretary of State based much of his rhetoric on the Yalta Declaration, Byrnes was only too aware that its specific terms justified Soviet rejection of American approaches. (*Speaking Frankly*, p. 34.)

For other information on the rights of the various powers under the Churchill-Stalin deal, the armistice arrangements, and the Yalta Declaration, see *Conference of Berlin*, I, pp. 211–17; Hull, *Memoirs*, II, p. 1458; Kennan, *Russia and the West*, p. 366; Roberts, *Rumania*, p. 266; Dennett and Johnson, *Negotiating with the Russians*, pp. 176–77.

* For more information on this question, see Grew Papers, May 12–June 12, 1945; Stimson Diary, same dates; Feis, *Between* (Continued on next page)

This firm action, however, was taken in an area of the Balkans which—despite the Churchill-Stalin agreement to share responsibility—was not directly related to vital Soviet interests. As Grew noted after a meeting with the President on May 14, "It was generally agreed that Tito was not very sure of himself and it was not believed that Stalin would give him unlimited support."*[61] In areas of the Balkans more intimately related to Soviet interests, Truman initially showed similar enthusiasm for a firm American approach, but soon his actions became more subtly involved in the broader strategy of delay.

In the first days of May, at a time when Truman was still committed to the immediate showdown approach in Poland, he suggested to Acting Secretary Grew that it would be wise for the United States to demonstrate its interest by calling home American representatives in protest over the situation in Rumania and Bulgaria.[62] Although the President quickly changed his mind and withdrew this proposal, he did not lose interest in Balkan affairs.[63] Even as he planned Hopkins's conciliatory mission to Moscow, the President ordered new State Department studies of the problem of the Balkans.[64] And despite the fact that Churchill personally informed Truman of his arrangement with Stalin, and despite the President's understanding that "Russian dominance in these countries had thus been recognized,"†[65] Truman now accepted the State Department's view that

---

(*Continued from preceding page*)
War and Peace, pp. 40–46; Feis, *Churchill, Roosevelt, Stalin*, pp. 627–30; Clark, *Calculated Risk*, pp. 443–45; Truman, *Truman Speaks*, pp. 70–71; Truman, *Year of Decisions*, pp. 244–45; Churchill, *Triumph and Tragedy*, pp. 552–55; Bryant, *Triumph in the West 1943–46*, p. 468.

* Truman's attitude is illuminated by Stimson's diary entry: "The Yugoslavs under Tito are retiring . . . and it has had such an inspiring effect upon our chief, the President, that he had given Grew instructions . . . to give them force if they sought to break back on the agreements. McCloy and I both thought that was a little overzealous . . . " (Diary, June 12, 1945.) This is another case which shows how Truman gave priority to establishing American influence in Eastern Europe and the Balkans. General Marshall's advice that a strong stand on the Polish question might jeopardize the Japanese war effort had been rejected in late April. Marshall advanced the same argument in mid-May against a

show of force regarding Trieste. Leahy noted that Marshall told the President that "every effort at any cost should be made to avoid a clash." (Leahy Diary, May 11, 1945, p. 81.) But Truman once more rejected his advice.

The point is of considerable importance for it is sometimes asserted that Truman's conciliatory diplomacy vis-à-vis Europe in late May and June derived from agreement with Marshall that the war effort might be jeopardized. As has been argued before, and as the Trieste incident shows again, Truman was not in agreement with Marshall on this point. (For another interpretation, see Feis, *Churchill, Roosevelt, Stalin*, pp. 599–600.)

† See also Byrnes's statement that "we knew they had reached the informal understanding that, if the British found it necessary to take military action to quell internal disorders in Greece, the Soviets would not interfere. In return, the British would recognize the right of the Soviets to take the lead in maintaining order in Rumania." (*Speaking Frankly*, p. 53.)

the Yalta Declaration provided a basis for American action in the liberated areas. Consequently, Truman devoted much time during the period from early May to early July to the study of ways in which he might reverse Roosevelt's decision and implement the broad ideals of the Declaration once the temporary period of conciliation had come to an end.[66]

In each country the situation facing the President was slightly different. Nowhere had the Russians installed Communist premiers. The State Department reported that in Hungary ("80 per cent" Soviet influence) power was exercised by "a coalition government headed by a conservative general [which] includes representatives of the five principal parties of the center and the left. . . . There has been no attempt . . . to substitute a purely leftist regime for the present coalition government." However, the State Department believed that Communist political strength was increasing due to the presence of the Red Army. There were also minor complaints that the American members of the Control Commission suffered from restrictions under the Soviet interpretation of the accepted rules of procedure.[67]

In Bulgaria ("80 per cent" Soviet influence), the situation appeared to be slightly less favorable to the West. Four days after the armistice had been signed in October 1944 a popularly supported *coup d'état* had installed a "Fatherland Front" government under Colonel Kimon Georgiev.[68] The new premier (whom the State Department's representative described as "a true conservative")[69] and four other Cabinet ministers were members of the moderately conservative Zveno party. Four other Cabinet posts were controlled by Agrarians, four by Communists, and three by Social Democrats.[70] Although the Fatherland Front enjoyed considerable popularity in the country, the State Department considered it to be Communist-dominated.[71] Fearing that an early election controlled by the government might give endorsement to the existing power distribution, the State Department had proposed tripartite observation to ensure free elections even while the war was in progress, but when this suggestion was rejected the matter had been taken no further.[72]

In Rumania ("90 per cent" Soviet influence), the Groza government installed by the Soviets shortly after Yalta had now consolidated its position. Although the government was responsive to the Soviet occupation authorities, the political situation was not clearly defined. Molotov had publicly proclaimed that the Soviet Union had no intention of "changing the existing social order";[73] Groza himself, a prosperous landowner and industrialist, had established a long anti-Communist record;*[74] and the Russians permitted widespread publicity for speeches by Cabinet members attacking Communist directives.[75] As in Bulgaria, however, the State Department believed the Groza government to be Communist-dominated.[76] In both Bulgaria and Rumania, the State Department was also disturbed because the Soviet Union had already concluded bilateral trading agreements which paid little heed to the Department's desire for more open, multilateral trading arrangements.[77]

During the conciliatory months of May and June, Truman made no major effort to intervene directly in Balkan affairs. The only manifestation of his interest was an attempt to take advantage of the provisions of the Hungarian and Bulgarian armistice agreements which hinted at increased American representation on the Control Commissions after German capitulation. The President attempted to make the most of these slight loopholes in the agreements which authorized Soviet predominance in the area: Although the degree of representation had not been defined for the "second phase," and although there was no basis for such a modification in the Rumanian armistice, Truman instructed Ambassador Harriman to propose that the United States and Britain be accorded veto power over the actions of the Soviet commander in all three countries.†[78]

This initial attempt to undo the Churchill-Stalin understanding and the armistice agreements was greeted skeptically in London. Many months earlier, the Foreign Office had concluded that to press the Russians in Southeastern Europe would endanger the hope of postwar cooperation. It was believed that since the area had never experienced Western democracy, and since the war had "proletarianized" the population, there was likely to be far greater internal demand for stability than for Western political institutions. Opposition to the Soviet Union in an area vital to its security would be of little service to British policy.[79] Indeed, until the death of Roosevelt, none of the Big Three had acted upon the assumption that Soviet predominance could

---

* Byrnes's later reference to Groza as "the Communist leader" is mistaken. (*Speaking Frankly*, p. 51.)

† Harriman made his approach regarding Hungary on June 1, Rumania on June 12, and Bulgaria on June 14. (*Conference of Berlin*, I, pp. 368, 399, 372–73, 364.)

be directly challenged. Now, of the Big Three, Truman alone wished to act. The American ambassador in London reported that the Foreign Office believed it "useless" to make an approach to the Russians —"Moscow would never allow itself to be maneuvered into position where Brit[ish] and Am[erican] Rep[resentatives] would be able to outvote Soviets. . . ."[80]

Truman disregarded this judgment and went ahead with his approach to Moscow. Undoubtedly to the surprise of the Foreign Office, the American initiative met with a favorable response. Stalin replied to Harriman's request with a major concession in the Balkans —he would agree to modify the armistice terms so as to permit a Western veto on the Hungarian Control Commission, and he proposed that American and British representatives be accorded the privilege of prior consultation in Bulgaria and Rumania.[81] Stalin's offer was made shortly after Hopkins had yielded on the Polish question— at a time when General Deane found a generally friendly atmosphere in Moscow[82]—but within a few weeks (during the Potsdam Conference) the Soviet Premier went even further: He accepted the full American proposal, agreeing that Western representatives in Bulgaria and Rumania would be accorded the same powerful veto position as in Hungary.[83]

Truman's successful attempt to increase the status of his representatives in the Balkan countries was only an interim measure. A far more important policy objective was the promotion of democratic, Western-oriented governments pledged to early free elections. Although the President had no doubts about the desirability of reorganizing the governments in Rumania and Bulgaria, he did not present this demand to Moscow during May and June. In Poland, the President had been forced to abandon a hastily conceived showdown over the same issue once Stimson's more subtle strategy had been accepted, and he did not make the mistake of attempting a premature confrontation on the Balkans. Instead, as in his handling of Far Eastern matters, Truman simply stalled.

Although the President made no official moves, he lost no interest in the problem. When, for example, on May 10 Grew brought him a long cable from George Kennan, the chargé d'affaires in Moscow, warning of the deeper implications of Soviet Balkan policy, Truman, much interested in the report, told the Acting Secretary he was already "fully alive" to the danger.[84] Similarly, although in early June he had told Grew and Ambassador Lane it would be desirable not to exercise too much pressure while Hopkins negotiated, the President made it absolutely clear that in due course he would act decisively to remove "the Soviet blackout" from the Balkans as well as the rest of Central and Eastern Europe.[85]

Although the President's summer strategy of delay in the Balkans dictated patience and the postponement of an American initiative, there were strong indications, even to those not privy to his private calculations, that Truman was not prepared to accept the *status quo*. The decision not to accept the Georgiev and Groza governments was carried forward by Truman's determined refusal to recognize either government after the collapse of Germany. Since opposition political leaders throughout the Balkans had already approached American representatives, searching for some sign that the United States might champion their cause against the Soviet Union, the negative act of refusing to accord diplomatic recognition took on ever-increasing importance in the domestic politics of each country. It now became possible to hope that the United States would not accept the established governments.* Because Truman's inaction was a powerful source of instability during the immediate postwar jockeying for political position, as the President's Balkan representative Mark Ethridge has written, "the withholding of its accord" became an "important American instrument of pressure."[86]

Fully aware that the absence of American recognition was a destabilizing force in the Soviet sphere, Stalin raised the matter directly with Truman three weeks after German capitulation: "More than eight months have passed since Rumania and Bulgaria broke off relations with Hitler Germany, signed an armistice with the Allied countries, and entered the war on the Allied side. . . . The Soviet Government deems it proper and timely right away to resume diplomatic relations."[87] But the strategy of delay in the Balkans, as elsewhere, was characterized by studied inaction. Although Truman did not judge it timely to press his own demands, neither would he yield anything of importance. His response to Stalin's plea arrived in Moscow on June 2, while Hopkins was still negotiating, but the Presiden-

---

* See below, pp. 256–58, 266–67.

tial representative, fearing that the cable might upset his conciliatory diplomacy, recommended that it be delivered only after he had left the Soviet Union.[88] Hence it was only on June 7 that Stalin received Truman's complaint that the governments were "neither representative of nor responsive to the will of the people." Truman did not reveal his demand that the governments be changed, however. Vaguely promising "it is my sincere hope that the time may soon come when I can accredit formal diplomatic representatives," Truman only suggested that it might be well to have discussions "in order to concert more effectively our policies and actions in this area."[89]

Stalin's response implicitly directed attention to the absence of free elections and the subservience to American and British forces of the governments in the West: "The opportunities for the democratic elements in Rumania and Bulgaria are not less than, say, in Italy, with which the Governments of the United States and the Soviet Union have already resumed diplomatic relations." The Soviet Premier once more demanded immediate diplomatic recognition,[90] but on June 19 Truman replied: "I am giving this matter further study. . . . I therefore propose that we discuss it at our forthcoming meeting."[91] Stalin's final pre-Potsdam communication was abrupt: "I maintain as heretofore that there is no justification for further delay in resuming diplomatic relations with Rumania and Bulgaria."[92]

Truman's basic attitude disturbed the Foreign Office. Just before Potsdam, in a conversation with Assistant Secretary of State James C. Dunn, Sir Alexander Cadogan "expressed disagreement with our reluctance to conclude peace with Bulgaria, Rumania and Hungary and reiterated UK view that treaties of peace would solve our difficulties in those countries. . . ."[93] Despite the British objections, however, as before, Truman simply ignored the advice. Thus, until the eve of the Potsdam meeting, on the one hand, the President refused to recognize the governments and, on the other, he held back his demand that they be changed. As in the Far East, he postponed action on the fundamental issue.

As has been shown, in general, Truman's strategy of delay was conceived in terms of the power the atomic bomb would eventually add to American diplomacy. From the very first, his decision to postpone a confrontation with Stalin had derived from the belief that the atomic bomb would relate not only to the Far East, but to European

issues as well. Both Secretary Stimson and Secretary Byrnes had urged
this view, and Byrnes, having stressed that the weapon might allow the
United States to dictate her own terms, had specifically argued that it
would make Russia more manageable in Eastern Europe. It is not
surprising, therefore, to find that the President's own view of the Balkan issue followed the logic of this approach.

Indeed, on June 6, Truman had been specific in stating to Stimson
that once the new weapon was demonstrated it would be useful in
achieving a satisfactory solution to the Balkan as well as to the Polish
and Manchurian problems. He said that in this area, too, he believed a
settlement would be reached when the Russians granted *quid pro quos*
in exchange for admitting them to partnership for international control of the new atomic force.[94]

At the same time that he offered this view, the President and his
Secretary of War had discussed the best tactics to employ in approaching the broad problem. As we have seen, Stimson had advised Truman
that "the greatest complication" would arise if the bomb had not been
conclusively demonstrated before the meeting with Stalin. Although
Truman had postponed the Potsdam Conference in order to give the
physicists more time, Stimson had "pointed out that there might still
be delay." He had also told the President the Interim Committee
recommended "that there should be no revelation to Russia or anyone
else of our work in [the atomic bomb] until the first bomb had been
successfully laid on Japan." If, as Stimson thought possible, this had
not occurred by the time of the meeting, and if "the Russians should
bring up the subject and ask us to take them in as partners," the
Secretary had urged that "our attitude was to . . . make the simple
statement that as yet we were not quite ready to do it."[95]

In this discussion Stimson had underscored a new and important
point. Although in mid-May he had urged only that Truman should
not "have it out with Russia" until he *knew* for certain "whether this
[was] a weapon in our hands or not," during the Interim Committee
discussions the strategy of delay had become much more specific. In
the first week of June, Stimson advised that mere knowledge of the
success of the atomic test would not be enough to influence the power
realities; it would first be necessary to publicly demonstrate the
weapon by "laying it on Japan" before Stalin could be expected to be
greatly impressed. If the heads-of-government meeting took place be-

fore the battle demonstration there would be "the greatest complication."

Truman's agreement with this new recommendation had profoundly ironic implications. Throughout the month preceding the Truman-Stalin meeting, Stimson's fear that the bomb might not be publicly demonstrated before the negotiations proved to be only too correct. Although, as J. Robert Oppenheimer has testified, "I don't think there was a time where we worked harder at the speed-up than in the period *after* the German surrender,"[96] by the end of June it was certain that the bomb would not be "laid on Japan" until early August.[97] Thus, Truman's twice-postponed meeting still would occur a few weeks too early for the atomic bomb to strengthen his diplomatic hand. In fact, as Stimson advised, the President should not even reveal the weapon to Stalin until it was shown in a dramatic battle demonstration.

The President now had no alternative but to go ahead with the arrangements for a mid-July heads-of-government conference. But it was clear that he could not yet press his diplomatic demands to a showdown. Ironically, the logic of his position ensured that the much heralded confrontation with Stalin could only be a modified continuation of the strategy of delay! Undoubtedly the hobbles the technological timetable now placed upon the President's diplomacy must have been extremely frustrating, for he was committed to a meeting which would take place a scant two weeks too early to be decisive. In a letter to his family written on July 3, Truman made no attempt to hide his feelings: "I am getting ready to go see Stalin and Churchill, and it is a chore. . . . Wish I didn't have to go, but I do, and it can't be stopped now."[98] On the voyage to Europe he wrote to complain again: "I wish this trip was over. I hate it. But it has to be done."[99]

POTSDAM

DESPITE THE DEEP IRONY that inevitably Truman would not be able to force matters to a showdown in his talks with Stalin, there was now no longer any reason why the President could not state the full American position. By the time the two heads of government had met, Truman would know the results of the atomic test, and the battle demonstration in Japan would be only a few weeks off. There would be no reason why the President should forego the opportunity to personally present the United States proposals. Thus, Truman carried with him a bluntly worded paper aimed at reversing the Churchill-Stalin arrangement, the armistice agreement, and Roosevelt's Yalta decisions.[100] The day Truman sailed from Norfolk, Virginia, Acting Secretary of State Grew revealed to the American ambassador in London that the previously rejected State Department position had now become official policy. Although Roosevelt had excised the operative clauses of the Yalta Declaration, Grew now cabled: "You may . . . tell Fo[reign] Off[ice] that . . . at forthcoming highest-level discussions we intend to press strongly proposals for implementation. . . ."[101]

The decision to state the full American case at Potsdam—at a time when a final showdown could not be expected to occur—produced a curious combination of firm demands, unyielding rejections of Soviet proposals, and most of all, continued willingness to postpone all questions in dispute. As is apparent, the subtleties involved in such a negotiating posture cannot easily be understood without reference to the atomic bomb. Nor can they be explained without recognizing that there had as yet been no reason to modify the existing strategy of delay. At the time, British diplomats found the American approach quite confusing—until they learned more of the atomic bomb.* It is not surprising that students of the problem who have not had access to previously classified information have also been confused. Undoubtedly, the scarcity of material (and the fact that the American approach ultimately failed) accounts for the poverty of scholarship in this matter,† and that, so far as I know, the American approach to Eastern Europe and the Balkans at Truman's only meeting with Stalin has not been adequately described.

Secretary of State Byrnes has written that both he and the President felt the attempt to reduce or eliminate Soviet influence in Southeastern Europe to be one of the most important objectives of American diplomacy at Potsdam.[102] As a matter of fact, once the Conference began, American proposals regarding this area precipitated the first prolonged discussions of the meeting.[103] Truman later described as the

---

* See below, pp. 200–2.
† See for example, Woodward, *British Foreign Policy*, pp. 552–53, 555–57. Note especially his mistaken view that the United States "gave up hope" of influencing the politics of the Balkans (p. 557).

"bitterest debate" of the entire meeting his arguments with Stalin over the issue.[104] And Admiral Leahy never qualified his statement that "Stalin suffered his greatest defeat" in connection with the Balkan discussions at Potsdam.[105]

Thus, unquestionably the American delegation ascribed great importance to its proposals involving the Soviet sphere of influence. Because *they* felt them to be far more important than have latter-day students of the problem, and because Truman's characteristic yet subtle approach to the Balkan issues provides a perfect illustration of the continued strategy of delay in action, it is useful to isolate, day by day, the attitudes and maneuvers of the President and his advisers and to relate them to the reports of the atomic bomb which flowed continuously from New Mexico and Washington to Berlin.

Truman arrived at ‾Potsdam during the late afternoon of Sunday, July 15.[106] As Stimson had promised, on Monday, July 16, at 5:30 A.M. (local time) the first successful atomic test took place at the Alamogordo site, in New Mexico.[107] A cryptic report reached the Secretary of War early the evening of the same day: "Operated on this morning. Diagnosis not yet complete but results seem satisfactory and already exceed expectations. . . ."[108] This message was immediately brought to the attention of the President and the Secretary of State. "Truman and Byrnes . . . were of course greatly interested," Stimson noted, "although the information was still in very general terms."[109]

The following day, after Stalin had suggested that Truman take the chair at the opening plenary session of the Conference, the President wasted no time in stating his full position. "Seizing this hoped-for opportunity to take the offensive," Admiral Leahy confided to his diary, Truman "presented at once, without permitting any interruption, the . . . proposals for the agenda which we had prepared. . . ."[110] In striking contrast to Roosevelt, who had habitually allowed Stalin and Churchill to take the lead,[111] Truman confidently produced detailed American proposals for the broad range of issues he intended to discuss during the Conference.* Taking up Eastern Europe, the President bluntly asserted that the obligations of the three governments undertaken in accord with the Yalta Declaration had not

---

* Compare Roosevelt's letter to Stalin before Yalta: "We understand each other's problems and as you know, I like to keep these discussions informal, and I have no reason for formal agenda." (Feis, *Churchill, Roosevelt, Stalin,* p. 497.)

been fulfilled. He quoted the State Department's prepared statement of steps required to implement the Declaration, demanding:

1. ". . . the immediate reorganization of the present governments in Rumania and Bulgaria . . ."
2. ". . . immediate consultations to . . . include representatives of all significant democratic elements . . ."
3. three power assistance ". . . in the holding of free and unfettered elections."[112]

In essence, the demands were precisely those which Truman had pressed in the first showdown over Poland: a reorganization of the government and immediate free elections.

The first plenary session, of course, was devoted only to listing items for the agenda.[113] The three foreign ministers were instructed to review the proposed items and to suggest specific questions for the heads of government.[114] Before discussion of the President's proposals by the foreign ministers, however, further word of the atomic test was received from New Mexico. Again the coded message was written in general terms, but it indicated far greater power than had been expected. It implied that the blast could be heard at a distance of fifty miles and seen at a distance of 250 miles.[115] "I at once took [the message] to the President, who was highly delighted, . . ." Stimson records. "The President was evidently very greatly re-enforced . . . and said he was very glad I had come to the meeting. . . ."[116]

The following day (July 19) at the foreign ministers' meeting, Byrnes requested that the President's paper on the implementation of the Yalta agreement be put on the agenda for the Big Three.[117] This was agreed to, but at the plenary session Stalin asked that the subject be put off because the Soviet delegation had a proposal of its own to make regarding this set of issues.[118] Consequently, discussion of the problem was once more briefly delayed. However, in private conversation with Churchill on the previous day, Stalin had already indicated his general reaction to the American proposal. As the Prime Minister reported it, Stalin was clearly affirming his continued adherence to the spheres-of-influence arrangement: The Soviet Premier ". . . said that he had been hurt by the American demand for a change in Government in Rumania and Bulgaria. He was not meddling in Greek affairs, and it was unjust of them."[119]

When Molotov took up the issue now referred to the July 20 foreign ministers' meeting, he gave a more detailed presentation of this basic response. Molotov introduced a new Soviet statement, which combined a rejection of the American proposal with a strong attack on the situation in Greece. The Soviet paper called attention to the fact that the governments in both Bulgaria and Rumania were fulfilling the armistice agreements. Rejecting the American suggestion for a reorganization of the governments, it stated that the Soviet government saw no reason for the powers to become involved in the domestic affairs of Bulgaria and Rumania. Molotov went on to urge restoration of diplomatic ties "in the nearest days." Then, switching to the offensive, he stated: "There is one country—Greece—in which no due order still exists, where law is not respected, where terrorism rages directed against democratic elements . . ." Molotov concluded that it was necessary to take action to establish democratic government in Greece.[120]

Despite this use of the Greek issue to underscore the abrogation of the spheres-of-influence agreement,* the primary focus of attention of the meeting was the status of the established Bulgarian and Rumanian governments. In fact, the general debate over recognition begun during May and June by Truman and Stalin was now brought to a climax by the foreign ministers. Molotov demanded immediate recognition of the Georgiev and Groza governments. Byrnes stated that the United States "could not recognize them at this time."[121] The Secretary of State repeated Truman's demand for reorganization of the governments and supervision of elections. He also urged that American press representatives be allowed to observe freely and to report on conditions in the countries.[122] Molotov steadily refused to alter the *status quo* or to accept supervision of the elections. However, he said he had "no objection to" improving the position of American press representatives, and he offered to consider written suggestions regarding both the elections and freedom of the press.[123]

While these were being drafted,[124] a third report on the atomic test arrived by special courier. This presented a detailed, full-length de-

---

* Another instance of this occurred after Attlee replaced Churchill. Stalin presented another series of charges against Greece in retaliation for a British paper on Yugoslavia. Bevin suggested they drop both issues, and Stalin immediately replied: "Yes, welcome." (Byrnes, *Speaking Frankly*, p. 75.)

scription of the test by General Leslie R. Groves, the project director. A brief excerpt offers a sense of the statement:

> . . . in a remote section of the Alamogordo Air Base, New Mexico, the first full scale test was made of the implosion type atomic fission bomb. For the first time in history there was a nuclear explosion. . . . The test was successful beyond the most optimistic expectations of anyone . . . I estimate the energy generated to be in excess of the equivalent of 15,000 to 20,000 tons of TNT; and this is a conservative estimate. . . .
>
> The feeling of the entire assembly was . . . profound awe. . . .*

The arrival of this report on July 21 was the psychological turning point of the Conference. "It was an immensely powerful document, clearly and well written and with supporting documents of the highest importance," Stimson noted. "It gave a pretty full and eloquent report of the tremendous success of the test and revealed far greater destructive power than we expected. . . ." Stimson's diary entry continues:

> I then went over to the "Little White House" and saw President Truman. I asked him to call in Secretary Byrnes and then I read the report in its entirety and we then discussed it. They were immensely pleased. The President was tremendously pepped up by it and spoke to me of it again and again when I saw him.

The Secretary of War concludes: *"He said it gave him an entirely new feeling of confidence and he thanked me for having come to the Conference and being present to help him in this way."*[125]

That the atomic report did help by producing a new sense of confidence in the President's power to secure his diplomatic objectives is evidenced by Truman's attitude at the plenary session which took place almost immediately after his meeting with Stimson. In the course of the discussion, Stalin decided to raise the Balkan issue directly with the President. He proposed an amendment to the American proposal, asking immediate recognition of the governments of the liberated countries.[126] Truman's confidence—and, indeed, his bluntness—is apparent even from the official third-person report of the discussion:

---

* For the entire report see *Conference of Berlin,* II, pp. 1361–71.

The President stated that the American Government was unable to recognize the governments of the other satellite countries. When these countries were established on a proper basis, the United States would recognize them and not before. The President stated that the meeting would proceed and that this question would be passed over.[127]

This declaration precisely stated Truman's basic view at Potsdam. He would not agree to the Soviet position; he had stated his own demand; and he was quite prepared to pass over the matter at this time.* Churchill was struck by Truman's new confidence, and the next day, after Stimson had read the full-length report to the Prime Minister, he reflected on the President's attitude. Stimson recorded:

> [Churchill] told me that he had noticed at the meeting of the Three yesterday that Truman was evidently much fortified by something that had happened and that he stood up to the Russians in a most emphatic and decisive manner, telling them as to certain demands that they absolutely could not have and that the United States was entirely against them. He said "Now I know what happened to Truman yesterday. I couldn't understand it. When he got to the meeting after having read this report he was a changed man. He told the Russians just where they got on and off and generally bossed the whole meeting." Churchill said he now understood how this pepping up had taken place and that he felt the same way. His own attitude confirmed this admission. . . .[128]

Thus, the first effect of the atomic bomb was a simple, yet profoundly important one—it confirmed the President's belief that he would have enough power to reverse Roosevelt's policy and attempt actively to influence events in the Soviet sphere of influence. It would, however, still be a few weeks before the battle demonstration of the new weapon. Hence, the full impact of the new weapon upon the diplomatic and power balance could not yet be tested. From Truman's point of view, therefore, after the July 21 meeting of the heads of government there was no reason to press matters any further. And, indeed, since Stalin and Truman both held their ground, no further

---

* See also the President's stand on July 24:

TRUMAN. We are asking reorganization of these governments along democratic lines . . .

TRUMAN. I have made clear we will not recognize these governments until they are reorganized . . .

TRUMAN. May I suggest that we again refer the matter to the Foreign Ministers?
—*Conference of Berlin*, II, pp. 371–72.

substantive progress was made on the Balkan issues. The final protocol recorded the agreement for improved Control Commission procedures discussed earlier and accepted in final form at the meeting. It stated that "the Three Governments have no doubt" that representatives of the Allied press would now enjoy full freedom to report; and it diplomatically papered over the stalemate on the fundamental issue: "The Three Governments agree to examine each separately in the near future, in the light of conditions then prevailing, the establishment of diplomatic relations . . ."*[129]

The American delegation was quite pleased with this outcome; the final issue had been successfully delayed and, as Admiral Leahy noted, although Stalin "tried every trick in the book, [he] did not succeed in getting the diplomatic recognition he sought."†[130] Truman, who had not really wanted to come to the inevitably premature Conference in the first place, was now convinced that nothing more could be accomplished at this time. "The United States was standing firm," he told Stimson on July 23. (The Secretary noted that "he was apparently relying greatly upon the information as to [the atomic bomb].")[131] And, the following day, "The President was frank about his desire to close the Conference and get away. . . ."[132]

A PROBLEM OF FRANKNESS

DESPITE THEIR OBJECTIONS, before the Potsdam meeting began, the Foreign Office had informed the State Department that "British officials at Potsdam would support the American view [of the Balkan issues] even though they had little hope that the Soviet Government would agree to it."[133] However, the First Secretary of the Embassy in Washington had told an American official "it was his understanding that if the Soviet Government does not agree to the U.S. position the British officials will then endeavor to persuade the U.S. to agree to the

---

* Note that early in the Conference Truman agreed that "observation" of the elections was as good as "supervision." (*Conference of Berlin*, II, p. 166; Truman, *Year of Decisions*, p. 362.)

For a detailed discussion of how these agreements were reached, see references provided under "Yalta Declaration," *Conference of Berlin*, II, p. 1643.

† His basic "trick" was to refuse to accept the American proposals for Italy unless his proposals for the Balkans were accepted. In the end, as might be expected, agreement was reached to postpone both issues. (See *Conference of Berlin*, II, pp. 168–69, 207, 1492.)

early recognition of the two governments."[134] This view, of course, reflected Churchill's appraisal (made in mid-1944 and held consistently until Potsdam) that the West would not be able substantially to influence Soviet policy in the Balkans.

The State Department's successful attempt to convince the Foreign Office to adopt an initially parallel position on Balkan and other questions, of course, marked the end of Truman's temporary effort to avoid "ganging up" against the Russians during the short period of conciliation.* However, Churchill was still nervous about breaking the spheres-of-influence arrangements he had promoted. On July 18, after the vague first report of the atomic test, the Prime Minister dined alone with Stalin and noncommittally replied to the Soviet Premier's protests by stating he had not yet seen the American proposals.[135] But when the full report of the successful test arrived, his reservations disappeared. "From that moment our outlook on the future was transformed," Churchill has testified. "We were in the presence of a new factor in human affairs, and possessed of powers which were irresistible."[136] The Foreign Office never made the projected effort to convince the United States to recognize the Bulgarian and Rumanian governments. Instead, they gave active and powerful support to the American Balkan demands.[137]

Churchill's unhesitating breach of the agreements he himself had originally proposed confirms the impact of the atomic bomb upon his estimate of the power realities. The Balkans, which had once seemed beyond the reach of Western diplomacy, now again seemed accessible.† Lord Alanbrooke's diary entry for July 22 offers a glimpse of Churchill's state of mind and an indirect reflection of American attitudes:

> [The Prime Minister] . . . had absorbed all the minor American exaggerations and, as a result, was completely carried away. . . . We

---

* See above, pp. 117–18.

† Churchill's action illuminates the difficult question of what Truman might have done had the atomic test failed. It is probable that Truman himself could not have answered this question in advance, for, unlike Churchill, Truman made his calculations on the basis of the extremely confident predictions of the Secretary of War. Nevertheless, Grew records that on May 31 Truman did ask for studies "of what points we should stand out for and on what points we could compromise or yield." (*Conference of Berlin*, I, p. 158*fn.*) Although Truman would probably have begun with the same proposals, it is difficult to judge which points he might have yielded at Potsdam—or subsequently—had the atomic test failed and the American Army been withdrawn from Europe. Churchill's preatomic view that the Balkans were the first place to yield, and his postatomic change, are probably the best guide to the Anglo-American judgment of the power realities at the time.

now had something in our hands which would redress the balance with the Russians. The secret of this explosive and the power to use it would completely alter the diplomatic equilibrium which was adrift since the defeat of Germany. Now we had a new value which redressed our position (pushing out his chin and scowling); now we could say, "If you insist on doing this or that, well . . ." And then where are the Russians![138]

Alanbrooke subsequently commented that Churchill

was already seeing himself capable of eliminating all the Russian centres of industry and population. . . . He had at once painted a wonderful picture of himself as the sole possessor of these bombs and capable of dumping them where he wished, thus all-powerful and capable of dictating to Stalin![139]

One result of Churchill's new confidence was, as Stimson noted, that the Prime Minister "not only was not worried about giving the Russians information of the matter but was rather inclined to use it as an argument in our favor in the negotiations."[140] It was only after he read the full report of the test that Churchill reached the conclusion that Stalin ought to be informed; but American officials had come to this view a few weeks earlier. In fact, the Interim Committee's initial recommendation that nothing should be said of the new weapon until it had been "laid on Japan" had been slightly modified on the eve of the Potsdam meeting.

Under pressure from nuclear scientists working at the University of Chicago, the scientific panel had reconsidered the initial recommendation at a meeting held on June 16.[141] The basic proposal of the scientists was presented in a report drafted by Dr. James Franck. The report argued that it was futile to hope the secret of the new weapon could be maintained. It stressed that an attempt to do so was bound to stimulate a desperate arms race, and that the United States, with its large centers of population and industry, would eventually be at a great disadvantage. It urged that the only hope lay in international control of the new force and concluded, therefore, that it would be unwise to use the weapon in a manner which might prejudice international cooperation. Suggesting a technical demonstration of the bombs, it strongly recommended against a surprise attack upon Japan: "Russia and even allied countries which bear less mistrust of our ways and intentions . . . may be deeply shocked by this step."*

Although the scientific panel rejected the basic proposal of the Franck report, it did agree that circumstances of the wartime use of the weapon might affect prospects for international cooperation.[142] It therefore recommended that the Soviet government be informed of the new weapon's existence before it was used.[143] This recommendation was unanimously approved by the Interim Committee on June 21.[144] On July 3, Stimson carried the final recommendation to the President:

> He should look sharp and, if he found that he thought that Stalin was on good enough terms with him, he should shoot off at him what we had arranged . . . simply telling him that we were busy with this thing working like the dickens and we knew he was busy with this thing and working like the dickens and that we were pretty nearly ready and we intended to use it against the enemy, Japan; that if it was satisfactory we proposed to ᴗhen talk it over with Stalin afterwards, with the purpose of having it make the world peaceful and safe rather than to destroy civilization. If he pressed for details and facts, Truman was simply to tell him that we were not yet prepared to give them. The President listened attentively and then said that he understood and he thought that was the best way to do it.[145]

The following day, July 4, Stimson mentioned this conclusion to the British members of the Combined Policy Committee: "If nothing was said . . . its subsequent early use might have a serious effect on the relations of frankness between the three great Allies. . . ."[146] The Secretary of War also took it up with Churchill at Potsdam on July 17—after the first cryptic report, but before the full-length report. At this point Churchill took a strong stand against mentioning the weapon to Stalin.[147] The next day Truman discussed it with the Prime Minister. Churchill reports: "On behalf of His Majesty's Government I did not resist his proposed disclosure of the simple fact that we have this weapon. He reiterated his resolve at all costs to refuse to divulge

---

* See *Bulletin of the Atomic Scientists,* May 1946, for full report. Also Hewlett and Anderson, *The New World,* p. 366; Feis, *Japan Subdued,* pp. 40–43; Smith, "Behind the Decision to Use the Atomic Bomb," *Bulletin of the Atomic Scientists,* XIV (October 1958).

Former President Eisenhower has recently disclosed that at Potsdam he too advised Stimson that Japan was "already defeated," that the atomic bomb should not be used, and that the United States should "avoid shocking world opinion." (See Eisenhower, *Mandate for Change,* pp. 312–13.)

any particulars. . . ."[148] As we have seen, once the full report came in, Churchill's attitude switched from opposition and passive acquiescence to strong approval of the idea.

Thus, it was with Churchill's agreement that on July 24—the day after he decided it was time to close the Conference as soon as possible—Truman casually mentioned to Stalin that a new weapon of unusual force had been developed.[149] However, he used neither the word "nuclear" nor the word "atomic," and Churchill, who was watching the encounter with intense interest, "was sure that [Stalin] had no idea of what he was being told."[150] Indeed, immediately after his conversation Truman boasted to the Prime Minister: "He never asked a question!"[151] Both Byrnes and Leahy confirm that, despite the recommendation of the Interim Committee and the Secretary of War, when the actual discussion took place Truman did not tell Stalin that an atomic weapon had been developed.*[152] Instead, apparently hoping that his action might allow him to rebut future charges that he had been less than frank with the Soviet ally, Truman offered only the vaguest hint of the weapon. As we shall see, for reasons intimately related to the fundamental logic of his strategy, the President had decided that the actual disclosure of the new force would also be delayed.†

---

* This is often misunderstood. See, for example, the erroneous statement that "Stalin was told of the new weapon . . ."

(Craven and Cate, *Air Forces in World War II*, Vol. V, p. 712.)
† See below, p. 231.

CHAPTER VI

The Tactics
of the
Potsdam
Conference (II)*

*[The atomic bomb] is tying in with what
we are doing in all fields . . .*
—SECRETARY OF WAR
HENRY L. STIMSON
July 23, 1945

As EARLY AS the first week of June it had been assumed that the atomic bomb would strengthen American diplomacy only after it was demonstrated in combat. This view was inevitably reinforced by the Potsdam decision to keep the atomic test secret from Stalin. From Truman's point of view, therefore, there was now even less reason to begin serious negotiations; the President was extremely impatient with the discussions, and he did not conceal his belief that there was little point to continuing the diplomatic sparring at Potsdam.† His desire to end the Conference as soon as possible was indicated to Stalin on July 24 (although as yet no major agreements had been reached) when Truman declared that "when there was nothing more upon which they could agree, he was returning home."[1] On the same day, Byrnes told Molotov that "the United States delegation wants to dispose of pending matters so that the Conference can end."[2]

Truman's attitude had important tactical implications. As one ob-

---

* The word "tactics" must be emphasized here even more than in the preceding chapter. The German reparations issue here considered involved extremely complicated negotiations which I have only attempted to summarize. If one bears in mind the limitations discussed in footnote on p. 219, it may be helpful to consult the more detailed summary in *Conference of Berlin*, II (pp. 940–49).

† Truman later recalled: "I was becoming very impatient, and on a number of occasions I felt like blowing the roof off the palace." (*Year of Decisions*, p. 369.)

server has noted, much of the remainder of the Conference was "conducted under the threat of imminent American departure, with or without agreement."[3] The President's desire to leave, of course, did not derive from a feeling of despair. On the contrary, as Stimson remarked at the time, the American delegation was in the best of spirits.[4] Ambassador Harriman also "commented on the increasing cheerfulness evidently caused by the news from us [of the atomic test]."[5] On July 24, Stimson recorded: "[The President] told me about the events of yesterday's meeting with which he seemed to be very satisfied."[6] And on July 28, Secretary of the Navy Forrestal noted: "[The President] said he was being very realistic with the Russians and found Stalin not difficult to do business with."[7] Later, Byrnes was to recall that even the difficult debate and the stalemate over Bulgaria and Rumania "perhaps should have stifled my optimism, but it didn't."*[8]

The American delegation's sense of satisfaction and confidence, apparent to all firsthand observers, also marked its approach to what Byrnes termed "the most difficult issue before us—Germany."[9] Considering that most writers have agreed with Byrnes's view that Germany was the most significant problem discussed at Potsdam, it is vital to recognize that Truman's July 23 decision to end the Conference quickly was taken *before* the heads of government or the foreign ministers had even begun serious consideration of the main issues in dispute. And, as both Truman and Byrnes were to make clear during the remainder of the Conference, if the Russians did not find the American proposals for Germany acceptable, the United States delegation was quite prepared to leave with no agreement; the matter could be taken up at a later date. Thus, the tactics followed in dealing with the Balkan issues were to be followed in the treatment of Germany as well.

The American approach to Germany was a logical extension of the basic desire to establish a stable Europe. Together with the Balkan demands, the proposals for Germany constituted the core of the policies Truman and Byrnes thought it important to urge at Potsdam.[10]

---

* It is true that some Americans were disturbed by Soviet suggestions for a base in the Dardanelles and for Soviet participation in a trusteeship for one of the Italian colonies. However, the President does not seem to have been greatly worried. After a discussion with Truman on July 23, Stimson recorded: "He evidently thinks a good deal of the new claims of the Russians are bluff . . ." (Diary, July 23, 1945.)

The combination offered the hope of a democratic, economically and politically stable Continental system.*

Truman found that there was not much disagreement with his suggested political principles for postwar Germany; with little dispute, the Conference endorsed the American proposal on July 18.[11] However, at the time Truman began to search for a way to close the Conference, the subcommittee considering the crucial economic issues reached a deadlock.[12] This caused some worry, for as Stimson had urged throughout the summer, and as American economic experts stressed, there was need for a cooperative settlement: "The Russian zone [is] the 'bread basket' of Germany, while the [Western] zones together constitute a deficit food area."[13] Accordingly, although Truman was prepared to leave Potsdam without an understanding,† he and Byrnes went to considerable lengths to attempt to force agreement on American terms.

Again, there was not much difficulty in the negotiations over general principles for the economic administration of Germany. The real controversy arose over the basic question of the scale and power to be permitted the postwar German economy. The level of reparation withdrawals was the heart of the matter, for a decision on this issue would determine what was to be left in Germany and would control a host of other subsidiary questions. At Yalta, Roosevelt had agreed to establish a Reparations Commission charged with responsibility for creating a detailed plan and for "the fixing of the total sum" of reparation payments to be made by Germany. It was agreed that the Commission would

> take in its initial studies as a basis for discussion the suggestion of the Soviet Government that the total sum of the reparation . . . should be 20 billion dollars and that 50% of it should go to the U.S.S.R.[14]

Roosevelt's commitment to twenty billion dollars as a basis for discussion was not a definitive statement of policy. Nevertheless, it established the order of magnitude for reparation withdrawals. Indeed, because the British Cabinet would not agree to such a commitment,

---

* For American views on the need to treat Europe as an integrated unit, see *Conference of Berlin*, I, pp. 257–61; II, pp. 754–57, 808–9.

† See below, p. 218.

Churchill refused to endorse this aspect of the agreement. (This is the one provision of the Yalta protocol which bears the signatures of Roosevelt and Stalin, but not of Churchill.)[15] More important than the precise figure, however, was Roosevelt's endorsement of the principle that a firm target for reparations would be established in advance. His agreement that "Germany must pay in kind for losses caused by her"[16] also endorsed the principle of "compensation"[17]—rather than the principle of "capacity to pay"—as the basic criterion to guide reparations negotiations. Since there was no question that Soviet damages had been much greater than one half of twenty billion dollars,[18] Roosevelt's agreement to very large-scale reparations was thus doubly confirmed.

This understanding gave first priority to establishing a target figure for reparation withdrawals. The accord treated only as a residual item the question of what industrial resources were to be left in Germany after the reparations had been paid, and it gave only secondary importance to the inevitable debilitating effect such withdrawals would have upon the German standard of living. Thus, it accepted Stalin's argument that the Germans should pay for some of the tremendous devastation their armies had caused in the Soviet Union.[19]

Even before Yalta, this approach had been severely criticized by Stimson and others who feared that weakening the German economy would seriously endanger European stability.[20] Roosevelt was fully aware of this difficulty and was also reluctant to agree to excessive withdrawals from the German economy.[21] But ultimately the President's decision had been taken with regard to other than purely economic considerations.

Throughout the last year of the war American policy makers had been faced with the difficult but unavoidable task of creating a viable plan for postwar European security. To most American leaders, the necessary condition of such a plan was a system of specific guarantees against the revival of German power. Unable to hope that the American public would permit retention of occupation forces in Europe for more than two years after the war's end,[22] Roosevelt had been forced to find a nonmilitary solution to the security problem. The President evolved two complementary approaches. The first was an attempt to work out a cooperative relationship with the Soviet Union. In Europe, this involved a coordinated effort to control Germany and was first expressed in the plans for a German Allied Control Council. "It is by now a commonplace," one State Department official characteristically noted, "that Germany cannot commit another aggression so long as the Big Three remain united."[23]

Roosevelt's second policy was based upon a calculated decision to weaken the industrial basis of German military power. Although Roosevelt disclaimed the "Morgenthau Plan" to remove 80 per cent of German industry,[24] in fact, the Yalta decision followed the fundamental logic of this approach. Massive reparations and what was termed the "industrial disarmament"[25] of Germany were two sides of the same coin. It may be true that Roosevelt underestimated the difficulties such a policy would create,[26] but as Byrnes knew, he had very little sympathy for those who urged a "soft" peace for the Germans.[27] On the eve of the Yalta meeting, the President somewhat overenthusiastically told his Cabinet that as far as he was concerned, the Germans "could live happily . . . on soup from soup kitchens."[28]

Roosevelt also felt that international control of the Ruhr industrial area would be a useful guarantee against a German military revival.[29] But the heart of his approach to the security problem was a melding of his two basic policies. Since Stalin desperately wanted industrial reparations to compensate for destruction wrought by Hitler's armies, at Yalta the agreement to extract large-scale reparations met Soviet requirements—thereby consolidating a cooperative relationship—at the same time that it reduced the industrial basis of German power.*[30]

This approach to the European security problem had obvious implications for the stability of the German economy. The hardened Russian answer to those who protested that there were not enough resources to meet Europe's needs, reparations, and German requirements, was: "Let the German standard of living be reduced."[31] In America, however, when Truman took office, those who feared the effects of such a policy urged the new President to reconsider Roosevelt's approach.[32] As we have seen, Truman was completely in accord

---

* Note how Roosevelt broke with Churchill over the question after being prompted by Hopkins that "the Russians have given in so much at this conference that I don't think we should let them down." (*Conferences at Malta and Yalta*, pp. 902, 920.)
Much of the information contained in the preceding analysis is taken from Paul Y. Hammond's excellent study, *Directives for the Occupation of Germany: The Washington Story*. This is presently available in mimeograph form from the author or from the Twentieth Century Fund, but is soon to be published.

with Stimson's advice that the German economic contribution to Europe should not be reduced.* Morgenthau's views were rejected, and by June 8 Grew was able to write: "There is no longer disagreement concerning the need for assuring such essential economic rehabilitation in Germany as is necessary to the fulfillment of the purposes of occupation."[33] One result of this change was that the United States continued to procrastinate on the reparations issue and, as we have seen, the American reparations representative began negotiating on the matter some three and a half months later than had been envisioned at Yalta.†

Even more significant, however, was the fact that only a short time after taking office, Truman asked for the resignation of Secretary of the Treasury Morgenthau—the primary architect of Roosevelt's policy.‡[34] On June 1, the new President also gave instructions to increase the production of German coal.[35] More specifically, the President felt that the Russian desire for large-scale reparations from Germany— "although morally she should have been made to pay"—could not be met.[36] "America was not interested in reparations for anybody,"[37] he later wrote. And, fearing that massive withdrawals from Germany would necessitate American assistance, on May 18, he instructed his "tough" reparations negotiator, Edwin Pauley, to oppose "any reparation plan based upon the assumption that the United States . . . will finance directly or indirectly any reconstruction in Germany or reparation by Germany."[38] Despite this attitude, however, before the Potsdam Conference, Truman refused to attempt openly to reverse Roosevelt's Yalta decision.

Instead, Pauley was instructed to try to secure Soviet agreement to a set of concepts to guide reparation withdrawals, which shifted emphasis away from the basic principles of Roosevelt's commitment but still paid lip service to the Yalta decision. Thus, Pauley was told: "It is and has been fundamental United States policy that Germany's war potential be destroyed, and its resurgence as far as possible prevented, by removal or destruction of German plants, equipment, and other

---

* See above, pp. 127–28.
† See above, pp. 133–34.
‡ Morgenthau had wanted to come to the Potsdam meeting because of his deep interest in the German economic issue. According to Truman, he threatened resignation over the matter. Truman recalls: " 'All right,' I replied, 'if that is the way you feel, I'll accept your resignation right now.' And I did. That was the end of the conversation and the end of the Morgenthau Plan." (*Year of Decisions*, p. 327.)

property."[39] At the same time, however, he was to urge a new approach to the determination of actual withdrawals: Experts should establish the amount of industry required to produce a German standard of living approximately equal to that of the surrounding nations; industrial resources in excess of the amount needed to produce this standard would then be distributed as reparations. Receipts from goods produced for export each year would be used, in the first instance, to pay for German imports; what was left after these claims had been met would be used to satisfy reparations requirements.[40] In this fashion the American interest in a reasonably strong German economy would be given first priority, while reparations would be treated as a residual. The Yalta principle of compensation would be replaced by the principle of "capacity to pay." Hence, in any conflict over the distribution of limited German resources, although the Yalta principle would have given preference to the claims of the invaded countries, the new approach would have favored the German standard of living.

When Pauley first brought forward this set of principles in the Moscow discussions during June, the new American approach was bitterly opposed by the Russians.[41] A debate first arose over the suggestion that yearly exports be used in the first instance to pay for imports rather than reparations.[42] The Russians argued that reparations could not be considered a mere residual.[43] Backed by Truman's firm decision that the United States would not pay for German reconstruction* and aided by the determination of the State and War Departments to avoid paying for German imports,[44] Pauley held his ground; the negotiations on the issue ended in stalemate.[45] While these discussions were going on, Pauley also asked the State Department to permit him to make a direct assault on the fixed-figure requirement, the heart of the Yalta agreement.[46] The Russian representative "keeps coming back to the 20 billion dollar sum," Pauley complained on June 19.[47] American policy, he argued, "should not fix any total figure in advance." Instead, "a formula [should] be adopted which will emphasize percentages, rather than dollars."[48]

Although Pauley's suggestion would have directly contradicted the

---

* Truman felt the United States had indirectly financed German reparations after World War I and he vowed not to allow this to happen again. (Truman, *Year of Decisions*, p. 307; Byrnes, *Speaking Frankly*, p. 82.)

Yalta decision, it was only a logical extension of Truman's instructions; if the level of German industry and the standard of living were to be established as fixed targets, reparations would automatically become a residual. Before Potsdam, however, Truman was not prepared so directly to countervene his predecessor's agreement. On July 2, Pauley was sent a somewhat ambivalent instruction: "The interest of this Government in questions of the total amount of reparations . . . is subservient to its interest in the firm application of those principles and procedures . . ." Despite this statement, however, Pauley was told that the United States would not take a stand against establishing a firm target figure. He was instructed that although the twenty-billion-dollar mark was too high, there was no objection to discussion of a figure in the twelve-to-fourteen-billion-dollar range.[49]

Interpreting these somewhat contradictory instructions along lines favoring his own approach, on his own initiative a few days before Potsdam, Pauley boldly told the Soviet reparations representative that he was no longer prepared to establish a fixed reparations target![50] This, of course, produced a deadlock. As Pauley reported on July 7, although some progress had been made, no agreement had been reached on "fundamental problems."[51] Hence, the reparations issue, which had taken up much of the Yalta Conference, and which, it had seemed, would be disposed of shortly thereafter, was now transferred to Potsdam.[52]

THE FIRM APPROACH TO REPARATIONS AND A NEW SOLUTION TO THE SECURITY PROBLEM

FROM ONE POINT OF VIEW, the discussion of the reparations issue in Berlin was bound to strengthen the basic American viewpoint. When American policy makers arrived in Germany they were appalled at both the destruction of the country and at what Stimson termed the "rather oriental" policies of the Russians.[53] At every turning they came across workers feverishly dismantling German industrial installations for immediate shipment to the Soviet Union.[54] But, although they were shocked by the scale and pace of these activities, during the first days of the Potsdam meeting, Truman and Byrnes made no alteration in their approach to reparations.

It was only after the full report of the atomic test arrived that they changed tactics. The confidence evidenced in the handling of the Balkan issues now appeared in the treatment of Germany as well. The need for Soviet cooperation, which had followed from the same considerations important to Roosevelt, and which had been expressed in Truman's troop withdrawal during the summer,* now ceased to be a decisive influence upon policy. A tremendous new assertiveness characterized the American attitude as Truman and Byrnes abandoned the ambivalence of the summer instructions. Although only four days before the American delegation had sailed for Potsdam they had told Pauley that a figure of twelve to fourteen billion dollars would be acceptable, now, the reparations negotiator was directed to refuse to adhere to the agreement that a fixed reparations figure be established.[55]

This direct assault upon the Yalta principles was in line with Pauley's earlier recommendation. However, the President also received powerful advice on the matter from other quarters. Significantly, the German problem was the one issue, besides the atomic bomb, which directly concerned Secretary Stimson.[56] Throughout the previous year he had argued against the destruction of German industry,† and now, during the first days of the Potsdam meeting he stressed the vital importance of a healthy German economy.[57] Using language which strikingly contrasted with his usual moderate style, he argued that "it would be foolish, dangerous and provocative of future wars to adopt a program calling for the major destruction of Germany's industry and resources."[58]

That responsibilities for policy regarding both the atomic bomb and the German issue were united in the person of the Secretary of War emphasizes (and symbolizes) the fact that it is extremely artificial to ignore the relationship between the new weapon and the Americans' confidence in their power to achieve solutions to diplomatic problems.‡ Stimson's July 23 comment that the atomic bomb "is tying in with what we are doing in all fields"[59] suggests the connection, and the fact is that the development was both psychologically and conceptually§ related to the American attitude toward Germany. The most obvious

---

* See above, p. 131.
† See above, p. 101.
‡ Although the State Department was also deeply involved, the War Department had a major share of the responsibility because of the military role in the occupation. (*Conference of Berlin*, II, p. 754.)
§ See below, pp. 220–21.

point, of course, was the sense of independence the new weapon gave the American negotiators; Stimson's basic approach and Pauley's specific policy now became the essence of an unyielding set of American proposals.

Secretary Byrnes made the position clear at a foreign ministers' session on July 23, two days after the full report of the test arrived. Objecting to the broad definitions the Russians wished to apply to "war booty," worried about the economic effects of Polish control of part of eastern Germany,* and, as always, fearing the effects of large-scale withdrawals, Byrnes stated unequivocally: "There will be no reparations until imports in the American zone are paid for. There can be no discussion of this matter."[60] True to his word, Byrnes refused to consider Molotov's suggestion that if German consumption were reduced, reparations and imports could both be paid for.[61] Nor would he consider the proposal that consumption, reparations, and imports, each be accorded an equal claim on export receipts so that a reduction in exports would affect all in the same proportion.[62] Moreover, he asked that the discussion of the fundamental target-figure question be postponed for a short while.[63]

Since the Russians held to the same views they had taken during the Moscow talks, it is not surprising that the July 23 negotiations ended in a stalemate. The Secretary of State was undoubtedly aware of the futility of the effort, for even before announcing his firm stand in the tripartite foreign ministers' meeting, he had come to the conclusion that quite a different handling of the dispute was necessary. His request that the target-figure question be postponed was directly related to his new appraisal, for, with the approval of the President, an hour earlier on the same day he had already approached Molotov privately

---

* Truman and Byrnes were disturbed that by turning over former German territories east of the Oder-Neisse line to Poland the Russians had seriously reduced Germany's economic resources and also her capacity to pay reparations. This matter took up considerable time at Potsdam and subsequently. However, the importance of the issue has probably been unduly emphasized, for (1) the entire area comprised only approximately (by American estimate) 5.9 per cent of Germany's movable assets, 6 per cent (or 9.7 per cent) of total manufacturing assets, 7.1 per cent of mining and manufacturing production; (2) the Yalta agreement provided that in any event much of the area would be given over to Poland after the peace treaty; and (3) most important, Stalin told Truman he was not committed to Polish administration of the area and seems at one point to have been willing to negotiate a compromise settlement. (See *Conference of Berlin*, I, p. 635; *Ibid.*, II, pp. 861–62, 879–81, 943, 1572.) Finally, of course, the facts of the Oder-Neisse dispute were well known throughout the summer and had not affected the State Department's willingness to discuss a twelve-to-fourteen-billion-dollar target before Potsdam.

with an alternative suggestion: "The Secretary said that under the circumstances he wondered whether it would not be better to give consideration to the possibility of each country taking reparations from its own zone." If the Russians wished industrial reparations from the West, they might pay for them with food and coal.[64]

For the remainder of the conference Byrnes directed his primary effort toward securing agreement to this zonal plan. Although he was prepared to continue discussion of the Yalta understanding that Germany would be treated as an economic unit for reparations purposes, he would do so only on the assumption that no fixed target would be established and that reparations would have last claim on export receipts.[65] Molotov was therefore faced with the choice of accepting the new zonal approach, or having to agree to an alteration of the Yalta agreement which eliminated the crucial target figure and which treated all reparations as residuals.

Byrnes was fully aware of the meaning of his negotiating stance: the Russians, who desperately wanted heavy industrial reparations, occupied a zone primarily devoted to raw-material production, agriculture, and light industry.[66] The Ruhr, in Western hands, was the key to the reparations issue; and the proposal that each side satisfy its claims from its own zone was an open threat to the understanding that the Russians would be allocated half of all reparations selected from the whole of Germany.*

Molotov soon bitterly "pointed out that if they failed to agree . . . the result would be the same as under Mr. Byrnes's plan. Each side would draw reparations from their respective zones. . . ."[67] And even United States Assistant Secretary of State William L. Clayton cautioned Byrnes: "Any decision to exclude them from any participation in the distribution of the heavy equipment in the Ruhr as reparations, would be considered by the Russians as a reversal of the Yalta and Moscow position, since no Allied understanding would be necessary to enable them to get reparations from their own zone."[68]

Indeed, taken together, the refusal to fix a target and the proposal that each side take reparations from its own zone all but eliminated the expectation that the Soviet Union would receive industrial repara-

---

* Byrnes also supported the zonal proposal with the argument that separate administration would avoid quarrels over actual reparation determinations. (*Conference of Berlin*, II, p. 274; *Speaking Frankly*, p. 83.)

tions from the Western zones.[69] Molotov strongly opposed the zonal proposal. He told Byrnes he was quite prepared to reduce the amount of Soviet claims, but that a fixed figure for the entire economy was absolutely essential.[70] With Byrnes still refusing to discuss such a figure, on July 27 Molotov asked point-blank "if the decision with regard to reparations which was taken at the Crimea Conference remained in force."[71]

Byrnes replied that Pauley had "considered the proposal and that in view of the circumstances now existing he regarded it as impractical." At Yalta, he added, "all that was done was to accept the proposal [regarding twenty billion dollars] as the basis for discussion. If he were asked for a million dollars and he said he would discuss it, this did not mean that he would write a check for it."[72] Molotov responded stressing the importance of establishing some fixed target, rather than the twenty-billion-dollar estimate itself; he would like "to know what remained from the Crimea decision as a basis for discussion. Mr. Byrnes knew that the Soviet delegation was willing to consider reducing the amount of reparations."[73] But Byrnes refused to adhere to the fixed-target principle. After careful consideration, he said, "he had determined that it was now in his opinion impractical."[74]

Byrnes's refusal to establish a fixed figure did not derive, of course, from technical considerations. Although it was difficult to obtain accurate statistics on Germany, even six months earlier Roosevelt had been prepared to agree to a rough estimate of twenty billion dollars for reparations, the State Department had already established twelve to fourteen billion as a reasonable target, and during the Potsdam meeting Pauley himself produced a slightly more conservative estimate of ten to twelve billion.* Byrnes's basic opposition to large-scale reparations was the underlying factor.[75] But his reluctance to negotiate, his refusal to consider any of Molotov's proposals to reduce the target figure (which at one point brought the Russian request within one billion dollars of the State Department estimate),† and his refusal

---

* On the rough assumption that half of the reparations would come from capital goods and half from current production, I have derived this figure by doubling Pauley's estimate that five to six billion dollars would be available from capital goods alone. (*Conference of Berlin*, II, p. 892.)

† At one point Molotov offered to reduce the Soviet claim to eight billion dollars. (*Conference of Berlin*, II, p. 297.) It seems likely that had Byrnes been prepared to bargain, Molotov might have reduced this unilateral offer further and, perhaps, might have accepted the State Department's seven-billion-dollar estimate (i.e., 50 per cent of fourteen billion).

to put forward his own estimates derived from tactical, not statistical, considerations—and from Pauley's suggestion that there was wisdom in delay.[76]

Consequently, with Molotov stubbornly insisting on the Yalta terms, and Byrnes completely unwilling to establish a firm target, on the substantive issue there was very little progress.[77] On more limited aspects of the problem, however, there was some forward movement. After a series of complicated negotiations, Molotov finally agreed in principle to Byrnes's proposal that each side satisfy its claims from its own zone.[78] However, he did so on condition that a certain percentage of industrial-capital reparations from the Western zone would be partly given, partly sold to the Soviet Union.*[79]

This understanding altered the form but not the substance of the fundamental issue. Since the Soviet zone comprised approximately 40 per cent of German industrial resources, supplemental payments from the Western zone would have to be made to meet the Yalta requirement that 50 per cent of German reparations be paid to the Soviet Union.[80] The question now was: Precisely how much would the Russians be given from the Western zone? Although certain percentages had been agreed, as Molotov stressed, a percentage "of an undetermined figure meant very little."[81] Thus, the debate over a fixed figure for the entire economy narrowed to a struggle over the more limited question of whether or not to establish a target for industrial reparations from the Western zone.[82]

Once again Byrnes refused to be pinned down; and once again it was not for technical or statistical reasons.[83] The Secretary of State had available to him expert estimates of the potential reparations available from the Western zone.[84] These were presented with Pauley's advice that the prudent sum for withdrawals from the Western zone "differs so widely from the figure which the Russians have in mind that I believe the mere mention of this figure at this time would preclude any agreement being made at all."[85] In fact, Pauley told Byrnes,

---

* During the Potsdam bargaining the precise percentages, and the zones to which they were applied, were constantly changed. In order to save space by avoiding a lengthy description of this process I have chosen to use the summary term "a certain percentage" throughout this essay. The interested reader will find the details of this aspect of the negotiations well summarized in *Conference of Berlin*, II, pp. 944–47.

he believed the West should pay only about 10 per cent of the reparations the Russians believed justifiable under the Yalta agreement.*

The Secretary of State received additional strong support for his refusal to return to the Yalta principle from the War Department when Assistant Secretary McCloy agreed that it would be a "great risk . . . if the amount of reparations . . . [were] absolutely fixed now."[86] But more important, as the controversy with Molotov reached a climax, the underlying fact that the American delegation was prepared to postpone final determination of the issue gave Byrnes a tremendous advantage.

In conversations with Admiral Leahy on July 26 and July 27, the President reaffirmed his decision to "depart for home at the earliest practicable date" and to "terminate" the Conference.[87] Although Stalin's illness and the British elections[88] caused some delay, the day after the British delegation returned to Potsdam, Truman and Byrnes decided to state the American case privately to Molotov.[89] On July 30, Byrnes made the position abundantly clear to the Soviet Foreign Minister: It was time to wind up all of the negotiations. Now the proposal that each side satisfy its reparations requirements from its own zone (with a certain percentage to be transferred to the Soviet zone from the West) was to be "conditional upon agreement on two other proposals." Byrnes brought forward previously discussed papers on lesser issues relating to the treatment of Italy and the satellite nations and the Polish western border. All three would have to be accepted as a package. If Molotov did not agree, Byrnes "was willing to report to the Big Three and they could decide whether to continue the discussion or refer the matter to some future conference."[90] The following day Byrnes was more explicit: "I told him we would agree to all three or none, and that the President and I would leave for the United States the next day."[91]

Thus, the American tactics on the German issue paralleled the approach they had taken to the Balkans. Roosevelt's previous understanding was abandoned, and the Russians were told that the position would have to be accepted or no agreement would be possible; Truman and Byrnes were more than willing to postpone a final settle-

---

* The figure was 214 *million* dollars in capital removals from the Western zone— i.e., about one tenth of the Russian estimate of 2 *billion*. (*Conference of Berlin*, II, pp. 297, 892.)

ment. Moreover, the basic conception of the April showdown now once again came to the fore; aware that the Russians desperately needed economic aid—from American credits or from Western-controlled German reparations—Byrnes now attempted to bargain industrial withdrawals for Soviet concessions on other diplomatic issues.

Although Stalin had rejected the demand that the governments of Bulgaria and Rumania be changed, he apparently reasoned that the promise of a percentage of Western industrial reparations (even though it was a percentage of an undetermined figure) was better than no reparations agreement at all. Hence, after bitterly criticizing Byrnes's tactics,[92] on July 31, agreeing to abandon the Yalta principle, he accepted the American reparations plan.[93] The tough-minded negotiator Pauley found "keen satisfaction" in the result.*[94] Admiral Leahy believed it one of the "major achievements" of the Conference.[95] And Secretary Byrnes was subsequently to boast that the United States "finally succeeded in eliminating from the agreed declaration any mention of a total amount."†[96]

The firm tactics and the decision to reverse Roosevelt's agreement undoubtedly were related to the "entirely new sense of confidence" which Truman told Stimson the atomic test had given him. There is no

---

* Truman's recollection is illuminating: "If Pauley had not been as tough as he is, we could never have got any reparations policy. . . . He is a tough, mean so-and-so. . . ." (Daniels, *Man of Independence*, p. 305.)

† It was also agreed that reparations from the Eastern zone would be used to meet not only Soviet but also Polish claims and that the Soviet Union would renounce its interest in German external assets in Western Europe, German gold captured by the Allied armies, and a share in corporate assets of German enterprises (such as railroads) which would necessarily be left in the country. (See *Conference of Berlin*, II, pp. 944–46, 1485–87.)

The reparations negotiations, as seen from the American viewpoint, are usefully summarized in *Conference of Berlin*, II, pp. 940–49. In using this State Department document, however, it is important to remember (1) that it was written two months after Potsdam; (2) that the State Department, of course, has no wish to emphasize Truman's break with Roosevelt's agreement; and (3) that the report incorporates a radically new interpretation of the zonal reparations agreement. The last point is of con-

siderable importance, for shortly after Potsdam both American and British policy makers were to hold that "the zone plan . . . did not contemplate separate reparations plans." (*Ibid.*, p. 944.) Specifically, it was later claimed that the agreement to treat the German economy as a unit precluded Soviet reparations extractions so long as there was a deficit in the import-export balance of the western zones. (Byrnes, *Speaking Frankly*, pp. 167, 189.) The publication of the Potsdam papers shows this claim to be false. At the time, Ernest Bevin was only too aware that the plan "cut across the agreement to treat Germany as a whole economy," but his objections were expressly overruled. As Byrnes told Molotov, "If the Soviets agreed to his plan they would have no interest in exports and imports from our zone . . ." (*Conference of Berlin*, II, pp. 490–91, 520–21.) Despite Byrnes's subsequent decision to break the agreement, he himself emphasized the meaning of his plan on numerous occasions at Potsdam, both to Bevin and to Molotov, and he proposed various modifications of the final protocol to clarify the point. (*Ibid.*; see especially pp. 291, 572, 827, 932; also pp. 450, 475, 487, 490, 491, 520, 822, 822*fn*.)

way, of course, to know if Truman and Byrnes would have taken such an unyielding line had they not been "greatly re-enforced" by the news. But it is vital to recognize that the new approach was adopted only after the atomic report was received. Moreover, in a more fundamental sense, the relationship between Truman's decision and the atomic bomb is greatly illuminated by considering that Truman inherited not only the Yalta agreement from his predecessor, but the basic problem of European security.

For both Roosevelt and Truman, the need to establish specific guarantees against the possibility of another German military revival was a fundamental condition of policy. Although he very much wished to maintain American troops in Europe,* Truman, like Roosevelt, was unable to count on Congressional authority for such action. Hence, he too had had to search for nonmilitary guarantees against a rebirth of German power. And despite his desire to maintain a strong German contribution to Continental economic stability, he had been forced to rely upon "industrial disarmament" and Soviet cooperation on the Control Council as the foundations of his policy.[97]

For this reason, during May and June, Hopkins had been authorized to tell Stalin that Truman, like Roosevelt, was prepared to agree to international controls for the Ruhr industry, and Pauley had also been allowed to discuss the matter.[98] Similarly, Pauley's first reparations plan emphasized (albeit to a lesser extent than Roosevelt's had) the destruction of selected German arms industries.[99] And, as we have seen, until the very eve of the Potsdam Conference, Truman continued to hold on to the major premise of Roosevelt's policy. Although the twenty-billion-dollar reparations figure was to be reduced to twelve to fourteen billion, until the atomic-test report Truman did not abandon the substance of Roosevelt's Yalta decision—a decision which had established the conditions of Soviet-American cooperation in Europe and of the industrial disarmament of Germany.

"The problem which presents itself . . ." Stimson advised Truman before details of the atomic test arrived, "is how to render Germany harmless as a potential aggressor, and at the same time enable her to play her part in the necessary rehabilitation of Europe."[100] The Secretary of War stated in precise terms the question which had confronted

---

* See below, p. 272.

both Roosevelt and Truman, but within hours of his statement the dilemma inherent in the problem had been resolved in a radical and dramatic way. As Truman explained to General de Gaulle shortly after Potsdam, there was no longer any need for international control of the Ruhr, nor for other specific and material guarantees against renewed aggression—"The German menace should not be exaggerated," for "the United States possessed a new weapon, the atomic bomb, which would defeat any aggressor."[101]

Thus, although Truman continued to endorse "industrial disarmament" as a way to achieve European security, he knew that the United States would never again greatly fear the threat of German military power.[102] Truman no longer required Soviet cooperation or massive reductions in German industry to achieve his primary objective. Acting in accord with his view of the undeniable merits of the American plan for European stability, the President could afford to ignore the German devastation of Russia and the Yalta agreement. There was no need to compromise; the reparations issue now took on a distinctly secondary importance. In the last analysis, therefore, the atomic bomb influenced the fundamental problem Truman faced to an even greater extent than it did his tactics; by revolutionizing the problem of European security the new weapon rendered trivial the considerations which had dominated Roosevelt's approach until his death.

DEADLOCK, CONFIDENCE AND DELAY

As HAS BEEN SHOWN, Truman's tactics on major issues at Potsdam were much the same: the President unveiled the full extent of the American demands, he refused to make important concessions, and he made it clear that if no agreement was reached, he was quite prepared to postpone consideration of the issue until a later date. "That was his position yesterday, that was his position today, and that would be his position tomorrow"—Truman's statement in the course of one of the debates provides a fitting summary of his approach.[103] Such an attitude combined the confidence derived from the new atomic weapon with the basic strategy postulate that it would be wise to delay final negotiations until after the atomic weapon had been demonstrated. That Stalin accepted the substance of the American proposal for Germany should not obscure the fact that Truman followed the same tactics on this issue as on others. Even the German settlement contained a considerable element of delay, for although the Russians were promised a percentage of industrial reparations from the western zone, the total to which this percentage would apply—and consequently the central issue of the agreement—would not be decided for many months.[104]

It had been clear even before the American delegation left Washington that the President had little real desire to begin serious negotiations at this time. Once at the Conference, neither Truman nor his Secretary of State attempted to wield the powerful bargaining leverage which had played such a crucial role in the first showdown over Poland; instead of following the plan to negotiate a large credit in exchange for Soviet diplomatic concessions, this effort had also been suspended for a few more weeks.* A Council of Foreign Ministers, established by the heads of government at Byrnes's suggestion, would meet to take up the diplomatic negotiations in less than a month.†[105] And, as Churchill has written, it would have much to do, for "a formidable body of questions on which there was disagreement was . . . piled upon the shelves."[106]

Thus, the only real agreements reached at Potsdam were on those questions over which there was little dispute (such as political principles for postwar Germany). On proposals concerning the American-controlled areas (such as Italy) to which Stalin would not agree, there was little progress;[107] on proposals concerning the Soviet-controlled area (such as the Balkans) there was postponement; on proposals concerning jointly controlled areas (such as Germany) there was either delay or an agreement along the broad lines of the American proposals written in vague and sometimes contradictory terms which, as it turned out, could be interpreted in a different way by each side.‡

---

* See below, pp. 271–72.

† It is probable that the American proposal to establish machinery for post-Potsdam negotiations was directly related to the expectation that there would be little likelihood of a settlement during the heads-of-government meeting. In the presently available material I have found no evidence on this point, and the American argument for the new Council of Foreign Ministers was put forward—and accepted—as the most efficient way to speed the peace settlement. Yet it is impossible to ignore the fact that

the American delegation was extremely interested in establishing a council to take up all the postponed issues immediately after the atomic bomb was to be demonstrated and only three weeks after the President was to return to America.

‡ The reparations and economic agreements are universally regarded as confused and were later the source of considerable dispute. (See McNeill, *America, Britain, and Russia, 1941–46*, p. 625; Ratchford and Ross, *Berlin Reparations Assignment*, pp. 44, 187; Penrose, *Economic Planning for the Peace*, p. 284.

Inevitably, the main result of the Conference was a series of decisions to disagree until the next meeting.[108] As Admiral Leahy has conveniently summarized the outcome, in addition to the Balkan issue, these were some of the "problems on which no agreement could be reached":

> (1) internationalization of major waterways (American proposal); (2) trusteeships of colonial possessions, principally Italy's holdings in Africa (Soviet proposal); (3) Macedonian-Greek frontier (British proposal); (4) settlement of Soviet claims for Turkish territory and control of the Dardanelles; (5) Russian seizure of British and American industrial property in Rumania; (6) Italian reparations; (7) naming of "high war criminals," although it was agreed that a special commission would make its "nominations" within a month; (8) Russian attempt to force Britain and America to sever diplomatic relations with Spain (the best Stalin got on that one was language in the communiqué which stated that Spain should not belong to the United Nations); (9) Stalin's effort to open up the question of control of Tangier and the Levant; and (10) Russian attempt to have the *status quo* in Yugoslavia accepted by the other two Allies.[109]

Reviewing the communiqué produced by the Potsdam Conference, General de Gaulle commented: " . . . We learned that it had concluded in a kind of uproar."*[110] His judgment of the result would have been correct, of course—*if* the American government had hoped to achieve a major negotiated settlement at this juncture. But, the whole point of strategy throughout the summer and throughout the Potsdam meeting, was to delay the settlement of controversial issues until the atomic bomb had been demonstrated. It is for this reason that the American delegation was not at all depressed with the seeming stalemate recorded in the Potsdam protocol. At the end of the Conference the President told Eisenhower he had achieved his objectives,[111] and as Byrnes has written, from the American point of view, the Conference could only be considered a success.[112] Byrnes believed that a few discussions at the foreign ministers' meeting, scheduled to meet only

---

* The British also felt this way. After reading the minutes of the Big Three on July 23, Alanbrooke confided to his diary: "One fact that stands out more clearly than any other is that nothing is ever settled!" (Bryant, *Triumph in the West 1943–46*, p. 478.) See also Churchill's comment: ". . . Frustration was the fate of this final Conference . . ." (*Triumph and Tragedy*, p. 668.)

three weeks after his return to Washington, would clear the way for a settlement in Eastern Europe.[113] The Potsdam protocol, in his view, provided a "basis" for the "early restoration of stability in Europe."[114] Attempts to erect a lasting structure upon this foundation and to settle all outstanding issues would only begin when the strategy of delay had reached its climax.*

CODA: CULMINATING TACTICS OF DELAY IN THE FAR EAST

THROUGHOUT JUNE AND JULY, Truman's approach to the Manchurian and Chinese diplomatic issues had followed a delaying strategy roughly similar to his approach to European issues. However, at Potsdam, once again the related issue of Soviet entry into the Japanese war complicated the tactical problem facing the President. There was no reason for Truman to conceal his views on European issues, for his ultimate goal was prompt agreement along the lines of American proposals. But despite his earlier plans to complete the Soviet-Chinese negotiations at Potsdam,† with the public demonstration of the new weapon still a few weeks off, Truman had no wish to reach a settlement which would also be the cue for an immediate Soviet declaration of war. Consequently, his approach to Far Eastern problems was far less candid than was his blunt assault upon the European issues.

As we have seen, in the weeks preceding Potsdam, Chinese Foreign Minister T. V. Soong had been carefully advised at each step of his negotiations with Stalin so as to maintain the insurance of Soviet participation in the war at the same time that final agreement and an actual declaration of war were delayed until the atomic test.‡ As this approach was followed it became increasingly evident that the Japanese were seeking an early end to the hostilities. American intercepts of cables between Tokyo and the Japanese ambassador in Moscow confirmed the "real evidence"§ that the Emperor—the one person all agreed could end the war—had now taken an active hand in the

---

* See below, pp. 248–52, 274. ‡ See above, pp. 168–74.
† See above, p. 169. § See above, p. 157.

matter.* In the week before Potsdam, formal decisions of the Imperial Conference to stop the fighting were revealed in the cables, and the Japanese ambassador begged for an interview with Molotov to discuss a special mission to be headed by Prince Konoye "carrying with him the personal letter of His Majesty stating the Imperial wish to end the war."[115] Molotov, however, refused an interview, and the ambassador was forced to carry his message to a subordinate official. He was then told that a response would undoubtedly be delayed because of the impending Big Three meeting.[116]

On July 17, the day of the first plenary session, another intercepted Japanese message showed that although the government felt that the unconditional-surrender formula involved too great a dishonor, it was convinced that "the demands of the times" made Soviet mediation to terminate the war absolutely essential.[117] Further cables indicated that the one condition the Japanese asked was preservation of "our form of government."[118] A message of July 25 revealed instructions to the ambassador in Moscow to go anywhere to meet with Molotov during the recess of the Potsdam meeting (caused by the British elections) so as to "impress them with the sincerity of our desire" to terminate the war.[119] He was told to make it clear that "we should like to communicate to the other party through appropriate channels that we have no objection to a peace based on the Atlantic Charter." The only "difficult point is the . . . formality of unconditional surrender."[120]

With the interception of these messages there could no longer be any real doubt as to Japanese intentions; the maneuvers were overt and explicit and, most of all, official acts. As Eisenhower told Stimson, "Japan was, at that very moment, seeking some way to surrender with a minimum loss of face!"[121] Even the covert, devious, and unofficial maneuvers made in Germany a few months earlier had been recognized as important opportunities to secure a surrender and had been

---

* It is impossible to determine whether the President saw every one of the intercepted cables. That he surely was familiar with the contents of the most important ones cannot be doubted, and he has confirmed that he saw the two crucial cables (July 12 and July 25). (*Conference of Berlin*, I, p. 873.) Moreover, both Stimson and Forrestal had full information regarding the intercepts. (*Conference of Berlin*, II, p. 1266; Stimson, *On Active Service*, p. 617; Forrestal, *Diaries*, pp. 20, 74–76.) Forrestal also made a special effort to bring a number of the texts to the attention of Byrnes at Potsdam. (Strauss, *Men and Decisions*, p. 188; Byrnes, *All in One Lifetime*, p. 297.)

rapidly exploited by American officials.* To be sure, the Japanese proposals had not yet been made in detail, and the unconditional-surrender formula would require some modification, but Truman had already determined that, if necessary, he would be quite prepared to modify the formula so as to allow the Japanese to maintain their Imperial institutions, and he reaffirmed this intention during the Potsdam Conference.[122]

Thus, the cables showed not only the Japanese desire to end the war, but the fact that the Japanese and American governments were not very far apart in their conception of final surrender terms. Most important, however, the cables also confirmed that the last frail hopes of the Japanese were now unmistakably focused upon the as yet indeterminate position of the Soviet Union. The insistent attempts to see Molotov were such obvious evidence of Japanese anxiety that at one point the ambassador in Moscow had to caution the foreign minister in Tokyo against moves "which would only result in exposing our uneasy emotion and would be of no benefit to us."[123]

Despite this advice and the continual reports that there was little reason for optimism concerning Russian intentions,[124] the Japanese government continued to cling to the belief that so long as Stalin remained uncommitted it might be possible to hope for Soviet mediation, or at least Soviet neutrality.[125] Undoubtedly, the Soviet enigma gave pause to even the most ardent Japanese peace advocates. The combination of uncertainty and hope precluded open peace maneuvers within governing circles, for as long as Soviet mediation was a possibility, no government could assume the dishonor and disadvantage of suing for peace on unconditional terms.†

Throughout the summer, the American government had recognized how this situation greatly enhanced the shock value of a Soviet declaration of war—it would eliminate the last hope and was likely to force capitulation.‡ Now the point was even more obvious. On July 16, Stimson advised the President that "the impending threat of Russia's participation" and "the recent news of attempted approaches on the part of Japan to Russia" had produced "the psychological moment" to attempt to warn Japan into surrender.[126] On July 18, Secretary Byrnes

---

* See McNeill, *America, Britain, and Russia, 1941–46*, pp. 569–70. Also my Appendix I, pp. 291–317.

† See Butow, *Japan's Decision*, pp. 112–41.

‡ See above, pp. 154–58.

also noted the dependence of the Japanese on Soviet actions, commenting that the recent Japanese maneuvers were quite evidently inspired by a fear of what Russia might do.[127]

This confirmation of earlier estimates of the crucial psychological and political role played by the Soviet Union was matched, at Potsdam, by renewed proof of Stalin's intentions. Since mid-May, American policy makers had been convinced that the Soviet Premier would enter the war, as pledged, as soon as the Soong negotiations were completed. Now, on July 17, Stalin once more reaffirmed his plans in a private talk with Truman and Byrnes; the Red Army would be prepared to cross the Manchurian border by mid-August and would do so as soon as the Chinese treaty was initialed.[128] On July 21, the Joint Chiefs of Staff informed the American commanders in the Pacific that they could expect a Russian declaration of war on or about August 15.[129]

Thus the alternatives which had emerged during the summer of delay were confirmed at the Potsdam Conference; if all that appeared necessary to force Japanese capitulation was a "tremendous shock," the United States could choose to accomplish the objective with either a Soviet declaration of war or the atomic bomb. Additionally, there was the possibility of a negotiated settlement involving guarantees for the Emperor.[130]

Truman did not hesitate. He had no wish to test the judgment that a Soviet declaration of war would probably force capitulation. Nor was he interested in attempts to negotiate. Instead, he simply followed through on earlier plans to use the atomic weapons as soon as possible. "The atomic bomb was no 'great decision,' " he later recalled, ". . . not any decision that you had to worry about";[131] and he has confirmed on numerous occasions that he "never had any doubt that it should be used."[132] Once the cables announcing the tremendous success of the New Mexico test began to flow into Potsdam, Truman was concerned only with operational details.* Formal British agreement to use the weapon had already been recorded on July 4,[133] and Chur-

---

* Since the story of the use of the atomic bomb against Japan has been described in detail elsewhere, I have eliminated interesting but well-known information relating to the various presidential and other decisions involved in the actual operations. For a good account, see Hewlett and Anderson, *The New World;* and Craven and Cate, *Air Forces in World War II,* Vol. V.

chill confirms: "The historic fact remains, and must be judged in the after-time, that the decision whether or not to use the atomic bomb . . . was never even an issue."[134]

Secretary of War Stimson records only that on July 22 the President "was intensely pleased" with word that the weapons might be delivered somewhat earlier than had been expected.[135] When more detailed information arrived stating "operation may be possible any time from August 1,"[136] Truman "said that was just what he wanted, that he was highly delighted."[137] And on July 25, the formal order to use the weapon in combat was issued by the Secretary of War.[138] As the President later recalled, "I . . . instructed Stimson that the order would stand unless I notified him that the Japanese reply to our ultimatum was acceptable."[139]

Having reaffirmed the decision—or assumption—which had guided policy since April, Truman turned to the problem of Soviet entry into the war. Again, he continued to follow the earlier tactics of delay. When on July 18 Stalin had personally brought copies of the latest Japanese messages to the President's attention,[140] Truman had made no attempt to follow up the Japanese overtures. Instead, he had simply agreed with Stalin's suggestion that "it might be desirable to lull the Japanese to sleep . . . [through an] unspecific answer."[141] When the full report of the unexpected power of the test reached the President, however, he went beyond the vagaries and ambivalence of his initial position.

As early as July 18, having heard from the President that "the war might come to a speedy end," Prime Minister Churchill was quite aware of a new confidence in Truman's approach to military problems in the Pacific.[142] When the full report of the test arrived, there could no longer be any question. On July 23, Alanbrooke noted one of the "American exaggerations" Churchill had absorbed and taken as his own: "It was now no longer necessary for the Russians to come into the Japanese war; the new explosive alone was sufficient to settle the matter."[143] Later the same day, reporting to the Cabinet on a conversation with Byrnes, Churchill cabled: "It is quite clear that the United States do not at the present time desire Russian participation in the war against Japan."[144]

Churchill's observation was completely accurate. As Byrnes has written, "The reports made it clear that the bomb had met our highest hopes and that the shock of its use would very likely knock our already wavering enemy out of the war."[145] On July 23, Stimson recorded that even the cautious General Marshall "felt, as I felt sure he would, that now with our new weapon we would not need the assistance of the Russians to conquer Japan."[146] This confirming view was reported to the President the next day,[147] and now there was unanimity; the ambivalent strategy of delay had paid off; it was no longer even necessary to attempt to maintain the insurance of a Soviet declaration of war. Thus, there was a double irony in the Potsdam meeting, for not only was it too early to settle European matters, but the only other reason for coming to the Conference—to insure a Soviet declaration of war—had now also disappeared.[148]

During June and early July American officials had agreed that a proclamation attempting to "warn Japan into surrender" would be issued from the Potsdam meeting. The warning had been conceived partly in the hope that if it were accepted the atomic bombing would be forestalled; but its primary objective had been to reinforce the impact of the bombing—for then, as Stimson had emphasized, although the atomic bomb would not be specifically mentioned in the declaration, the new weapon would be related to a demand for surrender, and it would serve as a "sanction" to the warning.[149] Thus, the primary aim of the proclamation was to encourage a prompt Japanese surrender, and the War Department, for its part, had supported the measure not only to end the war before an invasion, but more precisely, "before too many of our allies are committed there."[150]

Nevertheless, it was realized, as Stimson and Stettinius had specifically advised (and as was apparent to all concerned), that if the warning was endorsed by the Soviet Union its effectiveness would be multiplied manifold.[151] Before Potsdam, optional phrases including the Soviet Union as one of the signatory powers had been written into the warning at various points. These would be used if it was decided to invite Stalin to join in issuing the proclamation.[152] Similarly, before Potsdam, General Marshall and former Secretary of State Hull had particularly emphasized the great value of the Soviet "sanction" to the warning.[153] And Stimson's memorandum of advice to the President, reflecting the pre-Potsdam ambivalence, was replete with conditional phrases regarding the possibility of utilizing "the ominous threat of Russia" in conjunction with the proclamation.[154]

Now, however, greatly bolstered by the atomic test, Truman decided to strike out the tentative phrases and issue the proclamation without asking Stalin's participation.[155] During June, American leaders, aware that the Soviet Premier might not like to give the enemy advance indications of his intentions, had hesitated before suggesting that the United States Chiefs of Staff come to Potsdam; after the German defeat, military discussions could only be concerned with the Far East, and, "having in mind the possible Japanese reaction" to such a powerful hint of Russian plans, they were quite aware that Stalin might avoid military consultations.[156] Now, however, there was no fear of embarrassing the Soviet leadership or of prejudicing the military situation in Manchuria; much to the surprise and apparent anger of the Russians, the warning proclamation was issued from the site of the tripartite meeting even before the Russians were informed of its existence.[157]

Similarly, when on July 29 Molotov requested that the President provide a formal letter inviting Soviet participation in the war, Truman attempted to avoid the issue.[158] The Secretary of State and his assistant Benjamin Cohen spent the better part of the afternoon trying to devise a response to the Soviet request.[159] "We had, of course, begun to hope that a Japanese surrender might be imminent and we did not want to urge the Russians to enter the war," Byrnes has testified.[160] After considerable thought, finally the President sent Stalin a legalistic letter stating that he felt the new United Nations Charter (although not yet ratified) made it proper for the Russians to join in the war against an aggressor.[161] Undoubtedly aware of the limitations of this document, in a covering note Truman told Stalin: "If you decide to use it, it will be all right. However, if you decide to issue a statement basing your action on other grounds or for any other reason prefer not to use this letter, it will be satisfactory to me."[162] As General Deane has noted, " . . . Soviet participation was no longer an essential ingredient . . . we were in a position to be tough and indifferent."[163]

But avoiding the issue was only the most passive aspect of the American approach at Potsdam. By this time American leaders not only had little desire to maintain the possibility of a Russian declaration of war, but they were deeply concerned that the Red Army might cross the Manchurian border before the Japanese surrender. Secretary of the Navy Forrestal discussed the problem with the Secretary of State on July 28. His diary entry records: " . . . Byrnes said he was most anxious to get the Japanese affair over with before the Russians got in, with particular reference to [the Manchurian ports of] Dairen and Port Arthur. Once in there, he felt it would not be easy to get them out. . . ."[164] Moreover, as Byrnes has recently revealed, it was primarily for this reason that the earlier decision to inform Stalin of the successful atomic test had been rejected in practice; the vague statement that a powerful new weapon was available had been made because Truman and Byrnes feared that if Stalin were aware of the full power of the atomic test—and the possibility that the atomic bomb would end the war before Russia entered—the Soviet Premier might immediately order the Red Army to attack.*

And it was also for this reason that American policy makers—for the third time—shifted the emphasis of their approach to the Soong mission. No longer interested in preserving the possibility of an early declaration of war, Truman and Byrnes now hoped to use the negotiations only as a way to hold off the Red Army attack while the atomic bombs were brought into action. As General Deane has written, "It was a foregone conclusion that a satisfactory adjustment would be reached,"[165] but with the full report of the New Mexico test in hand, on July 23, the President and the Secretary of State, carefully trying to avoid the appearance of disregarding Roosevelt's pledges, cabled Chiang Kai-shek that they did not want him to make any concessions. They also declared that it was important for the Chinese to resume negotiations with Stalin.[166] "I had some fear," Byrnes later reported, "that if they did not, Stalin might immediately enter the war."[167]

Thus the strategy of delay continued. Despite the American interest in Sino-Soviet agreement on the complicated Chinese and Manchu-

---

* This information comes from Byrnes. Asked about the question many years later, Truman did not deny this intent, but stated that he did not remember such a consideration. (Feis, *Japan Subdued*, p. 89; also see above, p. 204.)

This fear may also partly account for the fact that despite Truman's desire to leave the Conference after July 23, he stayed on until August 2. Truman and Byrnes may well have wished to keep Stalin negotiating until the atomic bomb was used. At one point, it seemed the first attack could have taken place any time after August 1. Similarly, brief military conversations took place at Potsdam. Undoubtedly these were held though they were no longer needed, because cancellation of the talks would have aroused Soviet suspicions.

rian issues, the President had no wish to complete the negotiations until after the atomic bomb had been used and, as hoped, the Japanese war had ended. Although on July 17 the President informally discussed with Stalin the American desire to maintain the "Open Door" in Manchuria, and specifically, to treat Dairen as a free port, he did not pursue these matters during the remainder of the conference.[168] Similarly, although Stimson, Byrnes, and Harriman greatly feared that Russian control of the ports and railways of Manchuria might affect American commercial interests in the area, and although Stimson pressed his fears repeatedly in discussions with the President, Truman had no desire to attempt to secure new guarantees from Stalin at this juncture.[169] Finally, Truman rejected a proposal by State Department experts that Soong be summoned to Potsdam to conclude negotiations on the few remaining points in dispute.[170]

Even more obviously than in his handling of the European matters, the President made it clear that he had no wish to negotiate. His summer plans to complete the treaties in his talk with Stalin were suspended. The agenda items on the Far East were not taken up, and Truman did not press his earlier demand to be consulted before the Soviet Chinese treaty was signed. The "appropriate time"* had not yet arrived; first there would be an attempt to end the war. Then, with the Red Army stalled on the far side of the Manchurian border and—as Stimson had urged two months earlier—with the "master card" in hand, it would be time to "have it out with Russia on her relations to Manchuria and Port Arthur and various other parts of North China, and also the relations of China to us."†

During the last days of the Potsdam meeting, Stalin brought a further Japanese message to the attention of the President. Replying to the Soviet request for more definite information regarding the proposed Prince Konoye mission, the Japanese ambassador stated:

> The mission . . . was to ask the Soviet Government to take part in mediation to end the present war and to transmit the complete Japanese case in this respect. . . . Simultaneously, he wished to repeat that Prince Konoe (sic) was especially charged by His Majesty the Emperor to convey to the Soviet Government that it was exclusively

---

* See above, p. 172.　　　　　　　　　† See above, p. 146.

the desire of His Majesty to avoid more bloodshed by the parties engaged in the war. . . .*[171]

Though the message was still lacking in detail, there could be now no doubt that the Japanese government was seriously looking for a way to end the war. But again, the President had little interest in attempting to investigate the possibilities the Japanese approach offered. He simply agreed to the suggestion that the Russians should give a definite negative answer to the request that Prince Konoye be received, and he moved on to other business.†[172]

On the same day that Truman and Stalin discussed this matter (July 28), the Japanese Premier told a press conference that his government would *"mokusatsu"* the Potsdam warning.[173] Truman interpreted this as a rejection of the proclamation, taking the Japanese term to mean "ignore" or "regard as unworthy of public notice."[174] For this reason, earlier instructions to utilize the new weapons as soon as possible were not countermanded.

Truman permitted the bombing despite new cable intercepts which strongly indicated that the Japanese decision to *"mokusatsu"* did not mean an abandonment of the attempt to end the war. In fact, the cables suggested that the Premier had wished to convey by his ambiguous word the equally possible meaning, "withhold comment at this time."[175] A cable intercepted on the same day of the press conference showed that in the two days since the proclamation had been received the Japanese government had not yet reached a decision on how to treat the important question it raised. Truman's earlier decision to issue the warning proclamation without Soviet endorsement had been responsible to a considerable degree for the prolongation of Japanese indecision; despite the fact that the Soviet Union was not a belligerent, a proclamation from the Big Three Conference but signed only by Truman and Churchill (and Chiang Kai-shek) had increased the confusion with which the Japanese appraised the Soviet attitude. The cable to the Japanese ambassador stated: "The position taken by the Soviet Union in connection with the Potsdam joint declaration . . . will henceforth have a bearing on our planning and will be a

---

* Truman had already seen an intercepted copy of this message. (*Conference of Berlin*, I, p. 873; II, pp. 1262–63.)

† As can be seen the Russians for their own reasons were little interested in negotiations to end the war.

very important problem." It stressed that the Soviet attitude raised a number of questions which could not be immediately answered. "For the time being, countermeasures against the joint declaration will be decided after we receive and study the Soviet reply to our" latest message.*[176]

This intercepted cable was followed by another, on August 2, which stated: "The battle situation has become acute. There are only a few days left in which to make arrangements to end the war. . . . Since the loss of one day relative to this matter may result in a thousand years of regret, it is requested that you immediately have a talk with Molotov . . ."[177] But the President evidently had no interest in these cables, nor in potentially time-consuming attempts to explore the opportunity to bring the hostilities to an end.†

On the contrary, as T. V. Soong reached Moscow, the first days of August took on the air of a frenzied race for time. Although under the previously delivered orders the bombing could take place anytime after August 3, weather conditions in Japan frustrated the desire for an immediate strike.[178] Now, apparently worried that Stalin might become impatient with the continued stalling of the Chinese negotiators, or that Soong might yield, on August 5, Truman sent a final instruction to Ambassador Harriman asking him to tell Stalin that the United States believed the Chinese could be expected to go no further toward meeting the Soviet demands.[179]

Thus, as the President and his entourage aboard the cruiser *Augusta* reached mid-Atlantic on the return voyage from Potsdam, the strategy of delay entered its final phase. Truman and Byrnes (and

---

* There can be no doubt that the President and the Secretary of State were as well informed on this and subsequent cables as they were on the previous ones. Byrnes reports that on July 28, for example, "Secretary Forrestal arrived and told me in detail of the intercepted messages from the Japanese government to Ambassador Sato in Moscow, indicating Japan's willingness to surrender." (*All in One Lifetime*, p. 297.)

† It is sometimes argued that Truman had to use the atomic bomb because the Japanese would not accept "unconditional" surrender. (Byrnes, *Speaking Frankly*, pp. 211, 262.) This argument neglects the fact that early in the summer Truman had decided if necessary to permit a conditional surrender allowing the Japanese to maintain

the Imperial institutions. (See above, p. 158.) Hence, his use of the atomic bomb must be explained in other terms. See also Stimson's diary entry of July 24: "I then spoke [to Truman] of the importance which I attributed to the reassurance of the Japanese on the continuance of their dynasty . . . I hoped that the President would watch carefully so that the Japanese might be reassured verbally through diplomatic channels if it was found that they were hanging fire on that one point. He said he had that in mind, and that he would take care of it. . . ." (*Conference of Berlin*, II, p. 1272.) See Lord Alanbrooke's similar conclusions, and his suggestion that "an opportune moment to make it clear to the Japanese might be shortly after a Russian entry into the war." (*Ibid.*, p. 36.)

Stimson, already in America) fixed their attention on the much awaited battle test of the revolutionary new weapon.[180] Hopefully, it would end the war before the Red Army entered Manchuria. By its dramatic blast it would herald a new and unprecedented advance in American power and—if the logic followed throughout the summer of delay continued to hold true—its force would permit a new American initiative in European and Far Eastern diplomacy.

CHAPTER VII

American Diplomacy Takes the Offensive

Byrnes had already told me . . . that in his belief the bomb might well put us in a position to dictate our own terms at the end of the war.
—PRESIDENT HARRY S. TRUMAN on a conversation with James F. Byrnes in April 1945

THERE IS NO WAY to recapture the shock of the bombing of Hiroshima and Nagasaki. It requires an extraordinary feat of historical imagination to recreate the surprise and drama and horror of the day the world first learned of the atomic bomb. And it is all but impossible to recall the instant change in American thinking, the new sense of confidence and power the first atomic explosions engendered. To understand the impact of the new weapon upon diplomacy, one must go beyond the simple assertion that the added military power could be useful in war and in diplomatic maneuvering. In the first instance, its influence was psychological.

Truman's exuberance and Churchill's excitement at Potsdam show some of the emotional force of the new development. Though he had expected the bomb to be a success for many months, and despite the fact that at Potsdam he learned how greatly the test had exceeded expectations, when the President was informed of the successful bombing of Hiroshima, the effect was remarkable. Aboard the cruiser *Augusta*, Truman hurried back and forth telling officers and crew alike the news.[1] "I was greatly moved," the President has told us; and his sentiment was not remorse, but satisfaction. His first remark to those with him at the time was the unqualified assertion, "This is the greatest thing in history!"[2]

To the average American, as well as to most senior government officials, news of the atomic bomb came first from the newspapers. Here too the weapon's power was disclosed in a way which produced great emotion and optimism about its usefulness as an instrument of high policy. On August 7, newspapers were filled with banner headlines announcing the devastation of Hiroshima.[3] Not only was the development an unprecedented and amazing—indeed, at the time, fantastic*—scientific feat, but at once the bomb's seemingly incredible power for war and peace was dramatically disclosed. In less time than it took to read a newspaper, the American public learned that the bomb might reduce the Japanese war from a publicly estimated year and a half to a few short weeks or even days. Immediately, news of Nagasaki convinced those who might have doubted the extent of the new power. In less than a week, the war—which until then had been a long series of costly island-to-island battles against an enemy who fought to the death—was suddenly over. Not only was the atomic bomb spectacular in itself, but it immediately demonstrated its apparent capacity to force surrender upon a powerful enemy.†[4]

While the public at large was treated to the dramatic news of the weapon, the President and his senior advisers worked feverishly to end the Japanese war quickly. Ironically, the atomic bomb had not fulfilled one hope of the strategy of delay; with the Soong negotiations still stalled, on August 8—three months, to the day, after German capitulation—the Soviet Union declared war on Japan, and early the

---

* The *New York Herald Tribune* (Aug. 7, 1945) commented that the new force was "weird, incredible and somehow disturbing; one forgets the effect on Japan or on the course of the war as one senses the foundations of one's own universe trembling . . ."

† In recalling the effect of the bombing upon the American public I wish only to point out that most Americans did not doubt (and do not doubt) that the atomic bomb ended the war. (See, for example, Truman, *Year of Decisions,* p. 426; Byrnes, *Speaking Frankly,* p. 264; *All in One Lifetime,* p. 308.) Though a good case can probably be made that the Soviet declaration of war actually provided the *coup de grâce,* there is no need to argue the point,

nor can a final answer to this question ever be given. However, note that the Japanese Cabinet did not decide to surrender after the first atomic bomb, that the Cabinet fixed its hopes on the undetermined Soviet attitude until the very moment Stalin declared war, that the Russian entry hit where it counted (ending the hope of *the military leaders*), and that American propaganda directed at Japan after Hiroshima stressed the importance of the Russian attack. (Ehrman, *Grand Strategy,* pp. 283, 306–7; Hewlett and Anderson, *The New World,* p. 403; Craven and Cate, *Air Forces in World War II,* Vol. V, pp. 730–32; S. E. Morison, "Why Japan Surrendered," *The Atlantic,* October 1960, p. 47.)

next morning the Red Army crossed the Manchurian border.[5] In the few days between the Soviet declaration and the formal surrender of Japan, Stimson, Byrnes, and Truman continued to follow the basic line of strategy they had adopted during the summer. Stimson urged the President that "the thing to do was to get this surrender through as quickly as we can before Russia . . . should get down in reach of the Japanese homeland . . . It was of great importance to get the homeland into our hands before the Russians could put in any substantial claim to occupy and help rule it."[6]

Byrnes, of course, emphatically agreed.[7] But an August 10 Japanese message accepting the Potsdam Proclamation was conditional; it asked guarantees that the Emperor's position be respected.[8] Stimson urged that American assurances for the Emperor would produce a quick surrender.[9] Byrnes, agreeing with the objective, disagreed on tactics—such assurances might appear as a sign of weakness and could "cause much delay."[10] Finally, Truman accepted a suggestion by Forrestal that a message which implicitly recognized the Emperor's position but which was explicitly "unconditional" would be the best way to secure a prompt response.[11] In the meantime, "the President observed that we would keep up the war at its present intensity."*

Byrnes now attempted to arrange quick approval for this approach from the other Allies.[12] When Molotov asked for a day to consider the

---

* The tremendous desire to end the war quickly was expressed in many ways. Since the bomb dropped on Hiroshima accomplished the shock effect, the use of the second bomb against Nagasaki may well be explained by noting that Truman and Byrnes wished to leave absolutely no doubt about their resources or their intentions, and were anxious to avoid any time-consuming delays. Byrnes has testified they knew "the Japanese were patently anxious to surrender," but after the first Japanese acceptance message came in, Truman ordered conventional military operations to continue full force. At the Cabinet meeting on August 10, Stimson "suggested . . . that it would be a humane thing . . . that might affect the settlement if we stopped the bombing. . . ." However, his view was "rejected on the ground that it couldn't be done at once because we had not yet received in official form the Japanese surrender. . . ." Stimson's diary entry continues: "This of course was a correct but narrow reason, for the Japanese had broadcast their offer of surrender through every country in the world." (Stimson Diary, Aug. 10, 1945.) Forrestal's diary shows that Stimson also "cited the growing feeling of apprehension and misgiving as to the effect of the atomic bomb even in our own country," and that the Secretary of the Navy supported the advice that conventional bombing should cease. (Forrestal, *Diaries*, p. 83.) Truman refused to let up the pace even after the Japanese accepted the final American message, which implicitly acknowledged the position of the Emperor. Long after Radio Tokyo had broadcast acceptance of these terms (on August 14), but before the message had reached Washington through official channels, General Arnold (who wished to stage as big a *finale* as possible) was permitted to send 1,014 aircraft (approximately 800 B-29's and 200 fighters) to drop six thousand tons of conventional explosives on Honshu. (Byrnes, *All in One Lifetime*, p. 305; Truman, *Year of Decisions*, p. 423; Leahy, *I Was There*, pp. 434–36; Craven and Cate, *Air Forces in World War II*, Vol. V, pp. 699, 732–33; *New York Times*, Aug. 15, 1945.)

American message, Byrnes made it clear through Harriman that the United States was quite prepared to accept the surrender without the Soviet Union unless approval for the American message was immediately given.[13] Stalin quickly yielded to the American demand,[14] and the message was sent to the Japanese on August 11.[15] Now there was nothing to do except wait for the response.

Aware that each hour meant a further advance of the Soviet armies, and also some loss of life, American leaders now became extremely impatient.[16] "Never have I known time to pass so slowly!" Byrnes recalls.[17] When Japanese acceptance of the American message arrived, Byrnes abandoned all diplomatic requirements. Although the three powers had attempted to coordinate the acceptance and announcement of the German surrender,[18] Byrnes now cut consultations short and, giving the other Allies less than three hours' notice, he declared that the President would announce acceptance of the Japanese surrender at 7 P.M., August 14; the others could join in at that time if they wished.[19]

Thus, the war was ended five days after the Red Army entered Manchuria. Despite the fact that the atomic bomb did not prevent the attack, however, it did fulfill the other hope of the strategy of delay. Truman has characterized the result: "Our dropping of the atomic bomb on Japan . . . forced Russia to reconsider her position in the Far East."[20] Indeed, as Stimson had predicted, after the bombing the relative positions of the United States and the Soviet Union were radically altered. A new firmness immediately appeared in American diplomacy and, correspondingly a new willingness to yield appeared in the Soviet stance.

After the New Mexico test, Truman had decided to exclude the Soviet Union from a significant role in the occupation and control of Japan.[21] For this reason the August 11 message, as Stimson noted, "asserted that the action of the Emperor must be dominated by the Allied commander, using the singular to exclude any condominium."[22] When Harriman had demanded immediate Soviet agreement to the message, Molotov had asked for time to consider just this point.[23] But Moscow was in no position to dispute American prerogatives and by endorsing the American message the Soviet government formally paved the way for unilateral American control of Japan.[24]

Similarly, Stalin could do very little when Truman simply refused his request that the Red Army be allowed to take a token surrender in the Japanese homeland (on the northern half of the island of Hokkaido).[25] And Stalin's readiness to accept American conditions after Hiroshima was underscored a week after surrender when an American proposal for a Far Eastern Advisory Commission was accepted.[26] This body, unlike the Control Commissions governing the other ex-enemy states, was to be virtually powerless. Its location—in Washington—stressed the fact that it would have little control over the operating decisions of the Supreme Commander, General Douglas MacArthur, in Tokyo.[27] Thus, it was with the general approval of the Russians that Truman told the press on August 16 that Japan would not be divided into occupation zones, and declared in the first week of September that as far as Japan was concerned, "in the event of any differences of opinion [among the Allied powers] the policies of the United States will govern."*[28]

That the atomic bomb had strengthened the American hand was even more clearly demonstrated when the "tangled weave" of Manchurian issues was taken up. Japan, of course, was beyond the reach of the landlocked Red Army. But even in the area of Soviet military operations, Truman now found Stalin prepared to accept most American terms. The President had delayed the Manchurian negotiations all summer, and he had rejected the State Department's suggestion that they be concluded at Potsdam. However, as soon as the news of Hiroshima was made public, on August 7, 9, and 10, following his instructions, Harriman told Stalin and Soong that the United States believed the Chinese should make no further concessions.[29] With only a short debate, Stalin now conceded almost all of the points he had pressed so diligently during the past month of talks with Soong:†
Dairen was to become a free port under Chinese administration

---

* Later, during the London Conference, Stalin reversed his attitude, demanding a greater role in Japan. As Walter Lippmann, James Reston, the London *Times*, the *Christian Science Monitor*, and others noted at the time, his reversal was probably in retaliation to the pressure Byrnes put on the Soviet position in the Balkans. (*New York Herald Tribune*, Sept. 25; *New York Times*, Oct. 14; London *Times*, Oct. 2; *Christian Science Monitor*, Oct. 3, 1945.)

† See above, pp. 170–73.

(except in time of war),[30] and the jointly owned Manchurian railways were to be governed by a ten-man board of directors (five from each country) whose President was to be a Chinese Nationalist with decisive power to cast two votes.[31] A treaty was initialed on August 14 which "generally satisfied" Chiang Kai-shek,[32] and Ambassador Harriman cabled that T. V. Soong "was very grateful for our support and is convinced that unless we had taken an active part in the negotiations he would have had to accede to all Stalin's demands."*[33]

In Chungking, Ambassador Hurley was enthusiastic about the value of the treaties to internal Chinese politics. As in 1927, the Russians took a stand against the Chinese Communists:† "The publication . . . has demonstrated conclusively that the Soviet Government supports the National Government of China and also that the two governments are in agreement regarding Manchuria."[34] In America, most commentators expressed great satisfaction with the settlement in an area not administered by China for many years and under the direct military control of the Soviet Union.[35] On August 29, Madame Chiang visited Truman to thank him for his support. The President told his press conference: "She was very happy over the Russian-Chinese treaty, just as all of us are."[36]

To be sure, at a later date the hopes these successful negotiations produced were to be dissipated. But at the time—and for a very considerable period—Stalin respected the treaties.[37] Chiang Kai-shek's administrators were permitted to take over civilian control in the Red Army zone of operations[38] and the American Air Force and Navy ferried thousands of Nationalist troops (who had no independent way to reach the area)[39] to Manchuria to take over responsibilities from the Russians.[40] Although Stalin took advantage of his position to remove a number of Manchurian industries as "war booty,"‡[41] the Red Army withdrew in April 1946.[42] As the State Department later summarized the situation: "It was considered that Russia had accepted

---

* For the texts of the agreements, see Department of State, *Relations with China*, Annexes 51–59, pp. 585–96.

† And in 1959–1965?

‡ As I have noted, in the late autumn of 1945 a new Soviet *démarche* in the Far East seemed to be a direct response to the American effort in the Balkans. (See above, p. 240*fn.*) It may well be that the Soviet interest in industrial reparations and "war booty" from Manchuria was also a response to the West's reluctance to adhere to the Yalta reparations formula and the subsequent breakdown of German administrative arrangements.

definite limitations on its activities in China and was committed to withhold all aid from the Chinese Communists. . . ."*[43]

Thus the primary American objectives in the Far East were achieved. Moreover, as had been expected throughout the summer, now Truman and Byrnes began to take the initiative to secure further political and commercial concessions in Manchuria. At Stimson's suggestion, Truman had also deferred an approach to the Russians on these additional matters during the summer.† At Potsdam he had rejected the suggestion that negotiations begin while Stalin and he were together. However, now the "appropriate time"‡ had arrived. In his first approach to Molotov after Hiroshima, Harriman was instructed to attempt to secure a new public statement affirming Soviet support for America's traditional "Open Door" policy in the area.[44] Molotov initially responded that such a statement was superfluous, since Stalin had repeatedly confirmed his support for this policy.[45] But Truman and Byrnes persisted, on August 22 instructing Harriman to press the matter with Stalin himself.[46] This effort succeeded. On August 27 the Soviet Premier overruled his foreign minister and said he was prepared to issue the declaration sought by Washington.[47]

THE SECRET CLOSE-IN APPROACH

IN THE WHIRLWIND DAYS immediately after Hiroshima and Nagasaki, American diplomacy changed so swiftly that few observers have caught the sweep of all the policy decisions unveiled in a few short weeks. Secretary Byrnes, however, has emphasized the importance of this brief period. Underscoring the breadth and scope of new diplomatic departures, he has recalled: "Those . . . days . . . were full of action."[48] In fact, the sheer volume of work caused the Secretary of

---

* Although it is still a matter of dispute to what extent Stalin aided the Chinese Communists in the first postwar years, there is substantial agreement that his assistance, if of any importance at all, was extremely limited. (Beloff, *Soviet Policy*, pp. 42–43; Department of State, *Relations with China*, p. 121.) The Red Army withdrew from Manchuria in April 1946. (*Ibid.*, p. 147; McNeill, *America, Britain and Russia, 1941–46*, p. 709.) As late as June 1947, Byrnes made no complaints that Stalin was supporting the Chinese Communists. At that time

Byrnes was still able to write: "Whether Stalin will continue to resist the temptation . . . is a question which . . . remains in the balance." (Byrnes, *Speaking Frankly*, pp. 227–29, 293.) Similarly, as late as September 1947 the Chinese Foreign Minister wished to do nothing which might cause Stalin to reconsider his obligations under the Sino-Soviet treaty. (Department of State, *Relations with China*, p. 121.)

† See above, pp. 146, 149–51.

‡ See above, p. 172.

State to ask that the London foreign ministers' meeting set for September 1 be postponed until September 10.[49]

Amongst all the activities, however, unquestionably the most important concerned atomic energy. At precisely the same time American Far Eastern diplomacy was achieving its objectives, Truman and Byrnes also made it clear that the United States intended to maintain its atomic monopoly.

Truman's August 6 statement—released with the news of Hiroshima—revealed that "it is not intended to divulge the technical processes of production or all the military applications."[50] In his August 9 report to the nation, the President declared: "The atomic bomb is too dangerous to be loose in a lawless world . . . We must constitute ourselves trustees of this new force."[51] Within a week of the presidential statement, the War Department released a long report on atomic energy with the notice: "The best interests of the United States require the utmost cooperation by all concerned in keeping secret now and for all time in the future all scientific and technical information. . . ."[52] In another week Truman directed that no information on the nuclear development project be released without the specific approval of the President.*[53]

Thus, Truman made public his resolve to maintain the production secrets of the new weapon. His declarations revealed that Stimson's early idea of exchanging information on nuclear energy (and simultaneously establishing international controls) had been rejected. Instead of the theory that the new development might be used as a bargaining counter with which to obtain diplomatic *quid pro quos* from the Russians, there was to be what Stimson had once described as "the secret close-in attempted control of the project by those who control it now."[54] Although initially Truman had had to decide only that diplomacy would be delayed until the atomic weapons were demonstrated, by the end of July he had also resolved the nascent dispute between Stimson and Byrnes; the President had adopted the Secretary of State's more narrow view that a temporary monopoly of nuclear weapons, in itself, would be valuable to diplomacy.†

---

* Churchill praised this decision in the House of Commons. (5th Series, *Hansard*, Vol. 413, Commons, 76–86.) Shortly thereafter Stimson's successor, Robert Patterson, reassured Congress that "the President has already said that he would not reveal the atomic bomb itself at all . . ." (U.S. House of Representatives, *Hearings: Atomic Energy Act*, Oct. 9, 18, 1945, p. 66.)

† See above, pp. 110–12.

Indeed, although the policy decision was taken in late July and made public only on August 6, the crucial assumptions of the narrow view had been adopted as early as the first week of June; for, despite Stimson's hopeful discussion of diplomatic *quid pro quos*, the Interim Committee had been strongly influenced by the Secretary of State–designate. In the May 31 meeting of the Committee, the director of the Los Alamos laboratories, J. Robert Oppenheimer, had argued that under a system of controls the United States should offer the world free interchange of nuclear information, with special emphasis on peacetime uses. He had felt the nation would strengthen its moral position if it acted before using the bomb.[55] General Marshall and Assistant Secretary of State Clayton, however, had argued against putting faith in a system of inspection safeguards for international control.[56] General Marshall had added his opinion that it would be best to build up a combination of like-minded powers that would bring Russia into line by the very force of the coalition.[57] As the discussion progressed, Byrnes had intervened decisively; he argued against giving information to the Russians, even in general terms. He concluded that the best policy was to push production and research and make certain that the United States stayed ahead.[58]

Byrnes's prestige—and his status as personal representative of the President—had not been ignored. The Interim Committee unanimously concurred in his judgment: It would be best to push research and production, to maintain secrecy, and to establish a combination of democratic powers for cooperation in atomic energy.[59] Byrnes and the Committee also expressed hope that some form of cooperation with Russia could be worked out so that under a control system each country would make public whatever work was being done on the subject.[60] However, in reality the Committee's recommendations all but excluded the possibility of international control of atomic energy: The Russians were unlikely to accept continued American production and research without attempting to secure nuclear weapons for themselves, and the Committee had no specific control proposals to make. Aware of the limitations of this approach, even as Stimson had discussed *quid pro quos* with the President on June 6, he had acknowledged that the Committee's ideas were "imperfect" and that they "might not be assented to by Russia." But he had told the President that "we were far enough ahead of the game to be able to accumulate enough material to serve as insurance."[61]

Thus, in the end, even Stimson, who knew that a nuclear monopoly could not be maintained, and who was deeply concerned by the prospect of an arms race, had given priority to continued weapons production and research instead of an attempt to establish international controls. Stimson briefly took great interest in a proposal that further production of atomic weapons should be halted temporarily as evidence of good faith, so that an approach to Russia could be attempted, but he did not pursue the idea.[62] On June 21 the Interim Committee, preparing a statement to be issued by the President, struck out a proposed sentence which would have committed the United States to attempt to achieve international control of atomic energy.[63] Stimson accepted the draft,[64] but although he continued to be troubled that, as he had once expressed it, "modern civilization might be completely destroyed,"[65] apparently few other members of the Interim Committee shared his fears.*

Most important, the President's personal representative, Secretary Byrnes, had few doubts about the wisdom of the "close-in" approach.[66] He believed the temporary atomic monopoly would be a great advantage to American diplomacy.[67] In his view, the primary task was to establish a "lasting structure of peace."[68] A stable Europe, essential to world peace and American security alike, was the number-one goal.[69] Byrnes also believed that the nuclear monopoly could be maintained for at least seven years.[70] He appears to have been convinced that within this period, with the support of the revolutionary new weapon, his diplomacy could easily achieve its idealistic objectives. Thus, the weapon seemed a crucial factor in forcing agreement to an American plan for permanent peace—a plan which, *ipso facto*, would prevent another world war. Since this vision promised an end to all war it implicitly obviated the danger of an arms race. There seemed plenty of time to accomplish the task before the Russians might break the American monopoly.† In any case, as Byrnes has written, "no one

---

* Oppenheimer is an exception. See Atomic Energy Commission, *Oppenheimer Hearings* for repeated references to his personal depression during this period and his fear for the future.

† "Permanent peace," or "lasting peace," or "durable peace," seems to have been a universal objective of American policy makers. (See above, pp. 101, 126.) In retro-
(*Continued on next page*)

seemed too alarmed at the prospect, because it appeared that in seven years we should be far ahead of the Soviets in this field."[71]

Byrnes's arguments for secrecy and continued production of weapons convinced not only the Interim Committee but also the President. Although during June Truman also spoke optimistically of diplomatic *quid pro quos,* he accepted the recommendations presented to him. In mid-July, at Potsdam, the President told Churchill he would "at all costs . . . refuse to divulge any particulars."[72] He later wrote: "I had decided that the secret of the manufacture of the weapon would remain a secret with us."[73]

Indeed, during the Potsdam Conference both the President and Stimson lost the trace of interest in international controls each had evidenced earlier in the summer. Depressed by the omnipresent Soviet secret police in Berlin, both came to the conclusion that a control scheme could hope to succeed only if Russia were to become an open, democratic society.[74] As Harriman pointed out (and as Stimson soon realized),[75] to attempt to force the Soviet Union to change its national system would be to demand something no great power could consider.[76] However, once accepted, the idea that controls could be established only if Russia became a democracy inevitably destroyed even the meager remaining hope of international cooperation. Stimson's diary shows that this realization "troubled me a great deal,"[77] but as Truman has testified, the Secretary of War no longer urged the exchange of important information on the weapon.[78] And Stimson returned from Potsdam strongly opposed to the release of any atomic information.*[79]

The President later (in September) expressed some interest in meth-

---

(*Continued from preceding page*)
spect it is not surprising that leading officials, having personally experienced two world wars in one lifetime, should have aimed so consistently for a proper basis—as they defined it—which would eliminate a third world war. Nor, indeed, is it surprising that once given the unexpected power of the atomic bomb that they should have regarded the weapon as a means to achieve their goal. In this early period, Byrnes's view was the most straightforward, but compare Churchill's statement to the House of Commons, August 16, 1945: "The United States stand at this moment at the summit of the world . . . Let them act up to the level of their power . . . So far as we know, there are at least three and per-

haps four years before the concrete progress made in the United States can be overtaken. *In these three years we must remould the relationships of all men, wherever they dwell, in all the nations. . . ."* (5th Series, *Hansard,* Vol. 413, Commons, 80.) The newly available information on Byrnes's view also illuminates a previously enigmatic statement in his memoirs. Recalling discussions of the bomb with Churchill at Potsdam, Byrnes states: "In addition to his tremendous interest in the effect of the bomb on the war with Japan [Churchill] foresaw more clearly than many others the possibilities presented by the release of atomic energy." (*Speaking Frankly,* p. 262.)

For more information on Byrnes's view, see Hewlett and Anderson, *The New World,* ods for "controlling bomb warfare"[80] but the idea of sharing important information under a control scheme was dropped—"As far as I was concerned, this was not a matter for discussion."[81] Having accepted Byrnes's basic recommendations and having agreed that no control would be possible until the Soviet Union changed its system, Truman automatically—and apparently quite confidently—ended up strongly supporting the narrow view of his Secretary of State. Even before Potsdam there is little evidence that Truman showed much personal interest in promoting attempts to establish international controls. During the Conference he rejected the idea that frank relations and international cooperation required that he tell Stalin of the new weapon before using it.† After the Conference the President followed Byrnes's recommendations that no approach to the Russians be made. He told de Gaulle that because the United States had the only atomic bombs, "the peace problem . . . was therefore largely economic."[82] Stimson's Potsdam advice, which made control seem impossible, had bolstered Byrnes's conception of the role of the bomb in diplomacy; Truman concluded that so long as no "foolproof" method of control existed, "it was important to retain the advantage which the possession of the bomb had given us."‡[83]

---

pp. 354–60, 417, 418, 456, 458–59, 461, 469, 532; Atomic Energy Commission, *Oppenheimer Hearings*, p. 33; *The New York Times*, Sept. 6, 1945; Byrnes, *Speaking Frankly*, pp. 87, 179, 203, 261; *All in One Lifetime*, pp. 284, 303; Stimson Diary, Aug. 12–Sept. 3, Sept. 5, Sept. 11, 1945. The reader will note that I have not mentioned as one of the reasons for Byrnes's opposition to control schemes his belief that they were technically impossible. From all the evidence I have seen, it is quite clear that Byrnes *began* with the idea of basing his diplomacy on the atomic bomb (as his early April discussions with Truman show). Though he certainly distrusted the Russians, there is little evidence that at this time he opposed international control schemes because of doubts about their feasibility. Rather, he simply had no interest in any of the various schemes suggested which might have deprived him of the key factor in his diplomacy.

In 1947 Byrnes came to the conclusion that when the Russians caught up there would be little likelihood of war. Recalling that neither party used poison gas or germ warfare during the Second World War, he argued that a parallel situation would eventually be reached: "No nation dared use these terrible weapons because they knew the same weapons would be used against them." (*Speaking Frankly*, p. 276.) Though Byrnes failed to achieve his diplomatic objectives, if the present delicate balance of terror can be maintained, ironically Byrnes's prediction may be borne out.

* Stimson later reconsidered his entire viewpoint. See Appendix III.

† See above, pp. 204, 231.

‡ The last sentence is Truman's 1955 recollection. From the evidence I have seen, however, it appears that between April and August 1945 Truman never had more than a passing interest in the idea of international control. Despite his comments about *quid pro quos*, in practice he seems to have consistently agreed with Byrnes that the implied threat of the weapon could not be given up to an international control scheme. Available evidence does not permit a final determination of how Truman saw the problem at the time, but as I have shown, even taking Truman's recollection at its face value, by the time of Potsdam he had defined the control problem in a way which could not be resolved. Thus, on his own terms the "advantage which the possession of the bomb had given us" could only be the advantage urged by Byrnes.

In this way the ideas Byrnes had urged during the summer became American policy: When it came, the much delayed showdown would not be based upon exchanging an international control system for diplomatic *quid pro quos*. Instead the "advantage" of the weapon could only be its value as an "implied threat."* The consolidation of this viewpoint was confirmed privately at the same time the President offered his public pledges to guard the secrecy of the new development. In early August, immediately after Hiroshima and Nagasaki, Assistant Secretary of War McCloy found Byrnes resolutely against any negotiations looking toward the international control of atomic energy.[84] The Secretary of State reiterated that "in his opinion we should continue the Manhattan Project with full force."[85] Similarly, Byrnes, representing the President, transmitted a direction through General Groves to J. Robert Oppenheimer that the work at Los Alamos was not to let up.[86] Expenditures of the Manhattan Project rose during the first months of peace from 43 million dollars in August to 51 million in September to 59 million in October.[87]

Byrnes's dominant position in policy making was evidenced in other ways immediately after Potsdam. The scientific panel of the Interim Committee now reported that thermonuclear weapons might be developed, and that their power would greatly exceed the power of the fission weapons used in Japan. It was the panel's "unanimous and urgent recommendation" that such developments be controlled by international agreement. Again, however, the President's personal representative took a negative view of any attempt to approach the Russians. Oppenheimer, who had helped draft the report and had carried the panel's recommendation to Byrnes, was told that the "proposal about an international agreement was not practical and that he and the rest of the gang should pursue their work [on the hydrogen weapon] full force."[88]

REMOVING THE SOVIET BLACKOUT
FROM THE BALKANS

TRUMAN'S STATEMENT that the United States would act as "trustees" of the new force came in his August 9 report to the nation on

---

* The term is taken from Stimson's diary report of Byrnes's privately expressed view of the bomb. (See below, p. 303.) Within a month the Secretary of War came to oppose the Byrnes view. On September 11, he also argued against "a succession of express or implied threats or near threats in our peace negotiations." (Stimson, *On Active Service*, p. 645.)

the Potsdam Conference. Thus, just as the atomic bomb had been intimately related to his European policy throughout the summer, the disclosure of the President's approach to the new weapon was implicitly linked to his first postwar discussion of European issues. Once again, however, it is necessary to recall that American departures in European diplomacy, in Far Eastern diplomacy, and in atomic-energy policy were revealed simultaneously, and in a great rush in the crowded second, third, and fourth weeks of August.

Truman's August 9 report on Potsdam emphasized his sense of confidence and optimism about the future; the Allies would "continue to march together to a lasting peace and a happy world."[89] Although he was not yet able to report that all his European objectives had been achieved, the President offered a convincing argument that the ultimate goal, a politically and economically stable Europe, would be achieved. In the main, the American proposals for Germany had been accepted. Agreement on political principles had been reached and, most important, the economic issue, which was dominated by the reparations question, had been settled along the lines of American proposals: The "idea of attempting to fix a dollar value . . . was dropped."[90] The President looked forward to early agreement on various other proposals when the foreign ministers held their first peacetime meeting in London. Soon most of the issues postponed at Potsdam might be settled.[91]

At the time Truman was making these remarks cooperative relations with the Russians began on a hopeful note almost everywhere on the Continent. In Germany, Eisenhower and Zhukov quickly established a warm friendship and close working relations.[92] Plans for free interzonal politics and trade were laid (and soon implemented).*[93] In Austria, General Mark Clark was less successful in his personal relationships, but he too found a considerable degree of Soviet coopera-

---

* The moderate Soviet approach in Eastern Germany and elsewhere during the early autumn of 1945 has been noted by many observers; and the radical changes which took place later have yet to be adequately explained. In addition to the fact that free enterprise, free trade, free travel, and free politics were promoted by the Russians in East Germany during this period, in October the Red Army ripped up vital rail communications extending from the Soviet Union through Poland to Germany. For more information on this fascinating but unexplored period, see Slusser, *Soviet Economic Policy in Postwar Germany*, pp. 16, 19, 20, 42, 55; Nettl, *The Eastern Zone and Soviet Policy in Germany, 1945–50*, pp. 80, 81, 281, 292; Leonhard, *Child of Revolution*, pp. 352, 379, 391, 411, 413–15, 427; Eisenhower, *Crusade in Europe*, p. 444. Similarly, at this time the Red Army, which controlled the greater part of Czechoslovakia and Hungary, withdrew. (McNeill, *America, Britain and Russia, 1941–46*, p. 734; Betts, *Central and South East Europe*, p. 126.)

tion immediately after Potsdam.[94] In Poland—the original symbol of Truman's policy—there also seemed to be signs of hope. At Potsdam, Truman had again secured Stalin's support for an early free election and for unrestricted reporting by Western correspondents.[95] Assistant Secretary of State Clayton and Ambassador Harriman had carried forward talks regarding economic aid with the Polish government.[96] Immediately after Potsdam, American correspondents requested permission to enter the country. (The Polish government agreed on August 24, and the reporters soon enjoyed unrestricted freedom.)[97] Ambassador Lane laid plans to bring to a culmination the summer strategy of attempting to bargain American credits for early elections and unrestricted trade. And, just as Truman had been confident the approach would work in April, Lane seemed to find every reason to believe the approach would now succeed.*

Thus, there seemed a reasonable basis for Truman's hopeful review of most European questions. But in his Potsdam report to the nation the President also discussed Southeastern Europe. And here, as had been clear before and during the Potsdam meeting, the Russians were not so amenable to American plans. Consequently, once again from Truman's point of view Southeastern Europe presented the most immediate challenge to American European policy. Truman's Potsdam demand that the governments of Bulgaria and Rumania be changed had been refused, but the President had made it quite clear that he was willing to postpone, not withdraw, his demand. Now, immediately after Hiroshima and Nagasaki, he publicly declared: "These nations are not to be spheres of influence of any one power."[98]

This statement of American opposition to Soviet domination of the Balkans was of major political significance. Here was the first open and public break in the wartime alliance. And immediately the President and his Secretary of State demonstrated that the declaration meant what it said: The United States demanded that the governments subservient to Soviet influence be removed. From the American point of view, forcing agreement on this issue was important not only in

---

* Lane held his first explicit talks with the Poles on September 3. Hoping to secure early free elections and the elimination of disciminatory trading agreements, he carried forward the April strategy in discussions throughout the autumn. "With complete candor," he stated that economic aid would be forthcoming only if the American proposals were accepted; "I determined to take advantage of the eagerness of the Polish Government for economic assistance and to use it as a lever. . . ." (Lane, *I Saw Poland Betrayed*, p. 145.)

itself, but also because the issue, like the Polish question in April, now came to symbolize American opposition to a Soviet sphere of influence throughout Eastern Europe. The crucial decision of the summer had been to delay a confrontation on this fundamental question until the atomic bomb had been demonstrated, and although the Potsdam meeting had unavoidably come a few weeks too soon, now there was no longer any reason to wait.

As early as mid-April, Byrnes had told the President that in his belief the bomb might well put America in a position to dictate terms at the end of the war.[99] He had told one of the nuclear scientists that the demonstration and possession of the new weapon would make Russia more manageable in Eastern Europe, specifically mentioning Poland, Rumania, and Hungary.* Now Secretary Byrnes set about the task of implementing his own basic view. In Byrnes's approach to the Balkans, and in Truman's support for this approach—more than in any other single diplomatic effort—American leaders demonstrated that the strategy of delay had reached its long-awaited climax. Together with British leaders, American policy makers now attempted to fulfill the President's summer pledge to "insist on the eventual removal of the Soviet blackout."[100]

Truman's declaration of opposition to spheres of influence was what one observer termed "the first gun" in an "Anglo-American diplomatic offensive."[101] In a series of powerful statements other American and British leaders drove home the President's point. Prime Minister Clement Attlee told Parliament he "looked forward with hope to the emergence of democratic governments based on free elections" in the Balkans.[102] Foreign Minister Bevin, revealing the Potsdam change in the British approach, declared that he would refuse to recognize the governments of Hungary, Bulgaria, and Rumania until free elections were held.[103] He added that under Soviet control, in his opinion, "one kind of totalitarianism [was] being replaced by another."[104] Winston Churchill publicly introduced the term "the iron

---

* Before his death, Dr. Leo Szilard offered a few more details of his May 28 conversation with the Secretary of State-designate: "Byrnes was concerned about Russia's having taken over Poland, Rumania, and Hungary, and so was I. Byrnes thought that the possession of the bomb by America would render the Russians more manageable in Europe. I failed to see how. . . ." (*U.S. News & World Report*, Aug. 15, 1960, p. 69.)

curtain"* and demanded an end to the "police governments," in the area.[105] At the same time he told the Commons his belief that the atomic bomb gave the West "irresistible" powers.[106]

In these speeches the privately expressed confidence so apparent at Potsdam was publicly manifested. Churchill's speech in the Commons made no attempt to hide the relationship between the new weapon and his judgment that the West now had the power to force Soviet acceptance of their approach in the Balkans. Although American spokesmen were not so explicit in public, a number of commentators noted the direct relationship between the "entirely new sense of confidence" in diplomacy and the atomic explosions. Indeed, it was all but impossible to miss the connection, for Truman's disclosure of the confrontation in the Balkans was heralded by the commanding news of the two atomic bombings; and the destruction of Nagasaki and the President's attack upon spheres of influence were made public on precisely the same day, August 9.†

The Anglo-American assault upon Soviet predominance in the Balkans was made despite the Churchill-Stalin arrangement, the armistice agreements, and the Yalta decisions. In fact, Truman's public declaration was a unilateral act which contravened the assumptions of an understanding the President had signed only a week earlier.[107] At Potsdam, Truman had acknowledged the authority of the Allied Control Commissions in each country and had reaffirmed the

---

* It had been used in private cables earlier. (Churchill, *Triumph and Tragedy*, p. 573.) It is interesting to note that almost immediately after Churchill used the term in the Commons the original situation it was meant to describe changed. Churchill used the term specifically to mean that British officials were restricted in their movements in Poland and the Balkans ("an iron fence had come down around them"—*Conference of Berlin*, II, p. 362) and to mean that Western correspondents were not allowed free range. However, at Potsdam the Western representatives were given all the additional rights in the Soviet zone that they asked (*Conference of Berlin*, II, pp. 1494–95), and after Potsdam, Western correspondents were given free access to Poland, Rumania, and Bulgaria. (State Department *Bulletin*, Aug. 26, 1945, pp. 283–84; *New York Times*, Sept. 13, 1945.) Hungary, of course, never presented a major problem in this respect. Although Churchill introduced his term in the autumn of 1945, it was only

considerably later that a new "iron curtain" descended in the Soviet zone of Europe.

† C. L. Sulzberger, noting the "diplomatic offensive" in the Balkans, commented: "The disclosure of an effective atomic weapon, completely shifting the actual balance of military power . . . revised the entire over-all atmosphere and the realities of a situation in which two rival Allied pressures were operating against each other." (*New York Times*, Aug. 26, 1945.) James Reston also noted the new American confidence and related it to the atomic explosions, which disclosed "the actuality of preponderant military power." (*Ibid.*) The *New York Herald Tribune* (Aug. 29, 1945) commented on the widespread opinion "that it is the Truman firmness, backed by the atom bomb and the five-ocean navy, which has produced the very moderate Sino-Russian treaty, the about-face in Bulgaria, the non-interference . . . in the internal affairs of the new Polish state and similar manifestations."

principle of joint action through the Commissions. Indeed, he had emphasized his commitment by successfully urging that the status of American members of the Commissions be raised, and that they be given veto powers.[108] Now, simply bypassing the Commissions and the obligations of the armistice terms, Truman's statement made a unilateral appeal to public opinion in each country. And following the appeal, Secretary Byrnes began a campaign of direct intervention in the internal politics of Hungary, Bulgaria, and Rumania.

Hungary was the first problem, but the least difficult, for Churchill's understanding seemed to be operating fairly well. The Russians were working closely with a government headed by the conservative General Bela Miklos, a former supporter of the Horthy dictatorship.[109] The State Department believed "the present 'Provisional National Government' [to be] a coalition regime representing all important anti-Nazi parties."[110] However, Byrnes urged better facilities for free campaigning and demanded that the already scheduled elections be postponed until new arrangements could be made.[111] Even before Potsdam, the Russians had shown themselves willing to admit the Allies to equal power on the Hungarian Allied Control Commission, and new procedures, permitting a Western veto, had actually been put into operation by July 16.[112] Now the Russians quickly acceded to the American demand, postponing the election on August 29.[113] Budapest municipal elections were held on October 7. The Soviet pledge of free elections was strictly adhered to, and the Communist party suffered a resounding defeat. The Hungarian national election of November 4 produced a similar result.[114]

Thus, the Russians were apparently willing to yield to American demands in Hungary. In Bulgaria and Rumania, where Soviet interests were greater (80–20 and 90–10 respectively, in Churchill's calculations) Stalin had not yielded to Truman's main demands at Potsdam. Now, after Hiroshima, the President forced a test of the new power relationships. Bulgaria was first. Here domestic political conflicts had begun to take on international implications earlier in the year, but there had been little active maneuvering for position between the big powers and Soviet responsibility had not been directly challenged during the war. Nevertheless, it was already clear that politicians within the country had begun to look to one or another of the powers to back their various causes.[115]

When the Fatherland Front government was formed it originally had the support of the Agrarian and Social Democratic parties.[116] The most important political personality among these groups was Nikola Petkov, the Agrarian leader.[117] However, the alliance which had brought together the Agrarian and Zveno parties on the one hand, with the Social Democratic and Communist parties on the other, was extremely unstable.[118] During the winter of 1944–45 Petkov and his followers accused the Communists of attempting to use the joint Fatherland Front committees—which governed Bulgarian towns and cities—to increase their own political strength in the country.[119] The Communists denied the accusation and charged the conservative groups with working against the occupying Soviet troops, a contravention of the armistice agreement,[120] and a breach of faith which would undermine the Fatherland Front government.[121]

The tension caused by the political crisis was severe; it divided groups not only along party lines, but within the parties as well. The basic cleavage appeared over the general question of to what extent it was necessary to cooperate with the Soviet Union and the Communists.[122] The spokesman for those who believed cooperation essential was the Zveno party leader and prime minister, Kimon Georgiev. The American State Department representative, Maynard Barnes, found Georgiev "a true conservative in his views of the sacredness of private property (otherwise he could never have held highest political office in country) . . ."[123] However, the Prime Minister also felt it necessary to establish a working relationship with the Russians. On July 30, Barnes reported:

> [Georgiev] sees world as largely divided between three great powers and their respective spheres of influence. It is his belief Balkans fall squarely within Russian sphere. He considers himself too much of a realist to [accept] the view that spheres of influence are outmoded. . . .[124]

Georgiev and others believed cooperation with the Communists and the promotion of the Fatherland Front government the *sine qua non* of a viable Bulgarian political accommodation to the postwar power realities. However, others, like Petkov, disagreed. They distrusted the Communists and hoped that if an immediate "free" election could be held, their power among the conservative peasant groups would thrust them into a dominant political position. They hoped that the Western powers would take their side against the Soviet occupation forces and enable them to establish a new government which would implement their more conservative political program.[125] Nevertheless, Petkov was not the spokesman for a united group of conservative politicians. Like the Prime Minister Georgiev, many other conservatives within the Agrarian and Social Democratic parties believed the Fatherland Front the only possible course for Bulgaria.

In fact, throughout 1945 differences of opinion over this issue engendered violent debate and hostility, splitting the Agrarian party into "cooperation" and "anticooperation" factions.[126] A test of strength took place between the groups at the May 1945 congress of the party. Petkov denounced the congress and the "cooperative" line it espoused.[127] However, the congress elected the right-wing Alexander Obbov leader of the Agrarian party on a platform of cooperation with the Fatherland Front.[128] This split the Agrarians into an official Obbov wing promoting cooperation and the dissident Petkov wing urging a more and more critical view.[129]

Though still a member of the Cabinet, Petkov obviously needed all the political support he could find, for he faced the combined forces of the Russian occupation and the remainder of the Fatherland Front government. It was not surprising that he looked first to the American representative for help. In Maynard Barnes he found an extremely sympathetic ally. Almost from the first, Barnes took Petkov's side.[130] Because it also sympathized with Petkov's views, the State Department championed the opposition demand for immediate "free" elections.[131] The Russians exercised their power under the armistice to reject an American bid for supervision of the elections in mid-April while the war still continued, but they promised early free elections on the Finnish pattern soon after the war's end.[132] A few weeks after Germany collapsed, an election date—August 26—was set.[133]

From May to July the political struggle within Bulgaria focused on preparations for the coming election. The past history of democracy in the country was not very promising.[134] The opposition quite naturally feared that the Fatherland Front would manage the election so as to preclude a free campaign and they were extremely suspicious of the election plans.[135] Petkov and a small dissident faction of the Social Democratic party, with the support of Barnes, raised the Yalta pledge of free elections as their standard.[136] Together, Petkov's supporters and the American representative (who went to the limit—and perhaps beyond—of his instructions) urged that the election plans be liberalized.[137] Both the Agrarian leader and Barnes attempted to secure open American support for a vigorous campaign to promote three-power supervision—or at least observation—of the elections.

Barnes's strategy was to avoid any act which would increase the status of the Soviet-backed government. For this reason in June he vigorously opposed signing a peace treaty with the Georgiev government, and he disputed as "spurious" the British "contention that conclusion of peace with Bulgaria now would entail withdrawal of Soviet troops."[138] Instead, he argued that if a new government could be formed on the basis of a free election, American influence would be greatly increased: "In the event we raised the question with Russia of continued occupation of Bulgaria by its troops we could count not only upon having the mass of Bulgn people behind us, but also the Bulgn Govt."[139]

Searching for a political handhold, Barnes seized upon the conservative peasant vote: "As I see matters so far as Bulgaria is concerned, the hope of the democratic nations must be based on the wide mass of agrarian opinion in this country . . ."[140] Hence, he recommended a determined effort to promote free democratic elections as a means to support "this overwhelming mass of the Bulgn population in the only way that is left to us."[141] In sum, on the eve of Potsdam he argued: "There seems only one wise course, namely to do everything we can at present to assure the freest election possible with the widest democratic participation that pressure from U.S. at this time can effect."[142]

Barnes met "clandestinely" (to use his term) with Petkov and his followers even before Potsdam and encouraged them in their opposition to the Fatherland Front.[143] Though prevented from making a direct pledge of American support, Barnes discussed the election situation with high Bulgarian government officials, indicating the likelihood that the Allies might soon intervene to postpone the scheduled elections, and urging more rigorous safeguards for the opposition.[144] At the same time, Barnes begged his own government for an all-out effort to support Petkov and the other opposition politicians. Cabling home, he repeatedly reminded the State Department of its interpretation of the Yalta free election ideal:

> If democratic elements within and outside the [Fatherland] Front could be made aware of views to which I have referred and that such views will be re-iterated at Potsdam, they would be galvanized into a resistance against Communist designs, which in absence of public encouragement from US, could only appear futile and hazardous to them.[145]

As this appeal for a public declaration indicates, foreign intervention was the key to the Bulgarian political situation. Without an active American initiative, few politicians would attempt to oppose the Fatherland Front government. With it, there was a possibility that a political crisis could be promoted which would open the way to a new pattern of power within the country. Consequently, Barnes was almost frantic in his efforts to persuade Washington to come to his aid: "I am sorry to keep harping on this point . . ." he cabled on July 9.[146] And, again on July 30:

> I realize that this is a very long telegram on what may quite naturally appear to many in the Dept as a situation very remote from real and active American interests. I report at such length in the hope of still convincing the Dept of the desirability of some public statement. . . .[147]

The fact that the United States had not recognized the Fatherland Front government until Potsdam was enough to sustain hope of intervention. However, as the Big Three Conference drew to a close, politicians in Bulgaria began to despair of American support. In the midst of the Conference, Barnes reported:

> I found Petkov still full of courage but very fearful that if no sign is forthcoming from the US and UK and particularly from US, of favorable reaction to his resistance to the [Fatherland Front] rigged elections, the independents . . . will waver in their loyalty to his leadership in this matter.[148]

Petkov himself attempted to stimulate American intervention. On July 26 the Agrarian leader bypassed the established channels of authority under the armistice agreement and circulated an open letter to the Prime Minister requesting postponement of the election and Allied supervision.[149] At this point Petkov had two complementary objectives: to weaken the authority of the Soviet-dominated Control Commission, and to bring the Western Allies into support of his position. Quite aware of the significance of Petkov's audacious challenge to the Soviet occupation authority, the Fatherland Front government was deeply disturbed. Petkov's maneuver brought forth a response indicative of the tense political situation and the anxieties of the government. The Prime Minister accused the Agrarian leader of treason: "Petkov's sin had not been merely venial but had been a mortal sin, because he had distributed copies of his letter to members of the [Allied Control Commission], thus giving the British and Americans an opportunity to intervene."[150]

A few days later, on July 31, Petkov's resignation from the government was accepted.[151] Barnes, reporting just as the Potsdam Conference ended, said he had hoped that Petkov's resignation would provoke a government crisis. However, without American intervention, Barnes was extremely doubtful that Petkov's lead would be followed:

> I fear in absence of any encouraging signs from Washington, London and Potsdam of Anglo-American interest in Bulgarian election situation Petkov's "departure" may not be followed, as I had hoped it would be, by resignations of Stoyanov, Cheschmedjieff, Pavlov and Derzhanski. I feel very strongly that time has come when Dept must tell me what, if anything, the US Govt is really prepared to do about local political and election situation.[152]

As is evident from these cables, Barnes was deeply perplexed and frustrated by the ambivalence of the American position during the period of the long delay. With no way to know of the atomic bomb and the President's plans, he greatly feared that his own initiative would not be supported. In pleading for help for Petkov he thought he was urging something which might "quite naturally appear . . . very remote from real and active American interests."[153] In fact, as we have seen, Truman had pledged an active initiative in the Balkans months earlier and, at the very moment Barnes's despairing cables reached Potsdam, Truman had already gone beyond the representative's proposals: While Barnes asked only that elections procedures be improved, the President adamantly demanded of Stalin that the Georgiev government be changed.*

Thus, after Potsdam, Barnes found that his own views were not only sympathetically received, but that Washington was ready to intervene far more directly and actively than he could have hoped. The President's continued refusal to recognize the Georgiev government and his pointed declaration that the Balkans were not to be considered a sphere of influence for any one power (made against the background of mushroom clouds rising in the Pacific) were dramatic signals of American intentions. They transformed doubt into confidence; Bulgarian politicians who had been afraid to oppose the government without foreign support were now prepared to act.

Now all that was required was sufficient time to undertake a successful campaign against the government, and sufficient safeguards to insure that such a campaign would not be impeded. The first point involved the timing of the election. Since few politicians (except Petkov) had been prepared to criticize the government until after Truman's statement, as the August 26 election approached there had been virtually no political campaigning against Fatherland Front candidates.† As a result—with the election only three weeks off—even if conditions were absolutely free, there was little likelihood that the opposition could convey its message to the public in time to substantially affect the outcome of the poll. Only too aware of the need for prompt action, Barnes had begged for a public statement from Washington throughout July. However, Truman's need to wait for the atomic bomb had complicated the problems he faced in Bulgaria.[154]

To make up for his own delay, therefore, the President first had to attempt to postpone the Bulgarian election to allow time for serious campaigning. Secondly, he wished to improve the election statute. And thirdly, he wished to remove the existing government so that the election would be administered by men more independent and more favorable to the West. Four days after Nagasaki, Secretary Byrnes moved speedily to the task, forcefully unveiling the full extent of the American demands. Bypassing the recognized authority of the Soviet commander under the armistice terms, on August 13, Byrnes sent an

---

* See above, pp. 196, 199.

† Apparently a similar problem arose in

Yugoslavia; see Betts, *Central and South East Europe*, pp. 58–59.

open letter to Prime Minister Georgiev. He demanded that the elections scheduled for August 26—now less than two weeks off—be postponed.[155] Byrnes also gave notice that the United States would not recognize the Bulgarian government until it had been radically reorganized:

> The information available to the United States Government has not satisfied it that the first Provisional Bulgarian Government is adequately representative of the important democratic elements, of democratic opinion, or that the existing government has arranged for the scheduled elections to take place under conditions which will allow and insure the participation therein, free from the fear of force and intimidation, of all democratic elements.[156]

Byrnes's letter (which was followed by a similar British protest),[157] even more than the President's statement, was an explicit attempt to influence the political situation within the country. (Truman's Balkan representative later characterized the actions as "a major diplomatic effort.")[158] By committing American prestige to the main demand of the opposition, the Secretary of State's maneuver threw the Fatherland Front government into a state of frenzy. Its first reaction was a futile attempt to urge the American government to stand by the commitments it had made in signing the armistice agreement. Under that agreement, the government—which, of course, had no diplomatic relations with the United States—took orders from the Soviet chairman of the Allied Control Commission.* On August 23, Georgiev's Finance Minister, Petko Stainov, publicly stated the government's position: "The British and the United States Governments should rather have submitted notes to Moscow, reached an agreement, and then advised the Bulgarian Government."[159]

Despite this statement, the government was obviously weakened and much on the defensive. The four government ministers who had been unwilling to act without foreign help,† now told the Prime Minister that unless the elections were postponed and changes made in the electoral law, they would leave the government.[160] Georgiev refused to agree and accused the four of working with Barnes.[161] On August 17, the four resigned in protest over the plans for the forthcoming elec-

---

* See above, pp. 134, 140–141.   † See above, p. 210.

tion.[162] Georgiev countered the resignations with a firm declaration that the election would be carried out as scheduled.[163] He publicly attacked the four ministers and others who "allow themselves to be influenced by foreign powers."[164] New Cabinet members replaced the opposition group, and the government prepared to ride out the crisis.[165]

With the American government and the Petkov group of opposition leaders now publicly committed, there remained only the question of what action the Soviet Union would take to uphold a government it had sponsored for more than a year. Although Stalin, hoping to persuade Truman to act with him, had not recognized Georgiev before Potsdam,[166] after the President's statement attacking spheres of influence, the Soviet Premier had moved quickly to give strong support to the Fatherland Front. On August 15, Radio Moscow announced that the Soviet Union would accord diplomatic recognition to Georgiev.[167] Two days later, Moscow announced that the famous Bulgarian Communist Georgi Dimitrov would return from the Soviet Union to participate in—and lend his prestige to—the Bulgarian elections.[168] The return of Dimitrov, who had become famous during the Reichstag trial, further affirmed Soviet support for the elections and the government. *Izvestia* commented that the election plans were "most democratic."[169]

Thus the opposing positions of the various parties crystallized. "What must chiefly be regretted," observed the diplomatic correspondent of the London *Times* in Sofia, "is that a new complication is added to Allied relations. The Soviet Government has already recognized the Bulgarian Government and has sent an Ambassador to Sofia . . . A peace treaty can be made only with a recognized Government—and London and Washington appear to be committed not to recognize the Bulgarian Government. A deadlock appears inevitable."[170]

The implications of the conflict were also noted in Britain, where preparations for the first peacetime foreign ministers' meeting were underway. "The Bulgarian situation, it is said in official circles here, is likely to produce an early deadlock in the work of the new Council of Foreign Ministers,"[171] one American observed. Indeed, the challenge to Soviet influence in the Balkans seemed too obvious and too fundamental to permit of an easy reconciliation. The Foreign Office and others had been certain the Russians would not yield to the American demands before Potsdam, and once Soviet support had been publicly conveyed to Georgiev's rejection of the American note, there seemed no possible way to avoid a head-on collision. The Americans were adamant and the Russians were not likely to back down. Although the Soviet commander agreed to consult Moscow again, the Allied Control Commission meeting of August 22 produced no positive results.[172]

It was both a shock and a surprise, therefore, when on August 26—the very day of the election—radio Sofia interrupted its eleventh-hour appeals to voters and its denunciation of "foreign interference" to announce that the election had been postponed![173]

Truman's Balkan representative, Mark Ethridge, later boasted that the West's "determined action" had produced "remarkable results."[174] At the time, British Foreign Office officials were jubilant at the sudden success, telling reporters that the Bulgarian decision eased "considerably the Anglo-Soviet-American diplomatic tension."[175] Russian acquiescence in the American demand was an ignominious defeat for Soviet power in the Balkans.[176]

The dramatic *volte-face* and Stalin's apparent willingness to cooperate also greatly heartened the opposition politicians and the American officials in Bulgaria who were confirmed not only in their judgment of the situation, but also in their estimate of their own power to affect events. The opposition now presented a list of further conditions for the election and demanded that both the Prime Minister and the Minister of Interior resign.[177] The United States pressed the demand that the government be reorganized, and Barnes met with government and opposition leaders to attempt to reach agreement on changes in the government and preparations for the new election.[178]

The Georgiev government, helpless in the face of Soviet acquiescence to the Americans, could do little to repair the damage of the August 26 embarrassment. Instead, it began wholesale acceptance of various opposition proposals. Meetings were held with the American military representative and with Barnes to discuss requirements for the new election.[179] Pardons were granted to 302 political prisoners; another 400 had their sentences drastically reduced.[180] As Stalin had promised at Potsdam, American newsmen were allowed to enter the country and to report freely.[181] All four opposition parties were legally recognized and allowed to publish newspapers.[182] (It was necessary to give standing to those parties which, fearing to act without American support, had previously banded together in the Fatherland Front.)[183] Mixed committees, made up mostly of schoolteachers, were designated to oversee the elections.[184] The government proclaimed a series of administrative steps to insure free campaigning.[185]

In an attempt to close ranks, the government also invited the dissident opposition groups to reunite with the party leaders who had supported the Fatherland Front.[186] The move aimed at healing the breach between the two factions of the Agrarian and Social Democratic parties. However, the now confident opposition groups refused to reunite with their former colleagues. Instead, they demanded the dismissal of those Agrarian and Social Democratic ministers who had remained in the Cabinet,[187] and they began to hold public demonstrations to create public support for their position.[188] Once more they reiterated the demand that the Prime Minister and the Minister of the Interior resign. They now declared that unless this was agreed to, they would boycott the election.[189]

At this point the Georgiev government balked. Moscow and Sofia had yielded to the demand that the election be postponed and had agreed to a number of reforms to insure a free campaign.* However, the proposal that the government be changed, which had been refused when Truman first raised it at Potsdam, was apparently still too much to ask. As the London Conference approached, once more the Bulgarian political situation became tense. The American-supported groups were once more more in a direct confrontation with the Soviet-backed government. "The situation, therefore, remains on dead center," one observer noted.[190] Indeed, the renewed stalemate seemed even more rigidly defined than the original one had been.

Moreover, as the London Conference opened, the situation began to take on threatening overtones. Earlier, when the American demand

---

* Later the opposition boycotted the election, and the State Department declared that the election had not been freely conducted. However, this claim must be carefully examined, for (1) Truman's Balkan representative, who studied the problem in Bulgaria at the time, later wrote "it was by no means clear that the electoral boycott of the opposition was the best means of resolving the problem . . ."; (2) the British Foreign Office did not support the State Department's protests over the election; (3) most Western correspondents found little or no interference in the election; (4) at almost exactly the same time the Soviet-sponsored election in Hungary (which was not boycotted by the Hungarian opposition) was conducted in a "free" manner which met the State Department's standards. (Dennett and Johnson, *Negotiating with the Russians*, p. 191; *Sunday Times*, Nov. 18, 1945; *Christian Science Monitor*, Nov. 20, 1945; *Ibid.*, Sept. 20, 24; Oct. 12, 16, 17, 18; Nov. 17, 1945; Seton-Watson, *The East European Revolution*, p. 193; Betts, *Central and South East Europe*, p. 105.)

for a postponement of the elections had been received only four days after Nagasaki, there were scattered comments about the role of the atomic bomb in America's new-found "firmness."* Now, as the United States pressed the demand that the government be changed, mass meetings filled the streets of Sofia with defiant, repeated chants of "We don't fear the atomic bomb!"[191]

Thus, the fact that the atomic bomb had imparted an entirely new sense of confidence to American diplomacy was quickly recognized and interpreted in the most unfavorable light; it appeared as a menacing force—in brief, a threat. There were now also doubts as to the actual power of American diplomacy. It appeared that the diplomatic successes could only be attributed to the atomic bomb, for once it had been demonstrated, points at issue in Manchuria, Hungary, and Bulgaria which had not been yielded at Potsdam had now been accepted by the Russians. But now the failure to change the Bulgarian government seemed a sign that the diplomatic offensive which had scored so brilliantly might be losing its force. It remained to be seen to what extent Soviet policy would yield in a country far more vital to it than Hungary or Bulgaria.

DEADLOCK IN RUMANIA

EVEN CHURCHILL HAD DISTINGUISHED between the three ex-satellite countries, allocating, in the first instance, Soviet influence of "50 per cent" in Hungary, "75 per cent" in Bulgaria, and a full "90 per cent" in Rumania.† Though these figures had been modified in the bargaining process, from the Soviet point of view Rumania was obviously the most important Balkan country. Rumania occupied a key strategic position athwart the southwestern invasion route to Russia. Bulgaria had been able to wage war against the Soviet Union for only twenty-four hours;[192] but Rumania, in alliance with Hitler, had sent twenty-six divisions against the Soviets, devastating Russian territory, and penetrating as far into the interior as Stalingrad.[193] Moreover, Rumanians harbored traditional anti-Russian sentiments and were therefore more likely to use their strategic geographic position against the Soviet Union in any future hostilities.[194]

---

* See above, p. 252. † See above, p. 181.

American policy, however, recognized no distinctions in the Balkans.* In Rumania, too, American leaders had long planned to take the initiative to change the government. The demonstration of the atomic bomb and the end of the long wait meant that these plans could now be implemented. Here, as elsewhere, the first move in the diplomatic offensive was Truman's attack upon spheres of influence— a declaration which gave heart to conservative politicians in Rumania as it had in Bulgaria. Here there was even greater excitement for, unlike Bulgaria, in Rumania the deep tradition of anti-Russian feeling had been increased, not diminished, by war propaganda and the defeat suffered at Russian hands.[195]

Even during the spring, while the war was still on, among Peasant and Liberal leaders there was a constant hope that somehow the Western powers would come to their assistance. According to one American in the country at the time, "they were wholeheartedly anti-Russian, and a good many of their members continued to assume that the Western Allies would somehow intervene."[196] Although it seems that a number of conservatives had been offered posts in the Groza government, they had apparently refused to join the government after a dispute over estimates of their relative importance in the domestic political balance.[197] The leading politician in the conservative ranks, the seventy-year-old Juliu Maniu, leader of the Peasant party (a figure corresponding roughly to Petkov in Bulgaria), had retired from chairmanship of his party two weeks after Groza took office.[198]

However, Maniu, like Petkov in Bulgaria, did not retire from active participation in politics. As Potsdam approached and the powers continued to withhold recognition, Maniu and his associates also hoped

---

* As many observers have pointed out, Byrnes never seemed to understand a dilemma inherent in his policy. There is no reason to doubt his numerous assurances that in urging free elections and new governments he had no wish to support governments hostile to the Soviet Union; nevertheless, as Roberts has written, "a popularly elected Government [in Rumania] would in all probability be anti-Soviet." Thus, inevitably Byrnes's idealistic policy must have seemed a threat to the Russians. (Roberts, *Rumania*, p. 269.)

On the viability of democratic government in Rumania, see also the views cabled to the War Department by its representative in Bucharest shortly before Potsdam: "Even under normal peacetime conditions, a representative government in Rumania would find it difficult to maintain itself in power. Rumanians have had no experience in democracy for over ten years, and the ability of members of any coalition government to work in harmony for the common goal, regardless of personal or party problems must be open to question." (*Conference of Berlin*, I, p. 397. For additional views, see Wolff, *The Balkans in Our Time*, p. 286; McNeill, *America, Britain and Russia, 1941–46*, pp. 698–701; Allen, *Great Britain and the United States*, p. 872; Williams, *The Tragedy of American Diplomacy*, pp. 258–59.)

that the Soviet-sponsored government might be changed.[199] Because of the strength of anti-Russian sentiment in the country, they could go farther than Petkov in Slavophilic Bulgaria. The Peasant and Liberal parties decided to organize demonstrations to show that opposition to the National Democratic Front government was an effective force. They also hoped to forestall a Potsdam decision to recognize Groza or a slightly altered government.[200]

In open violation of the specific terms of the armistice, on July 18 Maniu boldly began his political offensive with a speech to university students demanding that the Groza government be dismissed: "The country must no longer tolerate dictatorial governments imposed from abroad."[201] The speech was followed by a brief demonstration in the Palace Square.[202] Two days later, Constantin Bratianu addressed about seven hundred members of his Liberal party's youth organization in the same vein.[203] Following his speech, a larger demonstration and parade took place.[204] This time the protesting demonstrators were met by Communists and others who supported the government. A brief struggle between the two groups took place and two people were injured and approximately thirty-two were arrested.[205]

The acting American representative in Bucharest, Roy Melbourne, reported that the Groza government was greatly disturbed by the demonstrations.[206] A hastily summoned conference between party leaders and the National Democratic Front evidenced increasing anxiety over the internal and the international situation. The hopes of the Peasants and Liberals, and the fears of the government, were directed toward Potsdam. The opposition apparently believed that the Big Three might eliminate the Groza government and open the way for new elections. Groups within the government too, according to Melbourne, were "expecting Cabinet changes and fearing shifts detriment[al]" to the National Democratic Front position.[207]

As in Bulgaria, the internal political situation was ruled not only by the relative strengths of the various political factions, but by the role the big powers played—or might be expected to play. In the midst of the Potsdam meeting, Maniu sought an interview with Melbourne in Bucharest to report that "he had counseled his party that U.S. and Great Britain . . . could secure Soviet acquiescence to a democratic interpretation of Yalta."[208] He said that in his belief the National

Peasants could confidently expect an overwhelming electoral majority if free elections were held.[209] He urged that Groza be removed from office so that a new government would supervise the elections.[210] He asked the War, Interior, and Propaganda ministries for his own party. The National Peasant party could be expected to be impartial, he explained, since "it would be to its interest to conduct the elections in an unbiased manner. . . . An inevitable large National Peasant majority" would emerge in any event.[211]

Having made his proposal, Maniu went on to hint at the possible consequences if he failed to achieve his aims. If the Groza government was retained, he stated, his party would organize energetic country-wide opposition, including demonstrations. According to Melbourne, "in measured words he said that for such . . . action he was certain of support from the dissatisfied Rumanian peasants who would unite with the townspeople. . . ."[212]

In view of earlier Rumanian riots and bloodshed (even during the war),* there were ominous overtones in this statement. In fact, it contained the distinct hint of a threat and offered the prospect of violent disturbances. The "measured words" meant that the opposition could, if it so chose, create an unstable and dangerous situation. Earlier, one reason Churchill had proposed his spheres-of-influence arrangement to Stalin was his knowledge that political feelings ran so high in Rumania and Greece that civil war was a very real possibility—especially if the powers began to support different factions.[213] In Greece, where anti-British feeling had already resulted in a short outburst of civil war in December 1944,† and in Rumania where riots and violence had been suppressed just before Groza's appointment in the spring of 1945, Churchill's judgment was apparently a fair assessment of realities. Maniu's statement did no more than recall and confirm this earlier estimate. Shortly thereafter, Molotov affirmed the same view, telling Byrnes that Rumanian politics could easily erupt into a civil war if the powers did not concert their policies.[214]

Maniu undoubtedly made his statement in the hope of forcing a

---

* These precipitated the Soviet intervention discussed on p. 184.
† See above, p. 182.

more explicit American commitment to his cause. However, during the summer of delay, and at the time of the Potsdam Conference, the American representative could give the Peasant leader very little direct encouragement. Like his colleague in Bulgaria, he did not know to what extent Truman was prepared to press the matter. Nor did he know of the atomic bomb. As soon as the Conference ended without recognition of the Groza government, however, the opposition had its signal.[215] And, as in Bulgaria, the series of speeches denouncing spheres of influence and "police governments" sparked tremendous political activity within the country.

In Rumania, the attack upon the Soviet-sponsored government centered around, and was led by, the young King Michael. The King had already secretly asked for American help before Potsdam.[216] Now, privately encouraged to act by American representatives,[217] Michael publicly demanded that Groza resign.[218] He then bypassed the Allied Control Commission and appealed directly to the three Allied powers to help him form a new government.[219] Adding emphasis to his demand, the King gave notice that until a new government was formed, he would refuse to sign government decrees.[220] Shortly thereafter, the Minister of Finance resigned. Michael seized the opportunity and, refusing to authorize the appointment of a replacement, made it impossible to pay the salaries of government employees.[221] Michael also refused to appear at important public celebrations, and, in a dramatic gesture of opposition, he left Bucharest to wait for the elimination of the Groza government.[222]

Melbourne let Michael know that if he persisted the United States would support him,[223] and Byrnes immediately responded to the King's appeal. On August 22, the Secretary of State met with representatives of the press, welcomed Michael's request for help to replace Groza, and pledged official American support for efforts to change the government. The United States would gladly lend "assistance with a view to the formation of a government, which, according to the report of the Conference of Berlin, might be recognized by the principal powers," Byrnes declared.[224] The Secretary of State's favorable response confirmed the American intention to bypass the Allied Control Commission and it publicly committed the United States to the demand that the Groza government be changed.

Some observers noted that the initial Soviet decision to yield to "the firmness of the Western Allies" in Bulgaria had given the American and British governments confidence in their approach to Rumania.[225] Though undoubtedly the first success in Bulgaria confirmed American leaders' estimates of their ability to force the Soviet hand in the Balkans, as we have seen, Truman and Byrnes had decided to intervene to remove the Soviet "blackout" many months earlier. During the period of the long wait, and at Potsdam, they had made their intentions quite clear and had also told Stalin that they would not yield on their demand that the Rumanian government be changed.

Thus, implementing their earlier plans, and now apparently quite confident of the wisdom of their course and their power to pursue it successfully, throughout August, American leaders pressed the attempt to remove Groza from office. As the London Conference of Foreign Ministers neared, however, no sign of Soviet willingness to yield appeared as it had in Bulgaria. Apparently the Russians felt that Rumania was different and, in fact, they had already indicated differences in attitudes toward the two countries.

Immediately after Potsdam (on August 4), Moscow had hastened to accord diplomatic recognition to Bucharest, although it was two weeks later—and only in the brief period before yielding to American demands—that Moscow had accorded the same recognition to Sofia.[226] Thus, even before the new American effort in Rumania, the Soviet Union had declared its commitment to Groza. After Michael's appeal and Byrnes's response to it, Moscow again promptly and dramatically demonstrated that it was not prepared to yield easily in Rumania. *Izvestia* criticized "some foreign newspapers" for their antagonism to Groza.[227] The Soviet-supported government announced a campaign against "hirelings of the former Premier Radescu." Twenty "terrorists" were arrested for attempting to overthrow the government. Those who were "trying to create discord among the United Nations and seeking foreign support for the realization of their personal political ambitions" were castigated by the government.[228]

On August 28, it was announced that the Soviet envoy in Rumania had been raised to the rank of full ambassador.[229] A week before the London Conference, Groza and his Deputy Prime Minister Tatarescu were invited to Moscow, where they were given celebrity treatment, including a state dinner by Stalin.[230] On September 4, the Soviet Union refused a proposal by Byrnes for consultations on the basis of

King Michael's appeal.[231] At the same time, Groza issued a bitter statement from Moscow attacking Maniu and Bratianu for their role in the crisis:

> Maniu and Bratianu have lost all contact with the realities of present-day political life in Rumania. They endeavor to provoke a Government crisis by artificial means and to sow discord between the Government and the people on the one hand, and the Head of State, King Michael, on the other, by recommending him to actions harmful to the national interest and to the crown.[232]

The following day, *Izvestia* accused Britain and America of trying to force Groza out of office, specifically identifying the local representatives of the two powers as prime movers in Michael's maneuver. Giving notice that the Soviet Union would hold to its support of Groza, *Izvestia* commented:

> American and British representatives began to insist on the resignation of the Rumanian Government without first placing the matter before the Allied Control Commission, thereby violating established procedure in the work of the Commission. If this is called implementation of a coordinated Allied policy, what might be called unilateral acts violating the coordination of Allied policy? . . . The viewpoint of Soviet public opinion is quite clear. It firmly maintains that interference . . . is inadmissible.[233]

Stalin now gave further evidence of his commitment to Groza, sending the Rumanian Premier back to his country with numerous politically useful concessions. Groza received promises of a Soviet loan of 150,000 tons of grain, the return of railroads to Rumanian direction, the return of a number of locomotives, railway freight cars, merchant ships, and even a few warships. Moreover, the Rumanian Premier was able to bring back from Moscow an agreement to reduce the reparations burden and a pledge to repatriate immediately all prisoners of war. Finally, Stalin agreed that Soviet troops stationed in Rumania would help reconstruct towns destroyed in the war.[234]

In this way, Moscow underscored its intention to stand by Groza on the eve of the London Conference. Now Britain and the United States on the one hand, and the Soviet Union on the other, were publicly committed to diametrically opposed positions in Rumania. Within the country, the opposition and the Groza government were similarly committed and, as London approached, Maniu and Bratianu burned their bridges behind them, openly attacking the Soviet Union in direct contravention of the armistice.[235]

TOWARD A TEST OF STRENGTH

THUS, ON THE EVE of the first peacetime meeting of the foreign ministers, the American offensive in the Balkans, which had been met by initial Soviet willingness to compromise, now had reached major obstacles in both Bulgaria and Rumania. The over-all question first posed in April and again at Potsdam was still the same: Did the United States have the power to force Soviet acquiescence to its demands deep within the Soviet area of influence? From the early summer American leaders had been convinced that, once demonstrated, the atomic bomb would permit them to demand major changes in the border areas of the Soviet Union. But now this conviction would be tested, and the relative power of the United States and the Soviet Union defined, when the foreign ministers met on September 10.

As Secretary Byrnes prepared to leave for London, the various instruments of diplomacy which had not been actively employed during the summer of delay were now again readied for use. Although neither the President nor the Secretary of State had discussed a large-scale credit with Soviet representatives since the late-April showdown, now, after the atomic bomb had been demonstrated, they were prepared to negotiate. At a meeting with the President and the Secretary of State shortly after the Japanese surrender, Leo Crowley urged that the Lend-Lease cutoff—first attempted, then repealed in May—should now be firmly implemented. Once again, though his recommendation was based upon the law's requirement that Lend-Lease cease at the end of hostilities, and though it would have implications for all the Allies, Crowley made it clear that the primary advantage of *immediate* action was that it would force the Soviet Union to look for other means to pay for American material assistance. Both the President and the Secretary of State agreed with Crowley, and Truman authorized him to act promptly.*[236] After Lend-Lease shipments were

---

* See Byrnes, *All in One Lifetime*, pp. 309–10, for a report which indicates that the primary reason for the *timing* of the August cutoff—like the May cutoff—was the desire to force the Soviet Union into a de- (Continued on next page)

halted on August 22, the Russians were informed that the Export-Import Bank would consider an application for a large credit. It was soon made clear that they would be expected to offer, as *quid pro quo,* concessions in Eastern and Southeastern Europe.[237]

Similarly, throughout the summer Truman and his advisers had regarded the presence of conventional troops as vital to their European diplomacy. The atomic bomb, as Stimson had expected, had helped stabilize the situation by ending the war long before redeployment had substantially weakened American strength on the Continent.* But now, looking to the future when demobilization would drain troops from Europe, Truman moved swiftly to attempt to preserve his position; on August 17—the third day of peace—he publicly declared his intention to ask Congressional approval for a universal-military-training program for all able-bodied young men.[238] On the eve of the London Conference he gave details of his proposals for peace, telling an August 31 Cabinet meeting "that the time had come to initiate a new military policy. If we were to maintain leadership among other nations, we must continue to be strong in a military way."†[239]

But, as before, economic aid and the presence of conventional troops were the least important elements in the American diplomatic posture. Throughout the summer the expectation of the atomic bomb had dominated diplomatic strategy. Now, in late August, as Byrnes prepared for his meeting in London, the Secretary of State made it clear that the bomb continued to play a predominant role in his calculations. In a long discussion with Byrnes, Assistant Secretary of War McCloy found him "quite radically opposed to any approach to Stalin whatever" to attempt to establish international control of

---

(*Continued from preceding page*)
pendent position in the next round of credit negotiations. And, as in May, the President apparently was not guided primarily by a belief that the legal provisions required immediate and unequivocal action, for he made a number of exceptions to the Lend-Lease cutoff. For a report of these, see McNeill, *America, Britain and Russia, 1941–46,* p. 785.

* See above, p. 165.

† Congress rejected Truman's proposal. Harriman was later to argue that this was the primary reason American diplomacy failed to achieve its European objectives:

"Only by keeping our military forces in being after Germany and Japan surrendered could we have attempted to *compel* the Soviet Union to withdraw from the territory it controlled. . . ." (*Congressional Record,* Aug. 27, 1951, p. A5416; emphasis added.) Similarly, Truman has written: "I am morally certain that if Congress had gone into the [military training] program thoroughly in 1945, when I first recommended it, we would have had a pool of basically trained men which would have made the Soviets hesitate in their program of expansion in certain strategic parts of the world." (*Year of Decisions,* pp. 511–12.)

atomic energy—"He was on the point of departing for the Foreign Ministers' meeting and wished to have the implied threat of the bomb in his pocket during the conference. . . ."[240]

And two days before sailing for London, Byrnes discussed the central role of the atomic bomb in his diplomacy with Secretary Stimson:

> Jim Byrnes had not yet gone abroad and I had a very good talk with him afterwards sitting in the White House hall . . . I took up the question which I had been working at with McCloy up in St. Hubert's, namely how to handle Russia with the big bomb. I found that Byrnes was very much against any attempt to cooperate with Russia. His mind is full of his problems with the coming meeting of foreign ministers and he looks to having the presence of the bomb in his pocket, so to speak, as a great weapon to get through the thing. . . .[241]

In this frame of mind Secretary of State Byrnes sailed for his first peacetime encounter with a representative of the Soviet Union. Since early April, the President and his senior advisers had focused their attention on political and economic conditions in Eastern Europe; they had never lost their active interest in reducing or eliminating Soviet influence in the area. In April the President had been able to back his diplomacy only with large-scale credits and the presence of the American army in Europe. Advised that there was much to gain if he would wait for the atomic bomb, Truman had decided to postpone a showdown over Eastern Europe.

Now, as Admiral Leahy has written, "it was no longer a theory. We had the bombs."[242] The firm approach so long in suspense could be resumed with the backing of unprecedented military power. For the first time since April, Secretary Byrnes was ready for a meeting with Molotov to discuss affairs in the Soviet zone of Europe. His immediate objective which, like the April showdown over Poland, was to have symbolic implications for all of Eastern Europe, was to force a change in the Balkan governments. The Secretary of State was extremely confident of success.[243] His meeting was to be, as he later wrote, "in a very real sense, a test of strength."[244]

CHAPTER VIII

Conclusions

> *One factor that was to change a lot of ideas, including my own, was the atom bomb . . .*
> —ADMIRAL WILLIAM D. LEAHY
> CHIEF OF STAFF
> TO THE PRESIDENT

BYRNES FIRMLY PRESSED his demand that the Bulgarian and Rumanian governments be changed, but when Molotov refused to yield at London, the first peacetime meeting of foreign ministers broke down completely—it was impossible even to agree upon a joint protocol recording the failure.* The initial climax of the post-Hiroshima struggle was a continued and open deadlock. "We had come to the crossroads," Byrnes recalls.[1] In forcing a public break over the issue, the Secretary of State's action was intended to be symbolic. As in the Polish dispute in April, American policy aimed not only at a favorable resolution of the specific points at issue, but at a reconsideration of fundamental political and economic arrangements throughout the Soviet-controlled zone of Europe—"Only by refusing to bow to Soviet domination could we establish sound relations for the future."[2]

Byrnes has written that "our attitude was a shock to them," and it is certain, as both he and John Foster Dulles (who assisted the Secretary of State at London) have emphasized, that postwar Soviet-American tension must be dated from the London Conference.[3] It is also undoubtedly true that the atomic bomb not only influenced the attitude American policy makers took in their approach to the confrontation,

---

* Technically, the Conference broke down over a procedural issue, but as Byrnes has written, in reality, "the chief cause" was the dispute over the governments of Rumania and Bulgaria. (*Speaking Frankly*, pp. 104–8; see also, Senate Committee on Foreign Relations, *A Decade of American Foreign Policy, 1941–49*, p. 55; Leahy Diary, Sept. 23, 1945, p. 163.)

but also, as Prime Minister Attlee cabled to President Truman at the time, the weapon completely overshadowed the discussions.[4]

The political developments after August 1945, like the later (mid-1946), ill-fated attempts to control atomic energy, cannot here be analyzed.* And, unfortunately, Admiral Leahy's summary judgment that the Cold War began in the Balkans can only be tested with further research.[5] However, at this point the major conclusions to be drawn from a study of American policy during the first five months of the Truman administration can be briefly summarized. It is also possible to attempt to define certain other problems which, with presently available materials, can be stated but cannot be conclusively resolved.

The most important point is the most general: Contrary to a commonly held view, it is abundantly clear that the atomic bomb profoundly influenced the way American policy makers viewed political problems. Or, as Admiral Leahy has neatly summarized the point, "One factor that was to change a lot of ideas, including my own, was the atom bomb . . ."[6] The change caused by the new weapon was quite specific. It did not produce American opposition to Soviet policies in Eastern Europe and Manchuria. Rather, since a consensus had already been reached on the need to take a firm stand against the Soviet Union in both areas, the atomic bomb *confirmed* American leaders in their judgment that they had sufficient power to affect developments in the border regions of the Soviet Union. There is both truth and precision in Truman's statement to Stimson that the weapon "gave him an entirely new feeling of confidence."[7]

This effect was a profoundly important one. Before the atomic bomb was tested, despite their desire to oppose Soviet policies, Western policy makers harbored very grave doubts that Britain and America could challenge Soviet predominance in Eastern Europe. Neither Roosevelt nor Truman could have confidence that the American public would permit the retention of large numbers of conventional troops in Europe after the war. (And Congressional rejection of Truman's

---

* The official history of the Atomic Energy Commission demonstrates how Byrnes opposed later attempts to control atomic energy, and how he finally agreed to approach the Russians with a control plan only after being assured that the proposal would guarantee continued American production of atomic weapons for some years. (Hewlett and Anderson, *The New World,* pp. 417, 456, 459–60, and especially 461.)

military-training program later confirmed the pessimistic wartime predictions.) Thus, at the time of the Yalta Conference, as Assistant Secretary of State William L. Clayton advised Secretary Stettinius, "a large credit . . . appear[ed] to be the only concrete bargaining lever for use in connection with the many other political and economic problems which will arise between our two countries."[8]

That this lever of diplomacy was not sufficiently powerful to force Soviet acceptance of American proposals was amply demonstrated during the late-April and early-May crisis over Poland. Despite Truman's judgment that "the Russians needed us more than we needed them,"[9] Stalin did not yield to the firm approach. Hence, without the atomic bomb it seemed exceedingly doubtful that American policy makers would be able substantially to affect events within the Soviet-occupied zone of Europe. It may well be that, had there been no atomic bomb, Truman would have been forced to reconsider the basic direction of his policy as Churchill had done some months earlier.

Indeed, Churchill's 1944 estimate of the power realities usefully illuminates the problems faced by Western policy makers as they attempted to judge their relative strength vis-à-vis the Soviet Union. As soon as Roosevelt rejected Churchill's desperate pleas for an invasion through the Balkans, the Prime Minister understood that he would have little power in Southeastern Europe, and that, indeed, the British position in Greece was seriously threatened. As he told Roosevelt, "the only way I can prevent [utter anarchy] is by persuading the Russians to quit boosting [the Communist-oriented] E.A.M."[10] Again, there was overwhelming logic in his parallel 1944 argument: "It seems to me, considering the Russians are about to invade Rumania in great force . . . it would be a good thing to follow the Soviet leadership, considering that neither you nor we have any troops there at all and that they will probably do what they like anyhow."[11] As he later recalled, before the atomic test, "the arrangements made about the Balkans were, I was sure, the best possible."[12]

As I have attempted to show, by the time of the Yalta Conference, somewhat reluctantly, and against the wishes of the State Department, Roosevelt came to the same conclusion. Even the State Department was forced to adopt the official view that "this Government probably would not oppose predominant Soviet influence in [Poland and the Balkans]."[13] And one high-ranking official went beyond this judgment; substituting his concern for Western Europe for the Prime Minister's specific fears about Greece, he stated: "I am willing to sponsor and support the Soviet arguments if it will save . . . the rest of Europe from the diplomacy of the jungle which is almost certain to ensue otherwise."[14] As Truman's Balkan representative recalled the Yalta Conference, it was "fateful that these discussions should have been held at a time when Soviet bargaining power in eastern Europe was so much stronger than that of the western allies."[15] But it remained for Byrnes to summarize the early-1945 relative strengths of the powers: "It was not a question of what we would *let* the Russians do, but what we could *get* them to do."[16]

As I have shown, this appraisal was radically changed by the summer of 1945. Since Byrnes advised Truman on both the atomic bomb and the need for strong opposition to the Russians in Eastern Europe before the President's first confrontation with Molotov, the new weapon's first impact possibly can be seen as early as the April showdown.* However, no final judgment can be rendered on this point, using the evidence presently available. But there is no question that by the middle of July leading American policy makers were convinced that the atomic bomb would permit the United States to take a "firm" stand in subsequent negotiations. In fact, American leaders felt able to demand *more* at Potsdam than they had asked at Yalta. Again, Churchill's post-atomic appraisal is in striking contrast to his view of the pre-atomic realities: "We now had something in our hands which would redress the balance with the Russians."[17] And Byrnes's new advice to Truman was quite straightforward: "The bomb might well put us in a position to dictate our own terms. . . ."[18]

Once the profound impact of the atomic bomb upon American judgments is recognized, considerable light is cast upon the complicated events of the summer of 1945. The curious reversals in American Polish policy and the Hopkins mission both become understandable. The period is one in which two groups of officials debated strategy. Although there were differences of emphasis, since all agreed on the broad objective of attempting to force the Soviet Union into cooperative relationships in Eastern and Central Europe, the real struggle was over timing. Those outside the War Department who had little knowledge or little faith in the as yet untested atomic weapon argued that an immediate showdown was necessary. In this their views

---

* See above, p. 111*fn.*

paralleled Churchill's, who, having come to terms on the Balkans, feared a further weakening of Western determination, combined with a withdrawal of American troops, would convince Stalin time was on his side if he dug in while the West melted away.[19]

Secretary Stimson, however, was able to counter this argument in two ways: He was able to show that conventional strength on the Continent would not be substantially reduced during the two months' delay until the atomic test; and he was able to promise that if a confrontation could be postponed the United States would soon be possessed of "decisive" powers.[20] After forcing a premature showdown on the symbolic Polish issue, Truman reversed himself and accepted Stimson's broad strategy. The price he paid for delay was not high; he was forced to yield the substance of the point at issue in the Polish controversy, and he had to withdraw American troops to the agreed zonal positions in Germany. Significantly, he later characterized his first attempt to utilize economic bargaining strength through the Lend-Lease cutoff as a "mistake."[21] From Truman's point of view, not only was the first showdown badly timed, but the need to reverse his public position and to send Hopkins on a mission of conciliation must have been a great personal embarrassment.

However, it is vital to recognize that Truman's conciliatory actions during late May, June, and early July did not represent his basic policy. He had demonstrated in the April showdown and in the decision to maintain American troop positions in Germany that his view of how to treat with Russia was far different from Roosevelt's. His decision abruptly to cut off Lend-Lease, his show of force over the Trieste dispute, his reconsideration of Roosevelt's Far Eastern agreement, his breach of the Balkans understandings, his refusal to adhere to the Yalta reparations accord—all these acts testify to the great gulf between his view and the view of his predecessor.

Those who argue that "Mr. Truman intended to continue the policy laid down by President Roosevelt"[*22] have focused attention on an extremely brief period when Truman did indeed adopt a more moder-

---

* Woodward, whose statement I have quoted, uncritically follows Truman's claim: "I stood squarely behind all commitments and agreements entered into by our late great President and . . . I would do everything I could to follow along that path." (*Year of Decisions*, pp. 75–76.) Feis makes the same mistake: "Truman felt faithful to the ideas and ideals of the war leader . . ." (*Churchill, Roosevelt, Stalin*, pp. 599–600.)

ate approach. But his actions during this period—symbolized by his attempt to avoid the appearance of "ganging up" with Britain against the Soviet Union—were only a manifestation of his tactical retreat. In a fundamental sense, even the conciliatory period can only be explained by recognizing that its primary purpose was not to continue Roosevelt's policy, but to facilitate a far different policy based upon the overwhelming power soon to be available. Truman replaced the symbolic April showdown over Poland with a parallel August and September effort in the Balkans. Both before and after the brief conciliatory period, the President's attitude is best summed up in the statement he made eight days after Roosevelt's death: He "intended to be firm with the Russians and make no concessions."[23] And both before and after the temporary period of no "ganging up," Truman's effort to coordinate policy with Britain was a hallmark of his approach. As Byrnes has written, Molotov's conclusion that American policy had changed after Roosevelt's death was "understandable."[24]

The Potsdam meeting clearly illustrates how the strategic decision to wait for the atomic bomb dominated American policy making from mid-May until early August. The primary reason most Western leaders began to call for another meeting with Stalin only three months after Yalta was their desire to have a confrontation on the important European questions then in tense dispute. But, as I have shown, Truman rejected the advice of his advisers and Churchill, and twice postponed a face-to-face meeting with Stalin because of his decision to wait for the atomic bomb. Ironically, however, in the end he committed himself to a meeting which was still a scant two weeks too early to be decisive. For this reason, to focus attention on the Potsdam meeting itself, as many writers have done,* is to completely misunderstand American policy. Indeed, the interesting question is not what happened at the meeting, but why very little happened at all.

Thus, the importance of the atomic bomb in American calculations is underscored by the negative result of the heads-of-government meeting; had the new weapon not played such a crucial role in American strategy, there would have been every reason for Truman to

---

* Note how both Woodward and Feis conclude their studies (*British Foreign Policy* and, *Between War and Peace*) with the Potsdam Conference, rather than the immediate post-conference diplomacy.

attempt to achieve a negotiated settlement as quickly as possible after the defeat of Germany. Assuming, as Churchill did until mid-July, that it was unwise to gamble on the possibilities of the as yet untested weapon, the Prime Minister was undoubtedly correct to argue that "the decisive, practical points of strategy" involved *above all,* that a settlement must be reached on all major issues between the West and the East . . . *before the armies of democracy melted . . .*" As he told Eden, the "issue . . . seems to me to dwarf all others."[25] Without the atomic bomb, Churchill believed, the only hope lay in an "early and speedy showdown."[26]

Just as he had hurried to arrange an understanding in the Balkans before the Russian position became overwhelmingly powerful in late 1944, he now searched for ways "we may be able to please them . . . as part of a general settlement."[27] Churchill sought to establish a *modus vivendi* before American conventional strength disappeared from the Continent. He wished to give priority to the German question, to recognize the Balkan governments, to settle all frontier issues, to complete the peace treaties quickly and to give only secondary attention to establishing new machinery for post-Potsdam discussions.[28]

Until the atomic test report arrived, Churchill must have thought it incomprehensible that the Americans were not interested in a negotiated settlement. Though they wished to state their case on all issues in dispute, the American delegation was far more concerned with establishing a Council to take up unsettled questions than they were in serious negotiations while the heads of government were together.[29] Thus, significantly, London met with no success in a pre-Potsdam effort to convince Washington of the seemingly obvious point that the German issue was more important than the procedural matter of arranging for new meetings of the foreign ministers.[30]

As we have seen, once the detailed report of the atomic test arrived at Potsdam, Churchill reversed himself completely: "We were . . . possessed of powers which were irresistible."[31] But Churchill's pre-Potsdam appraisal of Stalin's position was probably correct; for, unless the West was prepared to negotiate a settlement, the Soviet Premier undoubtedly calculated there was everything to gain if he waited until the American troops were withdrawn from the Continent.* Since Truman did not tell Stalin of the atomic bomb, it could not yet be expected to play a major role in Soviet-American relations. And, indeed, with no apparent changes in the power relationships, on most issues discussed at the Conference, *both* Truman and Stalin held their ground. The Potsdam Conference took place at a unique moment in history, when each side undoubtedly believed time was on its side. The logic of the situation ensured—as the final protocol showed—that the Conference could only end in deadlock.

Undoubtedly Soviet intelligence knew generally of the work being done on the atomic bomb. However, it is probable that Stalin had no specific knowledge of the New Mexico test—or that if he knew of it, he did not know in detail how greatly it had exceeded expectations. His post-Hiroshima reversals in Manchuria, Hungary, and Bulgaria testify to a new conviction that the power realities required him to yield considerably more than he may have originally thought necessary. It is probable that Truman had this in mind when he noted that by early September "our possession of the secret of harnessing atomic energy already had far-reaching effects on our relations with other nations."[32]

Undoubtedly the best concise summary of the position taken by the West at Potsdam has been provided by General de Gaulle: "The Americans and British hoped to recover in application what they had conceded in principle." De Gaulle believed that "the rapidity of the Sovietization [of Eastern Europe] was only the inevitable result of what had been agreed upon at the Crimea Conference."[33] For this reason, although he strongly opposed the Yalta decisions, de Gaulle felt that "the regrets the British and Americans now expressed [at Potsdam] were quite uncalled for."[34] He concluded that "there was every reason to foresee that on no issue would the Potsdam Conference realize any durable entente"; and that there would be "unlimited friction between the Soviet and Anglo-American participants."[35]

Truman would not have agreed with this judgment. He believed that the United States had sufficient power to force Soviet acceptance of the American plan for lasting world peace. Above all, his policy

---

* Compare Deutscher: By the time of the Potsdam Conference "Stalin's figure loomed incomparably larger on the European horizon." And "Stalin may have reckoned with a more or less rapid withdrawal of American power from the Continent and consequently with the further growth of Russian predominance." (*Stalin*, p. 532.)

required a stable Europe based upon democratic governments and a sound Continental economy. There were two fundamental reasons why the President believed the atomic bomb would permit him to implement his plan: On the one hand, after a new symbolic show-down, the bomb seemed likely to force Soviet agreement to American economic and political plans for Eastern Europe; and, on the other, its power meant that there was no need to fear another German re-vival—the German economic contribution to Continental stability could be given priority over industrial disarmament schemes.

Truman's own argument that a stable Europe was vital to world peace and to American security reveals the error of the common opin-ion that America had little active interest in European affairs until the 1947 Truman Doctrine and Marshall Plan. The President's mid-1945 declaration to his staff was an accurate statement of American policy: "We were committed to the rehabilitation of Europe, and there was to be no abandonment this time."[36] Indeed, much more must be said, for the American commitment to Europe was not restricted to the West-ern regions of the Continent. As George F. Kennan, the author of the "containment policy," has emphasized, American policy was "by no means limited to holding the line."[37] And as Byrnes has repeatedly stressed, in 1945 and 1946 senior American officials were not pri-marily concerned with a Soviet political or military threat to Western Europe;[38] their eyes were focused on conditions in the Soviet-occupied zone. Byrnes has been quite explicit; his policy always aimed at forc-ing the Russians to yield in Eastern Europe, and in mid-1947 he still continued to argue that the United States had it in its power to force the Russians to "retire in a very decent manner."*[39]

There is no question that Byrnes's policy derived from the best

---

* Compare Harriman's previously quoted remark that only the lack of sufficient conventional forces made it impossible "to compel the Soviet Union to withdraw." (*Congressional Record*, Aug. 27, 1951, p. A5416.)

By the time the President accepted his resignation in early 1947, Byrnes had not achieved his objective. Though the Red Army had indeed withdrawn from Manchu-ria, Iran, Hungary, and Czechoslovakia, measured by his own standard he was a failure as Secretary of State—American pol-icy had not been able to force Soviet with-drawal from the rest of Eastern Europe.

Byrnes left office complaining that the Rus-sians "don't scare." With straightforward logic that illuminated the consistency of his basic view and the ironic tragedy of his idealism, he then attempted to convince his fellow countrymen that "measures of the last resort" were the only way to secure lasting world peace. As is often forgotten, Byrnes, who recently endorsed the Presiden-tial candidacy of Senator Goldwater, was perhaps the most highly placed of those who urged a "preventive war" to force the Russians out of Europe. (Forrestal *Diaries*, p. 262; Byrnes, *Speaking Frankly*, p. 203.)

intentions and the highest ideals. And there is no reason to doubt Truman's statement that "the one purpose which dominated me in everything I thought and did was to prevent a third world war."[40] Nevertheless, the attempt to force Soviet withdrawal from Eastern Europe immediately after Hitler's invasion of Russia was an extremely difficult policy to implement. And, inevitably, the policy's problems were greatly multiplied when doubts were raised as to whether or not the industrial basis of German power would be weakened as had been agreed. It may well be true, as Walter Lippmann observed at the time, "that the best that was possible [was] an accommodation, a *modus vivendi*, a working arrangement, some simple form of cooperation, and that in demanding more than that we have been getting less than that, making the best the enemy of the good."[41]

Secretary Stimson seems to have shared this judgment and also to have recognized that the atomic bomb compounded the difficulties Truman's idealistic policy faced. By early September the Secretary of War had come full circle, concluding that "I was wrong" and that the attempt to use the atomic bomb to gain diplomatic objectives was "by far the more dangerous course."[42] In a profoundly ironic, but unsuccessful, attempt to change the policy he had launched, shortly before leaving office Stimson urged an immediate and direct approach to Moscow to attempt to establish international control of atomic energy which might head off "an armament race of a rather desperate character." Apparently greatly disturbed by the bombing of Hiroshima, and now openly opposed to Secretary Byrnes, he advised: *"If we fail to approach them now and merely continue to negotiate with them, having this weapon rather ostentatiously on our hip, their suspicions and their distrust of our purposes and motives will increase."**

At the same time Stimson offered this advice, Secretary Byrnes attempted to explain to Molotov that the United States was "not interested in seeing anything but governments friendly to the Soviet

---

* Stimson's emphasis. The Secretary of War recorded one of his last attempts to convince the President of what he now believed to be a fundamental error in his own previous advice and in American policy: "I described the talk that I had had with Byrnes and told him what our differences were. I told him that both my plan and Byrnes's plan contained chances which I outlined, and I said that I thought that in my method there was less danger than in his and also we would be on the right path towards world establishment of an international world, while on his plan we would be on the wrong path in that respect and (*Continued on next page*)

Union in adjacent countries." But the Soviet Foreign Minister was openly incredulous: "I must tell you I have doubts as to this, and it would not be honest to hide it."[43] Similarly, at this time former Soviet Foreign Minister Litvinov asked an American friend: "Why did you Americans wait till right now to begin opposing us in the Balkans and Eastern Europe? You should have done this three years ago. Now it is too late, and your complaints only arouse suspicions here."[44] And General Eisenhower, making a triumphal postwar visit to Moscow, sensed new and profound Soviet suspicions: "Before the atom bomb was used I would have said, yes, I was sure we could keep the peace with Russia. Now I don't know. . . . People are frightened and disturbed all over. Every one feels insecure again."[45]

To recall the judgments of Stimson and Eisenhower in the autumn of 1945 is to state the ultimate question of to what extent the atomic bomb affected the entire structure of postwar American-Soviet relations. But it is not possible at this juncture to test Secretary Stimson's September view that "the problem of our satisfactory relations with Russia [was] not merely connected with but [was] virtually dominated by the problem of the atomic bomb."[46] Nor can the issue of why the atomic bomb was used be conclusively resolved.

This essay has attempted to describe the influence of the atomic bomb on certain questions of diplomacy. I do not believe that the reverse question—the influence of diplomacy upon the decision to use the atomic bomb—can be answered on the basis of the presently available evidence. However, it is possible to define the nature of the problem which new materials and further research may be able to solve.

A fruitful way to begin is to note General Eisenhower's recollection of the Potsdam discussion at which Stimson told him the weapon would be used against Japan:

> During his recitation of the relevant facts, I had been conscious of a feeling of depression and so I voiced to him my grave misgivings,

(*Continued from preceding page*)
would be tending to revert to power politics." (Diary, Sept. 5, 1945.)
Stimson also reviewed the development of his thinking in a discussion with his successor, Robert P. Patterson: "I had a long talk with him. I told him how my view had been gradually formed; how in the beginning I was inclined to think we ought to hang on to the bomb . . . and its secrets; but

284

first on the basis of my belief that Japan was already defeated and that dropping the bomb was completely unnecessary, and secondly because I thought that our country should avoid shocking world opinion by the use of a weapon whose employment was, I thought, no longer mandatory as a measure to save American lives. It was my belief that Japan was, at that very moment, seeking some way to surrender with a minimum loss of "face."

"It wasn't necessary to hit them with that awful thing," Eisenhower concluded.[47]

Perhaps the most remarkable aspect of the decision to use the atomic bomb is that the President and his senior political advisers do not seem ever to have shared Eisenhower's "grave misgivings."* As we have seen, they simply assumed that they would use the bomb, never really giving serious consideration to not using it. Hence, to state in a precise way the question "Why was the atomic bomb used?" is to ask why senior political officials did *not* seriously question its use as Eisenhower did.

The first point to note is that the decision to use the weapon did not derive from overriding military considerations. Despite Truman's subsequent statement that the weapon "saved millions of lives,"[48] Eisenhower's judgment that it was "completely unnecessary" as a measure to save lives was almost certainly correct. This is not a matter of hindsight; *before the atomic bomb was dropped each of the Joint Chiefs of Staff advised that it was highly likely that Japan could be forced to surrender "unconditionally," without use of the bomb and without an invasion.* Indeed, this characterization of the position taken by the senior military advisers is a conservative one.

General Marshall's June 18 appraisal was the most cautiously phrased advice offered by any of the Joint Chiefs: "The impact of

---

that gradually I had found that I was wrong and that that would be by far the more dangerous course than to make an effort with Russia particularly to get on terms with us of confidence in which we would eliminate the manufacture of such bombs for war purposes—eliminate the development of the atomic energy of the explosive kind, and confine ourselves to its use and the development of its more controllable smaller powers for commerce . . ." (Diary, Sept. 17, 1945.)

Stimson left office at the end of September deeply disturbed at having failed to change the direction of the strategy he had launched. (Diary, Sept. 21, 1945.) For a memorandum in which he offered his final detailed views to the President, see Appendix III.

* But see: "I must say that personally I am not at all sure that we were well advised to use it." (Atomic Energy Commission, *Oppenheimer Hearings*, p. 367.)

Russian entry on the already hopeless Japanese may well be the decisive action levering them into capitulation . . ."[49] Admiral Leahy was
absolutely certain there was no need for the bombing to obviate the
necessity of an invasion.[50] His judgment after the fact was the same as
his view before the bombing: "It is my opinion that the use of this
barbarous weapon at Hiroshima and Nagasaki was of no material
assistance in our war against Japan. The Japanese were already defeated and ready to surrender . . ."[51] Similarly, through most of 1945
Admiral King believed the bomb unnecessary,[52] and Generals Arnold
and LeMay defined the official Air Force position in this way:
Whether or not the atomic bomb should be dropped was not for the
Air Force to decide, but explosion of the bomb was not necessary to
win the war or make an invasion unnecessary.*[53]

Similar views prevailed in Britain long before the bombs were used.
General Ismay recalls that by the time of Potsdam, "for some time
past it had been firmly fixed in my mind that the Japanese were tottering."[54] Ismay's reaction to the suggestion of the bombing was, like
Eisenhower's and Leahy's, one of "revulsion."[55] And Churchill, who
as early as September 1944, felt that Russian entry was likely to force
capitulation,[56] has written: "It would be a mistake to suppose that the
fate of Japan was settled by the atomic bomb. Her defeat was certain
before the first bomb fell . . ."[57]

The military appraisals made before the weapons were used have
been confirmed by numerous postsurrender studies. The best known is
that of the United States Strategic Bombing Survey. The Survey's conclusion is unequivocal: "Japan would have surrendered even if the
atomic bombs had not been dropped, even if Russia had not entered
the war, and even if no invasion had been planned or contemplated."†[58]

(*Continued from preceding page*)
  *At the time he argued against the use
of the atomic bomb, Eisenhower advised the
additional point that the war could easily
be ended before Soviet entry. (Eisenhower,
Crusade in Europe, pp. 441–42.)
  † See also Marshall's postwar statement
that the atomic bombs precipitated the surrender only "by months"; Bush's view that
"the war would have ended before long in
any case, for Japan had been brought
nearly to her knees"; Curtis LeMay's opinion that the war would have ended in two
weeks ("the atomic bomb had nothing to
do with the end of the war"); Claire
Chennault's view that the Russian declaration of war was the decisive factor; and the
arguments of Morton, Baldwin, Blackett,
and Craven and Cate, that the atomic
bomb was not needed to force a surrender
before an invasion. (J. P. Sutherland, "The
Story General Marshall Told Me," *U.S.
News & World Report*, Nov. 2, 1959, p.
52; Bush, V., *Modern Arms and Free Men*,
p. 101; *New York Herald Tribune*, Sept.
21, 1945; *New York Times*, Aug. 15, 1945;

That military considerations were not decisive is confirmed—and illuminated—by the fact that the President did not even ask the opinion of the military adviser most directly concerned. General Mac-Arthur, Supreme Commander of Allied Forces in the Pacific, was simply informed of the weapon shortly before it was used at Hiroshima.[59] Before his death he stated on numerous occasions that, like Eisenhower, he believed the atomic bomb was completely unnecessary from a military point of view.[60]

Although military considerations were not primary, as we have seen, unquestionably political considerations related to Russia played a major role in the decision; from at least mid-May American policy makers hoped to end the hostilities before the Red Army entered Manchuria. For this reason they had no wish to test whether Russian entry into the war would force capitulation—as most thought likely—long before the scheduled November invasion. Indeed, they actively attempted to delay Stalin's declaration of war.

Nevertheless, it would be wrong to conclude that the atomic bomb was used simply to keep the Red Army out of Manchuria. Given the desperate efforts of the Japanese to surrender, and Truman's willingness to offer assurances to the Emperor, it is entirely possible that the war could have been ended by negotiation before the Red Army had begun its attack. But, again, as we have seen, after Alamogordo neither the President nor his senior advisers were interested in exploring this possibility.

One reason may have been their fear that if time-consuming negotiations were once initiated, the Red Army might attack in order to seize Manchurian objectives. But, if this explanation is accepted, once more one must conclude that the bomb was used primarily because it was felt to be politically important to prevent Soviet domination of the area.

Such a conclusion is very difficult to accept, for American interests in Manchuria, although historically important to the State Department, were not of great significance. The further question therefore arises: Were there other political reasons for using the atomic bomb? In approaching this question, it is important to note that most of the men

Morton, "The Decision to Use the Atomic Bomb," *Command Decisions*, ed. K. R. Greenfield, p. 408; *Military and Political Consequences of Atomic Energy*, pp. 116–30; Baldwin, *Great Mistakes of the War*, p. 84; Craven and Cate, *Air Forces in World War II*, Vol. V, p. 726.)

involved at the time who since have made their views public always mention *two* considerations which dominated discussions. The first was the desire to end the Japanese war quickly, which, as we have seen, was not primarily a military consideration, but a political one. The second is always referred to indirectly.

In June, for example, a leading member of the Interim Committee's scientific panel, A. H. Compton, advised against the Franck report's suggestion of a technical demonstration of the new weapon: Not only was there a possibility that this might not end the war promptly, but failure to make a combat demonstration would mean the 'loss of the opportunity to impress the world with the national sacrifices that enduring security demanded.'* The general phrasing that the bomb was needed 'to impress the world' has been made more specific by J. Robert Oppenheimer. Testifying on this matter some years later he stated that the second of the two "overriding considerations" in discussions regarding the bomb was "the effect of our actions on the stability, on our strength, and the stability of the postwar world."[61] And the problem of postwar stability was inevitably the problem of Russia. Oppenheimer has put it this way: "Much of the discussion revolved around the question raised by Secretary Stimson as to whether there was any hope at all of using this development to get less barbarous relations with the Russians."[62]

Vannevar Bush, Stimson's chief aide for atomic matters, has been quite explicit: "That bomb was developed on time . . . " Not only did it mean a quick end to the Japanese war, but "it was also delivered on time so that there was no necessity for any concessions to Russia at the end of the war."[63]

In essence, the second of the two overriding considerations seems to have been that a combat demonstration was needed to convince the Russians to accept the American plan for a stable peace. And the crucial point of this effort was the need to force agreement on the main questions in dispute: the American proposals for Central and Eastern Europe. President Truman may well have expressed the key consideration in October 1945; publicly urging the necessity of a more conventional form of military power (his proposal for universal military

---

* The words set off are a quotation of the paraphrase provided by the historians of the U.S. Atomic Energy Commission. (Hewlett and Anderson, *The New World*, p. 367.)

training), in a personal appearance before Congress the President declared: "It is only by strength that we can impress the fact upon possible future aggressors that we will tolerate no threat to peace . . ."[64]

If indeed the "second consideration" involved in the bombing of Hiroshima and Nagasaki was the desire to impress the Russians, it might explain the strangely ambiguous statement by Truman that not only did the bomb end the war, but it gave the world "a chance to face the facts."[65] It would also accord with Stimson's private advice to McCloy: "We have got to regain the lead and perhaps do it in a pretty rough and realistic way. . . . We have coming into action a weapon which will be unique. Now the thing [to do is] . . . let our actions speak for themselves."[66] Again, it would accord with Stimson's statement to Truman that the "greatest complication" would occur if the President negotiated with Stalin before the bomb had been "laid on Japan."[67] It would tie in with the fact that from mid-May strategy toward all major diplomatic problems was based upon the assumption the bomb would be demonstrated. Finally, it might explain why none of the highest civilian officials seriously questioned the use of the bomb as Eisenhower did; for, having reversed the basic direction of diplomatic strategy *because* of the atomic bomb, it would have been very difficult indeed for anyone subsequently to challenge an idea which had come to dominate all calculations of high policy.*

At present no final conclusion can be reached on this question. But the problem can be defined with some precision: Why did the American government refuse to attempt to exploit Japanese efforts to surrender? Or, alternatively, why did they refuse to test whether a Russian declaration of war would force capitulation? Were Hiroshima and Nagasaki bombed primarily to impress the world with the need to

---

* It might also explain why the sober and self-controlled Stimson reacted so strongly when Eisenhower objected to the bombing: "The Secretary was deeply perturbed by my attitude, almost angrily refuting the reasons I gave . . ." (Eisenhower, *Mandate for Change*, p. 313.) Stimson's post-Hiroshima reversal, and his repeated references to the gravity of the moral issues raised by the new weapon, are evidence of his own doubts. Eisenhower's searching criticism may well have touched upon a very tender point, namely, Stimson's undoubted awareness that Hiroshima and Nagasaki were to be sacrificed primarily for political, not military, reasons.

See also Williams, *The Tragedy of American Diplomacy*, p. 254, and Fleming, *The Cold War*, I, pp. 296–302. Compare Irving's account of the bombing of Dresden. See especially his discussion of the precisely parallel argument that Churchill felt it politically important to impress Stalin with overwhelming air power when Central and Eastern European issues were discussed at Yalta. (*The Destruction of Dresden*, pp. 86–102.)

accept America's plan for a stable and lasting peace—that is, primarily, America's plan for Europe? The evidence strongly suggests that the view which the President's personal representative offered to one of the atomic scientists in May 1945 was an accurate statement of policy: "Mr. Byrnes did not argue that it was necessary to use the bomb against the cities of Japan in order to win the war . . . Mr. Byrnes's . . . view [was] that our possessing and demonstrating the bomb would make Russia more manageable in Europe. . . ."[68]

A Note on the Historical Debate Over Questions Concerning Truman's 1945 Strategy of Delay

ATOMIC DIPLOMACY WAS FIRST PUBLISHED in August 1965—a period when intense discussion of the early period of the Cold War was just getting under way. At that time and for some years thereafter the book stirred considerable debate. We have come a long way since 1965, and several of the main theses of the book have been accepted (sometimes in diluted form) by many authors. Part of the debate of the early period is, however, worth reviewing (even though it is rather technical for the nonprofessional), since new information has become available on important points dealt with in the book which have not yet been fully confronted.

As we saw in the Introduction to the 1985 Edition, the three fundamental arguments of *Atomic Diplomacy* are: (1) that the atomic bomb played a major role in American strategy toward the Soviet Union starting in the late spring of 1945; (2) that factors related to the Soviet Union were critical in the assumption-decision to bomb Hiroshima; and (3) that U.S. policy changes during the period April–September 1945 suggest a new point of departure for assessing the early dynamics of the Cold War.

Although some of the debate on *Atomic Diplomacy* dealt with the major issues, much of it concentrated on quite secondary or even tertiary points. The quality of the work was also highly uneven: Even the best researchers misinterpreted obvious statements, or offered trivial, erroneous, and sometimes extraordinarily petty comments.*

All of the rather voluminous academic literature on the book obviously cannot be taken up at this point. The issues I have selected for discussion have been chosen partly because they are somewhat more important than others (and have informed subsequent interpretations), partly because they have been treated responsibly, and partly because an illustrative consideration of the shortcomings of alternative views in these areas may offer readers a perspective on the debate over other, more limited points.†

GENERAL PROBLEMS

AT THE OUTSET a brief word about the availability of evidence for the 1945 period: As I have indicated in the Introduction to the 1985 Edition, there are considerable difficulties with problems of documentation concerning the early role of the atomic bomb in diplomacy. Given the great secrecy surrounding the weapon, and the unusual informal relationship between Truman and Byrnes from mid-April through June, "official" information is very skimpy on several important matters. Add to this the fact that Byrnes was congenitally secretive and had few scruples about doctoring the historical record, and the challenge facing those who wish to understand this period is formidable.

Given this situation, two alternative approaches, broadly speaking, have been open to serious historians: One is to regard as "truth" *only that for which a precise document can be found.* The second is to attempt to piece together, "detective style," what is known about various actors, decisions, and events with a view to establishing what happened at certain points *referred to* in the available evidence but not precisely documented by it.

---

* For instance, Warren F. Kimball, reviewing the narrow and "vindictive" approach Robert J. Maddox took in criticizing several authors and books (including *Atomic Diplomacy*), compared his attack to "Senator Joseph McCarthy's actions. . . ." Kimball provides a very useful overview of the kind of scholarship which was given attention about a decade ago. See his "The Cold War Warmed Over," pp. 1119–36. On Maddox, also see Krueger, "New Left Revisionists and Their Critics,"

pp. 463–66. For Maddox's attack on *Atomic Diplomacy*, see his "Atomic Diplomacy: A Study in Creative Writing and Communications," pp. 925–34; my response is on pp. 1062–67 of the same issue.

† Those interested in various other secondary and tertiary points raised in the literature will find the most important issues taken up in specific notes to this Appendix and to the Introduction to the 1985 Edition.

There are risks in both alternatives. The former inevitably makes the historian and the public the prisoners of officials who have an interest in withholding evidence. Before the Stimson diary and the records of the Manhattan Project were opened, for instance, the idea that the bomb was deeply involved in diplomatic calculations could not be "proved," and so, *if precise and absolute documentation were the test of historical truth,* what in fact was true about the actual history could not possibly be known.

But the second alternative inevitably leaves the historian open to the charge that there is *no* proof for certain precise points. Those who claimed very early after World War II that all the then available evidence pointed to a linkage between the use of the atomic bomb and U.S. diplomatic calculations *vis à vis* the Soviet Union were even attacked for alleged anti-Americanism, or worse; and their scholarship was repeatedly disparaged.

Nonetheless, in matters of great historical importance, especially when it is known that the key figures have an interest in distorting the record, there is no alternative except to attempt to piece together what is known—even in the absence of precise documentation on all points. The trick, of course, is to do this with care and precision, always stating carefully what is fact and what is inferred from fact.

Were I to rewrite *Atomic Diplomacy* today (as I suggested in the Introduction to the 1985 Edition), I would probably bring into the body of the main text much more of the kind of detailed argumentation presented in Appendix II (and in this Appendix) to establish certain points where precise documentation was not yet available. As the reader can see, what this involves is the careful fitting together of facts, conversations, dates, and so on, to demonstrate that events referred to in certain documents had to have taken place before they are subsequently mentioned; and it sometimes requires an inordinate amount of detailed analysis of various theoretically possible interpretations to discern which have and which do not have an adequate basis. I would probably also elucidate the meaning of short passages taken from certain documents to a greater extent than I did as a young graduate student. Although such an approach slows the development of the argument considerably (and often puts the reader to sleep), given the confusion that has occasionally arisen over one or two secondary points, on balance it is probably worth doing.

A REPRESENTATIVE CRITIQUE

BOTH TO DEAL with the several issues and to illustrate difficulties which must be confronted in historical debate over matters of evidence in 1945, let us initially review one representative critique of certain elements of *Atomic Diplomacy*'s interpretation of President Truman's decision to delay his confrontation with Stalin until after the atomic bomb was tested—that of Martin Sherwin, a responsible historian who has taken the trouble to spell out his differences with my views in more careful detail than many.

Sherwin's position, like a number of those who have taken up the problem, is in some ways curious: He makes something of an issue of his criticism, but in fact does not deny the important points— namely, that American policy makers did postpone their meeting with Stalin until after the bomb was tested, and that they saw the new weapon as likely to reinforce their diplomatic position greatly. (As we have seen in the Introduction to the 1985 Edition, Sherwin also comes quite close to *Atomic Diplomacy*'s interpretation of how the actual use of atomic weapons came about.).

Sherwin concentrates first on several subsidiary points, some of which are quite minor (and, in my view, erroneous). For instance, he quotes me correctly as saying that in early May 1945 "the Polish issue and the atomic bomb now became inextricably bound together. . . ." But he claims that "Alperovitz's description of Stimson's activities . . . is in error."[1] However, it is evident from the context, from preceding and subsequent paragraphs, and from repeated statements that I am talking about *Truman* (not Stimson), who was considering both matters of foreign policy (above all Poland) and the initial approach to nuclear policy during these days.[2]

Again, Sherwin quotes me correctly as saying that Truman was "extremely secretive about preparations . . . [for the Hopkins mission]." He then charges that this overlooks the fact "that Truman checked with Hull, Byrnes, and the State Department after Hopkins agreed to go."[3] But my full statement is: "Truman was extremely secretive about preparations . . . [for the Hopkins mission]. He did not consult the Secretary of State, the Acting Secretary of State, the Polish experts in the Department of State, or Admiral Leahy, *until the very eve of the trips. . . .*"*[4] The full quotation makes it clear that Sherwin has simply mischaracterized my position, which, like his, is that the checking occurred very late in the game.

One further illustration: Contrary to Sherwin, *Atomic Diplomacy* is quite straightforward in saying that Truman did check with Byrnes and the State Department.[5] I did not think it worth mentioning that the President checked with Hull, who was no longer in office. (However, my notes to the references given are to precisely the same paragraphs in the Truman Memoirs where this is reported along with the fact that Truman checked with Byrnes and the State Department.) As to whether Truman was secretive, as I suggested, here is information on the question (also presented in *Atomic Diplomacy* at precisely the point to which Sherwin refers): "As Arthur Bliss Lane, the designated ambassador to Poland, has written, all that was known in the Department of State was that 'suddenly and secretly, in the last days of May, Harry Hopkins left for Moscow.' "[6] *Atomic Diplomacy* also provides information at this point indicating that Truman did not even consult with his Chief of Staff, and that he ordered that all cables concerning the Hopkins mission be shown to only a very restricted group.[7]

Those not familiar with normal academic debate may be surprised at the intensity of conflict over such small issues. Sherwin's writing is, however, both moderate and intelligent. Nevertheless, just such points were often used to criticize portions of *Atomic Diplomacy*. Minor issues aside, Sherwin's most important point is related to precisely how and when President Truman received advice and took decisions which reflected the impact of the atomic bomb on strategy toward the Soviet Union. Sherwin feels that there was no conscious strategy involving the atomic bomb at the outset of Truman's Presidency, but instead "during the early weeks of May, the President was grasping at diplomatic straws, not scheming sophisticated diplomatic strategies. . . ."[8]

Let us examine the claim. Note first that the argument is about *the early weeks of May.* As I have said, Sherwin admits and agrees with

---

* Emphasis added.

the much more important argument of *Atomic Diplomacy* that Truman did base his strategy toward the Soviet Union during the summer of 1945 on an awareness that he was soon likely to have the new atomic weapon at his disposal. Sherwin's dating of Truman's acceptance of the strategy is sometime around May 16[9]—by the broadest possible interpretation a difference of between two and three weeks with my own suggested dating of the decision.

Within the time frame we are focusing on, Sherwin disputes my suggestion that *probably* Truman made his decision on April 25 or shortly thereafter. Sherwin's main argument is that Stimson's diaries (and other available documents) do not demonstrate that the decision occurred on these dates. "there is no evidence in the extant records of the [April 25] meeting that Stimson had such a strategy in mind or that Truman interpreted the Secretary's remarks as recommending such a policy."[10]

But *Atomic Diplomacy* did not claim that there was such evidence; or that the April 25 meeting was demonstrably the date at which the advice was given and the decision taken; nor, finally and most importantly, is either point crucial to the major or (as we shall see) several minor arguments concerning this general period. In fact, *Atomic Diplomacy* is quite specific on the pages referred to in Sherwin's critique (and elsewhere) that "we do not have precise information on the exact date on which Stimson advised the President to postpone diplomatic confrontations with the Russians."[11] Nor is there room for any doubt about this matter: The book devotes an entire Appendix (II) to precisely this point. *Atomic Diplomacy* does say that what evidence we have "suggests" that April 25 was the crucial date at which Stimson first advised delay, but it stresses: "Although available evidence establishes that Stimson recommended the delay of all disputes with Russia until the atomic bomb had been demonstrated, and that Truman followed this advice, the absence of complete information makes it difficult to pinpoint the exact dates on which the advice was offered and the decision was taken."[12] Again, this statement occurs at precisely the point to which Sherwin refers in his comment.

It is worth pursuing the dating question one step further: As indicated, Sherwin and other historians now agree that by May 16 Truman had accepted Stimson's advice and postponed his meeting with Stalin until the atomic bomb could be tested. This is the date on which Stimson responds to the President: "Therefore I believe that good and not harm would be done by the policy towards your coming meeting which you mentioned to me. We shall probably hold more cards in our hands later than now."[13] Sherwin believes that the President's decision cannot have taken place earlier than this date: "It is highly unlikely, considering how meticulous Stimson was about summarizing in his diary his thoughts on atomic energy and other matters he considered important, that he would have omitted other conversations with the President, or that he would have neglected to record as part of a conversation with him any suggestion that Soviet-American relations be governed by the Manhattan Project's schedule."[14] It is clear from the record, however, that many decisions were taken without Stimson's knowledge, and it is not clear that he recorded every decision and discussion with care. (And some of the conversations he reports include only very cryptic mention of the subject discussed.) Stimson was an old, frail man, who suffered from intense migraine headaches. To base an argument that *nothing occurred because it was not entered in a diary* is extraordinary, to say the least.

Moreover, note that when Stimson responds to Truman, it is in connection with a policy that the President *tells him about*—i.e., a policy he has *already decided upon.* Unless we are to assume that the President simply decided one of the most important matters before him suddenly and out of the blue, the discussions leading up to this date must have taken place, minimally, in the week preceding it.

That the decision, indeed, was not one which could have been made without careful consideration is evidenced by the fact that putting off the meeting with Stalin ran directly counter to the advice of virtually all the President's top advisers *who were not involved with the atomic bomb.*[15] From *their* standpoint, delay seemed incomprehensible: U.S. bargaining strength seemed to be weakening every day as the American Army was slowly withdrawn from Europe—a point men like Harriman, on the one hand, and Churchill, on the other, pressed repeatedly and intensely. (Only those who thought America's bargaining position would *improve,* not weaken, favored a strategy of putting off the meeting; and the most clearly documented advocate of this broad approach was Secretary Stimson, who based his thinking on the forthcoming atomic bomb.)

We know just a bit more about this issue, both through evidence Sherwin neglects and through evidence he knows about but attempts to discount. Truman's cable to Churchill proposing that the heads-of-government meeting be held after June 30 (it was subsequently shifted again, when there were technical delays in the atomic test) was sent on May 9. Sherwin believes that when Truman cabled Churchill he did not have the thought of the atomic bomb in mind. Referring to Stimson's diary entries of May 14, 15, and 16 he says, "Since these entries appear after May 9th . . . they indicate that the scheduled test of the atomic bomb became a consideration for Stimson only after Truman had already accepted the idea of a meeting with Churchill some time in July."[16]

Again, note that *because he does not find an entry* Sherwin believes that the two issues were not related. But there is strong evidence to the contrary. The undisputed date on which the bomb had entered both Truman's and Stimson's strategy toward the meeting fell on a Wednesday. Allowing for the weekend, there were only four intervening normal working days between Truman's cable to Churchill and May 16. Though Truman sent other cables to Churchill during these days, none changed the original date. Truman met with Stimson on Wednesday and told the Secretary that he had already adopted a policy of delay, *but there is no evidence recording such a decision other than the May 9 cable.* Without *some* evidence to the contrary there is no reason to doubt that what Truman is referring to is in fact *that* cable when he indicates to Stimson he has decided to delay the meeting.[17]

There is additional evidence that this cable is related to the bomb: Truman refers in it to having to wait until the end of the "fiscal year" before he can leave Washington. As we shall see, we know from the Davies diaries and other sources that Truman regularly used an excuse related to budget planning at the end of the fiscal year when he did not want to refer directly to the atomic bomb.

Sherwin states that other than brief telephone conversations on the membership of the Interim Committee in early May, "there is no indication . . . that [Stimson] discussed any of [his thoughts on atomic energy and diplomacy] with Truman until May 16."[18] In a more detailed account of this period he says of the May 16 meeting in which Truman confirms that the summit meeting would be timed to coincide with, or follow, the atomic test, "The conclusions Stimson had reached on May 14 and 15 had now become part of the effort to 'find some way of persuading Russia to play ball.' "[19] But this argument runs even more directly into conflict with the fact that Stimson is responding *to Truman* when he comments to the President on "the policy towards your coming meeting *which you mentioned to me.* . . ." How can it be that Stimson's private ideas have mysteriously culminated in the President's decision (which he mentions to the Secretary of War) if Truman and Stimson hadn't talked about them earlier?*

It appears, moreover, that Stimson also explained something of the role of the atomic bomb to Anthony Eden on May 14 when (as Stimson's diary shows) in a forty-five minute meeting "on general matters but especially [the atomic bomb]" he outlined "to him the progress which we have made and the timetable as it stood now, *and . . . its bearing upon our present problems of an international character.* . . ."†[20]

Nor is there any question about Stimson's overall viewpoint during *precisely* this period. On exactly the same day he talked with Eden, Stimson's diary (in the very next paragraph) delineates the Secretary of War's strategic conception of delaying major disputes, his belief that the atomic bomb will strongly aid such a strategy, and his belief, further, that the new weapon will ultimately allow the United States to take a tough position with the Russians. Here again is the Stimson diary entry quoted in the Introduction to this edition concerning a discussion with Assistant Secretary of War John J. McCloy after he had seen Eden:

> My own opinion was that the time now and the method now to deal with Russia was to keep our mouths shut and *let our actions speak for words.* The Russians will understand them better than anything else. It is a case where we have got to regain the lead *and perhaps do it in a pretty rough and realistic way.* They have rather taken it away from us because we talked too much and have been too lavish with our beneficences to them. I told him this was a

---

* See also below, pp. 356–58.
† Emphasis added.

place where we really held all the cards. I called it a royal straight flush and we mustn't be a fool about the way we play it. They can't get along without our help and industries and *we have coming into action a weapon which will be unique.* Now the thing is not to get into unnecessary quarrels by talking too much and not to indicate any weakness by talking too much; *let our actions speak for themselves.*[*21]

Moving back still further in the direction of the May 9 cable: Before the weekend, on Thursday, May 10, when Ambassador Harriman complained that Russia "is . . . going to try to ride roughshod over her neighbors in Europe . . . ," Stimson also "talked over very confidentially our problem connected with [the atomic bomb] *in this matter.*"[†22] Sherwin understandably has difficulty with this diary entry (he tries to explain it away as inconclusive) for it also strongly suggests that as of *this* date the strategy evidenced in diary entries on Tuesday and Wednesday was already in place, and that Truman's cable to Churchill the day before reflected this fact.

What the technical disagreements over the exact timing of Truman's decision center on is the question of just how calculated the President's strategy of delaying a confrontation with Stalin was, and when, precisely, it was adopted. My own view, as indicated, is that given the evidence we now have it is very hard to believe that Truman had not adopted something like Stimson's general view at a rather early point. Combining all of the information we have just reviewed—from the May 9 cable to the May 16 diary entry—it seems all but certain that Truman's strategic decision (*and the discussions leading to it*) had to have occurred either in the last week of April or the first week of May for the decision to have been embodied in the May 9 cable.

(To complete the story, three weeks later—on May 28—the President, as the official history of the Atomic Energy Commission put it, "thinking of the latest estimates from Los Alamos, suggested July 15" as the date for the Potsdam meeting. When Stimson met with Truman on June 6 to warn that the "greatest complication" would occur if the bomb had not been "laid on" Japan by the time of the

---

* Emphasis added.
† Emphasis added.

meeting, Truman reassured him, saying he had "postponed that until the 15th of July on purpose to give us more time."[23])

RELATED ISSUES

ALTHOUGH SHERWIN and a few other historians have made much of the argument about dates, to recall, the major theses put forward in *Atomic Diplomacy* do not stand or fall on the precise time of the decision within the April 25–May 16 three-week range, nor did the book make this claim. The exact date of the decision to delay the meeting with Stalin is of *some* significance (though again, it is not crucial) in connection with another aspect of *Atomic Diplomacy*'s thesis that has been disputed. This concerns the relationship of Truman's overall strategy to his decision to send Harry Hopkins to see Stalin and Joseph Davies to see Churchill.

In Chapters II, III, and IV of *Atomic Diplomacy* I attempted to show how an understanding of Truman's decision to postpone a confrontation with Stalin illuminates the President's decisions on a number of major issues, including the two diplomatic missions. Had Truman followed the advice of those urging an *immediate* showdown, an early heads-of-government meeting would have been the forum in which to deal with the then pressing issues. Putting off the meeting caused major difficulties: As Harriman put it to the President, "the longer the meeting was delayed the worse the situation would get. . . ."[24] Indeed, when Churchill heard about the latest delay (from Stalin), he was extremely upset. Even his cable does not disguise his emotion: "I consider that July 15th, repeat July, the month after June, is much too late. . . . I have proposed June 15th, repeat June, the month before July, but if that is not possible, why not July 1st, July 2nd, or July 3rd?" Stalin's reply was brief: "I should like to tell you again that July 15 was suggested by President Truman. . . ."[25]

As *Atomic Diplomacy* attempts to show, when Truman rejected Churchill's plea and decided to delay the meeting until the atomic bomb had been tested, the situational logic he faced demanded some interim or "bridging" strategy: Damage done during the initial tough fight over Poland had to be repaired; further Soviet *faits accomplis* had to be forestalled; Stalin's suspicions had to be allayed; cooperation had to be reestablished in the administration of Germany and Austria; and initiatives had to be attempted which might keep the door open to subsequent American influence. If Truman did nothing, things were likely to get worse. The Hopkins and Davies missions solved all of these problems.*

Rejecting the idea that the atomic bomb had already entered the President's calculations, Sherwin and some other writers feel there was no serious strategy at this point, that Truman was simply vacillating when he decided at first to be tough with the Russians and then to relax by sending the two men on their missions. That is why—in this interpretation—it is important to try to prove that Truman did not decide to postpone the Potsdam meeting until *after* he decided upon the missions. At one point Sherwin cautiously states that it "*seems* apparent" that the Hopkins mission (the main one) was not part of a subtle strategy based on the atomic bomb.[26] At other points, however, he argues with no qualification that the Hopkins and Davies missions had nothing whatsoever to do with the atomic bomb, but, rather, were simply conciliatory gestures designed to help arrange a conference with Stalin.[27] (And again this is a view other writers have echoed.)

Sherwin writes: "Upon the outcome of [the Hopkins-Stalin] meetings . . . rested the feasibility of arranging a meeting between Churchill, Stalin, and Truman."[28] He also states that the purpose of the Hopkins mission was to ascertain whether Stalin was willing to compromise on the issues then in dispute.[29]

As to the first point: Truman did not have to send a mission to Stalin to find out whether such a meeting was feasible; Churchill and others were literally begging Truman to arrange the meeting; there is no indication that any of Truman's top advisers thought it was not feasible. Even in the midst of the tense fight over Poland, Molotov indicated to Davies that Stalin would favor a meeting.[30] Second, it was *Truman*, not Stalin, who made the compromises—and they were very serious compromises indeed. There is a major flaw in the position taken by Sherwin and others in that it minimizes the gigantic fact that the Hopkins mission involved not simply a sounding operation, but a major reversal of fundamental policy—namely, a

---

* See above, pp. 116–38, and below, pp. 318–23.

U.S. decision to back down on the Polish question then in very tense dispute. This was the price that was paid for delay.

Virtually every major adviser other than Stimson, to say nothing of Churchill, had been pressuring Truman not to yield on the Polish problem up to this point; and the President had fully committed his own prestige to opposing Stalin's solution to the Polish problem. Indeed, things had gotten so tense that the United States had stated it would refuse further conversations until sixteen Polish resistance leaders who had been arrested were released. All of this was abandoned with the Hopkins mission. Once Hopkins got to Moscow, he made it clear that Poland was the key question, and very shortly thereafter the United States accepted the heart of the Soviet position on the distribution of power in the Polish government—*the central issue disputed at the highest level up to that point.* Again, Stimson was the only major adviser urging caution on the Polish problem, and, more generally, a subtle strategy of reducing tensions until after the bomb was demonstrated.[31]

Sherwin once more focuses on dates in attempting to make his argument; he believes the main source of the idea of reversing field on major issues with the Russians was former Ambassador Joseph Davies in conversations on April 30, May 13, and May 21. Davies did indeed urge conciliation toward the Russians, and it is true that on May 13 Truman asked the former Ambassador to go see Stalin. But note carefully: This conversation occurs *after* the May 9 cable in which (1) Truman agreed to the idea of a meeting with Stalin; and (2) said that he couldn't come until sometime in July. Sherwin's suggestion that Davies is the main influence behind Truman's decision rests on a misreading of these dates—and also an overestimation, in my view, of the importance of the conversation Truman and Davies had on April 30. Sherwin himself acknowledges that although Truman was extremely friendly to Davies on that date, it appears that the former Ambassador to Russia made very little headway with the President with his broad argument for a different approach to the Russians.[32] Between April 30 and the time he made his decision on May 9, there is no evidence that the President altered his tough stand in response to Davies' broad line of advice.[33]

Nor did Truman seek out Davies; it was the former Ambassador (not Truman) who initiated the second contact on May 13. Further doubt is cast on the idea that Truman is accepting *Davies'* approach in deciding to meet with Stalin by the fact that at their May 13 meeting *Truman did not tell the former Ambassador that four days earlier he had already sent Churchill the cable agreeing to meet.* If anything, Truman's lack of candor is evidence that something else is going on—and that the President's basic strategic thinking has been done elsewhere in consultation with others.[34] As to Truman's attitude, Eden's report of their meeting the very next day suggests it was anything but conciliatory: "Both Truman and [Acting Secretary of State] Grew referred bitterly to the failure of the Russians to keep their word. . . ."[35]

The record is not clear as to exactly when Truman asked Hopkins to undertake his mission to Stalin (as Sherwin and I both agree). We know it is before May 21, for Truman told Davies on that date that Hopkins would be going; and it is before May 19, when Truman met with Hopkins to go over final instructions. The contemporary records suggest that it must also have been *after* May 13, for Truman's diary and Davies' diary both say that the President first asked Davies to undertake the mission on that date—and Truman's says he asked Hopkins, on Harriman's recommendation, *only after Davies declined* due to illness.

Again, the date is not absolutely crucial, but Sherwin relies on Truman's 1955 recollection that he first asked Hopkins in very general terms to undertake a mission at some point either in mid-April (on the train to and from Roosevelt's funeral) or, more specifically, on May 4—and the *early* dates form part of his argument that Truman had determined upon the Hopkins mission *before* the discussions about the atomic bomb got serious.[36] However, both of the early dates are contradicted by contemporary evidence: We have just reviewed the diary evidence; and this is bolstered by the fact that Harriman suggested the Hopkins mission—and he could not have done so until his return from San Francisco on May 10. Recent research also indicates that Truman's Memoirs cannot be right about the mid-April date, for Hopkins was too sick to attend Roosevelt's funeral.*

---

* Truman's 1955 Memoirs are very confused on dates: For instance, he says he asked Davies to go see Churchill on April 30, but we now know that he did so on May 21. As indicated, he also says he

The request to Hopkins, as indicated, almost certainly occurred between May 13 and May 19. In any event, excepting mid-April, *all* of the *possible* dates are after Stimson's April 25 talk with Truman about the atomic bomb; and *all* coincide very closely with the time during which Truman was considering the relationship of the atomic bomb to his forthcoming meeting with Stalin: Even the first date for the specific proposal of the mission given in Truman's 1955 Memoirs (May 4) is in the period leading up to the May 9 cable; the only time when Harriman could have recommended Hopkins is after May 10 (May 10 is also the time when Stimson filled Harriman in on bomb-related issues); the main Stimson diary entries on strategy are May 14, 15, and 16; the date when Truman gave Hopkins his final briefing (May 19) is just after the May 16 Truman-Stimson meeting where there is no dispute that Truman has *already* decided to delay the heads-of-government meeting because of the bomb; and the first cable asking Stalin to see Hopkins was sent on May 19.

Even more difficult to explain for those who say there is no connection between the missions and Truman's decision to postpone his meeting until the atomic test is the fact that whatever the date at which the idea of the missions *first* occurred, *neither Hopkins nor Davies left for their respective destinations until just before the last week of May*—and by this time there is no disagreement that top U.S. policy makers had oriented their strategy to the forthcoming atomic test.[38] (When on May 28 Truman postponed the Potsdam meeting a second time to July 15 because of technical delays with the atomic test, moreover, it was while Hopkins was in Moscow, and the arrangments were made by Hopkins.)

Finally, the view that the Hopkins and Davies missions had nothing to do with the atomic bomb is very powerfully called into question by

asked Hopkins to go on May *4*, but it seems likely that this should read *May 14*—the day after Davies refused the request. This would accord with other evidence we have that Harriman and Bohlen raised the issue with Hopkins and only *thereafter* with Truman after May 10—and it would accord with Truman's contemporary diary entry, which confirms that Harriman suggested Hopkins. Further evidence from Harriman indicates that Truman refused Harriman's first suggestion of Hopkins, and then agreed several days later. This, too, would suggest a date three or four days after May 10—

i.e., around May 14, the day after Davies said he could not undertake the mission.

It also appears from Truman's Memoirs that if the President did in fact ask Hopkins to undertake a mission sometime in April, he did so *only in a very general sense.* Truman reports, moreover, that when he asked Hopkins in these terms, he refused, saying he was too sick. Harriman's report that Truman did not feel comfortable with the idea of sending Hopkins (and at first rejected it), however, casts additional doubt on the accuracy of this report.[37]

additional information made available since *Atomic Diplomacy* was first published. Although, again, we do not as yet have the full story, we now know there was an *express* linkage in the minds of the key actors at the time. As we have seen, the new evidence confirms that during his May 21, 1945, meeting with Davies, Truman quite clearly told the former Ambassador the reason why he had postponed the Potsdam meeting until July. To recall, in one version of his diary Davies puts an asterisk in his text after Truman's comment that this had to do with the "budget," noting: "The atomic bomb. He told me then of the atomic bomb experiment in Nevada (*sic*). Charged me with utmost secrecy." In another draft, he says in the text:

> To my surprise, he said he did not want it [the heads-of-government meeting] until July. The reason which I could assign was that he had his budget on his hands, and had to get that out. "But," he said, "I have another reason (*) which I have not told anybody."
> He told me of the atomic bomb. The final test had been set for June, but now had been postponed until July. I was startled, shocked and amazed.

Davies adds in the footnote referred to by the asterisk: "Uranium—for reason of security, I will have to fill this in later." Truman also took Davies into his confidence concerning Byrnes's role developing overall strategy in connection with the new weapon at this time.[39]

As to Hopkins, when Harriman and Bohlen met with him in mid-May to discuss the mission to see Stalin, we now also know that part of the conversation, on Hopkins' initiative, included the "big bomb" (which was clearly understood to be the new atomic weapon).[40] Since there is confusion about precisely when Truman first spoke to Hopkins, we do not know whether this discussion occurred after the President and Hopkins had their first meeting. The fact that Truman shared his strategy with Davies at this time suggests the strong probability that he also shared it with Hopkins either on May 4 or thereafter or subsequently on May 19. If so, Hopkins is probably reflecting those conversations. By this time, too, to recall, Harriman (on May 10) had also been taken into Stimson's confidence about nuclear matters as they related to Russia.

Exactly what was said in the Harriman-Bohlen-Hopkins conversation we do not know; nor do we know what else men like Hopkins and Davies, "charged . . . with utmost secrecy," were told by the President. *What we do know is that the conversations involving the Hopkins and Davies missions and strategy toward the forthcoming meeting with Stalin both included discussion of the role of the atomic bomb as well*—presumptive evidence (in the absence of proof to the contrary) that the idea the missions were in no way related to such considerations is in error.

In Appendix II I reviewed additional reasons why the Hopkins and Davies missions cannot be understood in isolation. Both for reasons stated there and in light of the above facts, it is clear that any interpretation of these events which ignores the atomic bomb seriously misconstrues the actual history of this period. Moreover, the most commonly held position—that the missions on the most important issue in dispute *were completely divorced from* the secret decision to delay negotiations until the atomic bomb was tested— appears to be a naive misreading of the men in positions of responsibility at the time and contrary to the clear thrust of the evidence presently available.[41]

OTHER POINTS

SHERWIN RAISES ONE other significant issue. This concerns how *Atomic Diplomacy* interprets Stimson's general approach. He says that what emerges from a careful reading of the various materials relating to the April 25 meeting is "a case for overall caution in American diplomatic relations with the Soviet Union—it was an argument against *any* showdown."[42] But again, first, as we have seen, the important issue is not what Stimson's advice was in precise terms on April 25. Second, there is no doubt whatsoever, as Sherwin himself acknowledges repeatedly, that during this general period Stimson clearly saw the atomic bomb as the "master card" of diplomacy, that he saw the bomb as playing a major role in connection with issues in both Europe and the Far East, that he advised Truman of this, and that Truman delayed Potsdam for such reasons. Perhaps Sherwin's difficulty is with the word "showdown" (which I took from both Churchill's and Forrestal's usage at the time); but it is hard to see how this differs from Stimson's judgment that "it may be necessary to have it out with Russia" or his further comment that this might have to be done in a "pretty rough and ready fashion. . . ."

It is true that Stimson urged a more cautious approach than many advisers and that he wanted "cooperation with the Soviets" (as he and others defined the requirements of cooperation). But to be clear about the matter, the description *Atomic Diplomacy* gave of Stimson's position is in accord both with his diaries and with the view Sherwin takes of him:

> Stimson's view that the atomic bomb would be "decisive" in diplomacy did not depend upon its use as a threat. . . . As early as December 1944, the Secretary searched for diplomatic *"quid pro quos"* which might be asked of Russia in exchange for information on nuclear energy and participation in a system of international control. . . . Discussing the problem with Truman at the April 25 interview, he declared: "The question of sharing [the atomic bomb] . . . and . . . upon what terms, becomes a primary question of our foreign relations."[43]

None of this negates the facts we have reviewed concerning Stimson's broad line of advice about delay and about possibly having to have it out with Russia. Nor, for that matter, do we know precisely what went on at the April 25 meeting itself. Though Stimson's formal memorandum suggests his primary concern was very broadly and generally stated, the meeting took place at the very height of the Polish dispute, *and was stimulated by it:* Immediately after Truman's tough confrontation with Molotov, Stimson asked for the meeting to discuss the bomb because it "has such a bearing on our present foreign relations and has such an important effect upon all my thinking in this field that I think you ought to know about it without much further delay." We know that the conversation did not center only on technical questions, but, rather, specifically on foreign affairs. Groves's memorandum summarizing the conversation contains a cryptic, enigmatic, and—in light of the context—highly suggestive sentence on the subject, namely: "A great deal of emphasis was placed on foreign relations and particularly on the Russian situation."[44] And Truman reports that at this meeting Stimson told him "the atomic bomb would be certain to have a decisive influence on our relations with other countries."[45]

One further point must be considered in connection with all of the above matters. Let us return once again to the May 16 diary entry concerning postponement of the meeting with Stalin until the atomic test—the one in which Stimson records his reply to Truman that "I believe that good and not harm would be done by the policy towards your coming meeting *which you mentioned to me.* We shall probably hold more cards in our hands later than now."* Sherwin is right to point out that there is no explicit record in the Stimson diary up to this point of a discussion with the President on the role of the bomb in diplomacy and of the idea of delaying the meeting. Let us ponder, once more, therefore, how it can be that Stimson talks about a policy which *Truman tells him about,* and not *vice versa.* It may be that this is simply confirming Stimson's earlier advice (not recorded in the diary) at the April 25 meeting or at other times (but, as we have seen, if it is, then it indicates that, contrary to Sherwin, there must have been discussions prior to May 16). It may also be that Truman is reporting to Stimson a policy decision which is his own idea (though in light of everything else we know, this seems unlikely). *Or it may be that when Truman tells Stimson about his policy, he is reflecting the fact that he has been conferring with someone else.* If so, the only other likely candidate is Byrnes, who briefed Truman on the Yalta understandings and was his personal representative on the Interim Committee.

There is almost no discussion of this possibility in the literature; nor, again, is it possible to prove at this point. But, as we have seen in the Introduction to this edition, we know that Byrnes had many private, unrecorded meetings with Truman during this period, and we know further that he kept his activities secret even from the close advisers with whom he usually shared information. When Stimson met with Truman on June 6 to report on the Interim Committee recommendations, Truman "said that Byrnes had reported to him already about it and that Byrnes seemed to be highly pleased with what had been done." (This is also the meeting at which Truman—four sentences later in Stimson's diary record—tells him that "he had postponed [the Potsdam meeting] to give us more time."[46]) Finally, we know Byrnes's general views about the relationship of nuclear matters to policy toward the Soviet Union—including the fact that it was Byrnes, not Stimson, who first advised Truman about the bomb almost immediately after the President took office.

---

* Emphasis added.

Byrnes was about to take on the mantle of Secretary of State, and it is not credible that he would not have been consulted on the most important issue in dispute prior to the forthcoming meeting with Stalin. We know that Truman directed that Davies report to Byrnes (even though he was not yet officially Secretary of State), and that he directed that atomic scientists like Szilard be sent to Byrnes as well (and not to Stimson, who was officially head of the Interim Committee). Truman also tells us that when he made the decision to send Hopkins, among those he consulted was Byrnes.[47]

Byrnes was by far the most complicated, "conniving" and devious of the President's top advisers, and, as I have suggested in the Introduction, it is highly likely that future research will show him to have been intimately involved in the major decision of this period—the decision to delay a meeting until the bomb had been tested. It is probable that his advice and Stimson's, though different in emphasis, converged on the recommendation of delay. However the idea of sending Hopkins and Davies on their missions first occurred, the decision to go forward with the plan would also accord with what we know of Byrnes's shrewd and calculating political approach. Indeed, the real question is whether it is possible to believe that the man charged with developing the President's strategy both on the atomic bomb and for the forthcoming meeting with Stalin was *not* involved in the decision to postpone that meeting—and in decisions concerning all important matters related to it during the summer.*

PROBLEMS OF INTERPRETATION

IT IS WORTH pausing briefly to note an obvious point: Most writers who have argued that the source of Truman's strange stops and starts in policy during 1945 was not advice concerning the atomic bomb but the President's vacillation because he was unsure of himself *have simply asserted this to be the case.* The proof for this

---

* In the Introduction to the 1985 Edition we have reviewed Byrnes's generally complex political-diplomatic strategy during the summer—what Robert Messer has termed an "elaborate international masquerade." If Byrnes was in fact involved in the Hopkins-Davies missions, it would accord well with this overall approach. Indeed, the missions are almost a perfect specific illustration of the general dual posture Byrnes had adopted on matters related to the Soviet Union at this time: A public and private display of apparent conciliation—combined with the secret preparation of a tough strategy based on the new weapon.

interpretation—an explanation so elastic it can be stretched to cover virtually any decision—has often simply been the casual, undocumented statement that this is or *must* have been what happened!

As I indicated at the outset, I have selected Sherwin's work because his comments are more careful and detailed than many others, because they center on the most important secondary issues in dispute, and because they have apparently been followed uncritically by several writers. It is abundantly clear, I believe, that any interpretation of the earliest period of the Truman Administration which ignores, or plays down, the role of the atomic bomb in the formulation of policy does not provide us with a full understanding of U.S. strategy and decision making during this time.

This is not to say that all questions of emphasis can be settled at this point; we are trying to understand what went on in connection with matters about which we simply do not as yet have the full story. Sherwin's account is far better than most in that it recognizes that the bomb did play some role in strategy at this point. It suffers, I believe, from its excessively narrow approach to documentation and from its unwillingness to confront the logical force of the totality of the evidence.

Beyond this, like so many studies which focus primarily on one aspect of policy—in this case, nuclear policy—Sherwin's work does not provide sufficient detail on policy decisions in other areas which occurred at precisely the same time and were not isolated from the context of the larger strategy by the people making decisions. There is, for instance, only the sketchiest treatment of questions policy makers thought absolutely vital—including decisions to reverse Roosevelt's policy on Bulgaria, Rumania, and Hungary and postwar plans for Germany.*

Atomic Diplomacy traced decision making from April to September in connection with diplomacy toward each of these nations (and Poland and Manchuria) to show that there was a clear and repeated

---

* For a review of the specific decisions reversing policy—and for an analysis of how policy makers thought this would allow them to achieve "cooperation with the Russians" *as they defined cooperation,* see above, pp. 71, 76, 76*fn,* 193–74, 178, 185, 205–24, 231–35, 278, and the detailed discussions referred to in these pages on Poland, the Balkans, Manchuria, German reparations, etc. See also Messer, *The End of an Alliance,* and Herken, *The Winning Weapon,* for information on the effect of the bomb on reversing U.S. policy toward the Balkans both at Potsdam and thereafter at London.

pattern which, step by step, could only be understood if one recognized that top American leaders were responding to different estimates *of their actual power to affect events.* In the first instance, they believed the only leverage they had was provided by the large (but fading) number of U.S. troops in Europe and the possibility of a loan to the Soviet Union. Their decision for an early showdown rested firmly on the assumption that it was better to have it out with the Russians sooner rather than later. The stop-start reversals of timing—and the resumption of the tough line immediately after Hiroshima—accords precisely with the shifts *in their understanding of their actual power,* and I believe can only be explained by it and the evidence we have of the impact of the bomb, not only on Stimson and Truman, but especially on Byrnes.

Quite apart from other issues related to the atomic bomb, very few historians have yet to confront the reality and import of the changing power estimates.

Instead, Sherwin and others rest much of their interpretation on *their assessment of Truman's personal psychological state.* Sherwin, in fact, even attributes the first showdown with Molotov to the fact that Truman was "emotionally unprepared and generally uninformed. . . ." We are told that the main reason Truman relied on his tough-minded advisers at the outset of his Administration was "to compensate for his lack of experience, his inadequate knowledge, and his profound concern over his ability to do the job. . . ." Further, "Truman felt compelled constantly to prove himself to those around him. . . ." "Inexperienced and insecure in the world of diplomacy," Truman did not relish facing Stalin, "a tough negotiator of considerable experience, the director, in Harriman's words, of a 'barbarian invasion of Europe' . . ." etc.[48]

It is probably true that Truman felt uncertain on many matters early in his Administration. However, the amount of attention and weight given *these* factors—as compared with the shifts in power and the actual pattern of decisions on the many specific diplomatic issues in question—is extraordinary. A major flaw in excessively psychological accounts of Truman at this time is that they seem to prefer to paint the President as a bumbler—ignoring the evidence we have that others found him very clear and firm in actual decision making. (Compare, for instance, this private report in mid-May 1945 to

Churchill from so astute an observer as Anthony Eden: "In general, I was struck by the President's air of quiet confidence in himself. He said at one point in our talk, 'I am here to make decisions, and whether they prove right or wrong, I am going to take them!' "[49])

Such accounts also tend to define the President and his top aides almost entirely in reactive terms, buffeted about by various conflicting pressures. In so doing they tend to devalue the simple fact that Truman, Secretary Stimson, and James Byrnes were also people who weighed matters of policy and politics—and thought seriously about their objectives and whether they had sufficient power to achieve them in light of the risks they entailed.

By comparison with Sherwin's writing, many accounts of this period are very poor indeed. (One historian has described the fairly widely known work of Lisle Rose, for instance, as "badly flawed by its firm conviction of the innocence and naivete of policy-makers and by its loosely-wrought pattern of analysis."[50]) Given the difficult problems of evidence, and the often highly emotional tone of reports on these controversial issues, some of the far less serious work in this area must be approached with considerable caution.*

Once the fundamental issue is understood—namely, that whatever the resolution of secondary points, Truman's early 1945 strategy toward the Soviet Union flowed in significant part from a belief that the atomic bomb, once tested, would strengthen the U.S. diplomatic position—a number of decisions during the summer become easier to understand. This is not the place to reproduce the detailed analysis presented in the body of the text on Truman's strategy in connection with Manchuria, the Balkans, German and Austrian issues, and so on. In some cases (e.g., the Manchurian issues), information currently available allows us to document how and when factors related to the new weapon affected policy with considerable precision, and how and when the strategy of delay was implemented. In other cases (e.g., the Balkans in May, as opposed, say,

---

* For a partial review of some of the literature, see Kimball, "The Cold War Warmed Over," and Bernstein, "The Atomic Bomb and American Foreign Policy." In the notes to the Introduction to the 1985 Edition and to this Appendix, I have attempted to deal with the main remaining points in the literature, and I have referred the reader to other work done by me and others which deals with a few additional points. In a number of cases, authors have presented alternative, if less precise, formulations of arguments similar to Sherwin's.

to July or, say, September[51]), the currently available information is more limited and we must use what we know about the general strategic approach, together with the available information on the specific cases, to build as much of an understanding as we can.

There is, however, a broader point involved in all of this: Reflecting back on the enormous amount written about the atomic bomb since 1945, I am struck by the recurrence of a kind of false pride, even arrogance in some of the accounts. Throughout the forty years—and especially at the height of the Cold War during the 1950s—those who questioned major aspects of the Hiroshima decision were regularly challenged for not having adequate "proof" of their interpretation of what happened. At the same time, defenders of the established view often presented as truth certain *apparent'* facts, and rarely questioned the official theory with the same degree of rigor.

Some of the key actors in the Hiroshima story were very prudent men who seem to have been unwilling to embarrass their superiors. Others were very secretive politicians who regularly resorted to subterfuge and dishonesty when it was in their interest. As early as 1948 (when some of the first important critical work appeared[52]), our lack of information should have been an invitation to more intense research and a warning that an open mind was the best approach to official interpretations. Instead, it was regularly used as if it were proof of an alternative theory, usually a theory less likely to cause official anger. There has also been an occasional tendency for ambitious scholars to offer petty criticism of others, especially those presenting nonconformist ideas, as a way to make their careers or prove their academic credentials.

Over the last forty years an excess of apparent but misplaced professionalism has thus regularly left the public at the mercy of those who controlled access to important information. Young historians who wish to write the story of what happened during this period could learn from investigative reporters, and from the kind of argumentation one finds in good legal presentations at well-prepared trials when all the facts are not available. In both instances the goal is to use what evidence *is* available to search out the truth . . . including the often very important fact that there are major and systematic holes in the known evidence.

Excerpts from a 1946 U.S. Intelligence Report

EXCERPTS FROM A TOP SECRET April 30, 1946 memorandum titled, "Use of the Atomic Bomb on Japan," prepared for the Chief of the Strategic Policy Section, Strategy and Policy Group, Operations Division (OPD) of the Army by the Intelligence Staff of the War Department of the Army.

Growth of Surrender Psychology. The Emperor had decided as early as 20 June 1945 to terminate the war. At a meeting on that date attended by the principal members of the Suzuki Cabinet, the Emperor is reported to have stated, "I think it necessary for us to have a plan to close the war at once, as well as one to defend the home islands." The latter part of this statement referred to the army plans for the defense of Japan. As a result of this statement by the Emperor, Premier Suzuki decided to stop the war. Unfortunately, Russia was chosen as the medium for arranging the peace, and Russia, for reasons of her own as well as acceding to Allied pressure, wanted to be an active participant against Japan in the final stages of the war. From 11 July, attempts to negotiate a peace were carried on through messages to Sato, the Japanese Ambassador to Russia. On 12 July, Prince Konoye was named as envoy and Sato informed the Russian Government that Konoye wanted to come to Moscow for the purpose of improving Russian-Japanese relations and to ask the USSR to use its good offices to end the war. Molotov and Stalin left for Potsdam without answering this request of the Japanese Government and on 26 July the Potsdam Declaration was issued. With this declaration the Japanese leaders Konoye, Kido, Suzuki, Yonai and others who had been the motivating agents in attempting to bring about the conciliaition [sic], knew the terms upon which Japan must surrender. The military leaders felt that the terms of the proclamation were too dishonorable and continued to procrastinate. While the Japanese were awaiting an answer from Russia, there occurred the disastrous event which the Japanese leaders regarded as utter catastrophe and which they had energetically sought to prevent at any cost – Russia declared war upon Japan and began moving her forces into Manchuria. Events had moved too swiftly for the Japanese, and Premier Suzuki, at about 0700, 9 August, presented the Emperor with two alternatives: to declare war on the Russians and continue the war, or to accept the Potsdam Declaration. The latter course was decided upon and the machinery was put into operation to implement this decision.

Investigation shows that there was little mention of the use of the atomic bomb by the United States in the discussions leading up to the 9 August decision. The dropping of the bomb was the pretext seized upon by all leaders as the reason for ending the war, but made it almost a certainty that the Japanese would have capitulated upon the entry of Russia into the war. The Emperor and the advisors immediately surrounding the throne had come to a decision to end the war as early as 20 June 1945 and by 9 August, the date of Russia's entry into the war, were actively attempting to carry out this decision. The above-mentioned group, the Cabinet, and presumably the majority of the people, knew how impossible it was to continue the war without all of Japan being destroyed and her people exterminated. The Japanese leaders had decided to surrender and were merely looking for sufficient pretext to convince the die-hard Army Group that Japan had lost the war and must capitulate to the Allies. The entry of Russia into the war would almost certainly have furnished this pretext, and would have been sufficient to convince all responsible leaders that surrender was unavoidable. …

The war would almost certainly have terminated when Russia entered the war against Japan.

Stimson's Unsuccessful Attempt to Change the Strategy of Delay Before Leaving Office*

September 11, 1945

DEAR MR. PRESIDENT:

In handing you today my memorandum about our relations with Russia in respect to the atomic bomb, I am not unmindful of the fact that when in Potsdam I talked with you about the question whether we could be safe in sharing the atomic bomb with Russia while she was still a police state and before she put into effect provisions assuring personal rights of liberty to the individual citizen.

I still recognize the difficulty and am still convinced of the ultimate importance of a change in Russian attitude toward individual liberty but I have come to the conclusion that it would not be possible to use our possession of the atomic bomb as a direct lever to produce the change. I have become convinced that any demand by us for an internal change in Russia as a condition of sharing in the atomic weapon would be so resented that it would make the objective we have in view less probable.

I believe that the change in attitude towards the individual in Russia will come slowly and gradually and I am satisfied that we should not delay our approach to Russia in the matter of the atomic bomb until that process has been completed. My reasons are set forth in the memorandum I am handing you today. Furthermore, I believe that this long process of change in Russia is more likely to be expedited by the closer relationship in the matter of the atomic bomb

---

* Taken from Stimson and Bundy, *On Active Service*, pp. 642–46. The emphasis was added by Stimson in 1947. He considered the first italicized passage the heart of the memorandum, and the second the most important point of all. (*Ibid.*, pp. 644–45.)

which I suggest and the trust and confidence that I believe would be inspired by the method of approach which I have outlined.

Faithfully yours,
HENRY L. STIMSON,
Secretary of War

THE PRESIDENT
The White House

MEMORANDUM FOR THE PRESIDENT

11 September 1945

Subject: Proposed Action for Control of Atomic Bombs.

The advent of the atomic bomb has stimulated great military and probably even greater political interest throughout the civilized world. In a world atmosphere already extremely sensitive to power, the introduction of this weapon has profoundly affected political considerations in all sections of the globe.

In many quarters it has been interpreted as a substantial offset to the growth of Russian influence on the continent. We can be certain that the Soviet Government has sensed this tendency and the temptation will be strong for the Soviet political and military leaders to acquire this weapon in the shortest possible time. Britain in effect already has the status of a partner with us in the development of this weapon. Accordingly, unless the Soviets are voluntarily invited into the partnership upon a basis of co-operation and trust, we are going to maintain the Anglo-Saxon bloc over against the Soviet in the possession of this weapon. Such a condition will almost certainly stimulate feverish activity on the part of the Soviet towards the development of this bomb in what will in effect be a secret armament race of a rather desperate character. There is evidence to indicate that such activity may have already commenced.

If we feel, as I assume we must, that civilization demands that someday we shall arrive at a satisfactory international arrangement respecting the control of this new force, the question then is how long we can afford to enjoy our momentary superiority in the hope of achieving our immediate peace council objectives.

Whether Russia gets control of the necessary secrets of production in a minimum of say four years or a maximum of twenty years is not nearly as important to the world and civilization as to make sure that when they do get it they are willing and co-operative partners among the peace-loving nations of the world. It is true if we approach them now, as I would propose, we may be gambling on their good faith and risk their getting into production of bombs a little sooner than they would otherwise.

To put the matter concisely, I consider the problem of our satisfactory relations with Russia as not merely connected with but as virtually dominated by the problem of the atomic bomb. Except for the problem of the control of that bomb, those relations, while vitally important, might not be immediately pressing. The establishment of relations of mutual confidence between her and us could afford to await the slow progress of time. But with the discovery of the bomb, they became immediately emergent. *Those relations may be perhaps irretrievably embittered by the way in which we approach the solution of the bomb with Russia. For if we fail to approach them now and merely continue to negotiate with them, having this weapon rather ostentatiously on our hip, their suspicions and their distrust of our purposes and motives will increase.* It will inspire them to greater efforts in an all-out effort to solve the problem. If the solution is achieved in that spirit, it is much less likely that we will ever get the kind of covenant we may desperately need in the future. This risk is, I believe, greater than the other, inasmuch as our objective must be to get the best kind of international bargain we can—one that has some chance of being kept and saving civilization not for five or for twenty years, but forever.

The chief lesson I have learned in a long life is that the only way you can make a man trustworthy is to trust him; and the surest way to make him untrustworthy is to distrust him and show your distrust.

If the atomic bomb were merely another though more devastating military weapon to be assimilated into our pattern of international relations, it would be one thing. We could then follow the old custom of secrecy and nationalistic military superiority relying on international caution to prescribe the future use of the weapon as we did with gas. But I think the bomb instead constitutes merely a first step in a new control by man over the forces of nature too revolutionary and dangerous to fit into the old concepts. I think it really caps the climax of the race between man's growing technical power for destructiveness and his psychological power of self-control and group control—his moral power. If so, our method of approach to the Russians is a question of the most vital importance in the evolution of human progress.

Since the crux of the problem is Russia, any contemplated action leading to the control of this weapon should be primarily directed *to* Russia. It is my judgment that the Soviet would be more apt to respond sincerely to a direct and forthright approach made by the United States on this subject than would be the case if the approach were made as a part of a general international scheme, or if the approach were made after a succession of express or implied threats or near threats in our peace negotiations.

My idea of an approach to the Soviets would be a direct proposal after discussion with the British that we would be prepared in effect to enter an arrangement with the Russians, the general purpose of which would be to control and limit the use of the atomic bomb as an instrument of war and so far as possible to direct and encourage the development of atomic power for peaceful and humanitarian purposes. Such an approach might more specifically lead to the proposal that we would stop work on the further improvement in, or manufacture of, the bomb as a military weapon, provided the Russians and the British would agree to do likewise. It might also provide that we would be willing to impound what bombs we now have in the United States provided the Russians and the British would agree with us that in no event will they or we use a bomb as an instrument of war unless all three Governments agree to that use. We might also consider including in the arrangement a covenant with the U.K. and the Soviets providing for the exchange of benefits of future developments whereby atomic energy may be applied on a mutually satisfactory basis for commercial or humanitarian purposes.

I would make such an approach just as soon as our immediate political considerations make it appropriate.

I emphasize perhaps beyond all other considerations the importance of taking this action with Russia as a proposal of the United States— backed by Great Britain but peculiarly the proposal of the United States. Action of any international group of nations, including many small nations who have not demonstrated their potential power or responsibility in this war would not, in my opinion, be taken seriously by the Soviets. The loose debates which would surround such proposal, if put before a conference of nations, would provoke but scant favor from the Soviet. As I say, I think this is the most important point in the program.

After the nations which have won this war have agreed to it, there will be ample time to introduce France and China into the covenants and finally to incorporate the agreement into the scheme of the United Nations. The use of this bomb has been accepted by the world as the result of the initiative and productive capacity of the United States, and I think this factor is a most potent lever towards having our proposals accepted by the Soviets, whereas I am most skeptical of obtaining any tangible results by way of any international debate. I urge this method as the most realistic means of accomplishing this vitally important step in the history of the world.

HENRY L. STIMSON,
Secretary of War

"Atomic Warfare and the Christian Faith": A Report from the Federal Council of Churches, 1946*

THE ATOMIC BOMB GIVES new and fearful meaning to the age-old plight of man. His proudest powers have always been his most dangerous sources of peril, and his earthly life has been lived always under the threat of eventual extinction. Christians of earlier times have felt these truths more keenly than modern men, whose growing control over physical forces has led many of them to believe that science and technology would in time assure human safety and well-being. This hope has been dashed. Our latest epochal triumph of science and technology may prove to be our last. The scientists who know most about the nature of atomic energy have been the first to declare themselves frightened men. With admirable restraint, but with impressive urgency, they have sought to awaken both military leaders and civilians to the alarming realities which as scientists they see more clearly than laymen who lack their special knowledge. The new weapon has destroyed at one blow the familiar conceptions of national security, changed the scale of destructive conflict among peoples, and opened before us all the prospect of swift ruin for civilization and even the possibility of a speedy end to man's life on earth.

There is little doubt that as knowledge of the new weapon becomes more widespread, and the earlier talk of some technical defense against it is clearly seen to be unrealistic clutching at straws, fear of these possibilities will be shared by more and more citizens and statesmen. Whether universal fear, one of the most powerful of all human motives, will help to save us or to

* Permission from the Federal Council of Churches   is gratefully acknowledged.
to reprint "Atomic Warfare and the Christian Faith"

push us the more quickly to destruction depends on how it is directed. The fear of God and His laws can indeed be a source of saving wisdom, but the fear of fellowmen or life or death or any created thing can be disastrous. In particular, blind panic is premature surrender to the evil that is feared. It may result either in mental and moral paralysis, or in acts of suicidal desperation. Death is the outcome, in either case.

By contrast, a more clear-sighted fear not of dangerous forces but of unrighteous use of them or capitulation to them, and of the consequences of such violation of God's will, can lead toward a sustaining faith which misdirected panic is sure to lose. In the face of atomic bombs and radio-active gases, no less truly than in the presence of smaller perils, the rule is: Seek first the Kingdom of God, and His righteousness, as the only sure ground of ultimate security. In a continuously perilous world, as on the battlefield, brave men who refuse to make personal safety their primary goal have a safety that cowards never know. A major task of the Church in the anxious months ahead will be to demonstrate a courageous fear of God and faith in His invincible goodness, in place of either complacency or panic before the awful energies now accessible for human use. Men have found new strength and wisdom to face repeated crises in the past. It seems right to reject despair and earnestly seek such needed strength once more.

It is a fundamental Christian conviction that amid all the perils of earthly life, the Lordship of God will prevail and His purpose of judgment and mercy will not be frustrated. Moreover, it has always been in moments of supreme despair, when men have turned to God in an agony of trust, that spiritual redemptive power has been released which has changed the shadow of night into a morning of new hope. Today also the prospects of man's life on earth are intimately bound up with the measure in which, through the gospel of Jesus Christ, the worldwide expansion and integrity of the Christian Church, and the diverse workings of the Holy Spirit, the lives of men become centered in God. The reality of God-centered thought and action, which it is the supreme task of the Church to cherish, is the one hope of securing a world order in which man's release of atomic energy would be employed for human welfare and not for world suicide. To develop such world order is a task of fearful urgency for both Church and State, for Christians and non-Christians alike – a task in which we must engage with mind, heart and strength as servants of God.

To that end, there is need first to face squarely the changes that the great discovery has made in our situation. The release of atomic energy brings new resources and a new kind of threat to civilized living. A new pattern of warfare has suddenly taken shape that may invalidate many traditional judgments about war. Certain theological problems have been set, almost overnight, in a new perspective. These changes must be examined briefly.

ATOMIC ENERGY AND TOTAL WAR

IT IS TOO early to weigh the possible benefits that may come to mankind from suitably controlled atomic energy; and a detailed appraisal would, in any event, be largely a task for physical scientists and engineers. Perhaps it is within proper bounds to notice that the chief benefits now regarded as immediately accessible are the opening of new avenues for research in the physical and biological sciences, and the provision of new tools for medical practice. Beyond these immediate benefits, it seems conceivable that constructive use of atomic energy could bring a more equitable distribution around the globe of labor-saving power, and the consequent freeing of additional millions of people from drudgery, with the chance for spiritual growth that is now denied to multitudes of human burden-bearers. This result would be the more likely (at the price of greatly increased peril) if ways should be found to release atomic energy from elements more plentiful and widespread than uranium. At all events, for the present it seems to be agreed that although power plants designed to utilize the heat liberated by atomic fission are not far away, the industrial benefits to be expected in the near future are pale beside the deadly threat to our tenure of life on earth.

The present fact is that neither the possible range of benefit from atomic energy nor the possible range of destruction to which we are henceforth exposed is accurately calculable. Even the physicists, chemists, and engineers who have developed the atomic bomb do not know how far the effects of a massive attack with such bombs, or with radioactive gases, might go toward making the earth uninhabitable. Some hold it theoretically possible, though highly improbable, that the entire atmosphere might be destroyed by atomic chain reactions. Somewhat greater, it would seem, is the chance that the atmosphere might be vitiated by radioactive gases, so that neither plants nor animals could live. Short of such total obliteration, we are quite certain at least that the industrial basis of civilized life is now largely at the mercy of weapons already in existence. Moreover, this threat is apparently permanent, beyond the reach of any technological defense now conceivable. As far as our best minds can see, the only promising defenses against atomic warfare are moral and political, not physical defenses. This momentous fact is fundamental in our present situation. The basis of any hope for the redemption of mankind simply through progress in the sciences and technology, always an unsound hope, has been permanently wrecked by the latest achievement in that very progress.

This judgment is underscored by the changes in the pattern of warfare as it can now be envisioned. The march toward total war, which this commission and other theologians have judged irreconcilable with Christian principles,* has been advanced a giant step further. For the new weapons are especially well suited to indiscriminate destruction. In purely tactical bombing of such targets as fighting ships, beach-heads, or fortifications, isolated from civilian areas, destruction might indeed be restricted to combatant units and equipment. But in the strategic bombing that has already become so large a factor in modern war, atomic weapons clearly belong with the tools for obliteration, not precision attack. A blast that incinerates four square miles of buildings at a time cannot be used to destroy a munitions plant or a railway yard and spare the city around it. Moreover, there is strong reason to expect that if another major war is fought, strategic bombing of key cities will have a still larger place from the very outset, and that rockets with atomic warheads, not piloted planes, will be the chief weapons for such attack. Since rockets and robots have even less precision than piloted bombers, whole cities and not simply factories or freight yards must be the targets, and all pretense of discrimination between military objectives and civilian homes would disappear. Even more all-inclusive would be attack with radioactive poison gases that were already known in 1940 as by-products of the work with uranium.† The logical end would be total war in grim truth.

The Premium Upon Aggression

FURTHER, THE NEW weapons alter in two morally fateful ways the balance between aggressive and defensive war. If two nations are armed with atomic weapons, both the incentive to strike a crippling blow first and

---

* See *The Relation of the Church to the War in the Light of the Christian Faith*, Nov. 1944, pp. 67–69. Cf. John C. Ford, S.J., "The Morality of Obliteration Bombing," *Theological Studies*, V, 261–309.

† H.D. Smyth *Atomic Energy for Military Purposes* (1945), 2.32, 4.26–4.28, 4.48. Cf. *Science News Letter*, 48:121 (Aug. 25, 1945).

the possibility of doing so are incalculably increased. The first phase of a future *Blitzkrieg* would require not days but minutes, and the destruction possible in the first blow is of a different order of magnitude from anything previously known. A premium is therefore placed on swift, ruthless aggression by any power that may believe itself in danger. Moreover, wholly new advantages can now be won through successful treachery. The planting of bombs by trained saboteurs in the key cities of a non-belligerent country can lay an effective basis for blackmailing or assassinating a neighbor so reduced to helplessness before a shot is fired. Thus, practices most revolting to ordinary human beings may well become accepted tactics of the new warfare, and conscientious statesmen may feel called upon to adopt them to forestall such action by a possible enemy. Finally, the uses of atomic weapons that can now be foreseen would make war not only more destructive and treacherous, but more irresponsible than ever. On the one hand, an aggressor who first employs such weapons in massive volume will be taking action the total result of which, as already noticed, is not now foreseeable, and certainly not controllable within predetermined limits. The immediate effects of single atomic bomb explosions are indeed localized within a few square miles. But the lethal effect of radioactive poisons would be vastly wider,* and total destruction or vitiation of the earth's atmosphere, however unlikely, is believed to be not impossible. Where the destructive effects of a massive concentration of atomic discharges might end is, therefore, in essential respects unpredictable. On the other hand, if a country were attacked with atomic bombs carried by rockets or planted by saboteurs, and attempted prompt retaliation, the reprisals might easily be directed against an offending third party, suspected but not guilty of the attack. In an atmosphere of general suspicion, atomic war would have, more than any previous form of combat, the character- istics of universal madness.

In this new perspective, both moral and theological problems raised by war assume new proportions and a new urgency. Hence, all men and Christians in particular are required to search their hearts and minds, to re-examine their principles and practices, and to seek with the greatest diligence for effective ways to abolish this diabolical horror. We can speak here only of some of the moral and social problems posed for the Church

---

* Professor M.L.E. Oliphant, leader of the British physicists in the joint research program, is repre- sented as declaring that a single gas attack with these poisons would destroy life over an area 1000 miles in radius. See *The Christian Century*, 62:1341 (Dec. 5, 1945).

by atomic warfare: problems arising from the past and possible future uses of the new weapons, the need for international controls, and the distinctive moral and social role of the Church. We shall speak also of what seem necessary restatements of our convictions about man's part in history, God's justice and mercy, and the hope of eternal life.

THE PAST USE OF THE ATOMIC BOMB

WE WOULD BEGIN with an act of contrition. As American Christians, we are deeply penitent for the irresponsible use already made of the atomic bomb. We are agreed that, whatever be one's judgment of the ethics of war in principle, the surprise bombings of Hiroshima and Nagasaki are morally indefensible. They repeated in a ghastly form the indiscriminate slaughter of non-combatants that has become familiar during World War II. They were loosed without specific warning, under conditions which virtually assured the deaths of 100,000 civilians. No word of the existence of atomic bombs was published before the actual blasting of Hiroshima. A prior demonstration on enemy soil (either in vacant territory or on a fortification) would have been quite possible and was actually suggested by a group of the scientists concerned. The proposed use of the atomic bomb was sure to affect gravely the future of mankind. Yet the peoples whose governments controlled the bomb were given no chance to weigh beforehand the moral and political consequences of its use. Nagasaki was bombed also without specific warning, after the power of the bomb had been proved but before the Japanese government and high command had been given reasonable time to reach a decision to surrender. Both bombings, moreover, must be judged to have been unnecessary for winning the war. Japan's strategic position was already hopeless, and it was virtually certain that she had not developed atomic weapons of her own.* Even though use of the new weapon last August may well have shortened the war, the moral cost was too high. As the power that first used the atomic bomb under these circumstances, we have sinned grievously against the laws of God and against the people of Japan. Without seeking to apportion blame among individuals, we are compelled to judge our chosen course inexcusable.

At the same time, we are agreed that these two specific bombing sorties cannot properly be treated in isolation from the whole system of obliter-

---

* Smyth, *op. cit.*, 13.3.

ation attacks with explosives and fire-bombs, of which the atomic raids were the stunning climax. We are mindful of the horrors of incendiary raids on Tokyo, and of the saturation bombings of Hamburg, Dresden, and Berlin. We are mindful also that protests against these earlier obliterative methods were met chiefly by appeals to military necessity, whereas the eventual report of the Air Force's investigators has now admitted the military ineffectiveness of much of this planned destruction. All things considered, it seems necessary to include in any condemnation of indiscriminate, excessive violence not only the use of atomic bombs in August, 1945, but the policy of wholesale obliteration bombing as practiced at first by the Axis powers and then on a far greater scale by the Allies. We recognize the grievous provocation to which the Allied leaders were subjected before they adopted the policy, and the persuasiveness of wartime appeals by military leaders to the superior competence of soldiers to decide military policy. But we have never agreed that a policy affecting the present well-being of millions of non-combatants and the future relationships of whole peoples should be decided finally on military grounds,* and we believe the right to criticise military policies on ethical grounds is freshly justified by the proved fallibility of competent professional soldiers in dealing with such problems in this war. In the light of present knowledge, we are prepared to affirm that the policy of obliteration bombing as actually practiced in World War II, culminating in the use of atomic bombs against Japan, is not defensible on Christian premises.†

---

* _The Relation of the Church to the War_, pp. 67–69.

† Some who concur in the foregoing judgment find their grounds primarily in the circumstances under which particular raids were carried out rather than in the practice of obliteration bombing or in the nature of the weapons employed. They agree that what has been done is wrong, and that it would be wrong for any nation in the future to take the initiative in using such measures for its own advantage; but they believe the way should be left open to regard the use of atomic weapons under some circumstances as right. For they believe that in the present state of human relations, if plans for international control of aggression should fail, the only effective restraint upon would-be aggressors might be fear of reprisals, and that this possible restraint should not be removed in advance. Others hold that even if belligerent action be regarded as, in extreme circumstances, unavoidable and justifiable, obliteration bombing and the atomic bomb as utilized for that purpose cannot be justified. Still others hold that the atomic bomb has revealed the impossibility of a just war, and has shown the necessity for repudiation of all support of war by the Church. They judge that since in fact belligerent powers are virtually certain to use any means that seems needed to insure victory, condemnation of obliterative bombing or of surprise attack with atomic weapons entails condemnation of all war.

POLICIES TO PREVENT ATOMIC WAR

WE ARE AGREED, further, on four major theses respecting future policy with regard to atomic warfare and other new methods for effecting mass destruction. First, these methods, more than the simpler combatant techniques of the past, lend themselves to belligerent practices that are intolerable to Christian conscience. They make it harder than ever before to give real effect to the traditional distinctions between combatants and non-combatants among the enemy, and between proportionate and excessive violence in conduct of the war. They tend to unlimited, indiscriminate destruction. They increase appallingly the problems of the aftermath of war, because indiscriminate destruction wrecks not only the military potential of the enemy but also his civil institutions, on which depend the reestablishment and maintenance of social order. Hence, it is more than ever incumbent upon Christians to resist the development of situations in which these methods are likely to be employed.

Secondly, the only mode of control that holds much promise is control directed to the prevention of war. We recognize the probable futility, in practice, of measures to outlaw atomic weapons while war itself continues. Use of the newer weapons might indeed be temporarily restrained, on the part of some belligerents by concern for humanity, on the part of others by fear of retaliation. But experience indicates that in a struggle for survival one side or the other will resort to whatever weapons promise victory, and its opponent will feel constrained to adopt counter-measures in kind. War itself must go.

Thirdly, in pursuit of this aim, we believe the Churches should call upon the government of the United States, as present holder of existing atomic bombs and plants for producing them, to move more swiftly toward allaying distrust respecting their possible use. Such distrust on the part of former enemies, neutrals, and even allies of this country seems to us understandable under present conditions. At the same time its existence is a barrier to international goodwill, and a possible cause of future conflict. We therefore call upon the Churches to urge, first, that all manufacture of atomic bombs be stopped, pending the development of effective international controls. We urge, secondly, that the Churches call upon the government of the United States to affirm publicly, with suitable guarantees, that it will under no circumstances be the first to use atomic weapons in any possible future war. Such measures are to be thought of not as adequate means of control but as aids to the development of a better state of international confidence, in which effective measures for the prevention of war may the more readily be worked out.

For we believe, fourthly, that the only conceivable road toward effective control of atomic warfare and other forms of mass destruction is the road of international comity and joint effort. Whatever be one's judgment respecting the pattern of future world society, it is clear that the war-making powers of national states must be given up, and the maintenance of justice and peace among nations become an international responsibility. In the present situation, we are agreed that progress toward this end may best follow two lines: the adoption of such political measures as may strengthen and improve the existing United Nations Organization, and unceasing effort to further the growth of spiritual world community.

Cooperation for International Control

AS TO THE former line of action, we are not competent to prescribe a political structure for international dealing with these problems. We are agreed, however, on two major propositions. First, exclusive trust in a political structure of any sort to solve the problems posed by atomic warfare would be a dangerous illusion. In particular, the hope for world government, useful as a guiding principle, cannot be turned into a program for immediate action without very serious confusion of aim. Although improvement of the United Nations Organization is imperative, world government in any literal sense of the term is not yet attainable, and rigid insistence on full world government now is in effect a vote for continued international anarchy. It might even tend to widen, not lessen, the distances among the Great Powers. Moreover, if world government could be imposed now, it would have to be by the overwhelming force wielded by a few powers in concert, and such forced rule would gravely imperil essential human liberty and growth. It is better to start with the imperfect accomplishments and promises of the provisional forms of cooperation that have actually begun to take shape, and earnestly to seek their improvement. For such improvement, the ideal of world government may indeed provide valuable guidance, to the end that as rapidly as possible reliance on force shall give place to reliance on common agreement and a growing body of law.

Secondly, international provision for the control of atomic research and its application to the problems of peace and war should fulfill certain elementary conditions. Ultimate control should be assigned to civilian, not military agencies. The development and use of atomic energies should be steadily held in the perspective of concern for the enhancement of human welfare, and both promotion and restrictions should be directed to that end. A major concern of the supervising agencies must be to assure a wide and equitable distribution of whatever economic benefits may result from the use of atomic energy, and to prevent monopolistic exploitation by cartels or other minority groups. The policies of supervision and control, moreover, should be calculated to safeguard intellectual freedom, both among responsible scientists of all nations and, as far as technical difficulties permit, among the peoples whose welfare is at stake. We can see only harm in a policy of attempted monopoly of either scientific research or political information by either national or international agencies. The only atmosphere in which growing rivalry and suspicion cannot thrive is an atmosphere of free and cooperative enterprise.

These demands for attention to the general welfare suggest the need that political and technical measures be sustained, directed and inspired by the development of spiritual world community. We know how vague and empty this term may seem, to many readers, without detailed elaboration for which there is no room here.* We recognize also that the essential nature and basis of community call for much more profound study. Here we may note four requirements for such a spiritual common life as the welfare of the peoples urgently demands. There must be established, in the midst of hostility and suspicion, a basis for mutual confidence. There must be evoked in every people a deep humility before God and men, a genuine readiness to acknowledge present faults and to learn better ways, a habit of self-criticism and of self-restraint toward others. There must be encouraged and increasingly satisfied a hunger and thirst after truth: the truth about men, their needs, shortcomings, common hopes, the truth about the world in which and with which they must live, the truth about God as the Beginning and the End of all human life. There must be made known, by word and deed, the sure ground of hope that Christians find in the God and Father of our Lord Jesus Christ. Only when the profound kinship of

---

* Cf. *The Relation of the Church to the War*, pp. 14–19, 54–60, 75–79.

common need, quest, achievement, failure, and hope becomes a living groundwork of men's efforts to achieve a world order can such efforts endure the strain of repeated disappointment. The more fully we recognize that other men have the same needs, the same fears, the same weaknesses as we, the better we shall understand our common failures and the more patiently we shall seek to help one another rise above them.

THE DISTINCTIVE ROLE OF THE CHURCH

THE MORAL AND social role of the Church in world affairs clearly is to help this spirit grow. This is not a political task. In essence it is a work of reconciliation among men, carried on in the spirit of Jesus Christ, in dependence on the power of God – a work that no political agency, partisan by its very nature, can perform as well. Precisely because the Church is ecumenical and supra-national in its being, worldwide in its membership and mission, it can speak directly to men and women of any nation in the name of one divine Father and one universal humanity.

Its first word in our present situation must be a call to active penitence, addressed to friends and former enemies alike. There is no useful place among us for sentimental self-accusation. But there is acute need for such humility as not many among victors or vanquished have yet shown: the humility of clear-headed, honest men who see how grievously they have squandered resources inherited from a long, laborious past and jeopardized what should have been a more enlightened future. We shall not rehearse here the sorry record of sin and misery of the years just ended.* But we must note with urgent concern the continuing abuses of power by the victorious great nations and the demonstrations of irresponsibility among both conquerors and conquered. That such faults are natural after an exhausting war is obvious. That they are excusable, not to say negligible, on that account is untrue. They call for genuine, effective repentance, in which Christians ought to take the lead.

The most appropriate and convincing expression of such repentance must be determined resistance to public policies of the victors that seek to cripple former enemy powers.† Military disarmament, as competent critics have insisted, is not the same as economic dismemberment. Destruction of the industrial basis of German and Japanese livelihood, already far

---

* See *The Relation of the Church to the War*, pp. 47–53, 10–21.

† Cf. *The Relation of the Church to the War*, pp. 67, 69.

advanced by strategic bombing and other military action, cannot now be completed on political grounds without adding heavily to the injustice already committed in the name of the Allied peoples. Against such compounding of injustice the Church must steadily protest, in the name of God and of the common sonship of all men.

Within the setting of Christian resistance to unjust public policies, there is need also for continual urging of more active provision for relief and rebuilding of devastated lands. Plainly the largest part of this load must be carried by governments, but the Christian Churches have a special duty to urge upon their members, their neighbors, and all appropriate public agencies the honoring of our obligations as victors. This is not optional generosity but plain justice. If it is right that aggressors be held to account for reparations, then it is only right that we make some specific amends for damage that has resulted from our wanton acts of destruction. We are well aware that to some of our fellow Americans, the matter appears very differently, and that any curtailment of the plenty to which we are accustomed is looked upon with resentment, even if it be for the benefit of needy or starving allies. Such callousness we are bound to view with shame. It is unwelcome further evidence of our corporate failure in human understanding or decency, and of our deep need for repentance.

We are well aware also of the inadequacy and the dangers of proposing specific acts of restitution: the inadequacy of singling out a few victims from among millions, the dangers of displaying in that way complacency, hypocrisy, or misunderstanding. To rebuild Hiroshima and Nagasaki, the victims of our most spectacular offenses, would be to restore only a small fraction of what our strategic bombings needlessly destroyed. To provide special aid for the survivors of those two murdered cities would be hardly more than a token of repentance. Yet we believe either would have lasting value for future human relations. The former task would require public funds or a large popular subscription. The latter could be undertaken by the Churches of the United States, and we hope that at least so much may be done. We do not forget that the fire-bombing of Tokyo and the area bombing in Germany entailed a greater mass of suffering, and we have no thought of suggesting that token reparations now can overbalance the harm done by excessive violence in wartime. Whatever we can do will be at best a belated effort to make some amends for past failure. All of us are too deeply in debt to appear as simple benefactors. A more realistic view of our role is essential to the growth of healthy community life. But even a small effort to right injustice, if the effort be sincere, can have reconciling value far beyond its intrinsic weight. Our refusal to accept a share of the Boxer indemnity has had that effect. Relief or remembrance for the first victims of atomic warfare might be misunderstood, or might be cherished as long as men remember the first atomic bomb.

One other task the Church has been performing throughout the war. It has maintained fellowship among Christians on both sides of the fighting lines, and around the globe. Now that the shooting has stopped, the evidence of persisting unbroken relationships within the Church is accumulating steadily. There have been, of course, large and painful losses, and these must as far as possible be made good through patient knitting up of broken threads, reestablishment of understanding and confidence, shared worship, and initiation of new common tasks. It is too early to judge how well the Church's ecumenical fellowship has come through the storm. It may prove to be in better case than anyone dared hope. And if that be so, Christians will give thanks first to God, who is not helpless in the presence of human strife.

ULTIMATE PROBLEMS FOR FAITH

To SPEAK THUS of God is to raise the final group of questions we have had to reconsider in relation to the new warfare: questions of Christian faith, which is the Church's ultimate recourse in times of extreme pressure. First, we have had to recognize important new light on man's part in history.* The release and utilization of atomic energy has given a quite fresh view of the scope of the effects that may result from his freedom. For on the one hand it would appear that by suitable directing of this new resource, man may be able to prolong the period during which the earth will sustain human life. If this be so, if man can actually extend earthly history beyond its natural term, then he can, in principle, transcend natural limits more fundamental and significant than any physical barrier he has hitherto surmounted. On the other hand, it seems at least as likely that by misdirection of atomic energy, man can bring earthly history to a premature close. His freedom, then, is more decisive and dangerous than we had

---

* For an account of our understanding of man,   *Relation of the Church to the War*, pp. 43–54, 30–32.
which in general we still believe to be valid, see *The*

suspected. In making man a little lower than the angels, God seemingly has laid on him a weight of responsibility that has not only personal but cosmic import.

This startling disclosure of the true dimensions of man's freedom raises again, in new perspective, the question of God's power, justice and mercy. We have held steadily that all these aspects of God's sovereignty are discernible in war as well as in peace.* We reaffirm that view here, with a somewhat wider frame of reference to match the wider scope that now seems ascribable to human freedom. We believe in God still as Creator and Sovereign of heaven and earth. We believe also that His judgment and His mercy are present inseparably in every moment of history. But our conceptions of divine judgment and mercy in history need to be carried a step further. Divine justice and judgment, we still believe, are to be seen in the steady maintenance of a natural and moral order such that men can live and thrive in it only on condition that they yield to it an adequate measure of voluntary obedience, as well as a great hidden body of unconscious adaptations. This order, with the obligations it entails for man, stands fast in peace and in war. If man should violate its demands so grievously as to destroy civilization or even to extinguish all earthly life, the inexorable justice of God would thus be vindicated, not impugned.

For divine justice is not the "distributive" or "retributive" justice of a human law-court, balancing claims and counter-claims, but primarily the unswerving maintenance of natural and moral law for mankind and the world as a whole. This, we believe, is the necessary basis of human learning and moral betterment. As such, it is intended as a manifestation also of divine mercy, which we believe is not to be separated, in the purpose of God, from divine judgment. Suppose then that in a sudden tempest of atomic warfare human civilization or even all earthly human life were extinguished, by the acts of some men. The fatal decisions would be human decisions, not divine fiats. In as far as divine justice contributed to the outcome, it would be through the active preservation of dependable order. Nothing else than this could be regarded as consistent with the dependability of God. But the persons thus suddenly ending their lives on earth would come to the end in very different roles, some as active aggressors, and others as relatively innocent victims. This contrast is always present in massive man-

---

* See *The Relation of the Church to the War*,
pp. 29–43, esp. 33–39.

made disasters, and poses in itself no new problem. But the inclusiveness and finality of a possible global annihilation puts the old problem with fresh urgency. How, in the face of such a cataclysm, is the mercy of God – nay, even the justice of God, in any personal sense – to be seen?

The Justice and Mercy of God

FIRST OF ALL, it must be remembered that the possible cataclysm is foreseeable, and such foresight can help to prevent the end from coming to pass. Such annihilation is possible only because of extraordinary gifts granted to man. Even if these gifts should be perverted, it is still right to recognize divine bounty in the grant itself, and in the opportunity to turn the gifts to good account rather than ill. Secondly, the saving power of God is such that from otherwise desperate situations in the past – the crucifixion of Jesus Christ and the scattering of his disciples, the persecution of the early Church, the submergence of the Roman Empire in a flood of barbarism – new life has been called forth. It is essential to remember that the new peril we confront today is not the impersonal closing down of an Age of Ice but a possible man-made disaster that will come, if at all, because of specific human decisions. These fateful decisions in turn will be made, if at all, because of underlying attitudes of fear, vengefulness, pride, or rashness. We know that the one good ground for hope that such human attitudes may be profoundly changed is the redemptive activity of God, and we are confident that as long as human life on earth goes on, there will be clear signs that His providence is steadily at work to change men's hearts and win them back from the edge of impending ruin. Finally, men of faith will find, even as time grows short, that strength is given them to live without panic – nay more, with quickened force and earnestness. In a word, until the possible disaster actually occurs, there is no great difficulty in seeing divine favor as well as divine rigor in our new situation.

If, in spite of all, through human malice or blundering a worldwide disaster should come, there is at least a fair chance that not all human life on earth would be destroyed. Urban civilization, dependent on heavy industry and on complex networks of communication and transport, would almost certainly be ended for a long time. The greater part of any survivors would most probably be agricultural or nomadic people in out-of-the-way places, who might not even know that a catastrophe had occurred. They could not, without straining terms, be regarded as a "faithful remant," saved by reason of obedience to God, even though civilization were thought of as destroyed because of fatal disobedience. They would be ignorant rather than obedient. Yet there is no reason to doubt that God could make them also become great peoples, and bring to realization through them new stretches of history, perhaps new levels of spiritual community.

At any rate, there is no need to question whether, as long as man's life on earth continues, the justice and mercy of God surround him and can sustain him. We confidently affirm again that they do. But if a premature end of history should come, then plainly the nature of the problem posed is different. The problem then is whether beyond the end of history God's justice and mercy are still a ground for hope, or whether the stultification of human life by a premature end is to be feared.

To this final question we can answer partly in terms of experience, partly in terms of our Christian faith and hope. First of all, even while earthly life lasts, men by God's grace rise above it in many ways: in devotion to truth and honor, in love for God and neighbor, in self-sacrifice, in martyrdom, even in Christlike life. Thus they achieve a dimension of living that is different in kind from sensation, natural impulse, and prudential self-interest. Such living is not stultified even if – as in martyrdom – it comes prematurely to a close. The quality of life so attained has become, we believe, a permanent gain, not subject to destruction by passage of time. This is true, secondly, because God lives and holds in eternal presence the life of His children in time. His creating and redeeming work will not end even if the earth be destroyed, and whatever men have done, whatever of human existence has been good, He will cherish forever. Finally, it is a part of our Christian faith that not only the high moments of men's lives but their very existence and fellowship as personal selves is safe in God's hands; that death is swallowed up in the victory we call resurrection, so that death has not the last word. How such triumph over death is best to be conceived, we do not know. No more than we can define or picture the being of God are we able to picture what He has in store for us. But we are confident that in it lies the answer to the final question concerning His justice and mercy. We trust in God, and look toward the future with sure hope.

NOTE

This Report was prepared at the request of the Federal Council of the Churches of Christ in America. It was not intended to be adopted by the Council and was therefore not considered for adoption. Its publication is authorized as an expression of the opinion of the signers.

The following members of the Commission on The Relation of the Church to the War in the Light of the Christian Faith have affixed their signatures to the report:

ROBERT L. CALHOUN, *Chairman*
Professor of Historical Theology,
Yale University

JOHN C. BENNETT, *Secretary*
Professor of Christian Theology and
Ethics, Union Theological Seminary

EDWIN E. AUBREY
President, Crozer Theological
Seminary

ROLAND H. BAINTON
Professor of Ecclesiastical History,
Yale University Divinity School

CONRAD J.I. BERGENDOFF
President, Augustana College and
Theological Seminary

B. HARVIE BRANSCOMB
Dean of the School of Religion and
Professor of New Testament, Duke
University

FRANK H. CALDWELL
President, Louisville Presbyterian
Seminary

ANGUS DUN
Bishop of the Washington Diocese
of the Protestant Episcopal Church

NELS F.S. FERRE
Professor of Christian Theology,
Andover-Newton Theological
Institution

THEODORE M. GREENE
McCosh Professor of Philosophy,
Princeton University

GEORGIA E. HARKNESS
Professor of Applied Theology,
Garrett Biblical Institute

WALTER M. HORTON
Professor of Systematic Theology,
Oberlin Graduate School of
Theology

JOHN KNOX
Professor of New Testament, Union
Theological Seminary

BENJAMIN E. MAYS
President, Morehouse College

JOHN T. McNEILL
Professor of Church History, Union
Theological Seminary

REINHOLD NIEBUHR
Professor of Applied Christianity,
Union Theological Seminary

H. RICHARD NIEBUHR
Professor of Christian Ethics, Yale
University Divinity School

WILHELM PAUCK
Professor of Historical Theology,
Chicago Theological Seminary

DOUGLAS V. STEERE
Professor of Philosophy, Haverford
College

ERNEST FREMONT TITTLE
Minister of First Methodist Church,
Evanston, Ill.

HENRY P. VAN DUSEN
President, Union Theological
Seminary

THEODORE O. WEDEL
Warden of the College of Preachers,
Washington Cathedral

Excerpts from "The Challenge of Peace": National Conference of Catholic Bishops' Pastoral Letter on War and Peace, 1983*

UNDER NO CIRCUMSTANCES may nuclear weapons or other instruments of mass slaughter be used for the purpose of destroying population centers or other predominantly civilian targets. Popes have repeatedly condemned "total war" which implies such use. For example, as early as 1954 Pope Pius XII condemned nuclear warfare "when it entirely escapes the control of man," and results in "the pure and simple annihilation of all human life within the radius of action." The condemnation was repeated by the Second Vatican Council:

> Any act of war aimed indiscriminately at the destruction of entire cities or of extensive areas along with their population is a crime against God and man itself. It merits unequivocal and unhesitating condemnation. ...

*

After the passage of nearly four decades and a concomitant growth in our understanding of the ever growing horror of nuclear war, we must shape the climate of opinion which will make it possible for our country to

* Excerpts are taken from *The Challenge of Peace: God's Promise and Our Response* Copyright © 1983 by the United States Catholic Conference, 3211 Fourth Street, N.E., Washington D.C. 20017-1194, U.S.A. All rights reserved. To purchase a copy of this publication, please write to the above address and ask for publication number 863-0.

express profound sorrow over the atomic bombing in 1945. Without that sorrow, there is no possibility of finding a way to repudiate future use of nuclear weapons or of conventional weapons in such military actions as would not fulfil just-war criteria. ...

*

Fundamentally, we are saying that the decisions about nuclear weapons are among the most pressing moral questions of our age. While these decisions have obvious military and political aspects, they involve fundamental moral choices. In simple terms, we are saying that good ends (defending one's country, protecting freedom, etc.) cannot justify immoral means (the use of weapons which kill indiscriminately and threaten whole societies). We fear that our world and nation are headed in the wrong direction. More weapons with greater destructive potential are produced every day. More and more nations are seeking to become nuclear powers. In our quest for more and more security, we fear we are actually becoming less and less secure.

*

In the words of our Holy Father, we need a "moral about-face." The whole world must summon the moral courage and technical means to say "no" to nuclear conflict; "no" to weapons of mass destruction; "no" to an arms race which robs the poor and the vulnerable; and "no" to the moral danger of a nuclear age which places before humankind indefensible choices of constant terror or surrender. Peacemaking is not an optional commitment. It is a requirement of our faith. We are called to be peacemakers, not by some movement of the moment, but by our Lord Jesus. The content and context of our peacemaking is set, not by some political agenda or ideological program, but by the teaching of his Church.

Bibliography
of Important
Sources

*No attempt is made to cover the enormous
volume of specialized materials relating to
all of the issues dealt with in this book.
The interested reader is referred to more
extensive bibliographies or bibliographical essays on specific questions in various
works cited.*

GOVERNMENT PUBLICATIONS

Butler, J. R. M., gen. ed. *Grand Strategy.* 6 vols. London: His Majesty's Stationary
Office, 1956. Vol. VI: *October 1944–August 1945,* by J. Ehrman.

Cline, R. S. *Washington Command Post: The Operations Division.* Washington,
D.C.: Office of the Chief of Military History, Department of the Army, 1951.

Ehrman, J. *October 1944–August 1945,* vol. VI of *Grand Strategy.* See Butler.

FRUS. See U.S. Department of State, *Foreign Relations of the United States:
Diplomatic Papers 1945.*

Great Britain. *Parliamentary Debates* (Commons), 5th Series. Vol. 413 (1945)
[Hansard].

Greenfield, K. R., ed. *Command Decisions.* Washington, D.C.: U.S. Dept. of the
Army, Office of Military History, 1960.

Morgenthau, H. *Morgenthau Diary (China).* Vol. II. Washington, D.C.: U.S.
Government Printing Office, 1965.

————. *Morgenthau Diary (Germany).* Vol. II. Washington, D.C.: U.S. Government Printing Office, 1965.

Morton, L. "The Decision to Use the Atomic Bomb (1945)." In *Command Decisions.* See Greenfield.

Public Papers of the President: Harry S. Truman, 1945–1953. Washington, D.C.:
U.S. Government Printing Office, 1961–1966.

Smyth, H. D. *Atomic Energy* (The Smyth Report). Washington, D.C.: U.S. Government Printing Office, 1945.

U.S. Atomic Energy Commission. *In the Matter of J. Robert Oppenheimer. Tran-
script of Hearing Before Personnel Security Board,* 12 April–6 May 1954. Washington, D.C.: U.S. Government Printing Office, 1954.

U.S. Department of Defense. "The Entry of the Soviet Union into the War against Japan: Military Plans, 1941–1945." Washington, D.C.: U.S. Government Printing Office, 1955.

U.S. Department of State. *Foreign Relations: Conference of Berlin (Potsdam) 1945.* 2 vols. Washington, D.C.: U.S. Government Printing Office, 1960.

U.S. Department of State. *Foreign Relations of the United States: The Conferences at Malta and Yalta 1945.* Washington, D.C.: U.S. Government Printing Office, 1955.

U.S. Department of State. *Foreign Relations of the United States: Diplomatic Papers 1945.* Vols. IV and V. Washington, D.C.: U.S. Government Printing Office, 1948, 1947.

U.S. Department of State, *Postwar Foreign Policy Preparation: 1939–45.* Washington, D.C.: U.S. Government Printing Office, 1949.

U.S. Department of State. *United States Relations with China 1944–49.* Washington, D.C.: U.S. Government Printing Office, 1949.

U.S. House of Representatives, Committee on Banking and Currency. *Hearings: Export-Import Bank Act of 1945.* 11, 12 July 1945. Washington, D.C.: U.S. Government Printing Office, 1945.

U.S. House of Representatives, Committee on Military Affairs. *Hearings: Atomic Energy Act.* 9, 18 October 1945. Washington, D.C.: U.S. Government Printing Office, 1945.

U.S. House of Representatives, Select Committee on Postwar Military Policy. *Hearings: Universal Military Training.* June 1945. Washington, D.C.: U.S. Government Printing Office, 1945.

U.S. Senate, Committee on Armed Services and Foreign Relations. *Hearings: Military Situation in the Far East.* May, June 1951. Washington, D.C.: U.S. Government Printing Office, 1951.

U.S. Senate, Committee on Banking and Currency. *Hearings: Export-Import Bank Act of 1945.* 17, 18 July 1945. Washington, D.C.: U.S. Government Printing Office, 1945.

U.S. Senate, Committee on Foreign Relations. *A Decade of American Foreign Policy.* Washington, D.C.: U.S. Government Printing Office, 1950.

U.S. Senate, Committee on Military Affairs. *Hearings: Demobilization of the Armed Forces.* 12, 13, 17, 18 September 1945. Washington, D.C.: U.S. Government Printing Office, 1945.

U.S. Senate, Special Committee on Atomic Energy. *Hearings: Atomic Energy Act of 1945.* January 1946. Washington, D.C.: U.S. Government Printing Office, 1946.

U.S. Senate, Special Committee on Atomic Energy. Testimony of A. Sachs. 79th Cong., 2d sess., pt. 5, 15 February 1946.

United States Strategic Bombing Survey. *Japan's Struggle to End the War.* 1 July 1946. U.S. National Archives, microfilm # M1013, roll 18.

BOOKS

Acheson, D. *The Pattern of Responsibility.* Ed. McG. Bundy. Boston: Houghton Mifflin, 1952.

BIBLIOGRAPHY OF IMPORTANT SOURCES

————. *Power and Diplomacy.* Cambridge, Mass.: Harvard University Press, 1958.

————. *Present at the Creation: My Years in the State Department.* New York: Norton, 1969.

————. *Sketches from Life of Men I Have Known.* New York: Harper, 1961.

Adams, H. H. *Witness to Power: The Life of Fleet Admiral William D. Leahy.* Annapolis, Md.: Naval Institute Press, 1985.

Albion, R. G., and Connery, R. H. *Forrestal and the Navy.* New York: Columbia University Press, 1962.

Allen, H. C. *Great Britain and the United States: A History of Anglo-American Relations (1783–1952).* London: Odhams Press, 1954; New York: St. Martin's, 1955.

Allen, J. S. *Atomic Imperialism: The State Monopoly and the Bomb.* New York: International Publishers, 1952.

Alperovitz, G. *Cold War Essays.* New York: Anchor Books, 1970.

Alsop, J. and S. *We Accuse! The Story of the Mismarriage of Justice in the Case of J. Robert Oppenheimer.* New York: Simon & Schuster, 1954; London: Gollancz, 1955.

Ambrose, S. E. *Eisenhower.* 2 vols. New York: Simon & Schuster, 1983, 1984.

————. *Rise to Globalism: American Foreign Policy Since 1938.* New York: Penguin Books, 1985.

Amrine, M. *The Great Decision.* New York: Putnam, 1959; London: Heinemann, 1960.

Anders, W. *An Army in Exile: The Story of the Second Polish Corps.* London: Macmillan, 1949.

Anderton, D. A. *Strategic Air Command: Two Thirds of the Triad.* New York: Scribner, 1960.

Arnold, H. H. *Global Missions.* New York: Harper, 1949.

Asada, S. "Japanese Perceptions of the A-Bomb Decision, 1945–1980." In *The American Military and the Far East: Proceedings of the Ninth Military History Symposiu..,* ed. J. C. Dixon. United States Air Force Academy, 1980.

Asbell, B. *When F.D.R. Died.* New York: Holt, Rinehart and Winston, 1961.

Attlee, C. R. *As It Happened.* London: Heinemann, 1954.

————. *Clem Attlee: The Granada Historical Records Interview.* London: Panther Books, 1967.

Ausubel, N., ed. *Voices of History, 1945–46: Speeches and Papers of Roosevelt, Truman, Churchill, Attlee, Stalin, DeGaulle, Chiang and Other Leaders.* New York: Gramercy Publishing, 1946.

Baker, P. R., ed. *The Atomic Bomb: The Great Decision.* New York: Holt, Rinehart and Winston, 1968.

Baldwin, H. *The Great Arms Race: A Comparison of U.S. and Soviet Power Today.* New York: Praeger, 1958; London: Atlantic Books, 1958.

————. *Great Mistakes of the War.* New York: Harper, 1950; London: Atlantic Books, 1950.

Balfour, M. "Germany." In vol. VIII of *Survey of International Affairs, 1937–1946.* See Toynbee.

Barclay, Sir R. *Ernest Bevin and the Foreign Office, 1932–1969.* London: Latimer, 1975.

Barnet, R. *Who Wants Disarmament?* Boston: Beacon Press, 1960.

Bartlett, C. J. *The Rise and Fall of the Pax Americana: United States Foreign Policy in the Twentieth Century.* London: Elek, 1974.

Baruch, B. M. *Baruch: The Public Years.* New York: Holt, 1960.

Batchelder, R. C. *The Irreversible Decision, 1939–1950.* Boston: Houghton Mifflin, 1962.

Bechhoefer, B. G. *Postwar Negotiations for Arms Control.* Washington, D.C.: Brookings Institution, 1961.

Becker, J. H. *The Decision to Divide Germany: American Foreign Policy in Transition.* Durham, N.C.: Duke University Press, 1978.

Bell, C. *Negotiation from Strength: A Study in the Politics of Power.* London: Chatto & Windus, 1962.

Beloff, M. *Soviet Policy in the Far East, 1944–1951.* London: Oxford University Press, 1953.

Berding, A. H. *Dulles on Diplomacy.* Princeton, N.J.: Van Nostrand, 1965.

Berger, J. "Hiroshima—A Portrait of Evil." In *First Harvest: The Institute for Policy Studies, 1963–1983,* ed. J. S. Friedman. New York: Grove Press, 1983.

Berle, A. A. *Navigating the Rapids: From the Papers of Adolf A. Berle.* New York: Harcourt Brace Jovanovich, 1973.

Bernstein, B. J., ed. *The Atomic Bomb: The Critical Issues.* Boston: Little, Brown, 1976.

――――, ed. *Politics and Policies of the Truman Administration.* Chicago: Quadrangle Books, 1970.

―――― and Matusow, A. J. *The A-Bomb Decision in the Truman Administration: A Documentary History.* New York: Harper & Row, 1966.

―――― and Matusow, A. J., eds. *The Truman Administration: A Documentary History.* New York: Harper & Row, 1966.

Betts, R. R., ed. *Central and South East Europe, 1945–48.* London: Royal Institute of International Affairs, 1950.

Birse, A. H. *Memoirs of an Interpreter.* London: Joseph, 1967.

Blackett, P. M. S. *Atomic Weapons and East-West Relations.* Cambridge: At the University Press, 1956.

――――. *Fear, War and the Bomb.* New York: Whittlesey House, 1949. (Originally published as *Military and Political Consequences of Atomic Energy.* London: Turnstile, 1948.)

――――. *Studies of War: Nuclear and Conventional.* Edinburgh: Oliver and Boyd, 1962.

Blum, J. M. *From the Morgenthau Diaries: Years of War, 1941–1945.* Boston: Houghton Mifflin, 1967.

――――, ed. *The Price of Vision: The Diary of Henry A. Wallace, 1942–1946.* Boston: Houghton Mifflin, 1973.

Blumberg, S. A., and Owens, G. *Energy and Conflict: The Life and Times of Edward Teller.* New York: Putnam, 1976.

Bohlen, C. E. *The Transformation of American Foreign Policy.* New York: Norton, 1969.

――――. *Witness to History, 1929–1969.* New York: Norton, 1973.

Bowles, C. *Promises to Keep: My Years in Public Life, 1941–1969.* New York: Harper & Row, 1971.

BIBLIOGRAPHY OF IMPORTANT SOURCES

Bradley, O. *A Soldier's Story*. New York: Holt, 1951; London: Eyre, 1951.

――― and Blair, C. *A General's Life: An Autobiography*. New York: Simon & Schuster, 1983.

Brooks, L. *Behind Japan's Surrender: The Secret Struggle That Ended an Empire*. New York: McGraw-Hill, 1968.

Brown, A. C., ed. *Dropshot: The United States Plan for War with the Soviet Union in 1957*. New York: Dial Press, 1978.

Brown, A. D., and Macdonald, C. B., eds. *The Secret History of the Atomic Bomb*. New York: Dial Press, 1977.

―――. *The Last Hero: Wild Bill Donovan*. New York: Times Books, 1982.

Bryant, A. *Triumph in the West, 1943-46*. (Based on diaries and autobiographical notes of Field Marshal Viscount Alanbrooke.) London: Collins, 1959.

Brzezinski, Z. K. *The Soviet Bloc: Unity and Conflict*. Cambridge, Mass.: Harvard University Press, 1960; New York: Praeger, 1961.

Buchanan, A. R. *The United States and World War II*. 2 vols. New York: Harper & Row, 1964.

Buell, T. B. *Master of Sea Power: A Biography of Fleet Admiral Ernest J. King*. Boston: Little, Brown, 1980.

Bullock, A. *Ernest Bevin: Foreign Secretary, 1945-1951*. London: Heinemann, 1983.

Burns, G. *The Atomic Papers: A Citizen's Guide to Selected Books and Articles on the Bomb, the Arms Race, Nuclear Power, the Peace Movement, and Related Issues*. Metuchen, N.J.: Scarecrow Press, 1984.

―――. "James F. Byrnes," In *An Uncertain Tradition: American Secretaries of State in the Twentieth Century*, ed. N. A. Graebner. New York: McGraw-Hill, 1961.

Bush, V. *Endless Horizons*. Washington, D.C.: Public Affairs Press, 1946.

―――. *Modern Arms and Free Men: A Discussion of the Role of Science in Preserving Democracy*. New York: Simon & Schuster, 1949; Kingswood: Heinemann, 1950.

―――. *Pieces of the Action*. New York: Morrow, 1970.

Butcher, H. C. *My Three Years with Eisenhower: The Personal Diary of Captain Harry C. Butcher*. New York: Simon & Schuster, 1946; London: Heinemann, 1946.

Butow, R. J. C. *Japan's Decision to Surrender*. Stanford, Calif.: Stanford University Press, 1954; London: Oxford University Press, 1957.

―――. *Tojo and the Coming of the War*. Princeton: Princeton University Press, 1961.

Byrnes, J. F. *All in One Lifetime*. New York: Harper, 1958.

―――. *Speaking Frankly*. New York: Harper, 1947.

Campbell, T. M., and Herring, G. C., eds. *The Diaries of Edward R. Stettinius, Jr., 1943-1946*. New York: New Viewpoints, 1975.

Carlton, D. *Anthony Eden: A Biography*. London: Allen Lane, 1981.

Carr, E. H. *Conditions of Peace*. London: Macmillan, 1942.

Chamberlain, W. H. *America's Second Crusade*. Chicago: Regnery, 1950.

Churchill, W. S. *The Hinge of Fate*. London: Cassell, 1951.

―――. *Triumph and Tragedy*. Boston: Houghton Mifflin, 1953.

Ciechanowski, J. *Defeat in Victory*. New York: Doubleday, 1950, 1947.

Clark, M. W. *Calculated Risk*. New York: Harper, 1950.

Clark, R. W. *The Birth of the Bomb*. New York: Horizon Press, 1961.

Clay, L. D. *Decision in Germany*. New York: Doubleday; London: Heinemann, 1950.

Clemens, D. S. *Yalta*. New York: Oxford University Press, 1978.

Clements, K. *James F. Byrnes and the Origins of the Cold War*. Durham, N.C.: Carolina Academic Press, 1982.

Cochran, T. B., et al. *Nuclear Weapons Datebook, Vol. I: U.S. Nuclear Forces and Capabilities*. Boston: Ballinger Publishing Co., 1984.

Coerr, E. *Saduko and the Thousand Paper Cranes*. New York: Putnam, 1977.

Coffey, T. M. *Hap: The Story of the U.S. Air Force and the Man Who Built It, General Henry H. "HAP" Arnold*. New York: Viking, 1982.

————. *Imperial Tragedy: Japan in World War II, The First Days and the Last*. New York: World Publishing Co., 1970.

Cohen, B. C. *The Political Process and Foreign Policy: The Making of the Japanese Peace Settlement*. Princeton: Princeton University Press, 1957.

Coit, M. L. *Mr. Baruch*. Boston: Houghton Mifflin, 1957.

Committee for the Compilation of Materials on Damage Caused by the Atomic Bombs in Hiroshima and Nagasaki. *Hiroshima and Nagasaki*. New York: Basic Books, 1981.

Compton, A. H. *Atomic Quest: A Personal Narrative*. New York: Oxford University Press, 1956.

Conant, J. B. *My Several Lives: Memoirs of a Social Inventor*. New York: Harper & Row, 1970.

Condit, K. W. *The History of the Joint Chiefs of Staff: The Joint Chiefs of Staff and National Policy*. Vols. I and II. Wilmington, Del.: M. Glazier, 1979.

Connally, T. T. *My Name Is Tom Connally*. New York: Crowell, 1954.

Corson, W. R. *The Armies of Ignorance: The Rise of the American Intelligence Empire*. New York: Dial Press, 1977.

Craig, W. *The Fall of Japan*. New York: Dial Press, 1967.

Craven, W. F., and Cate, J. L. *The Army Air Forces in World War II*. Chicago: University of Chicago Press, 1953. Vol. V: *The Pacific, Matterhorn to Nagasaki, June 1944 to August 1945*.

Current, R. N. *Secretary Stimson: A Study in Statecraft*. New Brunswick, N.J.: Rutgers University Press, 1954.

Dallek, R. *Franklin D. Roosevelt and American Foreign Policy, 1932–1945*. New York: Oxford University Press, 1979.

Dallin, A. *Soviet Conduct in World Affairs: A Selection of Readings*. New York: Columbia University Press, 1960.

Dalton, H. *High Tide and After: Memoirs, 1945–1960*. New York: Muller, 1962.

Daniels, J. *The Man of Independence*. Philadelphia: Kennikat Press, 1950; London: Gollancz, 1951.

Davis, L. E. *The Cold War Begins: Soviet American Conflict over Eastern Europe*. Princeton: Princeton University Press, 1974.

Deane, J. R. *The Strange Alliance*. New York: Viking, 1947.

DeGaulle, C. *War Memoirs*. 5 vols. New York: Simon & Schuster; London: Collins, 1951. Vol. III: *Salvation, 1944–1946*.

Dennett, R., and Johnson, J. E., eds. *Negotiating with the Russians*. Boston: World Peace Foundation, 1951.

BIBLIOGRAPHY OF IMPORTANT SOURCES

de Seversky, A. P. *Victory Through Air Power.* New York: Simon & Schuster, 1942.

Deutscher, I. *The Great Contest: Russia and the West.* London: Oxford University Press, 1960.

———. *Russia: What Next?* New York: Oxford University Press, 1953.

———. *Stalin: A Political Biography.* London: Oxford University Press, 1949.

Dewar, M. *Soviet Trade with Eastern Europe, 1945–49.* London: Royal Institute of International Affairs; New York, 1951.

Dinnerstein, H. S. *War and the Soviet Union.* New York: Praeger, 1959.

Divine, R. A. *Second Chance: The Triumph of Internationalism in America During World War II.* New York: Atheneum, 1967.

Djilas, M. *Conversations with Stalin.* New York: Harcourt Brace & World, 1962.

———. *The New Class.* New York: Praeger, 1957.

Donovan, R. J. *Conflict and Crisis: The Presidency of Harry S. Truman, 1945–1948.* New York: Norton, 1977.

———. *Nemesis: Truman and Johnson in the Coils of War in Asia.* New York: St. Martin's, 1984.

Dorwart, J. M. *Conflict of Duty: The U.S. Navy's Intelligence Dilemma, 1919–1945.* Annapolis, Md.: Naval Institute Press, 1983.

Druks, H. *Truman and the Russians.* New York: R. Speller, 1981.

Dulles, A. W. *The Secret Surrender.* New York: Harper & Row, 1966.

Dulles, J. F. *War or Peace.* New York: Macmillan, 1950; London: Harrup, 1950.

Eden, A. *The Reckoning: The Eden Memoirs by the Earl of Avon.* Boston: Houghton Mifflin, 1965.

Eisenhower, D. D. *Crusade in Europe.* Garden City, N.Y.: Doubleday, 1948.

———. *Letters to Mamie.* Garden City, N.Y.: Doubleday, 1978.

———. *The Papers of Dwight David Eisenhower.* 11 vols. Baltimore: Johns Hopkins Press, 1970–1984. Vol. VI: *Occupation, 1945,* ed. A. D. Chandler and L. Galambos.

———. *The White House Years: Mandate for Change, 1953–56.* Garden City, N.Y.: Doubleday, 1963.

Etzold, T. H., and Gaddis, J. L., ed. *Containment: Documents on American Policy & Strategy, 1945–1950.* New York: Columbia University Press, 1978.

Feis, H. *The Atomic Bomb and the End of World War II.* Princeton: Princeton University Press, 1966.

———. *Between War and Peace: The Potsdam Conference.* Princeton: Princeton University Press, 1960.

———. *The China Tangle: The American Effort in China from Pearl Harbor to the Marshall Mission.* Princeton: Princeton University Press, 1953.

———. *Churchill, Roosevelt, Stalin: The War They Waged and the Peace They Sought.* Princeton: Princeton University Press, 1957.

———. *From Trust to Terror: The Onset of the Cold War, 1945–1950.* New York: Norton, 1970.

———. *Japan Subdued: The Atomic Bomb and the End of the War in the Pacific.* Princeton: Princeton University Press, 1961.

Ferrell, R. H., ed. *The American Secretaries of State and Their Diplomacy.* New York: Cooper Square Publishers, 1965. Vol. XIV: *E. R. Stettinius, Jr.,* by R. L. Walker; *James F. Byrnes,* by G. Curry.

————, ed. *The Autobiography of Harry S. Truman.* Boulder: Colorado Associated University Press, 1980.

————, ed. *Off The Record: The Private Papers of Harry S. Truman.* New York: Harper & Row, 1980.

Finletter, T. K. *Power and Policy: U.S. Foreign Policy and Military Power in the Hydrogen Age.* New York: Harcourt Brace, 1954.

Fleming, D. F. *The Cold War and Its Origins, 1917–1960.* 2 vols. Garden City, N.Y.: Doubleday, 1961.

Forrestal, J. V. *The Forrestal Diaries.* Edited by W. Millis. New York: Viking, 1951; London: Cassell, 1952.

Francis-Williams, E. *Twilight of Empire: Memoirs of Prime Minister Clement Attlee.* Westport, Conn.: Greenwood Press, 1978.

————. *A Prime Minister Remembers: The War and Post-War Memoirs of the Rt. Hon. Earl Attlee.* London: Heinemann, 1962.

Frankel, J. *The Making of Foreign Policy: An Analysis of Decision-Making.* London: Oxford University Press, 1963.

Freeland, R. M. *The Truman Doctrine and the Origins of McCarthyism.* New York: Knopf, 1972.

Freund, G. *Germany: Between Two Worlds.* New York: Harcourt Brace, 1961.

Gaddis, J. L. *Russia, the Soviet Union, and the United States: An Interpretative History.* New York: Wiley, 1978.

————. *The United States and the Origins of the Cold War, 1941–1947.* New York: Columbia University Press, 1972.

Gardner, L. C. *Architects of Illusion: Men and Ideas in American Foreign Policy, 1941–1949.* Chicago: Quadrangle Books, 1970.

Garthoff, R. L. *The Soviet Image of Future War.* Washington, D.C.: Public Affairs Press, 1959.

————. *Soviet Strategy in the Nuclear Age.* New York: Praeger, 1958.

Giovannitti, L., and Freed, F. *The Decision to Drop the Bomb.* New York: Coward McCann, 1965.

Goldwin, R., ed. *Readings in Russian Foreign Policy.* New York: Oxford University Press, 1959.

Golovin, I. N., and Kurchatov, I. V. *A Socialist-Realist Biography of the Soviet Nuclear Scientist.* Bloomington, Ind.: Selbstverlag Press, 1968.

Goodchild, P. *J. Robert Oppenheimer, Shatterer of Worlds.* Boston: Houghton Mifflin, 1981.

Gosnell, H. F. *Truman's Crises: A Political Biography of Harry S. Truman.* Westport, Conn.: Greenwood Press, 1980.

Gowing, M. M. *Britain and Atomic Energy, 1939–1945.* New York: St. Martin's, 1964; London: Macmillan, 1964.

Grew, J. *Ten Years in Japan.* New York: Arno Press, 1972.

————. *Turbulent Era: A Diplomatic Record of Forty Years, 1904–1945.* 2 vols. Boston: Houghton Mifflin, 1952.

Groves, L. R. *Now It Can Be Told: The Story of the Manhattan Project.* New York: Harper, 1962.

Haines, G. K., and Walker, J. S., eds. *American Foreign Relations: A Historiographical Review.* Westport, Conn.: Greenwood Press, 1981.

Halle, L. J. *The Cold War as History.* New York: Harper & Row, 1971.

BIBLIOGRAPHY OF IMPORTANT SOURCES

Hammond, T. T. "Did the United States Use Atomic Diplomacy Against Russia in 1945?" In *From the Cold War to Detente*, ed. J. Potichny and P. Shapiro. New York: Praeger, 1976.

Harriman, W. A. *Peace with Russia?* New York: Simon & Schuster, 1959; London: Gollancz, 1960.

—— and Abel, E. *Special Envoy to Churchill and Stalin, 1941–1946.* New York: Random House, 1975.

Hayes, G. P. *The History of the Joint Chiefs of Staff in World War II: The War Against Japan.* Annapolis, Md.: Naval Institute Press, 1982.

Haynes, R. F. *The Awesome Power: Harry S Truman as Commander in Chief.* Baton Rouge: Louisiana State University Press, 1973.

Herken, G. F. "Atomic Diplomacy Reversed and Revised." In *The Atomic Bomb: The Critical Issues*, ed. B. J. Bernstein. Boston: Little, Brown, 1976.

——. *The Winning Weapon: The Atomic Bomb in the Cold War, 1945–1950.* New York: Knopf, 1980. References are to the first Vintage Books edition, 1982.

Herring, G. C. *Aid to Russia, 1941–1946: Strategy, Diplomacy, the Origins of the Cold War.* New York: Columbia University Press, 1973.

Hersey, J. *Hiroshima.* New York: Knopf, 1946.

Herz, M. *Beginnings of the Cold War.* Bloomington: Indiana University Press, 1966.

Hewlett, R. G., and Anderson, O. E. *The New World, 1939–1946.* Vol. I of *A History of the United States Atomic Energy Commission.* 2 vols. University Park: Pennsylvania State University Press, 1962.

Holmes, W. J. *Double-Edged Secrets: U.S. Naval Intelligence Operations in the Pacific During World War II.* Annapolis, Md.: Naval Institute Press, 1979.

Horowitz, D. *The Free World Colossus.* New York: Hill & Wang, 1971.

Hull, C. *Memoirs of Cordell Hull.* 2 vols. New York: Macmillan, 1948.

Iriye, A. "Continuities in US–Japanese Relations, 1941–49." In *The Origins of the Cold War in Asia*, ed. Y. Nagai and A. Iriye. New York: Columbia University Press, 1977.

Irving, D. J. *The Destruction of Dresden.* London: W. Kimber, 1963.

Ismay, H. L. *The Memoirs of General Lord Ismay.* London: Heinemann, 1960.

Japan Broadcasting Corporation (NHK), ed. *Unforgettable Fire: Pictures Drawn by Atomic Bomb Survivors.* New York: Pantheon, 1981.

Johnson, W. "Edward R. Stettinius, Jr. (1944–1945)." In *An Uncertain Tradition: American Secretaries of State in the Twentiety Century*, ed. N. A. Graebner. New York: McGraw-Hill, 1961.

Jones, F. C., Bolton, H., and Pearn, B. R. *The Far East, 1942–1946.* In *Survey of International Affairs, 1939–1946.* See Toynbee.

Jones, J. M. *The Fifteen Weeks.* New York: Viking, 1955.

Jungk, R. *Brighter Than a Thousand Suns: A Personal History of the Atomic Bomb.* New York: Harcourt Brace, 1958.

Kase, T. *Eclipse of the Rising Sun.* London: J. Cape, 1951.

——. *Journey to the Missouri.* New Haven, Conn.: Yale University Press, 1950.

Kaufmann, W. W., ed. *Military Policy and National Security.* Princeton: Princeton University Press, 1956.

Kennan, G. F. *American Diplomacy, 1900–1950.* Chicago: University of Chicago Press, 1951.

————. *Memoirs, 1925–1950*. London: Hutchinson, 1968.

————. *Russia and the West Under Lenin and Stalin*. Boston: Little, Brown, 1961.

————. *Russia, the Atom, and the West*. London: Oxford University Press, 1958.

Kertesz, S. D., ed. *The Fate of East-Central Europe: Hopes and Failures of American Foreign Policy*. Notre Dame, Ind.: University of Notre Dame Press, 1956.

Keynes, J. M. *The General Theory of Employment, Interest and Money*. London: Macmillan, 1957.

Khrushchev, N. *Khrushchev Remembers: The Last Testament*. Ed. S. Talbott. Boston: Little, Brown, 1974.

King, E. J., and Whitehill, W. M. *Fleet Admiral King: A Naval Record*. New York: Norton, 1952; London: Eyre, 1953.

Kirkendal, R., ed. *The Truman Period as a Research Field: A Reappraisal, 1972*. Columbia: University of Missouri Press, 1974.

Kissinger, H. A. *The Necessity for Choice: Prospects of American Foreign Policy*. New York: Harper, 1961.

————. *Nuclear Weapons and Foreign Policy*. New York: The Council of Foreign Relations, 1957.

Knebel, F., and Bailey, C. W. *No High Ground*. New York: Harper, 1960.

Kolko, G. *The Politics of War: The World and United States Foreign Policy, 1943–1945*. New York: Random House, 1968.

Kolko, J. and G. *The Limits of Power: The World and United States Foreign Policy, 1945–1954*. New York: Harper & Row, 1972.

Korb, L. C. *The Joint Chiefs of Staff: The First Twenty-five Years*. Bloomington: Indiana University Press, 1976.

Korbonski, S. *Warsaw in Chains*. London: Allen & Unwin, 1959.

Kovrig, B. *The Myth of Liberation: East-Central Europe in U.S. Diplomacy and Politics Since 1941*. Baltimore: Johns Hopkins University Press, 1973.

Kunetka, J. W. *Oppenheimer: The Years of Risk*. Englewood Cliffs, N.J.: Prentice-Hall, 1982.

Kuniholm, B. R. *The Origins of the Cold War in the Near East: The Great Power Conflict and Diplomacy in Iran, Turkey, and Greece*. Princeton: Princeton University Press, 1980.

LaFeber, W. *America, Russia and the Cold War, 1945–1984*. New York: Knopf, 1985.

————. "American Policy-Makers, Public Opinion, and the Outbreak of the Cold War, 1945–50." In *The Origins of the Cold War in Asia*, ed. Y. Nagai and A. Iriye. New York: Columbia University Press, 1977.

Lamont, L. *Day of Trinity*. New York: Atheneum, 1965.

Lane, A. B. *I Saw Poland Betrayed: An American Ambassador Reports to the American People*. Indianapolis: Bobbs-Merril, 1948. (Also published as *I Saw Freedom Betrayed*. London: Regency Publishers, 1949.)

Laurence, W. L. *Dawn over Zero: The Story of the Atomic Bomb*. New York: Knopf, 1946.

Lawrence, W. H. "The Second New York Times Report of the Hiroshima Blast." In *Hiroshima Plus 20*, prepared by *The New York Times*. New York: Delacorte Press, 1965.

Leahy, W. D. *I Was There: The Personal Story of the Chief of Staff to Presidents Roosevelt and Truman, Based on His Notes and Diaries Made at the Time*. New York: Whittlesey House, 1950.

BIBLIOGRAPHY OF IMPORTANT SOURCES

Lee, A. G. *Crown Against Sickle: The Story of King Michael of Rumania.* London: Hutchinson, 1950.

LeMay, C. E., with Kantor, M. *Mission with LeMay: My Story.* Garden City, N.Y.: Doubleday, 1965.

Leonhard, W. *Child of the Revolution.* Chicago: H. Regnery Co., 1958.

Lewin, R. *The American Magic: Codes, Ciphers and the Defeat of Japan.* New York: Farrar, Straus and Giroux, 1982.

Lieberman, J. I. *The Scorpion and the Tarantula: The Struggle to Control Atomic Weapons, 1945–49.* Boston: Houghton Mifflin, 1970.

Lifton, B. J., and Hosoe, E. *Return to Hiroshima.* New York: Atheneum, 1970.

Lifton, R. J. *Death in Life: Survivors of Hiroshima.* New York: Random House, 1967.

Lilienthal, D. E. *The Journals of David E. Lilienthal.* 7 vols. New York: Harper & Row, 1964–1983. Vol. II: *The Atomic Energy Years, 1945–1950.*

Lippmann, W. *The Cold War: A Study in U.S. Foreign Policy.* New York: Harper, 1947.

Love, R. W., Jr., ed. *The Chiefs of Naval Operations.* Annapolis, Md.: Naval Institute Press, 1980.

Lukacs, J. A. *The Great Powers and Eastern Europe.* New York: American Book Co., 1953.

———. *A History of the Cold War.* Garden City, N.Y.: Doubleday, 1961.

Lukas, R. C. *The Strange Allies: The United States and Poland 1941–1945.* Knoxville: University of Tennessee Press, 1978.

Lundestad, G. *The American Non-Policy Towards Eastern Europe, 1943–1947: Universalism in an Area Not of Essential Interest to the United States.* New York: Humanities Press, 1975.

Mackintosh, J. M. *Strategy and Tactics of Soviet Foreign Policy.* London: Oxford University Press, 1962.

Maddox, R. *The New Left and the Origins of the Cold War.* Princeton: Princeton University Press, 1973.

Maier, C. S. "Revisionism and the Interpretation of the Cold War Origins." In *The Origins of the Cold War and Contemporary Europe,* ed. C. S. Maier. New York: New Viewpoints, 1978.

Manchester, W. R. *American Caesar: Douglas MacArthur, 1880–1964.* Boston: Little, Brown, 1978.

Marx, J. L. *Nagasaki: The Necessary Bomb?* New York: Macmillan, 1971.

Mastny, V. *Russia's Road to the Cold War: Diplomacy, Warfare, and the Politics of Communism, 1941–1945.* New York: Columbia University Press, 1979.

May, E. R. "The Cold War." In *The Comparative Approach to American History,* ed. C. Vann Woodward. New York: Basic Books, 1968.

McCloy, J. J. *The Challenge to American Foreign Policy.* Cambridge, Mass: Harvard University Press, 1953.

McInnis, E., Hiscocks, R., and Spencer, R. *The Shaping of Postwar Germany.* New York: Praeger, 1960.

McLellan, D. S. *Dean Acheson: The State Department Years.* New York: Dodd, Mead, 1976.

McNeill, W. H. *America, Britain and Russia: Their Cooperation and Conflict, 1941–1946.* London: Royal Institute of International Affairs, 1953.

ATOMIC DIPLOMACY: HIROSHIMA AND POTSDAM

Mee, C. L., Jr. *Meeting at Potsdam.* New York: M. Evans, 1975.

Mendelsohn, E. "The Historian Confronts the Bomb." In *Proceedings of the Symposium: The Role of the Academy in Addressing the Issues of Nuclear War.* Geneva: Hobart and William Smith Colleges, 1982.

Messer, R. L. *The End of An Alliance: James F. Byrnes, Roosevelt, Truman, and the Origins of the Cold War.* Chapel Hill: University of North Carolina Press, 1982.

Mikolajczyk, S. *The Pattern of Soviet Domination.* London: S. Low, Marston, 1948. (Also published as *The Rape of Poland.* New York: Whittlesey House, 1948.)

Miller, L. H., and Pruessen, R. W., eds. *Reflections on the Cold War: A Quarter Century of American Foreign Policy.* Philadelphia: Temple University Press, 1974.

Miller, M. *Plain Speaking: An Oral Biography of Harry S. Truman.* New York: Berkley Publishing Corp., 1974.

——— and Spitzer, A. *We Dropped the A-Bomb.* New York: T. Y. Crowell, 1946.

Miller, W. *Arms and Men.* New York: Putnam, 1956.

———. *Arms and the State.* New York: Twentieth Century Fund, 1958.

Mills, C. W. *The Causes of World War Three.* New York: Simon & Schuster, 1958.

Moore, H. L. *Soviet Far Eastern Policy, 1931–1945.* Princeton: Princeton University Press, 1945.

Morgenthau, H. J. *In Defense of the National Interest.* New York: Knopf, 1951.

Morison, E. E. *Turmoil and Tradition: A Study of the Life and Times of Henry L. Stimson.* Boston: Houghton Mifflin, 1960.

Morison, S. E. *History of United States Naval Operations in World War II.* 15 Vols. Boston: Little, Brown, 1960. Vol. XIV: *Victory in the Pacific*, 1945.

Morray, J. P. *From Yalta to Disarmament: Cold War Debate.* New York: Monthly Review Press, 1961.

Mosley, L. *Dulles: A Biography of Eleanor, Allen, and John Foster Dulles and Their Family Network.* New York: Dial Press, 1978.

———. *Marshall, Hero for Our Times.* New York: Hearst Books, 1982.

Murphy, R. D. *Diplomat Among Warriors.* Garden City, N.Y.: Doubleday, 1964.

National Conference of Catholic Bishops. *The Challenge of Peace: God's Promise and Our Response.* Washington, D.C.: United States Catholic Conference, 1984.

Nettl, J. P. *The Eastern Zone and Soviet Policy in Germany, 1945–50.* London: Oxford University Press, 1951.

Nogee, J. L. *Soviet Policy Towards International Control of Atomic Energy.* Notre Dame, Ind.: University of Notre Dame Press, 1961.

Oppenheimer, J. R. *The Open Mind.* New York: Simon & Schuster, 1955.

———. *Robert Oppenheimer: Letters and Recollections.* Ed. A. K. Smith and C. Weiner. Cambridge, Mass.: Harvard University Press, 1980.

———. *Science and the Common Understanding.* New York: Simon & Schuster, 1954; London, 1954.

Paterson, T. G. *On Every Front: The Making of the Cold War.* New York: Norton, 1979.

———. *Soviet American Confrontation: Postwar Reconstruction and the Origins of the Cold War.* Baltimore: Johns Hopkins University Press, 1973.

BIBLIOGRAPHY OF IMPORTANT SOURCES

———, ed. *Cold War Critics: Alternatives to American Foreign Policy in the Truman Years*. Chicago: Quadrangle Books, 1971.

———, ed. *Containment and the Cold War: American Foreign Policy Since 1945*. Reading, Mass.: Addison-Wesley, 1973.

Patton, G. S. *War As I Knew It*. Boston: Houghton Mifflin, 1947; London: W. H. Allen, 1948.

Penrose, E. F. *Economic Planning for the Peace*. Princeton: Princeton University Press, 1953.

Phillips, C. *The Truman Presidency: The History of a Triumphant Succession*. New York: Macmillan, 1966.

Pickersgill, J. W., and Forster, D. F. *The Mackenzie King Record: 1944–1946*. 2 vols. Toronto: University of Toronto Press, 1968, 1970.

Pogue, F. *George C. Marshall: Organizer of Victory, 1943–1945*. New York: Viking, 1973.

Quester, G. H. *Deterrence Before Hiroshima: The Airpower Background of Modern Strategy*. New York: Wiley, 1966.

———. *Nuclear Diplomacy: The First Twenty-five Years*. New York: Dunellen Co., 1970.

Radosh, R. "Henry A. Wallace and the Open Door." In *Cold War Critics: Alternatives to American Foreign Policy in the Truman Years*, ed. T. G. Paterson. Chicago: Quadrangle Books, 1971.

Ratchford, B. U., and Ross, W. D. *Berlin Reparations Assignment: Round One of the German Peace Settlement*. Chapel Hill: University of North Carolina Press, 1947.

Reitzel, W., Kaplan, M. A., and Coblenz, C. G. *United States Foreign Policy, 1945–55*. Washington, D.C.: Brookings Institution, 1956.

Ridgway, M. B. *Soldier: The Memoirs of Matthew B. Ridgway*. New York: Harper, 1956.

Roberts, H. L. *Rumania: Political Problems of an Agrarian State*. New Haven, Conn.: Yale University Press, 1951.

———. *Russia and America: Dangers and Prospects*. New York: Council on Foreign Relations, 1956.

Rogow, A. A. *James Forrestal: A Study of Personality, Politics, and Policy*. New York: Macmillan, 1963.

Roosevelt, E. *As He Saw It*. New York: Duell, Sloan and Pearce, 1946.

Roosevelt, F. D. *F.D.R.: His Personal Letters, 1928–1945*. 3 vols. Ed. E. Roosevelt. New York: Duell, 1947–1950.

———. *The Public Papers and Addresses of Franklin D. Roosevelt*. Compiled by S. I. Rosenman. New York: Harper, 1950. Vol. XIII: *Victory and the Threshold of Peace*.

Rose, L. A. *After Yalta: America and the Origins of the Cold War*. New York: Scribner, 1973.

———. *Dubious Victory: The United States and the End of World War II*. Kent, Ohio: Kent State University Press, 1973.

Rothstein, A., ed. *Soviet Foreign Policy During the Patriotic War: Documents and Materials*. 3 vols. London: Hutchinson, 1947.

Rozek, E. J. *Allied Wartime Diplomacy: A Pattern in Poland*. New York: Wiley, 1958; London: Chapman, 1958.

Ryan, Cornelius. *The Last Battle.* New York: Simon & Schuster, 1966.

Schell, J. *The Fate of the Earth.* New York: Knopf, 1982.

Schlesinger, A. M., Jr., gen. ed. *The Dynamics of World Power: A Documentary History of United States Foreign Policy, 1945–1973.* New York: Chelsea House, 1973. Vol. II: *Eastern Europe and the Soviet Union,* by W. LaFeber.

Schnabel, J. F., and Watson, R. J. *The History of the Joint Chiefs of Staff: The Joint Chiefs of Staff and National Policy.* Vol. III, pts. 1 and 2. Wilmington, Del.: M. Glazier, 1979.

Schoenberger, W. S. *Decision of Destiny.* Athens: Ohio University Press, 1969.

Seton-Watson, H. *The East European Revolution.* New York: Praeger, 1951.

Sherry, M. S. *Preparing for the Next War: American Plans for Postwar Defense, 1941–1945.* New Haven, Conn.: Yale University Press, 1977.

Sherwin, M. J. *A World Destroyed: The Atomic Bomb and the Grand Alliance.* New York: Knopf, 1975. References are to the Vintage Books edition, 1977.

Sherwood, R. R. *Roosevelt and Hopkins: An Intimate History.* New York: Harper, 1950.

Siracusa, J. M. *New Left Diplomatic Histories and Historians: The American Revisionists.* Port Washington, N.Y.: Kennikat Press, 1973.

———— ed. *The American Diplomatic Revolution: A Documentary History of the Cold War, 1941–1947.* Port Washington, N.Y.: Kennikat Press, 1977.

Sivachev, N. V., and Yakovlev, N. N. *Russia and the United States: U.S.–Soviet Relations from the Soviet Point of View.* Chicago: University of Chicago Press, 1979.

Slusser, R. M., ed. *Soviet Economic Policy in Postwar Germany: A Collection of Papers by Former Soviet Officials.* New York: Research Program on the USSR, 1953.

Smith, A. K. *A Peril and a Hope: The Scientists Movement in America, 1945–1947.* Chicago: University of Chicago Press, 1965.

Smith, B. F., and Agarossi, E. *Operation Sunrise: The Secret Surrender.* New York: Basic Books, 1979.

Smith, P. M. *The Air Force Plans for Peace, 1943–1945.* Baltimore: Johns Hopkins Press, 1970.

Smith, W. B. *My Three Years in Moscow.* Philadelphia: Lippincott, 1950.

Smyth, H. D. *Atomic Energy for Military Purposes: The Official Report on the Development of the Atomic Bomb.* Princeton: Princeton University Press, 1945.

Snow, E. *Journey to the Beginning.* New York: Random House, 1958.

Social Science Research Council. *Public Reactions to the Atomic Bomb and World Affairs: A Nation-Wide Survey of Attitudes and Information.* Ithaca, N.Y.: Cornell University Press, 1947.

Spanier, J. "The Choices We Did Not Have: In Defense of Containment," in *Caging the Bear: Containment and the Cold War.* Ed. C. Gati. Indianapolis: Bobbs-Merrill, 1974.

Spector, R. H. *Eagle Against the Sun: The American War with Japan.* New York: Free Press, 1985.

Stalin, J. *Stalin's Correspondence with Churchill, Attlee, Roosevelt and Truman, 1941–45.* London: Lawrence & Wishart, 1958.

Stern, P. M. *The Oppenheimer Case: Security on Trial.* New York: Harper & Row, 1969.

BIBLIOGRAPHY OF IMPORTANT SOURCES

Stettinius, E. R. *The Diaries of Edward R. Stettinius, Jr., 1943-1946.* Ed. T. M. Campbell and G. C. Herring. New York: New Viewponts, 1975.

———. *Roosevelt and the Russians: The Yalta Conference.* Ed. W. Johnson. Garden City, N.Y.: Doubleday, 1949.

Stillman, E. O., and Pfaff, W. *The New Politics: America and the End of the Postwar World.* New York: Coward McCann, 1961; London: Secker & Warburg, 1962.

Stimson, H. L., and Bundy, McG. *On Active Service in Peace and War.* New York: Harper, 1948.

Strang, W. *Home and Abroad.* London: A. Deutsch, 1956.

Strauss, L. L. *Men and Decisions.* Garden City, N.Y.: Doubleday, 1962.

Szilard, L. *Leo Szilard, His Version of the Facts: Selected Recollections and Correspondence.* 2 vols. Ed. R. Weart and G. Szilard. Cambridge, Mass.: MIT Press, 1978.

Takayuki, I. "The Genesis of the Cold War: Confrontation over Poland, 1941–44." In *The Origins of the Cold War in Asia,* ed. Y. Nagai and A. Iriye. New York: Columbia University Press, 1977.

Teller, E., with Brown, A. *The Legacy of Hiroshima.* Garden City, N.Y.: Doubleday, 1962.

Theoharis, A. *The Yalta Myths: An Issue in U.S. Politics, 1945-1955.* Columbia: University of Missouri Press, 1970.

Thomas, G., and Witts, M. M. *Enola Gay.* New York: Stein and Day, 1977.

Thorne, G. G. *Allies of a Kind: The United States, Britain and the War Against Japan.* New York: Oxford University Press, 1978.

Togo, S. *The Cause of Japan.* New York: Simon & Schuster, 1956.

Toland, J. *The Last 100 Days.* New York: Random House, 1966.

———. *The Rising Sun: The Decline and Fall of the Japanese Empire, 1936-1945.* New York: Random House, 1970.

Toynbee, A. J. *The World and the West.* London: Oxford University Press, 1953.

———. gen. ed. *Survey of International Affairs, 1937-1946.* London: Oxford University Press, 1955, 1956. Vol. VII: *The Far East: 1942-1946,* by F. C. Jones, H. Barton, and B. R. Pearn; Vol. VIII: *Four Power Control in Germany and Austria, 1945-1946,* pt. 1, "Germany," by M. Balfour.

Truman, H. S. *Dear Bess: The Letters from Harry to Bess Truman, 1910-1959.* Ed. R. H. Ferrell. New York: Norton, 1983.

———. *Memoirs.* 2 vols. Garden City, N.Y.: Doubleday, 1955, 1956. Vol. I: *Year of Decisions.* Vol. II: *Years of Trial and Hope.*

———. *Mr. President.* Ed. W. Hillman. New York: Farrar, Straus and Young, 1952.

———. *Off the Record: The Private Papers of Harry S. Truman.* Ed. R. H. Ferrell. New York: Harper & Row, 1980.

———. *Strictly Personal and Confidential: The Letters Harry Truman Never Mailed.* Ed. M. M. Poen. Boston: Little, Brown, 1982.

———. *Truman Speaks.* New York: Columbia University Press, 1960.

Truman, M. *Harry S. Truman.* New York: Morrow, 1972.

Tucker, R. W. *The Radical Left and American Foreign Policy.* Baltimore: Johns Hopkins Press, 1971.

Tuttle, D. W. *Harry L. Hopkins and Anglo-American-Soviet Relations, 1941-1945.* New York: Garland, 1983.

Ulam, A. B. *Expansion and Coexistence: Soviet Foreign Policy, 1917–1973.* New York: Praeger, 1974.

———. "Re-reading the Cold War: Revising the Revisionists." In *The Atomic Bomb: The Critical Issues,* ed. B. J. Bernstein. Boston: Little, Brown, 1976.

———. *The Rivals: America and Russia Since World War II.* New York: Viking, 1971.

———. *Stalin: The Man and His Era.* New York: Viking, 1973.

Ullmann, W. *The United States in Prague, 1945–1948.* Boulder, Col.: East European Quarterly, 1978.

The United States and World War II: A Selected Bibliography. Tokyo: University of Tokyo, 1983.

Vandenberg, A. H., Jr., ed. *The Private Papers of Senator Vandenberg.* Boston: Houghton Mifflin, 1952; London: Gollancz, 1953.

Walker, J. S. "Historians and Cold War Origins: The New Consensus." In *American Foreign Relations: A Historiographical Review,* ed. G. K. Haines and J. S. Walker. Westport, Conn.: Greenwood Press, 1981.

Wallace, H. *The Price of Vision: The Diary of Henry A. Wallace, 1942–1946.* Ed. J. M. Blum. Boston: Houghton Mifflin, 1973.

Walton, R. J. *Henry Wallace, Harry Truman, and the Cold War.* New York: Viking, 1976.

Warburg, J. P. *Germany, Key to Peace.* Cambridge, Mass.: Harvard University Press, 1953; London: Deutsch, 1954.

Ward, P. D. *The Threat of Peace: James F. Byrnes and the Council of Foreign Ministers, 1945–1946.* Kent, Ohio: Kent State University Press, 1979.

Waskow, A. I. *The Limits of Defense.* Garden City, N.Y.: Doubleday, 1962.

Wedemeyer, A. C. *Wedemeyer Reports!* New York: Holt, 1958.

Welch, W. *American Images of Soviet Foreign Policy: An Inquiry into Recent Appraisals from the Academic Community.* New Haven, Conn.: Yale University Press, 1970.

Wheeler-Bennett, J. W. *John Anderson, Viscount Waverly.* New York: St. Martin's, 1962; London: Macmillan, 1962.

Williams, W. A. *American-Russian Relations, 1781–1947.* New York: Rinehart, 1952.

———. *Empire as a Way of Life: An Essay on the Causes and Character of America's Present Predicament.* New York: Oxford University Press, 1980.

———. *The Roots of the Modern American Empire.* New York: Random House, 1969.

———. *The Tragedy of American Diplomacy.* New York: Dell, 1962.

Willoughby, C. A., and Chamberlain, J. *MacArthur: 1941–1951.* New York: McGraw-Hill, 1954.

Wilmot, C. *The Struggle for Europe.* London: Collins, 1952.

Wilson, H. M. *Eight Years Overseas, 1939–1947.* London: Hutchinson, 1950; New York: Ryerson Press, 1950.

Wolff, R. L. *The Balkans in Our Time.* Cambridge, Mass.: Harvard University Press, 1956.

Woodward, L. *British Foreign Policy in the Second World War: History of the Second World War.* London: Her Majesty's Stationary Office, 1962.

BIBLIOGRAPHY OF IMPORTANT SOURCES

Wyden, Peter. *Day One: Before Hiroshima and After.* New York: Simon & Schuster, 1984.

Yergin, D. *Shattered Peace: The Origins of the Cold War and the National Security State.* Boston: Houghton Mifflin, 1977.

Zacharias, E. M. *Secret Missions: The Story of an Intelligence Officer.* New York: Putnam, 1946.

Zhukov, G. K. *The Memoirs of Marshall Zhukov.* London: Cape; New York: Delacorte Press, 1971.

ARTICLES AND PERIODICALS

Alperovitz, G. "Response." *Journal of American History,* March 1973.

Alsop, J., and Joravsky, D. "Was the Hiroshima Bomb Necessary? An Exchange." *The New York Review of Books,* 23 October 1980.

"The Atom and World Politics." University of Chicago *Roundtable,* 30 September 1945.

Attlee, C. "The Hiroshima Choice." *The Observer,* 6 September 1959.

Bard, R. A. "War Was Really Won Before We Used A-Bomb." *U.S. News and World Report,* 15 August 1960.

Bernstein, B. J. "The Atomic Bomb and American Foreign Policy, 1941–1945: An Historiographical Controversy." *Peace & Change,* Spring 1974.

———. "Cold War Orthodoxy Restated." *Reviews in American History,* December 1973.

———. "The Dropping of the A-Bomb." *The Center Magazine,* March/April 1983.

———. "Hiroshima Reconsidered—Thirty Years Later." *Foreign Service Journal,* August 1975.

———. "The Perils and Politics of Surrender: Ending the War with Japan and Avoiding the Third Atomic Bomb." *Pacific Historical Review,* February 1977.

———. "The Quest for American Security: American Foreign Policy and International Control of Atomic Energy, 1942–1946." *Journal of American History,* March 1974.

———. "Roosevelt, Truman, and the Atomic Bomb, 1941–1945: A Reinterpretation." *Political Science Quarterly,* Spring 1975.

———. "Unraveling a Mystery: American POW's Killed at Hiroshima." *Foreign Service Journal,* October 1979.

Bernstein, L. "Truman and the Bomb." *The New York Times,* 13 May 1984.

Black, C. E. "Soviet Policy in Eastern Europe." *Annals of the American Academy,* May 1949.

———. "The Start of the Cold War in Bulgaria." *The Review of Politics,* April 1979.

Boller, P. F., Jr. "Hiroshima and the American Left: August 1945." *International Social Science Review,* Winter 1982.

Boyle, P. G. "The British Foreign Office View of Soviet-American Relations, 1945–1946." *Diplomatic History,* Summer 1979.

Braker, Milton. "Chennault Holds Soviet Forced End." *The New York Times,* 15 August 1945.

Brodie, B. "The Atom Bomb as Policy Maker." *Foreign Affairs,* October 1948.

Brogan, D. W. "The Illusion of American Omnipotence." *Harper's,* December 1952.

Buck, P. S. "The Bomb—Did We Have to Drop It?" *American Weekly,* 8, 15, 22 March 1959.

Bundy, H. H. "Remembered Words." *The Atlantic,* March 1957.

Byrnes, J. F. "Actions Speak Louder Than Words." *Vital Speeches,* 1 April 1948.

Cary, O. "The Sparing of Kyoto—Mr. Stimson's Pet City." *Japan Quarterly,* October/December 1975.

Compton, A. H. "Hiroshima Revisited." *Science,* 1961.

Condon, E. Letter in *Science,* 4 December 1959.

Cousins, N., and Finletter, T. K. "A Beginning for Sanity." *Saturday Review of Literature,* 15 June 1946.

Dallek, R. "The Jimmy Byrnes Story." *Reviews in American History,* March 1983.

"Did Atom Bomb Help End War? Generals Differ." *New York Herald Tribune,* 21 September 1945.

"Did 'Big 3' Give Russia Too Much?" *U.S. News & World Report,* 10 September 1948.

Dulles, J. F. "Thoughts on Soviet Foreign Policy and What to Do About It.' *Life,* 3, 10 June 1946.

Eriksohn, K. "A Final Accounting of the Death and Destruction." *The New York Times Book Review,* 9 August 1981.

Feis, H. "Diplomacy of the Dollar—1947." *The Atlantic,* January 1947.

———. Letter in *Science,* 4 December 1959.

Ferrell, R. H. "Truman at Potsdam." *American Heritage,* June/July 1980.

Finney, N. S. "How FDR Planned to Use the A-Bomb." *Look,* 14 March 1950.

Franck, J. "A Report to the Secretary of War." *Bulletin of the Atomic Scientists,* May 1946.

Gaddis, J. L. "Containment: A Reassessment." *Foreign Affairs,* July 1977.

Garrett, S. A. "Images and Foreign Policy: The United States, Eastern Europe, and the Beginnings of the Cold War." *World Affairs,* Spring 1976.

Gimbel, J. "On the Implementation of the Potsdam Agreement: An Essay on U.S. Postwar Germany Policy." *Political Science Quarterly,* June 1972.

Glazier, K. M., Jr. "The Decision to Use Atomic Weapons Against Hiroshima and Nagasaki." *Public Policy,* Summer 1970.

Gormly, J. L. "Secretary of State Byrnes: An Initial British Evaluation." *South Carolina Historical Magazine,* July 1978.

Groom, A. J. R. "U.S.–Allied Relations and the Atomic Bomb in the Second World War." *World Politics,* October 1962.

Groves, L. R. "The Atom General Answers His Critics." *The Saturday Evening Post,* 19 June 1948.

———. Letter to the Editor, *Science,* 4 December 1959.

Gruber, C. S. "Manhattan Project Maverick: The Case of Leo Szilard." *Prologue: Journal of the National Archives,* Summer 1983.

Hammond, T. T. " 'Atomic Diplomacy' Revisited." *Orbis,* Winter 1976.

Harbutt, F. "American Challenge, Soviet Response: The Beginning of the Cold War, February–May 1946." *Political Science Quarterly,* 1981–82.

Harris, R. R. "The 'Magic' Leak of 1941 and Japanese-American Relations." *Pacific Historical Review,* February 1981.

BIBLIOGRAPHY OF IMPORTANT SOURCES

Haskins, C. P. "Atomic Energy and American Foreign Policy." *Foreign Affairs*, July 1946.

Herken, G. F. " 'A Most Deadly Illusion': The Atomic Secret and American Nuclear Weapons Policy, 1945–1950." *Pacific Historical Review*, February 1980.

"If It Didn't Work?" *Newsweek*, 17 April 1961.

Igarashi, T. "MacArthur's Proposal for an Early Peace with Japan and the Redirection of Occupation Policy Toward Japan." *The Japanese Journal of American Studies*, 1981.

"Ike on Ike." *Newsweek*, 11 November 1963.

Iokibe, M. "American Policy Towards Japan's 'Unconditional Surrender.' " *The Japanese Journal of American Studies*, 1981.

Jaffe, S. "Why the Bomb Didn't Hit Home." *Nuclear Times*, March 1983.

Kawai, K. "Mokusatsu: Japan's Response to the Potsdam Declaration." *Pacific Historical Review*, November 1950.

Kimball, W. F. "The Cold War Warmed Over." *American Historical Review*, October 1974.

Knebel, F., and Baily, C. W. "Secret Revealed After 18 Years: The Fight over the A-Bomb." *Look*, 13 August 1963.

Kramish, A. "Reviews of I. N. Golovin's *I. V. Kurchatov*." *Science*, 25 August 1967.

Krueger, T. A. "New Left Revisionists and Their Critics." *Reviews in American History*, December 1973.

Lapp, R. E. "The Einstein Letter That Started It All," *The New York Times Magazine*, 2 August 1964.

Laurence, W. L. "Atom Bomb Designers Bet in '45 It Would Fizzle." *The New York Times*, 29 July 1951.

———. "Would You Make the Bomb Again?" *The New York Times Magazine*, 1 August 1965.

Luft, J., and Wheeler, W. M. "Reaction to John Hersey's 'Hiroshima.' " *Journal of Social Psychology*, August 1948.

Maddox, R. J. "Atomic Diplomacy: A Study in Creative Writing and Communications." *The Journal of American History*, March 1973.

Mark, E. M. "Allied Relations in Iran, 1941–1947: The Origins of a Cold War Crisis." *Wisconsin Magazine of History*, Autumn 1975.

———. "American Policy Toward Eastern Europe and the Origins of the Cold War, 1941–1946: An Alternative Interpretation." *The Journal of American History*, September 1981.

———. "Charles E. Bohlen and the Acceptable Limits of Soviet Hegemony in Eastern Europe: A Memorandum of 18 October 1945." *Diplomatic History*, Spring 1979.

———. "The Question of Containment: A Reply to John Lewis Gaddis." *Foreign Affairs*, January 1978.

McFarland, S. I. "A Peripheral View of the Origins of the Cold War: The Crises in Iran, 1941–1947." *Diplomatic History*, Fall 1980.

Messer, R. L. "Paths Not Taken: The United States Department of State and Alternatives to Containment, 1945–1946." *Diplomatic History*, Fall 1977.

Miscamble, W. D. "Anthony Eden and the Truman-Molotov Conversations, April 1945." *Diplomatic History*, Spring 1978.

Morgenthau, H. J. "The End of an Illusion." *Commentary*, November 1961.
Morison, S. E. "Why Japan Surrendered." *The Atlantic*, October 1960.
Mosely, P. E. "Dismemberment of Germany: The Allied Negotiations from Yalta to Potsdam." *Foreign Affairs*, April 1950.
———. "The Occupation of Germany: New Light on How the Zones Were Drawn." *Foreign Affairs*, July 1950.
———. "Soviet-American Relations Since the War." *Annals of The American Academy*, May 1949.
Oppenheimer, J. R. "The Atomic Bomb as a Great Force for Peace." *The New York Times Magazine*, 9 June 1946.
———. Letter in *Science*, 4 December 1959.
———. "Niels Bohr and Atomic Weapons." *The New York Review of Books*, 17 December 1964.
Partin, J. W. "Roosevelt, Byrnes, and the 1944 Vice-Presidential Nomination." *Historian*, November 1979.
Paterson, D. S. "Recent Literature on Cold War Origins: An Essay Review." *Wisconsin Magazine of History*, Summer 1972.
Paterson, T. G. "The Abortive American Loan to Russia and the Origins of the Cold War, 1943–1946." *Journal of American History*, June 1969.
———. "Potsdam, The Atomic Bomb, and the Cold War: A Discussion with James F. Byrnes." *Pacific Historical Review*, May 1972.
———. "Presidential Foreign Policy, Public Opinion, and Congress: The Truman Years." *Diplomatic History*, Winter 1979.
Poole, W. S. "From Conciliation to Containment: The Joint Chiefs of Staff and the Coming of the Cold War, 1945–1946." *Military Affairs*, February 1978.
Quester, G. H. "Origins of the Cold War: Some Clues from Public Opinion." *Political Science Quarterly*, Winter 1978–1979.
Rabinowitch, Eugene. "James Franck and Leo Szilard." *Bulletin of the Atomic Scientists*, October 1964.
Resis, A. "The Churchill-Stalin Secret 'Percentages' Agreement on the Balkans, Moscow, October, 1944." *American Historical Review*, April 1978.
Richardson, J. L. "Cold War Revisionism: A Critique." *World Politics*, July 1972.
Schlesinger, A., Jr. "Origins of the Cold War." *Foreign Affairs*, October 1967.
Schoenfeld, H. F. A. "Soviet Imperialism in Hungary." *Foreign Affairs*, April 1948.
Sherwin, M. J. "The Atomic Bomb and the Origins of the Cold War: U.S. Atomic-Energy Policy and Diplomacy, 1941–45." *The American Historical Review*, October 1973.
Sigal, L. V. "Bureaucratic Politics and Tactical Use of Committees: The Interim Committee and the Decision to Drop the Atomic Bomb." *Polity*, Spring 1978.
Siracusa, J. M. "The Meaning of Tolstoy: Churchill, Stalin, and the Balkans, Moscow, October, 1944," *Diplomatic History*, Fall 1979.
Smith, A. K. "Behind the Decision to Use the Atomic Bomb, Chicago 1944–1945." *Bulletin of the Atomic Scientists*, October 1958.
———. "The Elusive Dr. Szilard." *Harper's*, July 1960.
Smith, D. M. "The New Left and the Cold War." *Denver Quarterly*, Winter 1970.
Snowman, D. "President Truman's Decision to Drop the First Atomic Bomb." *Political Science*, October, 1966.

BIBLIOGRAPHY OF IMPORTANT SOURCES

Steel, R. "Did Anyone Start the Cold War?" *The New York Review of Books,* 2 September 1971.

Stimson, H. L. "The Bomb and the Opportunity." *Harper's,* March 1946.

———. "The Decision to Use the Atomic Bomb." *Harper's,* February 1947.

Strauss, L. L. "I Proposed Bombing an Uninhabited Area." *U.S. News & World Report,* 15 August 1960.

" 'Superforts' Stage 6—Target Wind-Up." *The New Yor*ᵏ *ᴵ imes,* 15 August 1945.

Sutherland, J. P. "The Story General Marshall Tᶜ'ᴵ ᴵe." *U.S. News & World Report,* 2 November 1959.

Szilard, L. "Atomic Bombs and the Postwar Positioₙ of the United States in the World—1945." *Bulletin of the Atomic Scientists,* December 1947.

———. "A Personal History of the Atomic Bomb." University of Chicago *Roundtable,* 25 September 1949.

———. "Reminiscences." *Perspectives in American History,* vol. 2, 1968.

———. "Truman Did Not Understand." *U.S. News & World Report,* 15 August 1960.

Takemi, T. "Remembrances of the War and the Bomb." *The Journal of the American Medical Association,* 5 August 1983.

Teller, E. "Bombing of Hiroshima Was a Mistake." *U.S. News & World Report,* 15 August 1960.

Theoharis, A. "Atomic Diplomacy." *New University Thought,* May/June 1967.

———. "James F. Byrnes: Unwitting Yalta Myth-Maker." *Political Science Quarterly,* December 1966.

———. "Roosevelt and Truman on Yalta: The Origins of the Cold War." *Political Science Quarterly,* June 1972.

Truman, H. S. Letter in *The Atlantic,* February 1947.

Villa, B. L. "The U.S. Army, Unconditional Surrender, and the Potsdam Proclamation." *The Journal of American History,* June 1976.

"Was A-Bomb on Japan a Mistake?" *U.S. News & World Report,* 15 August 1960.

Williams, W. A. "The Cold War Revisionists." *Nation,* 13 November 1967.

Wither, L. S. "When CIA Hearts Were Young and Gay: Planning the Cold War (Spring 1945)." *Peace and Change,* Fall 1978.

Yavenditti, M. J. "John Hersey and the American Conscience: The Reception of 'Hiroshima.' " *Pacific Historical Review,* February 1974.

UNPUBLISHED MATERIAL

C.C.S. 643/3. Estimate of the Enemy Situation (as of 6 July 1945). C.C.S. 381 (6-4-43) Sect. 2, pt. 5, records of the U.S. Joint Chiefs of Staff. Record Group 218. U.S. Archives, Washington, D.C.

Davies, J. E. Diary (1945), Library of Congress, Washington, D.C.

Donovan, W. J. Memo for the President from Donovan, 21, 31 May 1945. Harry S. Truman Papers, Chron. file April/May 1945. Truman Library, Independence, Missouri.

Grew, J. C. Papers, Houghton Library, Harvard University, Cambridge, Massachusetts.

Hammond, P. Y. "Directives for the Occupation of Germany: The Washington Story." Twentieth Century Fund Study of Civil-Military Relations. Typewritten.

Herken, G. F. "American Diplomacy and the Atomic Bomb, 1945–1947." Ph.D. dissertation, Princeton University, 1974.

Hinckey, M. H. "The Frustration of the New Deal Revival, 1944–1946." Ph.D. dissertation, University of Missouri, 1965.

Leahy, W. D. Diary (1945), Library of Congress, Washington, D.C.

MacIssaac, D. "The United States Strategic Bombing Survey, 1944–1947." Ph.D. dissertation, Duke University, 1970.

"Magic Diplomatic Extracts." S.R.H.–040, July 1945. Records of the National Security Agency, Record Group 457. U.S. Archives, Washington, D.C.

Messer, R. L. "The Making of a Cold Warrior: James F. Byrnes and American-Soviet Relations, 1945–1946." Ph.D. dissertation, University of California, Berkeley, 1975.

Morgan, H. G. "Planning the Defeat of Japan: A Study of Total War Strategy." Office of the Chief of Military History, Department of the Army. Mimeographed.

Parten, J. R. Interviews, 26 December 1984, 5 January 1985.

Partin, J. W. " 'Assistant President' for the Home Front: James F. Byrnes and World War II." Ph.D. dissertation, University of Florida, 1977.

Preston, E. R. "Prelude to Cold War: American Reactions to the Growth of Soviet Power." Ph.D. dissertation, University of Virginia, 1979.

Sharp, E. F. "The Cold War Revisionists and Their Critics: An Appraisal." Ph.D. dissertation, University of North Carolina, 1974.

Sherwin, M. J. "The Atomic Bomb, Scientists and American Diplomacy During the Second World War." Ph.D. dissertation, University of California, Los Angeles, 1971.

Stimson, H. L. Diary, Yale University Library, New Haven, Connecticut.

Truman, H. S. Papers, Truman Library, Independence, Missouri.

Notes

INTRODUCTION TO THE 1985 EDITION
(*pp. 1–60*)

1. P. M. S. Blackett, William Appelman Williams, D. F. Fleming, and others had, of course, pointed to the role of diplomatic considerations in connection with the bombing of Hiroshima. Their important work, however, did not take up in detail the diplomatic-strategic debate within the U.S. government between Yalta and Potsdam. For a review of studies dealing primarily with the role of diplomatic considerations in the bombing itself, see Bernstein, "The Atomic Bomb and American Foreign Policy, 1941–1945," pp. 1–16.
2. Snow, *Journey to the Beginning*, pp. 360–61.
3. Sherwin, "The Atomic Bomb and the Origins of the Cold War," p. 963n.
4. See also Kimball, "The Cold War Warmed Over."
5. Feis, *Japan Subdued*, p. 181.
6. Feis, *The Atomic Bomb and the End of World War II*, p. 194.
7. See, for instance, Bernstein, *The Atomic Bomb: The Critical Issues;* Sherwin, *A World Destroyed;* Herken, *The Winning Weapon;* Messer, *The End of an Alliance.*
8. Messer, *The End of an Alliance*, p. 88.
9. See, for instance, Yergin, *Shattered Peace*, p. 132; see also Sherwin, *A World Destroyed;* Messer, *The End of an Alliance;* Herken, *The Winning Weapon;* and Bernstein, "Roosevelt, Truman and the Atomic Bomb." The argument is sometimes accepted with, sometimes without, direct citation. For instance, Messer's *The End of an Alliance*, from which the 1982 quotation in the text on the consensus that had been reached was taken, contains one or two critical remarks about *Atomic Diplomacy.* However, the unpublished doctoral dissertation at the Library of Congress upon which it is based includes the statement that although the author disagrees with aspects of my interpretation of Byrnes's thinking, the "fundamental argument of the bomb's influence on United States diplomacy at Potsdam put forth by Gar Alperovitz in *Atomic Diplomacy* . . . is persuasively supported by contemporary evidence. . . ." Messer, "The Making of a Cold Warrior" (Ph.D. dissertation), p. 491.
10. Truman, *Year of Decisions*, p. 87. There is dispute as to whether Byrnes is talking about the war against Japan or the Russians or both. In light of everything else we know about Byrnes, it seems likely he has the Russians in mind, though he may refer to both. See below, pp. 42–47.
11. Stimson Diary, May 15, 1945.
12. Stimson Diary, May 14, 1945. See below, p. 49, for a more complete extract from this entry.
13. Davies diary, May 21, 1945.
14. Daniels, *The Man of Independence*, p. 266. It is again not clear whether Truman is talking about Russia or Japan or both, but Truman's listeners believed Russia was at the very least one of the nations to whom he was referring.
15. Stimson Diary, July 22, 1945; Bryant, *Triumph in the West, 1943–46*, pp. 363–64. See also below, pp. 199, 201–2.
16. Ferrell, *Off the Record*, p. 53.
17. Byrnes, *Speaking Frankly*, p. 104; Stimson diary, Sept. 4, 1945.
18. For a typical misreading along these lines, see Hammond, " 'Atomic Diplomacy' Revisited," pp. 1403–28. Hammond also illustrates the bias of one line of particularly vitriolic criticism. After taking me to task for numerous alleged errors, he cites approvingly one of the studies even critical historians find least credible (by Robert Maddox in *The Journal of American History*, March 1973) but neglects to inform readers of my response in the same journal. For others who have misconstrued my position on the question of threats, and for additional specific comments on Hammond, see note 140.

19. Byrnes, for instance, left office complaining that the Russians "don't scare." (Forrestal, *Diaries*, p. 262.) See also Herken, *The Winning Weapon*, for general insights into this question.

20. See below, p. 278; see also Messer, *The End of an Alliance*, for a comprehensive account, and for numerous insights into Byrnes's awareness that he was attempting to reverse agreements reached previously by Roosevelt. Arthur Schlesinger, Jr., and others have uncritically taken Harriman's mid-April statement to Truman that he was glad the President was continuing Roosevelt's policies at face value in connection with the Polish crisis. (Schlesinger, "Origins of the Cold War," p. 24*fn.*) Leahy, Stimson, Byrnes, Davies, and others recognized that Truman's tough position was a major reversal here, as were the decisions to try subsequently to reverse the situation in the Balkans, and the specific changes in policy toward Manchuria and the then highly important German reparations issues. (For further information on these matters, see below, pp. 71, 76, 76*fn.*, 83–88, 139–74, 185, 205–24, 231–35, and 278; see also Messer, *The End of an Alliance*, p. 79; and Davies Diary, April 30, May 13, May 21, 1945.) Note, however, contrary to Schlesinger, *Atomic Diplomacy* makes it very clear that Harriman and others felt what they were doing was the best way to achieve cooperation, *as they conceived it.* See below, p. 71. As to Truman's willingness to continue Roosevelt's policies in other areas, see below, pp. 93 and p. 93*fn.* Related to this is the question of the U.S. decision to cut off Lend-Lease. *Atomic Diplomacy* was quite careful in stating that the decision to cut off aid *abruptly* was regarded by Truman and others as an error. Nevertheless, the *policy decision* was part of the "immediate showdown" strategy to bring pressure on the Russians at the time of the Polish dispute (see below, pp. 83–88, and especially the footnote on page 84). Recent research on this subject has confirmed that the Lend-Lease cut-off (despite its overzealous execution) was indeed part of an attempt to put pressure on the Russians. See Herring, *Aid to Russia 1941–46*, pp. 199–211. Though Herring criticizes revisionist accounts for not adequately considering domestic political factors, his research in no way contradicts the basic point, and, indeed, adds new documentation to *Atomic Diplomacy*'s argument that policy makers saw the cut-off as a way to bring pressure on the Soviets during the Polish crisis.

21. Bernstein, "Roosevelt, Truman and the Atomic Bomb," pp. 24, 42, 60, 48.

22. See below, p. 64.

23. Sherwin, "The Atomic Bomb and the Origins of the Cold War," pp. 966, 965. Though it is impossible to know precisely how significant *Atomic Diplomacy* was in stimulating the new thinking, a number of authors (even those critical of the book on other issues) have acknowledged its role in bringing about a revision of the previous, standard analyses. See Bernstein, "The Atomic Bomb and American Foreign Policy, 1941–1945," p. 9: "In what was to become one of the most influential books of Cold War revisionism . . . ," etc.

24. Truman, *Truman Speaks*, p. 67.

25. The U.S. Strategic Bombing Survey. *Japan's Struggle to End the War*, July 1, 1946, p. 13.

26. Department of Defense, "Entry of the Soviet Union into the War against Japan," p. 80.

27. Brooks, *Behind Japan's Surrender*, p. 134.

28. Department of Defense, "Entry of the Soviet Union into the War against Japan," p. 64.

29. *Ibid.*, p. 77. On June 29 the following item appeared on the agenda of the Joint Chiefs of Staff: "Prepare for sudden collapse of Japan." Leahy, *I Was There*, p. 385.

30. Butler, *Grand Strategy*, pp. 284–85.

31. Forrestal, *Diaries*, p. 74.

32. Dulles, *The Secret Surrender*, pp. 255–56. For a fuller account, see Toland, *The Rising Sun*, pp. 742–44, 755, 756, 758–60, 769–70. See also Butow, *Japan's Decision to Surrender*, pp. 103–11. See also Brown, *The Last Hero*, pp. 771–75.

33. Memos for the President from Donovan, May 12, 31, 1945. Truman Papers, Chron. file April–May 1945.

34. U.S. Dept. of State, *Conference of Berlin*, II, p. 460.

35. SRH-040. " 'Magic' Diplomatic Extracts," July 1945. Records of the National Security Agency, record group 457, see p. 071, "Item 3 not releasable"

(pp. -5- and -6-); still classified, January 1985. (Partial release of portions of document, April 1985, on F.O.I.A. request. Remainder still classified.) U.S. National Archives, Washington, D.C.

36. *Mandate for Change*, pp. 312–13; "Ike on Ike," p. 107; see also *Crusade in Europe*, pp. 443. John Eisenhower also reports on his father's conversation with Stimson in *Strictly Personal*, p. 97.

37. Bradley, *A General's Life*, p. 444. The argument that the assumption the bomb would be used was never challenged (see for instance Bernstein, "The Dropping of the A-Bomb," p. 8) ignores this evidence and minimizes other similar evidence. See notes 36, 38, 39, 40, 50, and 54.

38. Forrestal, *Diaries*, p. 79.

39. Leahy, *I Was There*, pp. 439–42.

40. *Ibid.*, p. 385.

41. Quoted in Boller, "Hiroshima and the American Left: August 1945," pp. 21–22.

42. Bradley, *A General's Life*, p. 444.

43. Leahy, *I Was There*, pp. 2, 438, 100–101; Messer, *The End of an Alliance*, p. 113.

44. Leahy Diary, June 18, 1945.

45. For the military judgments cited above (and others), see King and Whitehall, *Fleet Admiral King*, p. 621; Ismay, *Memoirs*, p. 401; Sutherland, "The Story General Marshall Told Me," p. 52; Bush, *Modern Arms and Free Men*, p. 101; "Did Atom Bomb Help End War? Generals Differ"; Braker, "Chennault Holds Soviet Forced End"; Morton, "The Decision to Use the Atomic Bomb," in Greenfield, ed., *Command Decisions*, pp. 393–410; Blackett, *Military and Political Consequences of Atomic Energy*, pp. 116–30; Baldwin, *Great Mistakes of the War*, pp. 88–108. See also references in next note.

46. Cline, *Washington Command Post*, p. 346; Craven and Cate, *Army Air Forces in World War II*, Vol. V, pp. 711, 741; Giovannitti and Freed, *The Decision to Drop the Bomb*, pp. 35–36, 244, 308–9; Knebel and Bailey, *No High Ground*, p. 111.

47. Churchill, *Triumph and Tragedy*, p. 646.

48. Leahy, *I Was There*, p. 385.

49. Eisenhower, *Mandate for Change*, p. 313.

50. For information on Bard, see: Wyden, *Day One*, pp. 158, 174–75, 228n; Hewlett and Anderson, *The New World*, p.

370; Strauss, *Men and Decisions*, pp. 192, 270; Giovannitti and Freed, *The Decision to Drop the Bomb*, pp. 144–46; Sherwin, *A World Destroyed*, pp. 215–17, 307–8; Bard, "War Was Really Won Before We Used A-Bomb," pp. 73–75; Smith, *A Peril and a Hope*, p. 52.

51. Giovannitti and Freed, *The Decision to Drop the Bomb*, p. 145; Strauss, *Men and Decisions*, pp. 193, 270.

52. Wyden, *Day One*, p. 159fn.

53. *Ibid.*, p. 159; Messer, *The End of an Alliance*, p.87. Also see above, pp.42–44.

54. In the Hyde Park agreement of 1944, this language is used: "when a 'bomb' is finally available, it *might perhaps*, after mature consideration, be used against the Japanese. . . ." (Emphasis added.) Here also are some of the doubts expressed by Roosevelt as Bush recorded them a few days after the agreement:

> "The President raised the question of whether . . . [the bomb] should actually be used against the Japanese or whether it should be used only as a threat with full-scale experimentation [noncombat demonstration?] in this country."

In the Hyde Park agreement, and in the above conversation recorded by Vannevar Bush, and in a further discussion with Dr. Alexander Sachs in December 1944, Roosevelt apparently was also thinking about a warning as well as a demonstration. According to Sachs, Roosevelt agreed that a warning should be given before using the bomb against the enemy area, from which humans and animals would be evacuated. Some scholars have raised questions about Sachs's report, but the Hyde Park agreement does also include general language concerning a warning. See pp. 32–33 in Bernstein, "Roosevelt, Truman and the Atomic Bomb." See also below, note 136.

55. Smith, "Behind the Decision to Use the Atomic Bomb," p. 297; Feis. *Japan Subdued*, pp. 44–45.

56. Forrestal, *Diaries*, p. 20.

57. Churchill, *Triumph and Tragedy*, pp. 154, 215.

58. Department of Defense, "Entry of the Soviet Union into the War against Japan," p. 70.

59. Cline, *Washington Command Post*, p. 344.

60. Department of Defense, "Entry of the Soviet Union into the War against Ja-

pan," p. 79. Barton Bernstein and others have attempted to downplay this and related evidence. However, Truman's diary (see above, pp. 24–25 and also pp. 32–33) clearly shows he fully understood the significance of a Soviet declaration of war. See Bernstein, "Roosevelt, Truman, and the Atomic Bomb," pp. 43, 47, 47n. Bernstein also claims (pp. 47, 55) that *Atomic Diplomacy* argues that Truman deviously tried to avoid a surrender *in order to be able to use the atomic bomb.* Elsewhere (p. 53) he says that I "imply" this. Both characterizations constitute very serious misreadings and distortions of my published views.

61. Ferrell, *Off the Record*, p. 47.
62. Department of Defense, "Entry of the Soviet Union into the War against Japan," p. 84.
63. Ferrell, *Off the Record*, p. 53. Also see below, p. 34. On the timing of the reports, see Hewlett and Anderson, *The New World*, pp. 385–90; Wyden, *Day One*, pp. 222–24. Neither Truman nor Byrnes reacted strongly to the first reports so far as we can tell; only after the full report arrived by plane on July 21 did they seem to feel the full impact of the new weapon.

Note that Bernstein ("The Dropping of the A-Bomb," p. 14) ignores this evidence of Truman's personal understanding of the importance of a Soviet declaration of war. Bernstein's earlier writings, of course, also downplay the Soviet declaration, but they were written before the Truman diary became available.
64. See below, pp. 229–30, 233–34.
65. Butler, *Grand Strategy*, p. 292; U.S. Dept. of State, *Conference of Berlin*, II, p. 276.
66. Forrestal, *Diaries*, p. 78.
67. Ferrell, *Off the Record*, p. 53.
68. Byrnes, *All in One Lifetime*, p. 291. See also below, pp. 229–35, for more on this subject.
69. Byrnes, *All in One Lifetime*, pp. 305–7.
70. Stimson Diary, Aug. 10, 1945; Forrestal, *Diaries*, pp. 82–83.
71. Byrnes, *All in One Lifetime*, p. 305; Truman, *Year of Decisions*, p. 423; Leahy, *I Was There*, pp. 434–36; Craven and Cate, *Army Air Forces in World War II*, V, pp. 699, 732–33; " 'Superforts' Stage 6—Target Wind-Up." .

72. Butow, *Japan's Decision to Surrender*, p. 130.
73. C.C.S. 643/3. *Estimate of the Enemy Situation (as of 6 July 1945)*, C.C.S. 381 (6-4-43) sect. 2, pt. 5, Records of the U.S. Joint Chiefs of Staff. Record Group 218, p. 10.
74. *Ibid.*, p. 11.
75. *Ibid.*, pp. 40–41.
76. *Ibid.*, pp. 40–42.
77. Grew, *Turbulent Era*, II., pp. 1423, 1434; but see also 1421–38.
78. Forrestal, *Diaries*, p. 69.
79. Department of Defense, "Entry of the Soviet Union into the War against Japan," p. 84.
80. Leahy, *I Was There*, p. 385.
81. Churchill, *Triumph and Tragedy*, p. 642; Butler, *Grand Strategy*, p. 303.
82. U.S. Dept. of State, *Conference of Berlin*, II, p. 1272n.
83. See, for instance, Hewlett and Anderson, *The New World*, pp. 384, 392. Political considerations may possibly have played some tactical role in this matter, especially after the atomic bombs were used. In attempting to argue that such considerations were of primary (rather than secondary) importance, Barton Bernstein ("The Perils and Politics of Surrender") plays down the abundant evidence that Truman himself did not regard a change in the unconditional surrender formula as a fundamental issue, politically or morally. He also minimizes the fact that the *context* of decision making was one of overwhelming haste—and that this itself *in late July and August was a product of concern about the advance of the Soviet Union into Manchuria.*
84. Grew, *Turbulent Era*, II, p. 1406.
85. Leahy, *I Was There*, p. 419.
86. Butler, *Grand Strategy*, p. 291.
87. Ferrell, *Off the Record*, pp. 53–54. This entry also refutes the thesis of historians like Barton Bernstein that Truman did not believe the bomb would produce a speedy surrender. See Bernstein, "Roosevelt, Truman, and the Atomic Bomb," p. 52. Bernstein also ignores this evidence of the President's personal belief in work published after the Truman diaries became available. See his "The Dropping of the A-Bomb," pp. 13 and 14.
88. Forrestal, *Diaries*, pp. 78–79.
89. Leahy Diary, May 20, 1945, p. 86.

90. *Ibid.*, June 4, 1945, p. 92.
91. See Messer, "The Making of a Cold Warrior" (Ph.D. dissertation), for a discussion of this problem in general.
92. Hewlett and Anderson, *The New World*, p. 343; Sherwin, *A World Destroyed*, p. 293.
93. Sherwin, *A World Destroyed*, p. 293.
94. *Ibid.*, pp. 293–94; Truman, *Year of Decisions*, p. 87.
95. Hewlett and Anderson, *The New World*, p. 352.
96. *Ibid.*, p. 364.
97. Davies Diary, May 21, 1945.
98. Interviews with J. R. Parten, December 26, 1984; January 5, 1985.
99. See, for instance, Clements, ed., *James F. Byrnes and the Origins of the Cold War*. See also Herken, *The Winning Weapon*, and Partin, " 'Assistant President' for the Home Front" (Ph.D. dissertation).
100. Ferrell, *Off the Record*, p. 49. Messer, *The End of an Alliance*, p. 70. Messer writes of Byrnes's "almost pathological obsession with concealing his thoughts from public and even possible historic exposure . . ."; he describes Byrnes in "The Making of a Cold Warrior" as a "man whose life-long political philosophy was fundamentally one of opportunism—an opportunism directed above all at political survival and fed by an ambition to succeed, or at least to seem to succeed . . . ," pp. 15, 18–19.
101. The information cited is taken from Messer, "The Making of a Cold Warrior," pp. 12, 13, 5, 6, 10, 11.
102. The information cited follows Messer, "The Making of a Cold Warrior," pp. 1–19; see also Herken, *The Winning Weapon*, p. 47. Many of Byrnes's distortions of the record seem to have been designed to show him as a tough anti-Communist public official and to corroborate the view of his time in office that he presented in his own autobiographies. We simply do not know the limits of these distortions; that they almost certainly applied to his role in connection with potentially embarrassing aspects of the atomic bomb decision is highly likely, given what we know about his political practices. On the secrecy Byrnes maintained in connection with his work on the atomic bomb and his relationship to Truman

during April, May, and June 1945, see Messer, "The Making of a Cold Warrior," p. 483 note 38.
103. Messer, "The Making of a Cold Warrior," p. 483 note 38.
104. The information in this paragraph follows closely Messer, *The End of an Alliance*, Chapter IV.
105. But Forrestal, in fact, did the actual "sending for" on April 12, the day of Roosevelt's death. Truman made it clear he wanted to see Byrnes "first thing in the morning." See Messer, "The Making of a Cold Warrior," p. 200.
106. This is based on Messer, "The Making of a Cold Warrior," p. 201. Also see Messer, *The End of an Alliance*, Chapters IV and V.
107. Messer, "The Making of a Cold Warrior," pp. 200–201.
108. Messer, "The Making of a Cold Warrior," pp. 202–4.
109. Truman, *Year of Decisions*, p. 87.
110. Szilard, "A Personal History of the Atomic Bomb," pp. 14–15.
111. This account follows Hewlett and Anderson, *The New World*, pp. 347–73; Messer, "The Making of a Cold Warrior," pp. 279–81; Messer, *The End of an Alliance*, pp. 86–89; and Sherwin, *A World Destroyed*, Chapters VII and VIII and various appendices in which "Notes" of the Interim Committee are printed along with supporting memoranda and other documents. Also see Wyden, *Day One*.
112. Messer, *The End of an Alliance*, p. 88.
113. *Ibid.*, p. 88. See also Hewlett and Anderson, Sherwin, and Wyden, all cited in note 111, for further details on the Interim Committee meetings.
114. Szilard, "Reminiscences," pp. 127–28.
115. Quoted in Messer, *The End of an Alliance*, p. 105.
116. *Ibid.*, p. 105.
117. *Ibid.*, p. 105.
118. Quoted in Sherwin, *A World Destroyed*, p. 224.
119. Quoted in Messer, *The End of an Alliance*, p. 107.
120. Stimson Diary, August 12–Sept. 3, 1945.
121. Stimson Diary, Sept. 4, 1945.
122. The information in this paragraph also follows Messer closely; see his *The End of an Alliance*, Chapter III, and "The Making of a Cold Warrior," Chapters

V, VI, VII. The quotations are cited on p. 207 of the latter work. But see also p. 66 of the former.

123. Quoted in Messer, "The Making of a Cold Warrior," p. 213, and in abbreviated form in *The End of an Alliance*, p. 68.

124. Messer, *The End of an Alliance*, p. 119.

125. See the three previous notes for details, especially Chapter VII of "The Making of a Cold Warrior"; see Messer in general for a careful description of the complicated ins and outs of Byrnes's maneuvering during this period. As to Byrnes's awareness of what he was doing, see, for instance, his conversation with Davies in early June on the Polish issue in which (as Messer writes) Byrnes "privately admitted that virtually everything he had been saying since his first highly-publicized press conference in February, was a distortion of the reality of Yalta" (p. 235).

126. See especially Messer, "The Making of a Cold Warrior," Chapter VII. The quotation is from p. 253. On the matter of Lippman and Davies: It is difficult to tell precisely how much Byrnes was sincerely interested in the opinions of the two men. Messer credits him with sincere interest. But the fact that we have a clear picture of Byrnes on the Interim Committee and with Szilard and others taking a very hard line on Soviet issues during precisely the period he was attempting to seem "cooperative" with Lippman and Davies—to say nothing of the fact that Byrnes was preparing his tough position for Potsdam at this time—strongly suggests that his show of interest (as in so much of what Byrnes did) was probably mainly political: He obviously was aware that both influential men could be helpful or harmful to him in building his new image as Secretary of State. His letter to Lippman at a time he was aware he would probably be appointed is almost fawning (p. 224). His flattering "offer" of the Ambassadorship to Britain to Davies is also difficult to take seriously: All parties knew Davies was a very sick man not likely to take on such an arduous post (pp. 230–33). Nor is it likely that Byrnes did not understand the obvious unreality of appointing as Ambassador to London a man so openly identified as opposed to Churchill's position and in favor of a conciliatory approach to the Soviet Union. That Byrnes may have thought it shrewd to flatter Davies—and possibly use him, symbolically, to show that the United States wished to *appear* conciliatory—is a possibility explored also in the new Appendix V, A Note on the Historical Debate Over Questions Concerning Truman's 1945 Strategy of Delay (see pp. 356–58).

127. Wyden, *Day One*, p. 131.

128. Stimson Diary, June 6, 1945.

129. *Ibid.*, May 13, 1945.

130. *Ibid.*, May 15, 1945.

131. *Ibid.*, May 14, 1945.

132. Ferrell, *Off the Record*, p. 49.

133. Harriman, *Special Envoy to Churchill and Stalin*, p. 488.

134. See Yergin, *Shattered Peace*, pp. 109, 113. See also Herken, *The Winning Weapon*, p. 47.

135. Churchill, *Triumph and Tragedy*, p. 639; Truman, *Truman Speaks*, pp. 67, 93.

136. Some authors believe that the source of the assumption that the bomb would be used derives from the legacy of the Roosevelt Administration, and that Truman was simply carrying out Roosevelt's assumption. See, for instance, Bernstein, "Roosevelt, Truman and the Atomic Bomb." Perhaps. But it is difficult to reconcile this with the language of the Hyde Park agreement of 1944 or doubts apparently expressed to Bush and Sachs previously cited. (See above, note 54.) At best, Roosevelt's position on whether and how to use the bomb was ambiguous before his death; and if anything, the record shows that he had considerable doubts. The evidence is much stronger that Truman was carrying out Roosevelt's policy on the question of international control of atomic energy.

The more important point is that whatever assumptions about the actual use of the weapon were inherited from Roosevelt, the fact is that in the final months before Hiroshima, the situation changed radically, and in view of the evidence, it is very difficult to argue that the old assumptions were the guiding motivation *at this point*. On this issue, Sherwin's conclusion that the Russian factor is inextricably bound up with the decision is, I believe, closer to the truth than Bernstein's view that it was only a bonus.

In assessing Bernstein's argument that Truman "neither wished to abandon, nor could easily escape" from policies he inherited from Roosevelt (p. 24), it is especially important to remember that we now know that by mid-July *Truman clearly recognized that other options were available to him to end the war quickly without using the bomb.* (see above, pp. 23–25, 33). That factors related to the Soviet Union played a very large role during this period is now also beyond question. That one of Roosevelt's most important advisers, Leahy, was strongly against the use of the bomb casts further doubt on the argument that it was impossible to go against "inherited policies." We also know that the Supreme Commander Truman inherited from Roosevelt, Eisenhower, personally urged Truman not to use the atomic bomb (see above, p. 14). Finally, we know that Truman's most important adviser, Byrnes, had few qualms about altering Roosevelt's policies when he felt it important to do so. (And, of course, the Russian factor played a central, not marginal, role in Byrnes's thinking.)

In this connection it is also important to focus special attention on the final four weeks before Hiroshima was destroyed: First, because it was during this period that evidence concerning Japan's collapse flowed in with increasing force (and that U.S. intelligence estimates and advice reflected this fact); and second, because it was at this time that Byrnes became particularly important in advising the President—especially once the two men were out of Washington after July 7 on the ship to Potsdam and at the Conference site itself.

While it is not yet possible to fully resolve all matters of emphasis on this matter, each new bit of information discovered in the last few years—and particularly the Truman diary—has further weakened the argument that the Roosevelt legacy was the determinative factor in the final period leading up to Hiroshima. Bernstein's acknowledgment (p. 24) that "impressing the Soviet Union . . . constitute[d] a subtle deterrent to reconsidering combat use of the bomb and to searching for alternative

means of ending the war," is itself, of course, a major (if as yet partial) step in the direction of this difficult conclusion. For further discussion, see also footnotes 54, 60, 63, and 87.

137. Interviews, December 26, 1984 January 5, 1985.
138. Blum, ed., *The Price of Vision*, p. 474.
139. For a review, see, for instance, Bernstein, "The Atomic Bomb and American Foreign Policy"; Maier, "Revisionism and the Interpretation of Cold War Origins"; Walker, "Historians and Cold War Origins: The New Consensus."
140. See Herken, *The Winning Weapon*, Chapter III; Messer, *The End of an Alliance*, Chapter VII.

Several authors have wrongly concluded that because there was no *explicit* threat the bomb could not have informed U.S. attitudes. For such views, see Ulam, *The Rivals*, p. 82 (also in "Re-reading the Cold War: Revising the Revisionists," p. 122); Spanier, "The Choices We Did Not Have," pp. 131–32; Black, "The Start of the Cold War in Bulgaria," pp. 195–96. For a related argument, see Davis, *The Cold War Begins*, p. 320*fn*. See Herken, "Atomic Diplomacy Reversed and Revised," for a discussion of Byrnes's view of the bomb as an *implied threat*, and for information which supports the general argument on this point presented in *Atomic Diplomacy* and adds additional detail from materials not available in 1965. (For Bernstein's comments on Ulam, see Bernstein, *The Atomic Bomb: The Critical Issues*, pp. 121–22.)

On some small points in connection with Bulgaria and Rumania: *Atomic Diplomacy* was written before many State Department records for August and September 1945 became available. One or two details have been clarified with newer documents. For instance, while the information available twenty years ago correctly indicated that the U.S. representative in Bulgaria demanded (successfully) that the August Bulgarian elections be postponed, we now know that he did so initially on his own initiative. After Byrnes made public a strong statement indicating the United States would not recognize the existing government, Barnes demanded that the elections be postponed. *The*

New York Times and others correctly described this as part of an "Anglo-American diplomatic offensive. . . ."

At the very last minute, *well after Washington had been notified of the initiative of the local representative, and too late to reverse the election postponement*, a telegram saying the initiative was not authorized was sent from Washington. Barnes was amazed, since he had informed the Department earlier and had not been told *not* to proceed. He cabled on August 25:

> Before requesting General Crane to communicate with Chairman Allied Control Commission I reread with great care all instructions received from Department back to and including . . . March 29. . . . I remain at a loss to understand what prompted the Department's telegram. Obviously the purpose of expressing the views of the US Government was to forestall rigged elections and consequent formation of a government that US could not recognize. . . .

See also Lundestad, *The American Non-Policy Towards Eastern Europe*, p. 269, who observes that calling for a postponement was "a natural progression of the view that the forthcoming elections would not be satisfactory. . . ." (But note that Lundestad, like Hammond and others, does not indicate the fact that the demand for a postponement had been reported to Washington on August 22.)

Byrnes apparently wanted to avoid the charge that the United States had *directly and explicitly* intervened at this point; he also apparently wanted to take the matter up directly with Molotov at the forthcoming London Foreign Ministers meetings: Telling several associates that he was bolstered by the atomic bomb, he made Bulgaria (and Rumania) a major focus of his diplomacy there. (See below, pp. 271–74; also Herken, *The Winning Weapon* and "Atomic Diplomacy Reversed and Revised," and Messer, *The End of an Alliance*.)

The cable to Barnes may well have been a formality to "put on the record" a defense that the United States had not *explicitly authorized* the demand at this point just before the Foreign Ministers were to meet—supposedly to attempt to work out a coordinated approach to the peace settlements in general.

Hammond's report in " 'Atomic Diplomacy' Revisited" (p. 1417) that an "immediate" reprimand was sent is inaccurate as to dates, and, more important, as to implication: The cable went out only after three cables (August 22, 23, and 24) from Barnes informed Washington of exactly what he was doing—and it reached Bulgaria only on the very day before the election (August 25). *Before* this cable went out (midnight Sofia time), Barnes sent a cable (which may have crossed the Washington cable) telling Washington that the Bulgarian government had in fact decided to postpone the election.

Davis, *The Cold War Begins*, pp. 309–10, also misses these points, as does Rose, *After Yalta*, p. 117. See also Lundestad, *The American Non-Policy Towards Eastern Europe, 1943–1947*, p. 269. For the various cable documents, see *FRUS* 1945, IV, pp. 304–6, 308–12.

Hammond also finds no evidence that Truman and Byrnes initiated a major effort designed to reduce or eliminate Soviet influence in Rumania (p. 1419). (Davis, pp. 299–306, takes a similar position.) This is also in error: The United States continued and intensified the effort it had begun earlier to change the power relations in Rumania. After King Michael asked Groza to resign, Byrnes also bypassed the Control Commission and went public, telling the press about notes he had recently sent to Moscow and London asking for consultations to replace the Rumanian government. U.S. broadcasts to Rumania with information on the crisis were also increased to bring the information to popular attention. As Lundestad writes, the United States "hoped that a combination of local opposition strength, moderation on both sides in composing a new government, and American-British pressure would succeed in toppling the Groza government" (p. 239).

However, the British government expressed concern that King Michael's call for Groza's resignation was "ill timed as it would have been more effective if it had coincided with meeting of Foreign Ministers" (*FRUS* 1945,

V, p. 589). Byrnes then instructed U.S. representatives to avoid any action "which might seem to give ground for Soviet suspicion that crisis was brought about by 'Anglo-American intervention.' Contact . . . should be avoided at present stage" (*ibid.*, p. 594). However, eleven days later, while still wishing to avoid any sign of *direct* interference, Byrnes cabled that there was now no longer any reason to avoid contact "with the King, his advisers, members of the Government . . ." (*ibid.*, p. 608). The conflict was then transferred to the London Council as expected.

These twists and turns of policy clarify minor details about U.S. strategy during the last half of August when Byrnes apparently hoped for a short while that he might achieve his objectives without an open break. However, they in no way alter the conclusion that, contrary to the decisions which had been made at Yalta and earlier, U.S. policy now sought major changes in the Balkans, that its public initiatives bypassed the Control Commission procedures previously endorsed, and that at London Byrnes pressed these issues with the firm conviction that the atomic bomb gave him new power to radically reduce Soviet influence in the area. (See Messer, *The End of an Alliance*, and Herken, *The Winning Weapon* and especially "Atomic Diplomacy Reversed and Revised.")

On several related points Hammond builds a straw man by mischaracterizing my position. Thus, he says, "Alperovitz gives the impression that Byrnes, emboldened by the success of the atom bombs on Japan, put forward new and sweeping demands regarding Bulgaria" (p. 1417). However, my position is not that Byrnes made sweeping "*new* demands," but, rather, that *the policy developed during the summer of delay and stated at Potsdam was now put forward with new seriousness and force.* This is stated clearly at several points: "Truman's Potsdam demand that the governments of Bulgaria and Rumania be changed had been refused, but the President had made it quite clear that he was willing to postpone, not withdraw his demand. . . ." "In Byrnes's approach to the Balkans . . . American leaders demonstrated that the strategy

of delay had reached its long-awaited climax . . . [they] now attempted to fulfill the President's summer pledge to 'insist on the eventual removal of the Soviet blackout . . .' " (*Atomic Diplomacy*, pp. 250–51; see also p. 253).

Hammond also directly misquotes me in saying that I give the impression that Truman's post-Potsdam speech does not give Truman's sense of optimism about cooperation between the major powers (p. 1416). See *Atomic Diplomacy* p. 249, for just the opposite view: "Truman's [speech] emphasized his sense of confidence and optimism about the future; the Allies would 'continue to march together to a lasting peace and a happy world. . . .' "

Incidentally, Hammond is right that the date of Byrnes's open letter is given inaccurately in *Atomic Diplomacy;* the correct date is August 18, not 13. See the new Appendix V, A Note on the Historical Debate Over Questions Concerning Truman's 1945 Strategy of Delay, for a general treatment of views similar to those presented by Hammond on the overall strategy of delay and the role the atomic bomb played in it.

141. See previous note.
142. Forrestal, *Diaries*, p. 262; Byrnes, *Speaking Frankly*, p. 203.
143. Lippmann, *The Cold War*, p. 29.
144. Quoted in Messer, *The End of an Alliance*, p. 107.
145. Quoted in Herken, *The Winning Weapon*, p. 36.
146. World Day of Peace Message, quoted in National Conference of Catholic Bishops, *The Challenge of Peace: God's Promise and Our Response*, p. 40.

PREFACE (*pp. 61–65*)

1. Truman, *Year of Decisions*, p. 85.
2. *Ibid.*, pp. 85, 87.
3. Stimson Diary, May 16, 1945.
4. Feis, *Churchill, Roosevelt, Stalin*, pp. 599–600.
5. Byrnes, *All In One Lifetime*, p. 389.
6. Byrnes, *Speaking Frankly*, p. 104.
7. Feis, *Between War and Peace*, p. 180.
8. Stimson Diary, July 21, 1945.
9. Truman, *Year of Decisions*, p. 87.
10. Snow, *Journey*, p. 357.
11. Stimson, *On Active Service*, p. 644.
12. Truman, *Truman Speaks*, p. 67.

13. *Newsweek*, November 11, 1963, p. 107.
14. Keynes, *The General Theory*, p. viii.

CHAPTER I (*pp. 67–88*)

1. Leahy, *I Was There*, p. 352.
2. Woodward, *British Foreign Policy*, pp. xxxix, 519.
3. *Stalin's Correspondence*, I, p. 244; II, pp. 188–89.
4. *Conference of Berlin*, II, p. 1579.
5. Leahy, *I Was There*, p. 352.
6. Churchill, *Triumph and Tragedy*, p. 486.
7. *Stalin's Correspondence*, II, pp. 215–17.
8. Leahy, *I Was There*, pp. 315–16.
9. Feis, *Churchill, Roosevelt, Stalin*, p. 575.
10. Stettinius, *Roosevelt and the Russians*, p. 302.
11. Truman, *Year of Decisions*, p. 76.
12. *Ibid.*, pp. 70–72.
13. *Ibid.*, p. 70.
14. *Ibid.*, p. 71.
15. Forrestal, *Diaries*, p. 40.
16. Truman, *Year of Decisions*, p. 71.
17. Feis, *Churchill, Roosevelt, Stalin*, p. 598.
18. Forrestal, *Diaries*, p. 41; Truman, *Year of Decisions*, p. 15; *Conferences at Malta and Yalta*, pp. 310–12, 319, 323, 610.
19. Truman, *Year of Decisions*, p. 70.
20. *Ibid.*, p. 71.
21. *Ibid.*, p. 321.
22. *Ibid.*, p. 17.
23. Stimson Diary, May 10, 1945.
24. Forrestal, *Diaries*, p. 41; Vandenberg, *Papers*, p. 176; Grew memorandum of conversation, May 11–12, 1945.
25. Leahy, *I Was There*, p. 351; Leahy Diary, April 19, 1945.
26. Forrestal, *Diaries*, pp. 47–49.
27. Deane, *The Strange Alliance*, p. 9; Woodward, *British Foreign Policy*, p. xxxvi.
28. Byrnes, *Speaking Frankly*, p. 23.
29. Butler, *Grand Strategy*, p. 149.
30. Grew, *Turbulent Era*, II, p. 1485*fn.*
31. *Ibid.*, p. 1446.
32. *Ibid.*, p. 1485*fn.*
33. Stimson Diary, April 3, 1945.
34. Forrestal, *Diaries*, p. 51; Truman, *Year of Decisions*, p. 78.
35. Truman, *Year of Decisions*, p. 78.
36. Forrestal, *Diaries*, p. 50.
37. Truman, *Year of Decisions*, p. 78.
38. Leahy, *I Was There*, p. 351.
39. Stimson Diary, April 23, 1945.
40. Truman, *Year of Decisions*, p. 50.
41. *Ibid*, pp. 70–71.
42. *Ibid.*, p. 71.
43. *Ibid.*, p. 72; Woodward, *British Foreign Policy*, p. 509.
44. Forrestal, *Diaries*, p. 50.
45. *New York Times*, June 24, 1941.
46. Deane, *The Strange Alliance*, p. 265.
47. *Ibid.*, p. 262.
48. *Ibid.*, pp. 84–86, 98.
49. *Ibid.*, pp. 84–86.
50. Stimson Diary, April 23, 1945; Forrestal, *Diaries*, p. 40.
51. Deane, *The Strange Alliance*, p. 84.
52. *Ibid.*, p. 85.
53. *Ibid.*, pp. 85–86.
54. *Ibid.*, pp. 264–66.
55. *Ibid.*, p. 265; Feis, *Churchill, Roosevelt, Stalin*, pp. 599–600.
56. Deane, *The Strange Alliance*, pp. 261–65.
57. *Ibid.*, p. 263.
58. *Ibid.*, p. 265.
59. *Ibid.*, Department of Defense, "Entry of the Soviet Union into the War against Japan," pp. 60–61.
60. Deane, *The Strange Alliance*, p. 265.
61. Department of Defense, "Entry of the Soviet Union into the War against Japan," p. 61.
62. *Ibid.*, p. 50.
63. *Ibid.*, p. 67.
64. *Ibid.*
65. *Ibid.*, p. 68.
66. Deane, *The Strange Alliance*, p. 265.
67. Truman, *Year of Decisions*, p. 79.
68. *Ibid.*
69. Leahy, *I Was There*, p. 351.
70. Truman, *Year of Decisions*, p. 79.
71. *Ibid.*, p. 80.
72. Stettinius, *Roosevelt and the Russians*, p. 302.
73. Truman, *Year of Decisions*, p. 82.
74. *Ibid.*
75. *Ibid.*, pp. 80–82.
76. Leahy, *I Was There*, p. 352.
77. *Ibid.*, p. 413.
78. Leahy Diary, April 23, 1945, p. 63.
79. *Stalin's Correspondence*, II, pp. 219–20; Woodward, *British Foreign Policy*, p. 509.
80. Vandenberg, *Papers*, p. 176.

81. Truman, *Year of Decisions*, p. 109.
82. Feis, *Between War and Peace*, p. 223.
83. *Conference of Berlin*, II, p. 1580.
84. Woodward, *British Foreign Policy*, p. 511.
85. *Ibid.*
86. Truman, *Year of Decisions*, p. 24; Churchill, *Triumph and Tragedy*, pp. 424–26.
87. Lane, *I Saw Poland Betrayed*, p. 67; Woodward, *British Foreign Policy*, pp. 511–12.
88. Truman, *Year of Decisions*, p. 109.
89. *Ibid.;* Feis, *Between War and Peace*, p. 89; *Stalin's Correspondence*, II, pp. 228–29.
90. Grew memorandum of conversation, May 7, 1945; Truman, *Year of Decisions*, p. 255.
91. Forrestal, *Diaries*, p. 41.
92. Deane, *The Strange Alliance*, p. 98.
93. Leahy, *I Was There*, p. 351.
94. Deane, *The Strange Alliance*, pp. 84–86, 98.
95. Forrestal, *Diaries*, p. 41; *New York Times*, July 18, 1945; *Conference of Berlin*, I, p. 181.
96. Deane, *The Strange Alliance*, p. 86.
97. Grew memorandum of conversation, May 11, May 11–12, 1945; Leahy, *I Was There*, p. 351; Feis, *Between War and Peace*, p. 28; Stimson Diary, May 11, 1945.
98. Feis, *Between War and Peace*, pp. 27–28; Truman, *Year of Decisions*, p. 228.
99. Truman, *Year of Decisions*, p. 228.
100. Feis, *Between War and Peace*, pp. 28, 329.
101. Truman, *Year of Decisions*, p. 228.
102. Forrestal, *Diaries*, p. 41.
103. Grew memorandum of conversation, May 11, 1945.
104. Stimson Diary, May 11, 1945.
105. *Ibid.*, May 14, 1945.
106. Grew memorandum of conversation, May 11, 1945.
107. *Ibid.*
108. Truman, *Year of Decisions*, p. 228.
109. Feis, *Between War and Peace*, p. 331; *Conference of Berlin*, II, p. 341.
110. *Stalin's Correspondence*, II, p. 232.
111. Leahy, *I Was There*, p. 367.
112. *Conference of Berlin*, I, p. 13.
113. Churchill, *Triumph and Tragedy*, pp. 491–92.
114. *Ibid.*
115. *Ibid.*, pp. 456–57. Emphasis in original.
116. *Conference of Berlin*, I, pp. 5–9.
117. Churchill, *Triumph and Tragedy*, p. 503.
118. *Conference of Berlin*, I, p. 11.

CHAPTER II   (*pp. 89–109*)

1. *Conference of Berlin*, I, p. 597.
2. Wilmot, *The Struggle for Europe*, pp. 798–800.
3. Feis, *Churchill, Roosevelt, Stalin*, pp. 633–34; Churchill, *Triumph and Tragedy*, p. 512.
4. Churchill, *Triumph and Tragedy*, pp. 511–12.
5. *Ibid.*, pp. 512–13.
6. *Ibid.*, p. 503; *Conference of Berlin*, I, p. 165.
7. Churchill, *Triumph and Tragedy*, p. 513.
8. Butler, *Grand Strategy*, pp. 152–53.
9. Churchill, *Triumph and Tragedy*, p. 513.
10. *Ibid.*, pp. 514–15.
11. Truman, *Year of Decisions*, p. 62.
12. Feis, *Between War and Peace*, p. 74; Feis, *Churchill, Roosevelt, Stalin*, p. 609.
13. Mosely, "The Occupation of Germany," p. 602.
14. Butler, *Grand Strategy*, p. 153.
15. Churchill, *Triumph and Tragedy*, p. 516; Truman, *Year of Decisions*, p. 214.
16. Truman, *Year of Decisions*, p. 215.
17. *Ibid.*
18. *Ibid.*, p. 217.
19. Bryant, *Triumph in the West*, p. 469.
20. Eisenhower, *Crusade in Europe*, p. 474.
21. Feis, *Churchill, Roosevelt, Stalin*, p. 623–24.
22. *Ibid.*, p. 624–25.
23. *Conference of Berlin*, I, p. 334.
24. *Ibid.*, pp. 334–35; Truman, *Year of Decisions*, p. 218.
25. Truman, *Year of Decisions*, p. 217; Feis, *Churchill, Roosevelt, Stalin*, pp. 623–25; Feis, *Between War and Peace*, p. 67.
26. Truman, *Year of Decisions*, p. 218;

Churchill, *Triumph and Tragedy*, p. 519.
27. Churchill, *Triumph and Tragedy*, p. 502.
28. Truman, *Year of Decisions*, p. 218; *Conference of Berlin*, I, pp. 3–4.
29. *Conference of Berlin*, I, p. 4.
30. *Ibid.*, p. 5.
31. *Ibid.*, p. 9; Churchill, *Triumph and Tragedy*, p. 574.
32. Mosely, "Dismemberment of Germany," p. 497; Nettl, *The Eastern Zone and Soviet Policy in Germany*, p. 41; Smith, *My Three Years in Moscow*, p. 20; Leahy, *I Was There*, p. 363.
33. Feis, *Between War and Peace*, pp. 76–77.
34. *Ibid.*
35. Truman, *Year of Decisions*, p. 77.
36. See Stimson, *On Active Service*.
37. *Ibid.*, p. 604.
38. Truman, *Year of Decisions*, p. 78.
39. Forrestal, *Diaries*, p. 49.
40. Stimson Diary, April 23, 1945.
41. *Ibid.*, April 16, 1945.
42. *Ibid.*, April 26, 1945.
43. *Ibid.*
44. Truman, *Year of Decisions*, pp. 78–79; Forrestal, *Diaries*, p. 49.
45. Stimson Diary, April 23, 1945.
46. Truman, *Year of Decisions*, p. 79.
47. Stimson Diary, April 2, 1945.
48. *Ibid.*, April 3, 1945.
49. *Ibid.*
50. *Ibid.*, April 23, 1945.
51. *Ibid.*
52. *Ibid.*, May 16, 1945.
53. *Conference of Berlin*, II, p. 808–9.
54. Stimson, *On Active Service*, p. 589.
55. Truman, *Year of Decisions*, p. 236.
56. *Conference of Berlin*, II, p. 809.
57. *Ibid.*, p. 808.
58. Stimson, *On Active Service*, p. 571.
59. *Ibid.*, p. 573.
60. *Conference of Berlin*, II, pp. 754–57, 991.
61. *Ibid.*, p. 755.
62. Stimson, *On Active Service*, p. 567.
63. Truman, *Year of Decisions*, p. 102.
64. Forrestal, *Diaries*, p. 48.
65. Stimson, *On Active Service*, p. 583.
66. Stimson Diary, April 16, 1945.
67. *Ibid.*, April 4, 1945.
68. Feis, *Between War and Peace*, p. 77.
69. *Conference of Berlin*, II, p. 757.

70. Stimson Diary, April 30, 1945.
71. *Ibid.*, May 14, 1945.
72. Truman, *Year of Decisions*, p. 85.
73. Stimson, *On Active Service*, p. 635.
74. Byrnes, *All In One Lifetime*, p. 282; *Speaking Frankly*, p. 259; Truman, *Year of Decisions*, p. 87.
75. Hewlett and Anderson, *The New World*, p. 343.
76. *Ibid.*; Truman, *Year of Decisions*, p. 87.
77. Truman, *Year of Decisions*, p. 10.
78. *Ibid.*, p. 85.
79. *Ibid.*, p. 87.
80. Stimson Diary, March 15, 1945.
81. Truman, *Year of Decisions*, p. 85.
82. Stimson Diary, May 15, 1945.
83. *Ibid.*, May 16, 1945.
84. *Ibid.*, May 15, 1945.
85. *Ibid.*
86. *Ibid.*, May 10, 1945.
87. *Ibid.*, May 14, 1945.
88. Stimson, *On Active Service*, p. 643.
89. *Ibid.*, p. 635.
90. *Ibid.*
91. *Ibid.*, p. 636.
92. *Ibid.*
93. Hewlett and Anderson, *The New World*, p. 335.
94. *Ibid.*, p. 338.
95. Stimson, *On Active Service*, p. 636.
96. Truman, *Year of Decisions*, p. 87.
97. Stimson Diary, May 3, 1945.
98. Hewlett and Anderson, *The New World*, p. 345.
99. Stimson Diary, June 6, 1945.
100. *Ibid.*, May 14, 1945; Churchill, *Triumph and Tragedy*, p. 575.
101. Stimson Diary, May 16, 1945.
102. *Ibid.*, June 6, 1945.
103. *Ibid.*, May 14, 1945.

CHAPTER III (*pp. 110–138*)

1. Butler, *Grand Strategy*, p. 277.
2. Hewlett and Anderson, *The New World*, p. 345.
3. Stimson Diary, May 3, 1945.
4. Leahy, *I Was There*, p. 441; Leahy Diary, May 20, 1945, p. 85.
5. Truman, *Year of Decisions*, pp. 10–11.
6. Byrnes, *Speaking Frankly*, p. 261.
7. Truman, *Year of Decisions*, p. 87.
8. *Conference of Berlin*, I, pp. 6–7.
9. Forrestal, *Diaries*, p. 49.
10. Truman, *Year of Decisions*, p. 85.
11. *Ibid.*, p. 87.

12. *Ibid.*, p. 25; *Conference of Berlin*, I, p. 13.
13. Truman, *Year of Decisions*, p. 10.
14. *Conference of Berlin*, I, p. 4.
15. Stimson Diary, May 16, 1945.
16. *Conference of Berlin*, I, p. 13.
17. *Ibid.*, p. 8.
18. Churchill, *Triumph and Tragedy*, p. 575.
19. *Ibid.*, p. 574.
20. *Ibid.*, pp. 572–74; *Conference of Berlin*, I, pp. 8–9.
21. *Ibid.*, p. 13.
22. *Ibid.*, p. 11.
23. *Ibid.*, p. 10.
24. Stimson Diary, May 10, 14, 1945.
25. Churchill, *Triumph and Tragedy*, p. 575; *Conference of Berlin*, I, p. 13.
26. *Conference of Berlin*, I, p. 13.
27. Truman, *Year of Decisions*, p. 224.
28. Stimson Diary, May 16, 1945.
29. Truman, *Year of Decisions*, pp. 257–58.
30. Woodward, *British Foreign Policy*, p. 521.
31. Stettinius, *Roosevelt and the Russians*, p. 319.
32. Forrestal, *Diaries*, p. 58.
33. Lane, *I Saw Poland Betrayed*, pp. 68–71; Truman, *Year of Decisions*, p. 258.
34. Truman, *Year of Decisions*, pp. 22, 258.
35. Lane, *I Saw Poland Betrayed*, pp. 68–71.
36. Woodward, *British Foreign Policy*, p. 512; Sherwood, *Roosevelt and Hopkins*, p. 913.
37. Sherwood, *Roosevelt and Hopkins*, p. 913.
38. Truman, *Year of Decisions*, p. 110.
39. Lane, *I Saw Poland Betrayed*, p. 84.
40. Feis, *Churchill, Roosevelt, Stalin*, p. 650; Churchill, *Triumph and Tragedy*, p. 577.
41. Churchill, *Triumph and Tragedy*, p. 479.
42. *Ibid.*
43. Truman, *Year of Decisions*, p. 75.
44. *Ibid.*, p. 94.
45. Woodward, *British Foreign Policy*, p. 519; Truman, *Year of Decisions*, p. 333.
46. *Conference of Berlin*, I, pp. 8, 63, 65; Grew, *Turbulent Era*, II, p. 1463;

Feis, *Churchill, Roosevelt, Stalin*, p. 649; Butcher, *Three Years with Eisenhower*, p. 712.
47. Truman, *Year of Decisions*, pp. 110, 257.
48. Woodward, *British Foreign Policy*, p. 512; Churchill, *Triumph and Tragedy*, p. 555.
49. *Conference of Berlin*, I, pp. 21–22, 63.
50. *Ibid.*, p. 22; Grew memorandum of conversation, May 21, 1945; Leahy Diary, May 20, 1945, p. 86; Lane, *I Saw Poland Betrayed*, p. 71.
51. Forrestal, *Diaries*, p. 58.
52. Lane, *I Saw Poland Betrayed*, p. 71.
53. Forrestal, *Diaries*, pp. 66–67.
54. Truman, *Year of Decisions*, p. 259.
55. Sherwood, *Roosevelt and Hopkins*, p. 888.
56. *Ibid.*, p. 890.
57. *Ibid.*, pp. 890, 899, 909.
58. *Ibid.*, p. 890.
59. *Ibid.*, p. 889.
60. *Ibid.*, p. 892.
61. *Conference of Berlin*, I, p. 28.
62. *Ibid.*
63. Sherwood, *Roosevelt and Hopkins*, p. 893.
64. *Conference of Berlin*, I, p. 32.
65. Sherwood, *Roosevelt and Hopkins*, p. 894.
66. *Conference of Berlin*, I, pp. 33–38.
67. Sherwood, *Roosevelt and Hopkins*, p. 898.
68. *Ibid.*, pp. 905–6.
69. *Conference of Berlin*, I, pp. 55–56.
70. *Ibid.*, p. 40.
71. Feis, *Between War and Peace*, p. 103.
72. *Ibid.*, p. 105.
73. Sherwood, *Roosevelt and Hopkins*, p. 908.
74. Leahy, *I Was There*, p. 377; Forrestal, *Diaries*, p. 68; Byrnes, *Speaking Frankly*, pp. 63–64.
75. Feis, *Between War and Peace*, p. 208.
76. *Ibid.*; Mikolajczyk, *The Pattern of Soviet Domination*, pp. 140–43.
77. Sherwood, *Roosevelt and Hopkins*, p. 909.
78. *Stalin's Correspondence*, I, p. 326; II, p. 216.
79. Mikolajczyk, *The Pattern of Soviet Domination*, p. 128; Rozek, *Allied*

Wartime Diplomacy, pp. 384–86.
80. Sherwood, Roosevelt and Hopkins, pp. 908–10.
81. Ibid., pp. 909–10.
82. Conference of Berlin, I, p. 716.
83. Ibid., pp. 716, 722–23.
84. Ibid., p. 735.
85. Ibid.
86. Truman, Year of Decisions, p. 17.
87. Ibid., p. 45.
88. Forrestal, Diaries, p. 48.
89. Truman, Year of Decisions, p. 102.
90. Ibid., p. 105.
91. Ibid., p. 308.
92. Ibid., pp. 236–38; Stimson Diary, May 16, 1945.
93. Truman, Year of Decisions, p. 45.
94. Ibid., p. 496.
95. Truman, Years of Trial and Hope, p. 68.
96. Truman, Year of Decisions, p. x.
97. Ibid., p. 308.
98. Ibid., p. 464.
99. Ibid., p. 46.
100. Ibid., p. 262.
101. Ibid., p. 236.
102. Ibid., p. 306.
103. Ibid., p. 235; Grew memorandum of conversation, May 10, 1945.
104. Feis, Between War and Peace, p. 56fn; Clay, Decision in Germany, p. 16; Hammond, "Directives for the Occupation of Germany," p. 312.
105. Truman, Year of Decisions, pp. 105–6.
106. Ibid., p. 308.
107. Stimson Diary, July 2, 1945.
108. Truman, Year of Decisions, p. 300.
109. Feis, Between War and Peace, p. 77.
110. Sherwood, Roosevelt and Hopkins, p. 891.
111. Conference of Berlin, I, pp. 28–29.
112. Sherwood, Roosevelt and Hopkins, p. 891.
113. Ibid., pp. 901–2.
114. Feis, Between War and Peace, p. 140.
115. Conference of Berlin, I, p. 51.
116. Mosely, "The Occupation of Germany," pp. 599–603; Truman, Year of Decisions, p. 302; Feis, Between War and Peace, p. 142.
117. Feis, Between War and Peace, pp. 52–56.
118. Conference of Berlin, I, p. 39.
119. Truman, Year of Decisions, p. 301.
120. Churchill, Triumph and Tragedy, p. 557.
121. Feis, Between War and Peace, p. 141.
122. Conference of Berlin, I, p. 53.
123. Truman, Year of Decisions, p. 302; Feis, Between War and Peace, p. 141; Clay, Decision in Germany, pp. 22–23.
124. Conference of Berlin, I, p. 348.
125. Truman, Year of Decisions, p. 301.
126. Ibid., p. 302.
127. Churchill, Triumph and Tragedy, p. 604.
128. Feis, Between War and Peace, p. 142.
129. Ibid., p. 142fn.
130. Truman, Year of Decisions, p. 302.
131. Ibid., pp. 303–4.
132. Ibid., p. 303.
133. Stalin's Correspondence, II, pp. 245–46; Leahy, I Was There, p. 382.
134. Mosely, "The Occupation of Germany," p. 601; Feis, Between War and Peace, p. 144.
135. Conference of Berlin, I, p. 348fn.
136. Ibid., II, p. 244.
137. Feis, Between War and Peace, p. 241.
138. Grew Papers, message dated June 6, 1945.
139. Forrestal, Diaries, p. 68.
140. Grew, Turbulent Era, II, p. 1518.
141. Leahy, I Was There, p. 383. See also Byrnes, Speaking Frankly, p. 61.
142. Conference of Berlin, I, p. 62.
143. Churchill, Triumph and Tragedy, pp. 576–81.
144. Truman, Year of Decisions, p. 229.
145. Sherwood, Roosevelt and Hopkins, p. 897; Feis, Between War and Peace, p. 101fn.
146. Feis, Between War and Peace, pp. 329–30.
147. Ibid., p. 138fn.; Woodward, British Foreign Policy, p. 527.
148. Feis, Between War and Peace, pp. 60, 137–38.
149. Conference of Berlin, I, p. 36.
150. Ibid., p. 562fn.
151. Ibid., p. 33.
152. Ibid., pp. 33–34.

153. *Ibid.*, p. 53.
154. *Ibid.*, p. 157.
155. Feis, *Between War and Peace*, p. 330.
156. Truman, *Year of Decisions*, p. 310; *Conference of Berlin*, II, p. 940.
157. *Conference of Berlin*, I, p. 563.
158. Truman, *Year of Decisions*, p. 233.
159. *New York Times*, Jan. 18, Mar. 2, 3, April 2, May 9, 1946.
160. *Conference of Berlin*, I, p. 181.
161. *Ibid.*, pp. 785–87.
162. *Ibid.*, pp. 786–87.
163. *Ibid.*, p. 726.
164. *Ibid.*, pp. 788–89.
165. *Ibid.*, p. 784.
166. *Ibid.*, p. 715.
167. Szilard, "A Personal History of the Atomic Bomb," pp. 14–15. See also "Was A-Bomb on Japan a Mistake?", p. 69.
168. Leahy, *I Was There*, p. 441.
169. Stimson Diary, June 6, 1945.
170. *Ibid.*
171. Truman, *Year of Decisions*, p. 321.
172. Grew, *Turbulent Era*, II, pp. 1464–65. Emphasis added.
173. *Conference of Berlin*, I, p. 728.
174. Grew Papers, letter to Paul V. Bacon, June 4, 1945.

CHAPTER IV (*pp. 139–174*)

1. Grew, *Turbulent Era*, II, pp. 1455–56; Department of State, *Relations with China*, pp. 113–14.
2. *Conference of Berlin*, I, p. 860.
3. *Congressional Record*, Aug. 27, 1951, p. A5413.
4. *Ibid.;* Leahy, *I Was There*, p. 318.
5. *Congressional Record*, Aug. 27, 1951, p. A5412.
6. Leahy, *I Was There*, p. 318.
7. Deutscher, *Stalin*, pp. 399–402; Beloff, *Soviet Policy*, p. 36.
8. Department of State, *Relations With China*, p. 99.
9. *Ibid.*, p. 96.
10. Truman, *Year of Decisions*, pp. 280–81.
11. Feis, *Japan Subdued*, p. 168.
12. Feis, *China Tangle*, 286*fn.*
13. Butler, *Grand Strategy*, p. 214.
14. Feis, *China Tangle*, pp. 280–85; Department of State, *Relations With China*, pp. 95–96.
15. Truman, *Year of Decisions*, p. 66.

16. *Ibid.*, p. 76.
17. Department of State, *Relations With China*, pp. 97–98; *Congressional Record*, Aug. 27, 1951, p. A5414.
18. Department of Defense, "Entry of the Soviet Union into the War Against Japan," p. 67.
19. Truman, *Year of Decisions*, pp. 84–85.
20. *Congressional Record*, Aug. 27, 1951, p. A5414; Feis, *China Tangle*, p. 304.
21. Forrestal *Diaries*, p. 55.
22. Leahy Diary, May 11, 1945, p. 82.
23. Forrestal *Diaries*, p. 56.
24. *Ibid.*
25. Grew, *Turbulent Era*, II, pp. 1455–57; Department of Defense, "Entry of the Soviet Union into the War against Japan," pp. 68–70.
26. Truman, *Year of Decisions*, p. 85.
27. *Ibid.*, p. 266.
28. Grew, *Turbulent Era*, II, pp. 1460–61.
29. Stimson Diary, May 13, 1945.
30. *Ibid.*, May 14, 1945.
31. *Ibid.*, May 15, 1945.
32. Grew, *Turbulent Era*, II, pp. 1457–59.
33. Feis, *Between War and Peace*, pp. 80–81.
34. Grew, *Turbulent Era*, II, pp. 1457–59.
35. *Ibid.*
36. *Conference of Berlin*, I, p. 14.
37. Hewlett and Anderson, *The New World*, p. 351.
38. *Ibid.;* Stimson Diary, May 15, 16, 1945.
39. Stimson Diary, May 15, 1945.
40. *Conference of Berlin*, I, pp. 13–14.
41. Stimson Diary, May 16, 1945.
42. *Ibid.*, June 6, 1945.
43. Atomic Energy Commission, *Oppenheimer Hearings*, p. 31.
44. *Ibid.;* Feis, *Japan Subdued*, p. 32.
45. *Conference of Berlin*, I, p. 19.
46. Hewlett and Anderson, *The New World*, p. 375.
47. *Ibid.*, p. 352; *Conference of Berlin*, I, p. 87.
48. Stimson Diary, June 6, 1945.
49. *Conference of Berlin*, I, pp. 19–20; *Stalin's Correspondence*, I, p. 361.
50. *Ibid.*, pp. 361–63; Woodward, *British Foreign Policy*, p. 523.
51. *Conference of Berlin*, I, pp. 41–52.

52. Department of Defense, "Entry of the Soviet Union into the War against Japan," p. 73.
53. *Conference of Berlin*, I, p. 62.
54. Stimson Diary, June 6, 1945.
55. Department of Defense, "Entry of the Soviet Union into the War against Japan," p. 72.
56. Feis, *China Tangle*, pp. 311–12.
57. *Conference of Berlin*, I, p. 162.
58. Stimson Diary, May 15, 1945.
59. Leahy, *I Was There*, p. 318.
60. Deane, *The Strange Alliance*, p. 247; Forrestal, *Diaries*, p. 12; Churchill, *Triumph and Tragedy*, p. 218.
61. Churchill, *Triumph and Tragedy*, pp. 229, 238.
62. Department of Defense, "Entry of the Soviet Union into the War against Japan," p. 35.
63. Leahy, *I Was There*, p. 335.
64. Feis, *China Tangle*, p. 285.
65. Truman, *Year of Decisions*, p. 76.
66. *Ibid.*, p. 79; Forrestal *Diaries*, pp. 12, 55; Deane, *The Strange Alliance*, p. 247; Leahy, *I Was There*, p. 369.
67. *Congressional Record*, Aug. 27, 1951, p. A5415; Stimson Diary, May 15, 1945.
68. Stimson Diary, May 15, 1945.
69. Feis, *Between War and Peace*, pp. 80–81.
70. Department of Defense, "Entry of the Soviet Union into the War against Japan," p. 72.
71. Forrestal, *Diaries*, p. 79.
72. Hewlett and Anderson, *The New World*, p. 348.
73. Craven and Cate, *Air Forces in World War II*, Vol. V, p. 644.
74. *Ibid.*, pp. 617, 756.
75. Knebel and Bailey, *No High Ground*, p. 111.
76. Craven and Cate, *Air Forces in World War II*, Vol. V, p. 728.
77. *Ibid.*, p. 740.
78. Feis, *Japan Subdued*, pp. 168–69; Butow, *Japan's Decision*, pp. 82–85.
79. Butow, *Japan's Decision*, pp. 58–59, 77, 85–86; Craven and Cate, *Air Forces in World War II*, Vol. V, pp. 728, 729.
80. Feis, *Japan Subdued*, pp. 168–73; Butow, *Japan's Decision*, pp. 77–78; Forrestal, *Diaries*, p. 20.
81. Forrestal, *Diaries*, p. 89; Toynbee, *The Far East 1942–46*, pp. 126–27.

82. U.S. Senate, *Military Situation in the Far East*, pp. 2432–33.
83. Butow, *Japan's Decision*, pp. 65–66.
84. *Ibid.*, pp. 86–91; Feis, *Japan Subdued*, pp. 168–73.
85. Feis, *Japan Subdued*, pp. 168–77; Butow, *Japan's Decision*, pp. 30–166.
86. U.S. Senate, *Military Situation in the Far East*, p. 561; Strauss, *Men and Decisions*, p. 188; Stimson, *On Active Service*, pp. 617–18; Grew, *Turbulent Era*, II, p. 1423*fn.*
87. Department of Defense, "Entry of the Soviet Union into the War against Japan," p. 68.
88. Churchill, *Triumph and Tragedy*, pp. 154, 215.
89. Department of Defense, "Entry of the Soviet Union into the War against Japan," p. 49.
90. Cline, *Washington Command Post*, p. 343.
91. Feis, *Japan Subdued*, p. 15*fn.*
92. Department of Defense, "Entry of the Soviet Union into the War against Japan," p. 64.
93. Stimson, *On Active Service*, pp. 626–28; Butler, *Grand Strategy*, pp. 302–4.
94. Cline, *Washington Command Post*, p. 343.
95. Leahy, *I Was There*, pp. 384–85; *Conference of Berlin*, I, p. 909.
96. Grew, *Turbulent Era*, II, pp. 1438–42.
97. *Conference of Berlin*, I, pp. 891–92.
98. Feis, *Japan Subdued*, p. 169; King, *Fleet Admiral King*, pp. 597–99, 623; Butow, *Japan's Decision*, pp. 58, 76.
99. Butler, *Grand Strategy*, pp. 284–85.
100. *Conference of Berlin*, I, pp. 875–76.
101. Forrestal, *Diaries*, p. 74.
102. Leahy, *I Was There*, p. 419; Grew, *Turbulent Era*, II, p. 1406.
103. Grew, *Turbulent Era*, II, p. 1458; *Conference of Berlin*, I, pp. 44–45; "Entry of the Soviet Union into the War against Japan," p. 74.
104. Cline, *Washington Command Post*, p. 344.
105. *Conference of Berlin*, I, p. 905.
106. *Ibid.*, II, p. 36*fn.*
107. Truman, *Year of Decisions*, p. 416; Grew, *Turbulent Era*, II, pp. 1421–23, 1434.
108. Grew, *Turbulent Era*, II, p. 1434.

109. Department of Defense, "Entry of the Soviet Union into the War against Japan," p. 63.
110. *Conference of Berlin*, I, p. 892; Leahy, *I Was There*, pp. 384–85; Forrestal, *Diaries*, pp. 68–69; Grew, *Turbulent Era*, II, p. 1429.
111. Truman, *Year of Decisions*, p. 417; King, *Fleet Admiral King*, pp. 396, 398; Sutherland, "The Story General Marshall Told Me."
112. Leahy, *I Was There*, p. 245.
113. *Conference of Berlin*, I, p. 906.
114. *Ibid.*, p. 909.
115. McCloy, *Challenge to American Foreign Policy*, p. 41; Forrestal, *Diaries*, p. 68.
116. Leahy, *I Was There*, pp. 318, 336, 385.
117. Deane, *The Strange Alliance*, pp. 263–65; King, *Fleet Admiral King*, p. 606; Morton, "The Decision to Use the Atomic Bomb," *Command Decisions*, K. R. Greenfield, ed., p. 509; Forrestal, *Diaries*, pp. 55, 68, 69, 70, 78–79; Byrnes, *All in One Lifetime*, pp. 291, 298, 300; Grew, *Turbulent Era*, II, pp. 1444–46; Byrnes, *Speaking Frankly*, p. 208; Truman, *Year of Decisions*, p. 425; Stimson Diary, Aug. 10, 1945.
118. Byrnes, *Speaking Frankly*, p. 208.
119. Byrnes, *All in One Lifetime*, p. 300. Emphasis added.
120. "Was A-Bomb on Japan a Mistake?" *U.S. News and World Report*, Aug. 15, 1960, p. 66.
121. Cline, *Washington Command Post*, p. 345.
122. Byrnes, *Speaking Frankly*, p. 208.
123. Butler, *Grand Strategy*, p. 214.
124. Blackett, *Military and Political Consequences*, p. 117.
125. Butler, *Grand Strategy*, pp. 276, 297.
126. Truman, *Year of Decisions*, p. 419; Wilson, *Eight Years Overseas*, p. 259; Churchill, *Triumph and Tragedy*, p. 639.
127. U.S. Senate, *Military Situation in the Far East*, p. 563.
128. Feis, *Japan Subdued*, pp. 10–11; Sutherland, "The Story General Marshall Told Me."
129. Byrnes, *Speaking Frankly*, p. 260; Hewlett and Anderson, *The New World*, p. 356.
130. Hewlett and Anderson, *The New World*, pp. 356–60; Leahy, *I Was There*, pp. 440–41.
131. Stimson, *On Active Service*, p. 617.
132. U.S. Senate, *Military Situation in the Far East*, p. 562.
133. Compton, *Atomic Quest*, p. 238.
134. *Ibid.*, p. 230; Department of Defense, "Entry of the Soviet Union into the War against Japan," p. 72.
135. Smith, "Behind the Decision to Use the Atomic Bomb," p. 297; Feis, *Japan Subdued*, pp. 44–45.
136. Hewlett and Anderson, *The New World*, pp. 356–60.
137. *Ibid.*, p. 358.
138. *Ibid.*, p. 352; Stimson Diary, May 29, 1945.
139. Stimson, *On Active Service*, p. 617.
140. *Ibid.* Emphasis added.
141. Hewlett and Anderson, *The New World*, pp. 365, 692.
142. Byrnes, *All in One Lifetime*, p. 286; Byrnes, *Speaking Frankly*, p. 262.
143. Byrnes, *Speaking Frankly*, p. 262.
144. Truman, *Year of Decisions*, p. 420.
145. Byrnes, *Speaking Frankly*, p. 262.
146. Craven and Cate, *Air Forces in World War II*, Vol. V, p. 709.
147. Truman, *Year of Decisions*, p. 262.
148. Butler, *Grand Strategy*, p. 223.
149. Truman, *Year of Decisions*, p. 235.
150. *Ibid.*, pp. 235–37; Feis, *Japan Subdued*, p. 38; Stimson Diary, May 16, 1945.
151. Stimson Diary, May 15, 1945.
152. Stimson, *On Active Service*, p. 618: King, *Fleet Admiral King*, p. 621.
153. Forrestal, *Diaries*, p. 70.
154. *Ibid.*, p. 83; Hewlett and Anderson, *The New World*, p. 364.
155. *Conference of Berlin*, I, p. 909.
156. Grew, *Turbulent Era*, II, p. 1458.
157. Leahy, *I Was There*, p. 383; King, *Fleet Admiral King*, pp. 395–96.
158. Department of Defense, "Entry of the Soviet Union into the War against Japan," p. 61.
159. *Ibid.*, p. 67.
160. Leahy, *I Was There*, p. 385; *Conference of Berlin*, I, p. 911.
161. *Conference of Berlin*, I, pp. 194–95; Department of Defense, "Entry of the Soviet Union into the War against Japan," p. 72.

162. *Conference of Berlin,* I, p. 910.
163. Byrnes, *All in One Lifetime,* p. 291.
164. *Ibid.*
165. *Ibid.,* p. 300.
166. Forrestal, *Diaries,* p. 70; Truman, *Year of Decisions,* p. 314.
167. Grew, *Turbulent Era,* II, p. 1465.
168. Grew memorandum of conversation, June 11, 1945.
169. Feis, *China Tangle,* p. 313.
170. *Ibid.,* p. 314.
171. *Ibid.*
172. Grew, *Turbulent Era,* II, p. 1468.
173. *Conference of Berlin,* I, p. 176.
174. *Ibid.,* p. 201.
175. Truman, *Year of Decisions,* p. 269; Feis, *China Tangle,* p. 315.
176. Feis, *China Tangle,* p. 312.
177. *Ibid.*
178. *Ibid.,* p. 315; Truman, *Year of Decisions,* pp. 318–19.
179. Feis, *China Tangle,* p. 316.
180. Truman, *Year of Decisions,* p. 319.
181. *Congressional Record,* Aug. 27, 1951, p. A5415. Emphasis added.
182. *Ibid.*
183. Feis, *China Tangle,* p. 317; Truman, *Year of Decisions,* pp. 315–16.
184. Department of State, *Relations with China,* p. 117.
185. Truman, *Year of Decisions,* pp. 316–17.
186. *Congressional Record,* Aug. 27, 1951, p. A5414.
187. Truman, *Year of Decisions,* p. 315.
188. *Ibid.,* p. 316.
189. *Ibid.,* pp. 315–18; Department of State, *Relations with China,* pp. 116, 123; *Congressional Record,* Aug. 27, 1951, p. A5414.
190. *Conference of Berlin,* I, p. 867.
191. Truman, *Year of Decisions,* p. 317.
192. Byrnes, *Speaking Frankly,* p. 205.
193. *Ibid.*
194. Truman, *Years of Trial and Hope,* p. 64.
195. Feis, *China Tangle,* p. 319.
196. Truman, *Year of Decisions,* p. 317.
197. *Ibid.,* pp. 317–18.
198. *Conference of Berlin,* I, p. 231.
199. Feis, *China Tangle,* p. 319; *Congressional Record,* Aug. 27, 1951, p. A5415.
200. Knebel and Bailey, *No High Ground,* p. 122.

201. Butler, *Grand Strategy,* p. 298; *Conference of Berlin,* I, p. 941.
202. Department of Defense, "Entry of the Soviet Union into the War against Japan," p. 75; Feis, *Between War and Peace,* p. 28.
203. *Conference of Berlin,* II, p. 34.
204. *Congressional Record,* Aug. 27, 1951, p. A5415.
205. Feis, *China Tangle,* pp. 318–19.
206. *Ibid.,* p. 319; Truman, *Year of Decisions,* p. 319.
207. Feis, *China Tangle,* p. 319; *Conference of Berlin,* I, pp. 862–63.
208. *Conference of Berlin,* I, p. 231.
209. Feis, *Japan Subdued,* p. 61.
210. Feis, *China Tangle,* p. 320.
211. *Ibid.; Conference of Berlin,* I, pp. 231, 862–63.
212. *Conference of Berlin,* I, p. 864.
213. Daniels, *Man of Independence,* p. 266.
214. Department of Defense, "Entry of the Soviet Union into the War against Japan," pp. 54, 67; Truman, *Year of Decisions,* p. 417.
215. Department of State, *Relations with China,* p. 93.

CHAPTER V (*pp. 175–204*)

1. Grew, *Turbulent Era,* II, p. 1464.
2. Leahy, *I Was There,* p. 382; Leahy Diary, June 15, 1945.
3. *Conference of Berlin,* II, pp. 1097–98.
4. *New York Times,* July 6, 1945.
5. *Conference of Berlin,* I, p. 704.
6. Grew, *Turbulent Era,* II, p. 1488.
7. *Conference of Berlin,* I, p. 181. Emphasis in original. See also *New York Times,* Feb. 15, 1950.
8. House Committee on Banking and Currency, *Hearings: Export-Import Bank Act of 1945;* Senate Committee on Banking and Currency, *Hearings: Export-Import Bank Act of 1945.*
9. *New York Times,* July 18, 1945; Senate Committee on Banking and Currency, *Hearings: Export-Import Bank Act of 1945,* p. 6.
10. Woodward, *British Foreign Policy,* pp. 539–40; *Conference of Berlin,* I, pp. 171, 359; II, pp. 633–34.
11. Truman, *Year of Decisions,* p. 415.

12. Daniels, *Man of Independence*, p. 266.
13. Truman, *Year of Decisions*, p. 245.
14. *Conference of Berlin*, I, pp. 257, 369, 373.
15. *Ibid.*, pp. 360–62.
16. Senate Committee on Banking and Currency, *Hearings: Export-Import Bank Act of 1945*, p. 9. House Committee on Banking and Currency, *Hearings: Export-Import Bank Act of 1945*, pp. 51–54.
17. *Conference of Berlin*, I, pp. 357–62.
18. McNeill, *America, Britain, and Russia, 1941–46*, pp. 325–26, 417, 421, 425, 476, 609; Woodward, *British Foreign Policy*, pp. 516–18.
19. Lukacs, *The Great Powers and Eastern Europe*, p. 658; *Conference of Berlin*, I, p. 358*fn.*
20. *Conference of Berlin*, I, pp. 334–35.
21. Feis, *Churchill, Roosevelt, Stalin*, p. 569; Betts, *Central and South-East Europe*, pp. 50, 170, 178. See also *Conference of Berlin*, I, p. 318.
22. *Conference of Berlin*, II, p. 193.
23. *Ibid.*, I, p. 728; II, pp. 1130–31.
24. Byrnes, *Speaking Frankly*, p. 294.
25. *New York Times*, March 4, 1945; McNeill, *America, Britain, and Russia, 1941–46*, p. 476.
26. *Conference of Berlin*, I, p. 262.
27. *Ibid.*
28. *Ibid.*, pp. 169–70, 361–62.
29. Churchill, *Triumph and Tragedy*, pp. 227–33.
30. Woodward, *British Foreign Policy*, pp. 293–94; Churchill, *Triumph and Tragedy*, p. 77; Hull, *Memoirs*, II, p. 1458; Dennett and Johnson, *Negotiating with the Russians*, pp. 176–77.
31. Feis, *Churchill, Roosevelt, Stalin*, pp. 415–16, 450–51; Allen, *Great Britain and the United States*, pp. 870–73; Churchill, *Triumph and Tragedy*, pp. 75–77; McNeill, *America, Britain, and Russia, 1941–46*, p. 493.
32. Woodward, *British Foreign Policy*, p. 307; Sherwood, *Roosevelt and Hopkins*, pp. 833–34.
33. Feis, *Churchill, Roosevelt and Stalin*, pp. 450–51.
34. *Ibid.*, pp. 415–16.
35. *Conference of Berlin*, I, p. 215.
36. Kennan, *Russia and the West*, p. 366; Feis, *Churchill, Roosevelt, Stalin*, pp. 415–16; *Conferences of Malta and Yalta*, p. 445; Senate Committee on Foreign Relations, *A Decade of American Foreign Policy*, pp. 482, 487, 494.
37. *A Decade of American Foreign Policy*, p. 455; *Conferences at Malta and Yalta*, p. 246.
38. *A Decade of American Foreign Policy*, pp. 487–91.
39. Woodward, *British Foreign Policy*, p. 308.
40. Churchill, *Triumph and Tragedy*, pp. 283–325.
41. *Ibid.*, p. 293.
42. *Ibid.*, p. 420.
43. *Ibid.*
44. Hull, *Memoirs*, II, pp. 1458–61.
45. *Conferences at Malta and Yalta*, pp. 97–108.
46. *Ibid.*, pp. 97–99.
47. Byrnes, *Speaking Frankly*, p. 33.
48. *Conferences at Malta and Yalta*, p. 503.
49. Byrnes, *Speaking Frankly*, p. 33.
50. *Conferences at Malta and Yalta*, pp. 503, 977; Byrnes, *Speaking Frankly*, pp. 32–33.
51. *Conferences at Malta and Yalta*, pp. 873, 909; Byrnes, *Speaking Frankly*, pp. 32–33; Lukacs, *The Great Powers and Eastern Europe*, p. 649; Kertesz, *Fate of East-Central Europe*, p. 266.
52. Dennett and Johnson, *Negotiating with the Russians*, p. 180.
53. *Conference of Berlin*, I, p. 374; Byrnes, *Speaking Frankly*, p. 50; Feis, *Churchill, Roosevelt, Stalin*, pp. 565–67.
54. *Conference of Berlin*, I, p. 398*fn.*
55. Byrnes, *Speaking Frankly*, p. 53; *Conference of Berlin*, I, p. 374.
56. Stimson Diary, May 10, 1945.
57. *Ibid.*
58. Grew memorandum of conversation, May 2, 1945.
59. Clark, *Calculated Risk*, pp. 442–48.
60. *Ibid.;* Truman, *Truman Speaks*, pp. 70–71.
61. Grew memorandum of conversation, May 14, 1945.
62. *Ibid.*, May 2, 1945.
63. *Ibid.*
64. *Ibid.*, May 4, 1945.
65. Truman, *Year of Decisions*, p. 254.
66. Grew memorandum of conversation, May 10, 1945; *Conference of Berlin*,

I, pp. 158–59, 169–70, 210–11.
67. *Conference of Berlin*, I, pp. 367, 369–70; Betts, *Central and South-East Europe*, p. 207.
68. Betts, *Central and South-East Europe*, p. 29.
69. *Conference of Berlin*, II, p. 729.
70. Betts, *Central and South-East Europe*, p. 29.
71. Feis, *Churchill, Roosevelt, Stalin*, p. 567.
72. *Ibid.*, p. 568; *Conference of Berlin*, I, p. 365.
73. McNeill, *America, Britain and Russia, 1941–46*, p. 422.
74. Roberts, *Rumania*, p. 260.
75. *Conference of Berlin*, I, p. 413.
76. *Ibid.*, p. 374.
77. *Ibid.*, pp. 422–23.
78. *Ibid.*, pp. 364*fn.*, 368, 372*fn.*
79. Woodward, *British Foreign Policy*, p. 517; Churchill, *Triumph and Tragedy*, pp. 76–79.
80. *Conference of Berlin*, I, pp. 393–94.
81. *Ibid.*, pp. 372*fn.*, 687; II, pp. 582, 1494.
82. Deane, *The Strange Alliance*, p. 268.
83. *Conference of Berlin*, II, p. 582.
84. Grew memorandum of conversation, May 10, 1945.
85. Grew, *Turbulent Era*, II, p. 1465; Roberts, *Rumania*, p. 264.
86. Dennett and Johnson, *Negotiating with the Russians*, p. 181.
87. *Stalin's Correspondence*, II, p. 239.
88. Feis, *Between War and Peace*, p. 110.
89. *Stalin's Correspondence*, II, pp. 241–42; *Conference of Berlin*, I, p. 358*fn.*
90. *Conference of Berlin*, I, p. 358*fn.*; *Stalin's Correspondence*, II, pp. 243–44; Churchill, *Triumph and Tragedy*, p. 115.
91. *Conference of Berlin*, I, p. 182; *Stalin's Correspondence*, II, pp. 248–49.
92. *Stalin's Correspondence*, II, p. 250; *Conference of Berlin*, I, p. 387.
93. *Conference of Berlin*, I, p. 417.
94. Stimson Diary, June 6, 1945.
95. *Ibid.*
96. Atomic Energy Commission, *Oppenheimer Hearings*, pp. 32, 33. Emphasis added.
97. Craven and Cate, *Air Forces in World War II*, Vol. V, p. 709; Hewlett and Anderson, *The New World*,
pp. 374–80.
98. Truman, *Year of Decisions*, p. 331.
99. *Ibid.*, p. 338.
100. *Conference of Berlin*, II, pp. 643–44.
101. *Ibid.*, I, pp. 400, 413.
102. *Speaking Frankly*, Byrnes, pp. 67–68.
103. *Conference of Berlin*, II, pp. 150–55.
104. Truman, *Year of Decisions*, p. 384.
105. Leahy, *I Was There*, p. 428.
106. *Conference of Berlin*, II, p. 8.
107. *Ibid.*, p. 1361.
108. *Ibid.*, p. 1360.
109. Stimson Diary, July 16, 1945.
110. Leahy Diary, p. 110, July 17, 1945.
111. McNeill, *America, Britain and Russia, 1941-46*, p. 615; Byrnes, *Speaking Frankly*, p. 31.
112. *Conference of Berlin*, II, pp. 53, 643–44.
113. *Ibid.*, pp. 52–63.
114. *Ibid.*, p. 56.
115. *Ibid.*, pp. 1360–61, Hewlett and Anderson, *The New World*, p. 386.
116. Stimson Diary, July 18, 1945; *Conference of Berlin*, II, p. 1361.
117. *Conference of Berlin*, II, p. 106.
118. *Ibid.*, p. 127.
119. Churchill, *Triumph and Tragedy*, p. 636.
120. *Conference of Berlin*, II, pp. 146–55, 698, 1044.
121. *Ibid.*, p. 151.
122. *Ibid.*
123. *Ibid.*, pp. 151–55.
124. *Ibid.*, p. 186.
125. Stimson Diary, July 21, 1945; *Conference of Berlin*, II, p. 1361. Emphasis added.
126. *Conference of Berlin*, II, p. 207.
127. *Ibid.*
128. Stimson Diary, July 22, 1945; *Conference of Berlin*, II, p. 225.
129. *Conference of Berlin*, II, pp. 1492–94.
130. Leahy, *I Was There*, p. 428.
131. Stimson Diary, July 23, 1945.
132. *Ibid.*, July 24, 1945.
133. *Conference of Berlin*, I, p. 413.
134. *Ibid.*, pp. 413–14.
135. Churchill, *Triumph and Tragedy*, p. 636.
136. *Hansard*, 413, H. C. Deb. 5s. (1945), pp. 78–79.
137. *Conference of Berlin*, II, pp. 361–

64; Woodward, *British Foreign Policy*, 539*fn.*
138. Bryant, *Triumph in the West 1943–46*, pp. 477–78.
139. *Ibid.*, p. 478.
140. Stimson Diary, July 22, 1945.
141. Hewlett and Anderson, *The New World*, pp. 367–69.
142. *Ibid.*, p. 367.
143. *Ibid.*; Feis, *Japan Subdued*, pp. 40–43.
144. Hewlett and Anderson, *The New World*, p. 369.
145. Stimson Diary, July 3, 1945; Hewlett and Anderson, *The New World*, p. 372.
146. *Conference of Berlin*, I, p. 942.
147. Hewlett and Anderson, *The New World*, p. 384; Stimson Diary, July 17, 1945; *Conference of Berlin*, II, p. 47.
148. Churchill, *Triumph and Tragedy*, p. 641.
149. Truman, *Year of Decisions*, p. 416.
150. Churchill, *Triumph and Tragedy*, pp. 668–70.
151. *Ibid.*, pp. 669–70; *Conference of Berlin*, II, p. 379.
152. Byrnes, *Speaking Frankly*, p. 263; Leahy, *I Was There*, p. 429. See also Craven and Cate, *Air Forces in World War II*, Vol. V, pp. 712–13.

CHAPTER VI   (*pp. 205–235*)

1. *Conference of Berlin*, II, p. 367.
2. *Ibid.*, p. 330.
3. McNeill, *America, Britain and Russia, 1941–46*, p. 622.
4. Stimson Diary, July 24, 1945.
5. *Ibid.*, July 23, 1945.
6. *Ibid.*, July 24, 1945.
7. Forrestal, *Diaries*, p. 78.
8. Byrnes, *Speaking Frankly*, p. 72.
9. *Ibid.*, p. 79.
10. *Ibid.*, p. 68.
11. Feis, *Between War and Peace*, p. 241–44; *Conference of Berlin*, II, pp. 72–76, 94.
12. *Conference of Berlin*, II, p. 795.
13. *Ibid.*, I, p. 611.
14. *Conferences at Malta and Yalta*, p. 983.
15. *Ibid.*
16. *Ibid.*, p. 982.

17. *Ibid.*, pp. 622, 937, 971.
18. *Ibid.*, p. 322.
19. *Ibid.*, p. 909.
20. Stimson, *On Active Service*, pp. 572–83.
21. *Conferences at Malta and Yalta*, p. 632.
22. *Ibid.*, p. 628.
23. *Conference of Berlin*, I, p. 504; see also Byrnes, *Speaking Frankly*, p. 37.
24. Stimson, *On Active Service*, p. 581; see also Churchill, *Triumph and Tragedy*, p. 156.
25. *Conference of Berlin*, I, pp. 228, 507; II, pp. 752, 832, 869, 1484.
26. Penrose, *Economic Planning for the Peace*, p. 268.
27. Byrnes, *Speaking Frankly*, p. 181.
28. Stimson, *On Active Service*, p. 573.
29. Hammond, "Directives for the Occupation of Germany," p. 213; Leahy, *I Was There*, p. 219; Toynbee. *Four-Power Control of Germany, 1945–46*, p. 145; Churchill, *Triumph and Tragedy*, p. 351.
30. Byrnes, *Speaking Frankly*, p. 26.
31. *Conference of Berlin*, II, p. 281.
32. Stimson, *On Active Service*, p. 583; Diary, May 16, 1945.
33. *Conference of Berlin*, I, p. 524*fn.*
34. Truman, *Year of Decisions*, p. 327.
35. *Ibid.*, p. 496; *Conference of Berlin*, I, p. 612–13.
36. Truman, *Year of Decisions*, p. 323.
37. *Ibid.*, p. 398.
38. *Conference of Berlin*, I, p. 520*fn.*
39. Truman, *Year of Decisions*, p. 309; see also *Conference of Berlin*, I, p. 452–53.
40. *Conference of Berlin*, I, pp. 520–21.
41. *Ibid.*, p. 510; Truman, *Year of Decisions*, pp. 310–11.
42. Stimson, *On Active Service*, p. 582; *Conference of Berlin*, I, pp. 539, 540, 547–48; II, pp. 833, 896.
43. *Conference of Berlin*, I, p. 547.
44. *Ibid.*, pp. 468–71, 524–25.
45. *Ibid.*, p. 540; II, pp. 870, 896.
46. *Ibid.*, I, pp. 530–31.
47. *Ibid.*, p. 510.
48. *Ibid.*, pp. 510–11.
49. *Ibid.*, pp. 519–20.
50. *Ibid.*, pp. 522–23.
51. *Ibid.*, pp. 530–31; II, pp. 870–71.
52. *Ibid.*, I, p. 532; II, p. 871.
53. *Ibid.*, II, p. 809; Byrnes, *Speaking*

Frankly, pp. 68, 82; Leahy, *I Was There,* pp. 395–96; Truman, *Year of Decisions,* p. 341.

54. Truman, *Year of Decisions,* p. 357; *Conference of Berlin,* II, pp. 873–76.
55. *Conference of Berlin,* II, pp. 428, 871.
56. *Ibid.,* pp. 754–57, 808–9; Stimson Diary, July 2, 1945.
57. *Conference of Berlin,* II, p. 755.
58. *Ibid.,* pp. 754–56, 808.
59. Stimson Diary, July 23, 1945.
60. *Conference of Berlin,* II, p. 279–80.
61. *Ibid.,* p. 280–81.
62. *Ibid.,* pp. 279, 810.
63. *Ibid.,* pp. 277–78.
64. *Ibid.,* p. 275; Byrnes, *Speaking Frankly,* pp. 83–84.
65. *Conference of Berlin,* II, pp. 428–31, 490–91, 947.
66. *Ibid.,* pp. 872, 877–85, 900.
67. *Ibid.,* p. 430.
68. *Ibid.,* p. 901.
69. *Ibid.,* pp. 900–1.
70. *Ibid.,* pp. 275, 296–97.
71. *Ibid.,* p. 428.
72. *Ibid.,* p. 429.
73. *Ibid.*
74. *Ibid.*
75. Byrnes, *Speaking Frankly,* p. 82; *Conference of Berlin,* II, p. 297.
76. *Conference of Berlin,* I, pp. 510–11.
77. *Ibid.,* II, pp. 451–52.
78. *Ibid.,* p. 473.
79. *Ibid.,* pp. 473–76.
80. *Ibid.,* pp. 486–87, 841, 855, 877–78, 880, 884.
81. *Ibid.,* pp. 473, 886–87.
82. *Ibid.,* pp. 473, 487.
83. *Ibid.,* p. 487.
84. *Ibid.,* pp. 877–85, 892.
85. *Ibid.,* p. 892.
86. *Ibid.,* p. 926.
87. Leahy Diary, July 26, 27, 1945, pp. 126, 130.
88. Truman, *Year of Decisions,* pp. 389, 394; *Conference of Berlin,* II, p. 471.
89. *Conference of Berlin,* II, pp. 471–77.
90. *Ibid.,* pp. 484–85.
91. *Ibid.,* p. 510; Byrnes, *Speaking Frankly,* p. 85.
92. *Conference of Berlin,* II, p. 514.
93. *Ibid.,* pp. 510–14.
94. Penrose, *Economic Planning for the Peace,* p. 287.
95. Leahy, *I Was There,* p. 427.

96. Byrnes, *Speaking Frankly,* p. 82.
97. *Conference of Berlin,* I, pp. 228, 507; II, pp. 752, 775–80, 832, 869, 1484.
98. *Ibid.,* I, p. 50; II, pp. 183–84, 482.
99. *Ibid.,* I, pp. 520–21; Truman, *Year of Decisions,* p. 309.
100. *Conference of Berlin,* II, p. 756.
101. De Gaulle, *Salvation,* U.K., pp. 285–86.
102. *Conference of Berlin,* II, pp. 1481–85.
103. *Ibid.,* p. 251.
104. *Ibid.,* pp. 515, 1486.
105. *Ibid.,* pp. 52, 186, 609–10, 1479–80.
106. Churchill, *Triumph and Tragedy,* p. 672.
107. *Conference of Berlin,* II, pp. 1086, 1492–93.
108. McNeill, *America, Britain and Russia, 1941–46,* pp. 627–28.
109. Leahy, *I Was There,* p. 428.
110. De Gaulle, *Salvation,* U.K., p. 230.
111. Forrestal, *Diaries,* p. 78; see also Truman, *Year of Decisions,* p. 411.
112. Byrnes, *Speaking Frankly,* p. 87.
113. *Ibid.,* p. 72.
114. Byrnes, *All in One Lifetime,* p. 303.
115. *Conference of Berlin,* I, p. 879.
116. *Ibid.,* I, pp. 879–80.
117. *Ibid.,* II, p. 1249.
118. *Ibid.,* p. 1250.
119. *Ibid.,* p. 1260.
120. *Ibid.,* p. 1261.
121. Eisenhower, *Mandate for Change,* p. 313.
122. Truman, *Year of Decisions,* p. 417; Grew, *Turbulent Era,* II, pp. 1423, 1434; *Conference of Berlin,* II, p. 1272fn.
123. *Conference of Berlin,* II, p. 1294.
124. *Ibid.,* pp. 1260–64.
125. *Ibid.,* pp. 1260–61.
126. *Ibid.,* p. 1266.
127. *Ibid.,* pp. 87, 1588.
128. *Ibid.,* pp. 45, 1585.
129. Department of Defense, "Entry of the Soviet Union into the War against Japan," p. 106; see also Butler, *Grand Strategy,* p. 303; Leahy, *I Was There,* p. 397.
130. Butler, *Grand Strategy,* p. 291.
131. Truman, *Truman Speaks,* pp. 67, 93.
132. *Ibid.,* p. 93; Truman, *Year of Decisions,* p. 419.
133. *Conference of Berlin,* I, pp. 941–42.

134. Churchill, *Triumph and Tragedy*, p. 639; see also Wilson, *Eight Years Overseas*, p. 259.
135. Stimson Diary, July 22, 1945; *Conference of Berlin*, II, p. 1373*fn*.
136. *Conference of Berlin*, II, p. 1374.
137. Stimson Diary, July 24, 1945.
138. Knebel and Bailey, *No High Ground*, pp. 124–25; Hewlett and Anderson, *The New World*, p. 394.
139. Truman, *Year of Decisions*, p. 421.
140. *Conference of Berlin*, II, pp. 87, 1587–88.
141. *Ibid.*, pp. 1587–88.
142. *Ibid.*, p. 81; Butler, *Grand Strategy*, pp. 302–3.
143. Bryant, *Triumph in the West 1943–46*, pp. 477; Feis, *Between War and Peace*, p. 172.
144. Butler, *Grand Strategy*, p. 292; *Conference of Berlin*, II, p. 276.
145. Byrnes, *Speaking Frankly*, p. 206.
146. Stimson Diary, July 23, 1945.
147. *Ibid.*, July 24, 1945.
148. Forrestal, *Diaries*, pp. 78–79; Byrnes, *All in One Lifetime*, p. 297; Hillman, *Mr. President*, p. 123; Truman, *Year of Decisions*, p. 411; "Was A-Bomb on Japan a Mistake?" *U.S. News and World Report*, Aug. 15, 1960, pp. 62–76.
149. *Conference of Berlin*, I, p. 889; Stimson Diary, June 19, 1945; Hewlett and Anderson, *The New World*, p. 365, and *especially* p. 403.
150. Cline, *Washington Command Post*, p. 345; Morton, "The Decision to Use the Atomic Bomb," *Command Decisions*, K. R. Greenfield, ed., p. 499.
151. *Conference of Berlin*, I, pp. 173, 891.
152. *Ibid.*, pp. 893, 897.
153. *Ibid.*, II, p. 1267; Stimson Diary, June 19, 1945.
154. *Conference of Berlin*, I, pp. 889–90.
155. *Ibid.*, II, pp. 449–50, 460, 1284.
156. *Ibid.*, I, pp. 110, 125.
157. *Ibid.*, II, pp. 449–50, 460, 1284; Byrnes, *Speaking Frankly*, p. 207.
158. Byrnes, *Speaking Frankly*, pp. 207–9; Truman, *Year of Decisions*, pp. 401–4; *Conference of Berlin*, II, p. 476; Byrnes, *All in One Lifetime*, pp. 297–98.
159. Byrnes, *All in One Lifetime*, p. 298; *Speaking Frankly*, p. 208.
160. Byrnes, *All in One Lifetime*, p. 298.
161. Truman, *Year of Decisions*, pp. 403–4; *Conference of Berlin*, II, pp. 1333–34.
162. *Conference of Berlin*, II, pp. 1333–34.
163. Deane, *The Strange Alliance*, pp. 267–68.
164. Forrestal, *Diaries*, p. 78.
165. Deane, *The Strange Alliance*, p. 270.
166. *Conference of Berlin*, II, pp. 276, 1241; Byrnes, *All in One Lifetime*, p. 291.
167. Byrnes, *All in One Lifetime*, p. 291.
168. *Conference of Berlin*, II, pp. 43–47, 1582–87.
169. *Ibid.*, pp. 1223–24, 1240–41, 1586.
170. *Ibid.*, pp. 1227–30.
171. *Ibid.*, p. 460.
172. *Ibid.*
173. *Ibid.*, p. 1293.
174. *Ibid.*, p. 1293*fn*.
175. Hewlett and Anderson, *The New World*, p. 396; Butow, *Japan's Decision*, pp. 140–41, 143–49.
176. *Conference of Berlin*, II, pp. 1292–93.
177. Strauss, *Men and Decisions*, p. 189; Feis, *Japan Subdued*, pp. 103–4; Butler, *Grand Strategy*, p. 308.
178. Hewlett and Anderson, *The New World*, p. 401; Truman, *Year of Decisions*, p. 420.
179. Truman, *Year of Decisions*, pp. 423–24; Byrnes, *All in One Lifetime*, p. 304; Hewlett and Anderson, *The New World*, p. 398; Feis, *China Tangle*, pp. 330–31; *Congressional Record*, Aug. 27, 1951, p. A5415.
180. Leahy, *I Was There*, p. 430; Hewlett and Anderson, *The New World*, p. 401.

CHAPTER VII (*pp. 236–273*)

1. Byrnes, *Speaking Frankly*, p. 264; Truman, *Year of Decisions*, pp. 421–22; Leahy, *I Was There*, p. 430.
2. Truman, *Year of Decisions*, p. 421.
3. *New York Times, New York Herald Tribune*, Aug. 7, 1945.
4. *Ibid.*; *New York Times*, Aug. 8–10, 1945.
5. Morton, "The Decision to Use the

Atomic Bomb," *Command Decisions*, Greenfield, ed., p. 516; Truman, *Year of Decisions*, p. 425; Hewlett and Anderson, *The New World*, p. 403.

6. Stimson Diary, Aug. 10, 1945.
7. *Ibid.*, Aug. 8–10, 1945; Byrnes, *All in One Lifetime*, p. 305.
8. Byrnes, *All in One Lifetime*, p. 305; Truman, *Year of Decisions*, pp. 427–29; Stimson Diary, Aug. 10, 1945.
9. Stimson Diary, Aug. 10, 1945; Truman, *Year of Decisions*, p. 428; Byrnes, *All in One Lifetime*, p. 305.
10. Byrnes, *All in One Lifetime*, p. 305; Forrestal, *Diaries*, p. 83.
11. Forrestal, *Diaries*, p. 95; Truman, *Year of Decisions*, p. 428; Hewlett and Anderson, *The New World*, pp. 404–5; Stimson Diary, Aug. 10, 1945.
12. Byrnes, *All in One Lifetime*, pp. 305–6.
13. *Ibid.*; Hewlett and Anderson, *The New World*, p. 405.
14. Byrnes, *All in One Lifetime*, p. 306; Truman, *Year of Decisions*, p. 430–31.
15. Truman, *Year of Decisions*, p. 432.
16. Byrnes, *Speaking Frankly*, p. 210; *All in One Lifetime*, p. 306.
17. Byrnes, *All in One Lifetime*, pp. 305–7.
18. Truman, *Year of Decisions*, p. 205.
19. Byrnes, *Speaking Frankly*, p. 210.
20. Truman, *Year of Decisions*, p. 425.
21. *Ibid.*, pp. 142, 432, 439.
22. Stimson Diary, Aug. 10, 1945.
23. Truman, *Year of Decisions*, pp. 430–31; Byrnes, *All in One Lifetime*, p. 306.
24. Byrnes, *All in One Lifetime*, p. 306; Truman, *Year of Decisions*, p. 439.
25. Truman, *Year of Decisions*, pp. 440–43; *Stalin's Correspondence*, II, pp. 266–68.
26. Byrnes, *Speaking Frankly*, pp. 213–15; Dennett and Johnson, *Negotiating with the Russians*, p. 120.
27. Dennett and Johnson, *Negotiating with the Russians*, p. 121.
28. *New York Times*, Aug. 17, 1945; Senate Committee on Foreign Relations, *A Decade of American Foreign Policy, 1941–49*, p. 628.
29. Truman, *Year of Decisions*, p. 423; Feis, *China Tangle*, pp. 342–45; Department of State, *Relations with China*, p. 117.
30. Department of State, *Relations with China*, p. 589.
31. *Ibid.*, p. 594.
32. *Ibid.*, p. 120; Feis, *China Tangle*, pp. 344–47.
33. Department of State, *Relations with China*, p. 118fn.
34. *Ibid.*, pp. ix, 99, 120; *Congressional Record*, Aug. 27, 1951, p. A5413.
35. Feis, *China Tangle*, p. 347; *New York Times*, Aug. 28, 1945.
36. Truman, *Public Papers of the Presidents*, I, p. 248; Department of State, *Relations with China*, p. 121.
37. U.S. Senate, *Military Situation in the Far East*, p. 2934.
38. Department of State, *Relations with China*, pp. 119, 137, 147; Beloff, *Soviet Policy*, p. 37.
39. Truman, *Year of Decisions*, p. 448.
40. Department of State, *Relations with China*, pp. 119, 122, 124, 137, 147, 149.
41. *Ibid.*, pp. 123–24.
42. *Ibid.*, Truman, *Year of Decisions*, p. 424; Beloff, *Soviet Policy*, pp. 39–40; Wedemeyer, *Wedemeyer Reports!*, p. 347.
43. Department of State, *Relations with China*, p. ix.
44. *Ibid.*, pp. 118–19; Feis, *China Tangle*, pp. 342–43; Truman, *Year of Decisions*, pp. 423–24.
45. Department of State, *Relations with China*, p. 118.
46. Feis, *China Tangle*, pp. 342, 349–50.
47. *Ibid.*, pp. 349–50; Department of State, *Relations with China*, pp. 118–19.
48. Byrnes, *Speaking Frankly*, p. 92.
49. *New York Times*, Aug. 23, 1945; see also Truman, *Year of Decisions*, p. 483.
50. Truman, *Year of Decisions*, p. 423; *Public Papers of the Presidents*, I, p. 199.
51. Truman, *Public Papers of the Presidents*, I, pp. 212–13.
52. Hewlett and Anderson, *The New World*, p. 407.
53. Truman, *Year of Decisions*, p. 524.
54. Stimson, *On Active Service*, p. 616; Diary, March 15, 1945.
55. Hewlett and Anderson, *The New*

World, p. 357.

56. *Ibid.*

57. *Ibid.*

58. *Ibid.*

59. *Ibid.*, pp. 357–58.

60. *Ibid.*, pp. 357–58, 360–61; Stimson Diary, June 6, 1945.

61. Stimson Diary, June 6, 1945; Hewlett and Anderson, *The New World*, pp. 360–61.

62. Hewlett and Anderson, *The New World*, p. 355.

63. *Ibid.*, p. 368.

64. *Ibid.*, pp. 398–99; Truman, *Year of Decisions*, pp. 422–23.

65. Stimson Memo, April 25, 1945.

66. *Ibid.*, Aug. 12–Sept. 5; Sept. 11, 12; Dec. 11, 1945; Hewlett and Anderson, *The New World*, pp. 357–58, 417, 456, 458–59, 460–61, 469.

67. *Ibid.*, pp. 355, 417, 418; Truman, *Year of Decisions*, p. 87; Stimson Diary, Aug. 12–Sept. 3; Sept. 5, 1945; Szilard, "A Personal History of the Atomic Bomb"; "Was A-Bomb on Japan a Mistake?" *U.S. News and World Report*, Aug. 15, 1960, p. 69.

68. Byrnes, *Speaking Frankly*, p. 179.

69. *Ibid.*, pp. 87, 179, 203; *All in One Lifetime*, p. 303; Senate Committee on Foreign Relations, *A Decade of American Foreign Policy, 1941–49*, pp. 51–58.

70. Byrnes, *Speaking Frankly*, p. 261; *All in One Lifetime*, p. 283.

71. Byrnes, *All in One Lifetime*, p. 284.

72. *Conference of Berlin*, II, p. 82; Churchill, *Triumph and Tragedy*, p. 641.

73. Truman, *Year of Decisions*, p. 525.

74. Hewlett and Anderson, *The New World*, p. 388; Stimson Diary, July 19–22, 1945; *Conference of Berlin*, II, pp. 1155–57.

75. *Ibid.*, p. 1156*fn.*; Stimson, *On Active Service*, p. 642.

76. *Conference of Berlin*, II, p. 1155–56; Stimson Diary, July 20, 1945.

77. Stimson Diary, July 20, 1945; *Conference of Berlin*, II, p. 1156*fn.*

78. Truman, *Year of Decisions*, p. 525.

79. Hewlett and Anderson, *The New World*, p. 401.

80. Truman, *Year of Decisions*, p. 526.

81. *Ibid.*, p. 525.

82. Hewlett and Anderson, *The New World*, pp. 455–56, 458–59; Stimson Diary, Sept. 21, 1945; de Gaulle, *Salvation*, U.K. pp. 207, 287.

83. Truman, *Year of Decisions*, p. 524.

84. Hewlett and Anderson, *The New World*, p. 417.

85. *Ibid.*

86. Atomic Energy Commission, *Oppenheimer Hearings*, p. 33.

87. Hewlett and Anderson, *The New World*, p. 724.

88. *Ibid.*, p. 417.

89. Truman, *Public Papers of the Presidents*, I, p. 214.

90. *Ibid.*, p. 207.

91. For details see *ibid.*, or *New York Times*, Aug. 10, 1945.

92. Deane, *The Strange Alliance*, p. 212; Smith, *Moscow Mission*, pp. 10–12; Eisenhower, *Crusade in Europe*, pp. 438, 444; Clay, *Decision in Germany*, pp. 33–34.

93. Clay, *Decision in Germany*, p. 34; Nettl, *The Eastern Zone and Soviet Policy in Germany*, pp. 65, 260, 262–63; Toynbee, *Four-Power Control in Germany and Austria, 1945–46*, p. 17.

94. Clark, *Calculated Risk*, p. 461.

95. Truman, *Year of Decisions*, p. 354; *Conference of Berlin*, II, p. 1491.

96. *Conference of Berlin*, II, pp. 403, 419.

97. *Ibid.*, pp. 193, 506; Lane, *I Saw Poland Betrayed*, pp. 179–82; *New York Times*, Aug. 25, 1945.

98. Truman, *Public Papers of the Presidents*, I, p. 210.

99. Truman, *Year of Decisions*, p. 87.

100. Grew, *Turbulent Era*, II, p. 1465.

101. *New York Times*, Aug. 26, 1945.

102. *Hansard*, 413, H.C. Deb. 5s. (1945), p. 102.

103. *Ibid.*, pp. 291–92.

104. *Ibid.*

105. *Ibid.*, pp. 82–85.

106. *Ibid.*, p. 79.

107. *Conference of Berlin*, II, pp. 1494–95.

108. *Ibid.*

109. *Ibid.*, p. 690; Lukacs, *The Great Powers and Eastern Europe*, p. 632; Seton-Watson, *The East European Revolution*, pp. 104–5.

110. *Conference of Berlin*, I, pp. 367, 370.

111. Fleming, *The Cold War*, I, p. 310; *New York Times*, Aug. 30, 1945.
112. *Conference of Berlin*, II, pp. 687, 690.
113. *New York Times*, Aug. 30, 1945; Fleming, *The Cold War*, I, p. 310.
114. Fleming, *The Cold War*, I, p. 310; Seton-Watson, *The East European Revolution*, p. 193; McNeill, *America, Britain and Russia, 1941–46*, p. 702; Betts, *Central and South East Europe*, p. 105.
115. Betts, *Central and South East Europe*, pp. 31–32; *New York Times*, June 3, 1945.
116. Seton-Watson, *The East European Revolution*, p. 213; Dennett and Johnson, *Negotiating with the Russians*, p. 187; Betts, *Central and South East Europe*, p. 29.
117. Betts, *Central and South East Europe*, p. 31; Seton-Watson, *The East European Revolution*, p. 213.
118. Seton-Watson, *The East European Revolution*, pp. 213–15; Betts, *Central and South East Europe*, p. 31.
119. Betts, *Central and South East Europe*, p. 32.
120. Senate Committee on Foreign Relations, *A Decade of American Foreign Policy, 1941–49*, pp. 484–85.
121. Seton-Watson, *The East European Revolution*, p. 212; Betts, *Central and South East Europe*, pp. 31, 32.
122. Betts, *Central and South East Europe*, p. 32; Seton-Watson, *The East European Revolution*, pp. 213–14.
123. *Conference of Berlin*, II, p. 729.
124. *Ibid.*
125. *Ibid.*, pp. 730–31; Betts, *Central and South East Europe*, p. 32.
126. Betts, *Central and South East Europe*, p. 32; Seton-Watson, *The East European Revolution*, p. 213.
127. *Ibid.*
128. *Ibid.*
129. *Ibid.*
130. *New York Times*, June 3, 1945; *Conference of Berlin*, I, p. 384.
131. *Conference of Berlin*, I, pp. 357–67.
132. *Daily Telegraph*, May 21, 1945; Truman, *Year of Decisions*, p. 50; *New York Times*, March 11, 1945.
133. *New York Herald Tribune*, June 18, 1945; Betts, *Central and South East Europe*, p. 32; Seton-Watson, *The East European Revolution*, p. 214.
134. Seton-Watson, *The East European Revolution*, p. 212; Fleming, *The Cold War*, I, p. 311; Woodward, *British Foreign Policy*, pp. 516–18.
135. *Conference of Berlin*, II, p. 731.
136. *Ibid.*, p. 723; Seton-Watson, *The East European Revolution*, p. 214.
137. *Conference of Berlin*, II, pp. 716–18, 730.
138. *Ibid.*, I, p. 383.
139. *Ibid.*, pp. 383–84.
140. *Ibid.*, p. 384.
141. *Ibid.*
142. *Ibid.*, I, p. 384; II, p. 695.
143. *Ibid.*, II, p. 730.
144. *Ibid.*, pp. 716–18.
145. *Ibid.*, pp. 694–95.
146. *Ibid.*, I, p. 403.
147. *Ibid.*, II, p. 731.
148. *Ibid.*, pp. 730–31.
149. *Ibid.*, pp. 722–25.
150. *Ibid.*, p. 730.
151. *Ibid.*, p. 735; Dennett and Johnson, *Negotiating with the Russians*, p. 189.
152. *Conference of Berlin*, II, p. 734.
153. *Ibid.*, p. 731.
154. Dennett and Johnson, *Negotiating with the Russians*, p. 190.
155. *New York Times*, Aug. 19, 1945; Wolff, *The Balkans in Our Times*, p. 296; Betts, *Central and South East Europe*, p. 33.
156. Betts, *Central and South East Europe*, p. 33; *New York Times*, Aug. 19, 1945; Wolff, *The Balkans in Our Times*, p. 296; State Dept. *Bulletin*, Aug. 19, 26, 1945.
157. *New York Herald Tribune*, Aug. 22, 1945; Betts, *Central and South East Europe*, p. 33; Seton-Watson, *The East European Revolution*, p. 214.
158. Dennett and Johnson, *Negotiating with the Russians*, p. 190.
159. London *Times*, Aug. 24, 1945.
160. *Ibid.*, Aug. 20, 1945; *Manchester Guardian*, Aug. 20, 1945; *New York Times*, Aug. 17, 18, 1945.
161. *New York Times*, Aug. 17, 18, 1945; *Daily Telegraph*, Aug. 17, 1945.
162. *Daily Telegraph*, Aug. 17, 1945; *New York Times*, Aug. 18, 1945;

Dennett and Johnson, *Negotiating with the Russians,* p. 189; *New York Herald Tribune,* Aug. 20, 1945.

163. *New York Herald Tribune,* Aug. 20, 1945.

164. *New York Times,* Aug. 20, 1945.

165. *Manchester Guardian,* Aug. 20, 1945.

166. *Conference of Berlin,* I, p. 383.

167. *New York Herald Tribune,* Aug. 16, 1945.

168. London *Times,* Aug. 21, 1945.

169. *New York Times,* Aug. 26, 1945.

170. London *Times,* Aug. 21, 1945.

171. *New York Herald Tribune,* Aug. 22, 1945.

172. *Ibid.,* Sept. 16, 1945; *New York Times,* Aug. 26, 1945.

173. *New York Times,* Aug. 26, 1945; Wolff, *The Balkans in Our Time,* p. 296; Seton-Watson, *The East European Revolution,* p. 214; *New York Herald Tribune,* Aug. 26, 1945; London *Times,* Aug. 27, 1945; Betts, *Central and South East Europe,* p. 33.

174. Dennett and Johnson, *Negotiating with the Russians,* p. 190.

175. *New York Herald Tribune,* Aug. 26, 1945.

176. Dennett and Johnson, *Negotiating with the Russians,* p. 190.

177. *New York Herald Tribune,* Aug. 30–31, 1945; *New York Times,* Sept. 4–10, 1945.

178. *New York Times,* Sept. 4–10, 1945; *New York Herald Tribune,* Aug. 30–31, 1945.

179. *New York Herald Tribune,* Aug. 29, 1945; *New York Times,* Sept. 7, 1945.

180. *New York Times,* Sept. 10, 1945.

181. *Conference of Berlin,* II, pp. 1492–93; State Department *Bulletin,* Aug. 26, 1945, pp. 283–84.

182. Betts, *Central and South East Europe,* pp. 33–34; *New York Times,* Sept. 10, 1945; Dennett and Johnson, *Negotiating with the Russians,* p. 190; Seton-Watson, *The East European Revolution,* p. 214.

183. Dennett and Johnson, *Negotiating with the Russians,* p. 190.

184. *New York Times,* Sept. 10, Nov. 20, 1945.

185. *Ibid.,* Sept. 10, 1945.

186. *New York Herald Tribune,* Aug. 30, 1945.

187. *Ibid.,* Aug. 31, 1945; *New York Times,* Sept. 8, 1945; Betts, *Central and South East Europe,* p. 33.

188. *New York Herald Tribune,* Aug. 30, 1945.

189. *Ibid.,* Aug. 31, Sept. 10, 1945; Betts, *Central and South East Europe,* p. 33.

190. *New York Times,* Sept. 9, 1945.

191. *Ibid.,* Sept. 20, 1945.

192. Seton-Watson, *The East European Revolution,* p. 97; Betts, *Central and South East Europe,* p. 29; Lukacs, *The Great Powers and Eastern Europe,* p. 616.

193. Churchill, *Triumph and Tragedy,* p. 233; Fleming, *The Cold War,* I, p. 251; Betts, *Central and South East Europe,* p. 2.

194. Betts, *Central and South East Europe,* pp. 2, 203.

195. *Ibid.,* p. 203; Roberts, *Rumania,* pp. 264–65.

196. Roberts, *Rumania,* pp. 264–65, *Conferences at Malta and Yalta,* p. 248; Lee, *Crown against Sickle,* pp. 111–12.

197. Lee, *Crown against Sickle,* pp. 110–12; Betts, *Central and South East Europe,* p. 7.

198. *New York Times,* March 23, 1945.

199. *Conference of Berlin,* II, p. 714.

200. *Ibid.,* pp. 700, 714–15.

201. *Ibid.,* p. 700; *Senate Committee on Foreign Relations: A Decade of American Foreign Policy 1941–49,* pp. 483–84.

202. *Conference of Berlin,* II, p. 700.

203. *Ibid.*

204. *Ibid.*

205. *Ibid.*

206. *Ibid.,* pp. 700–1, 714.

207. *Ibid.,* p. 701.

208. *Ibid.,* p. 714.

209. *Ibid.*

210. *Ibid.*

211. *Ibid.*

212. *Ibid.,* pp. 714–15.

213. Churchill, *Triumph and Tragedy,* p. 76.

214. Byrnes, *Speaking Frankly,* p. 98.

215. Seton-Watson, *The East European Revolution,* p. 207; Lee, *Crown*

against Sickle, pp. 121–22.

216. Lee, *Crown against Sickle*, pp. 109–10; Feis, *Between War and Peace*, p. 191.

217. Lee, *Crown against Sickle*, pp. 122–24, 126, 129.

218. *Ibid.*, p. 122; London *Times*, *New York Times*, *New York Herald Tribune*, Aug. 23–24, 1945.

219. *New York Herald Tribune*, *New York Times*, London *Times*, Aug. 23, 24, 1945; Seton-Watson, *The East European Revolution*, p. 207; Lee, *Crown against Sickle*, p. 123; Betts, *Central and South East Europe*, p. 9.

220. Betts, *Central and South East Europe*, p. 9; Seton-Watson, *The East European Revolution*, p. 207; Lee, *Crown against Sickle*, p. 123.

221. *New York Times*, Sept. 19, 1945.

222. Betts, *Central and South East Europe*, p. 9.

223. Lee, *Crown against Sickle*, p. 124.

224. *Ibid.*, pp. 124, 126; State Department *Bulletin*, Aug. 26, 1945, p. 281; London *Times*, Aug. 23, 1945; *New York Herald Tribune*, Aug. 25, 1945; *Daily Telegraph*, Aug. 23, 1945; *New York Times*, Aug. 23, 1945.

225. *New York Times*, Aug. 27, 1945.

226. Betts, *Central and South East Europe*, p. 9; Grew memorandum of conversation, Aug. 6, 1945.

227. *New York Times*, Aug. 24, 1945; *Christian Science Monitor*, Aug. 23, 1945.

228. London *Times*, Aug. 29, 1945.

229. *New York Times*, Aug. 29, 1945; Lee, *Crown against Sickle*, p. 127.

230. Lee, *Crown against Sickle*, p. 128; *New York Times*, Sept. 5, 1945; *New York Herald Tribune*, Sept. 9, 1945; Betts, *Central and South East Europe*, p. 9.

231. London *Times*, Sept. 5, 1945.

232. *Manchester Guardian*, Sept. 6, 1945; Lee, *Crown against Sickle*, p. 128.

233. *New York Times*, Sept. 9, 1945.

234. London *Times*, Sept. 13, 20, 1945.

235. *New York Herald Tribune*, Sept. 13, 1945.

236. Byrnes, *All in One Lifetime*, p. 309.

237. McNeill, *America, Britain and Russia, 1941–46*, p. 691; *New York*

Times, Oct. 1, 1945, Jan. 18, March 2, 3, April 2, 20, 21, May 9, 1946; *Wall Street Journal*, March 18, 20, 21, 1946; Truman, *Year of Decisions*, pp. 475–76; see also Byrnes, *Speaking Frankly*, pp. 113–14.

238. Truman, *Public Papers of the Presidents*, I, p. 227; *New York Times*, Aug. 17, 1945.

239. Truman, *Year of Decisions*, p. 510.

240. Stimson Diary, Aug. 12–Sept. 3, 1945.

241. *Ibid.*, Sept. 4, 1945.

242. Leahy, *I Was There*, p. 431.

243. Byrnes, *All in One Lifetime*, pp. 313–14; *Speaking Frankly*, pp. 97–101, 105, 107, 108.

244. Byrnes, *Speaking Frankly*, p. 105.

CONCLUSIONS (*pp. 274–290*)

1. Byrnes, *Speaking Frankly*, p. 104.

2. *Ibid.*, p. 105.

3. *Ibid.*; *All in One Lifetime*, p. 317; *New York Times*, Oct. 7, 1945.

4. Hewlett and Anderson, *The New World*, p. 456.

5. Leahy, *I Was There*, p. 416.

6. *Ibid.*, p. 429.

7. *Conference of Berlin*, II, p. 1361*fn*.

8. *Conferences at Malta and Yalta*, p. 319.

9. Truman, *Year of Decisions*, p. 71.

10. Churchill, *Triumph and Tragedy*, pp. 72, 76, 77, 78.

11. *Ibid.*, p. 76.

12. *Ibid.*, p. 238.

13. *Conferences at Malta and Yalta*, p. 234.

14. *Ibid.*, p. 95.

15. Dennett and Johnson, *Negotiating with the Russians*, p. 178.

16. Black, "Soviet Policy in Eastern Europe," p. 155. Emphasis in original.

17. Bryant, *Triumph in the West 1943–46*, pp. 477–78.

18. Truman, *Year of Decisions*, p. 87.

19. *Conference of Berlin*, I, p. 10.

20. Truman, *Year of Decisions*, p. 87.

21. *New York Times*, Feb. 15, 1950.

22. Woodward, *British Foreign Policy*, p. 519.

23. Truman, *Year of Decisions*, p. 71.

24. Byrnes, *Speaking Frankly*, p. 104.

25. Churchill, *Triumph and Tragedy*, pp. 457, 574; emphasis in original.

26. *Conference of Berlin*, I, p. 7.
27. Churchill, *Triumph and Tragedy*, p. 503.
28. *Ibid.*, pp. 637, 649, 650, 655, 672; *Conference of Berlin*, I, pp. 295, 359, 380, 417; Feis, *Between War and Peace*, pp. 223–24, 238.
29. Feis, *Between War and Peace*, pp. 155–56.
30. *Conference of Berlin*, I, p. 295.
31. *Hansard*, 413, H. C. Deb. 5s (1945), p. 78.
32. Truman, *Year of Decisions*, p. 524.
33. De Gaulle, *Salvation*, U.K., pp. 229–30.
34. *Ibid.*, p. 230.
35. *Ibid.*
36. Truman, *Year of Decisions*, p. 262.
37. Kennan, *American Diplomacy 1900–1950*, p. 123.
38. See for example, Byrnes, *Speaking Frankly*, pp. 294–95.
39. *Ibid.*, p. 295.
40. Truman, *Year of Decisions*, p. x.
41. *New York Herald Tribune*, Nov. 27, 1945.
42. Stimson Diary, Sept. 17, 1945.
43. Byrnes, *Speaking Frankly*, p. 98.
44. Snow, *Journey*, p. 357.
45. *Ibid.*, p. 361.
46. Stimson, *On Active Service*, p. 643.
47. Eisenhower, *Mandate for Change*, pp. 312–13; "Ike on Ike," *Newsweek*, Nov. 11, 1963, p. 107.
48. Truman, *Truman Speaks*, p. 67.
49. *Conference of Berlin*, I, p. 905.
50. Leahy, *I Was There*, pp. 245, 259, 269, 384–85.
51. *Ibid.*, p. 441.
52. King and Whitehill, *Fleet Admiral King*, p. 621.
53. Knebel and Bailey, *No High Ground*, p. 111; Craven and Cate, *Air Forces in World War II*, Vol. V, pp. 711, 741.
54. Ismay, *Memoirs*, p. 401.
55. *Ibid.*
56. Churchill, *Triumph and Tragedy*, p. 215.
57. *Ibid.*, p. 646.
58. U.S. Strategic Bombing Survey, *Japan's Struggle to End the War*, p. 13.
59. Knebel and Bailey, *No High Ground*, pp. 73, 89, 141–42, 222.
60. See for example, *New York Times*, Aug. 22, 1963.
61. U.S. Atomic Energy Commission, *Oppenheimer Hearings*, p. 34.
62. *Ibid.*
63. *Ibid.*, p. 561.
64. State Department *Bulletin*, Oct. 28, 1945, p. 659.
65. Craven and Cate, *Air Forces in World War II*, Vol. V, pp. 712–13.
66. Stimson Diary, May 14, 1945.
67. *Ibid.*, June 6, 1945.
68. L. Szilard, "A Personal History of the Atomic Bomb," University of Chicago *Roundtable*. No. 601 (Sept. 25, 1949), pp. 14–15. Byrnes has not denied this statement, but see his recollection of a different aspect of the conversation with Dr. Szilard. (*All in One Lifetime*, pp. 284–85.) See also Hewlett and Anderson, *The New World*, p. 355; and *U.S. News and World Report*, Aug. 15, 1960, p. 69.

APPENDIX I   (*pp. 291–317*)

1. Sherwin, *A World Destroyed*, p. 188*fn.*
2. See above, pp. 112–13.
3. See below, p. 312, note 44.
4. See above, p. 118.
5. See above, p. 117; p. 397, notes 33, 34, 35.
6. See above, p. 119.
7. See above, p. 119. Incidentally, Sherwin is correct that there is an error in the text of *Atomic Diplomacy* on page 319 of Appendix II (this edition) in the sentence stating that Stimson spoke with Truman on May 1, 2, 3, and 4, 1945. The correct dates, as he indicates, were May 2, 3, and 4. On May 1, Stimson spoke with Marshall, Harrison, and Bundy about the bomb.
8. Sherwin, "The Atomic Bomb, Scientists and American Diplomacy During the Second World War" (Ph.D. dissertation), p. 256. Sherwin's interpretation on this point has been followed in numerous works. See, for instance, Yergin, *Shattered Peace*, p. 433.
9. Sherwin, "The Atomic Bomb, Scientists, etc.," p. 267.
10. Sherwin, *A World Destroyed*, p. 163.
11. See above, p. 107.
12. See below, p. 318.
13. Stimson Diary, May 16, 1945.
14. Sherwin, "The Atomic Bomb, Scientists, etc.", p. 267.
15. See above, pp. 114–16.

16. Sherwin, "The Atomic Bomb, Scientists, etc.," pp. 267–68.

17. Sherwin attempts to make much of his idea that the meeting could not have taken place much earlier than June 30 as a way to discount this cable (*ibid.*, p. 259). However, the proposal that the meeting occur earlier is not an invention of *Atomic Diplomacy*. Whatever Sherwin's view of the feasibility of an earlier meeting, strong pressure for this was in fact put forward—even a few weeks or days earlier—and it came from Churchill and many of the President's top advisers. Harriman, for instance, begged the President to hold the meeting in *early* June. See above, pp. 88, 113–17. (U.S. Dept. of State, *Conference of Berlin*, I, p. 14.)

A very weak case might possibly be made (Sherwin does not attempt to do it) that the decision is embodied in Truman's cable to Churchill on May 14 (*Conference of Berlin*, I, p. 11), but this cable simply indicates that Truman will await a report from his Embassy in Moscow before deciding upon a time. The only cable which clearly embodies a decision not to meet until July is the May 9 cable. Even if the May 14 cable were the important one, of course, it occurred before the May 16 meeting, and does not alter the above argument that Truman's acceptance of the idea of delay had to have occurred earlier than May 16.

18. Sherwin, *A World Destroyed*, p. 188.

19. Sherwin, "The Atomic Bomb, Scientists, etc.," p. 267.

20. Stimson Diary, May 14, 1945.

21. *Ibid.*

22. Stimson Diary, May 10, 1945; Sherwin, "The Atomic Bomb, Scientists, etc.," pp. 262–63.

23. Hewlett and Anderson, *The New World*, p. 352; Stimson Diary, June 6, 1945.

24. U.S. Dept. of State, *Conference of Berlin*, I, p. 13. The quotation is from an official summary report.

25. See above, p. 149.

26. Sherwin, "The Atomic Bomb, Scientists, etc.," p. 256. Emphasis added.

27. *Ibid.*, pp. 267–69.

28. Sherwin, *A World Destroyed*, p. 184.

29. *Ibid.*, p. 186.

30. Davies Diary, May 13, 1945.

31. See above, pp. 116–25.

32. Sherwin, *A World Destroyed:* "It is not likely that Davies changed the President's mind . . ." (p. 174). Sherwin also cites Davies' May 13 remark (in connection with Stalin's action when he had believed there was a hostile capitalistic alliance ganging up on him in 1939): "This impressed him. He got it more clearly, it appeared, than when I talked to him last" (p. 183).

33. Quite the contrary, this is a period of continuing tension and the President approved several tough moves which were in line with the views of those who favored a nonconciliatory approach. See above, pp. 87–88, 89–97, 111–13, 128–30.

34. Davies Diary, May 13, 1945.

35. Eden, *The Reckoning*, p. 621.

36. Sherwin, "The Atomic Bomb, Scientists, etc.," p. 256.

37. Evidence on the dates is to be found in Truman, *Year of Decisions*, pp. 30–32, 110, 257–58; Ferrell, *Off the Record*, p. 35; Sherwood, *Roosevelt and Hopkins*, p. 885; Davies diary, May 21, 1945; Harriman and Abel, *Special Envoy*, p. 459; Herring, *Aid to Russia, 1941–1946*, pp. 202–3. See also Tuttle, *Harry L. Hopkins and Anglo-American Soviet Relations, 1941–1945*, p. 275 note 26, which reports that Hopkins was so ill he did not attend Roosevelt's funeral.

38. U.S. Dept. of State, *Conference of Berlin*, I, pp. 21–22. Hopkins left Washington on May 23. (Tuttle, *Harry L. Hopkins*, p. 279.)

39. Davies Diary, May 21, 1945. See also entry for June 5, 1945.

40. Bohlen, *Witness to History: 1929–1969*, p. 236. Sherwood indicates that Harriman and Bohlen first sounded Hopkins and that Harriman proposed the idea to Truman after these soundings. Harriman was in San Francisco until May 10. If the sounding occurred after that date, this is a direct contradiction of Truman's account that he talked to Hopkins on May 4. At some point, however, either in the May 4 meeting with the President (if it occurred) or at another time, Hopkins obviously learned that the atomic bomb was involved with thinking about the ongoing diplomatic problems with the Soviet Union. Two possible explanations (beyond the implausible notion of a very strange coincidence) are: (1) Truman told Hopkins about the bomb and the postponement of the meeting, just as he

did Davies—and Bohlen's report reflects this fact. (In this case the idea that Hopkins did not believe Truman would send him, as reported in Sherwood, is in error.) Alternatively, (2) Bohlen has his dates slightly confused and the conversation about the bomb took place at another discussion with Hopkins (after May 19) and not during the first sounding discussion. For Sherwood's report of Hopkins' attitude, see *Roosevelt and Hopkins*, p. 887. On Harriman's dates, see Herring, *Aid to Russia*, pp. 201–2.

41. See, for instance, Tuttle, *Harry L. Hopkins*, pp. 304–5.
42. Sherwin, *A World Destroyed*, p. 163.
43. See above, pp. 106–7.
44. See above, p. 61; Sherwin, *A World Destroyed*, p. 293.
45. Truman, *Year of Decisions*, p. 87.
46. Stimson Diary, June 6, 1945.
47. Truman's 1955 memoirs indicate that Byrnes opposed the Hopkins trip, but Truman's diary entry of the time (May 22) says *only that he consulted Byrnes* (among others). According to Truman, he had first wanted to use Davies for the mission, but decided on Hopkins only when Davies declined. There is other evidence that Byrnes thought he could work with Davies. And there are reasons Byrnes may not have wanted to work with Hopkins. (Hopkins had led a group opposed to appointing Byrnes as Secretary of State when Roosevelt was alive; and Hopkins was involved in the complicated maneuvers which first seemed to promise the Vice-Presidency and then gave it to Truman in 1944.) If Byrnes was advising Truman on overall diplomatic strategy and the decision to send missions to Moscow and London, it may be that Truman's recollection that Byrnes opposed Hopkins simply records his preference for another person—i.e., Davies. Or it may be that Truman's 1955 recollection is simply in error. Truman's contemporary diary strongly suggests that the issue was not whether the mission should be sent, but *who* to send from the "political standpoint." (See Truman, *Year of Decisions*, p. 258; Messer, *The End of an Alliance*, pp. 21–22, 35, 74–75; Ferrell, *Off the Record*, p. 35.)
48. Sherwin, *A World Destroyed*, pp. 143, 148, 186–87, 221–22.
49. Eden, *The Reckoning*, p. 621.

50. Bernstein, "The Atomic Bomb and American Foreign Policy," p. 12. Bernstein also comments that Rose's work "criticized Alperovitz in two sometimes meandering and unclear chapters that slipped past some key issues, failed occasionally to answer its own explicit questions, and overlooked some important problems of interpretation." (p. 12).
51. This is another area where some critics attempted to make much of minor alleged errors of fact or interpretation while ignoring the central issue. Although new documents not available twenty years ago help round out *Atomic Diplomacy*'s treatment of the Balkans, the most recent research overwhelmingly confirms the book's fundamental argument in connection with this issue. See note 140 to the Introduction to the 1985 Edition.
52. E.g., Blackett, *Military and Political Consequences of Atomic Energy.*

Index

Alanbrooke, Viscount, 7, 201–2, 223*fn.*, 228, 234*fn.*
Anderson, Clinton, 2
Anderson, Sir John, 104*fn.*
Arnold, Gen. Henry H., 17–18, 26, 164, 167*fn.*, 172, 238*fn.*, 286
Atlantic Charter, 225
atomic bomb: its role in U.S.–Soviet diplomacy, 1–60, 61–64, 103–6, 145–52, 178, 199–202, 205, 206, 212–13, 219–21, 239, 240, 243, 258, 259, 284, 288; Stimson's and Byrnes's views on, 1, 4, 5, 6, 8, 14, 18, 26, 31–37, 42–45, 51, 55–56, 103–4, 110–11, 136, 137, 192, 212–13, 251, 277, 283; its use decided or assumed, 9, 52, 64, 104, 161, 164, 227–29, 284–89; its use not necessary, 19–27, 64, 158, 284–87; moral issues and, 15–16, 54; military's view of, 16–19; Interim Committee, 19, 21, 38, 42, 43–44, 48, 107, 110, 162–64, 165*fn.*, 192, 202–4, 244–46, 248, 288; demonstrations suggestion, 21, 163; secrecy and distortion in documents about, 34–40; monopoly or international control; 43, 58*fn.*, 106–8, 111, 136–37, 148, 202, 203, 243–48, 283; basis for delayedshowdown strategy, 49–50, 105–9, 112–14, 118, 128, 132, 133, 137, 164–66, 173, 174, 191–94, 198, 224, 229, 231, 234, 251, 258, 259, 278–81, 289; postwar Europe and Asia, 53, 56–57, 249, 251, 252, 264, 265, 271–77, 282, 290; modern power relations and, 59–60; test blast, 104, 107, 113, 166, 173, 175, 176, 178, 192, 193, 195–201, 206, 212–13, 220, 221, 224, 228, 231, 280, 281; postwar

development of, 248; its use on Japan, *see* Japan
Atomic Diplomacy (1965 edition): three controversial issues addressed in, 1–2; public and academic debate generated by, 2–3, 23*fn.*, 47; reinterpretation of early postwar period as response to, 3–5; newly available historical documents and, 4, 7, 10, 12, 13, 27; 30, 34, 38, 44, 46, 47, 50, 53, 55; diplomacy issues in bombing decisions seen as central controversy in, 8–10; reliance on diaries as problem, 34–36; Byrnes's crucial role and, 47–50; new research as confirmation of arguments in, 47, 50, 55
Atomic Energy Commission, 37, 245*fn.*, 146*fn.*, 275*fn.*, 285*fn.*, 288*fn.*
Attlee, Clement, 197*fn.*, 251, 215
Augusta, U.S.S., 173, 234, 236
Austria, 57, 90–96, 101–3, 128, 130, 131, 178–79, 249

Baldwin, Hanson W., 286*fn.*
Balkans, 4*fn.*, 55, 95, 137, 180*fn.*, 184, 223; diplomatic recognition, 178, 190, 191, 197–200, 280; spheres of influence in, 180–86, 188–89, 194, 197, 199, 201, 259, 265, 267; British policy on, 181–83, 188–89, 191, 196, 199–201; armistice agreements, 182, 183, 188–89, 197, 252, 253; U.S. intervention in, 185–86, 188, 192, 194–200, 206, 213, 218, 240*fn.* 250–53, 262, 271, 273, 275, 279, 284; *see also* Bulgaria; Greece; Rumania; Yugoslavia
Bard, Ralph A., 19–20, 165*fn.*
Barnes, Maynard, 254–62 *passim*